WITHDRAWN

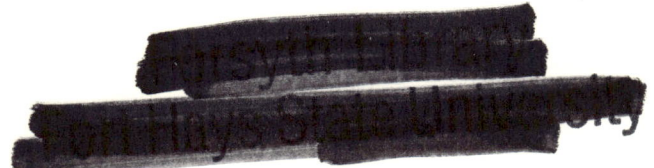

The PLO and Israel

From Armed Conflict to Political Solution, 1964–1994

Edited by Avraham Sela
and Moshe Ma'oz

St. Martin's Press
New York

*Dedicated to the memory of Yehoshafat Harkabi,
a soldier-philosopher, mentor, and colleague.*

THE PLO AND ISRAEL: FROM ARMED CONFLICT TO POLITICAL SOLUTION, 1964-1994
Copyright © Avraham Sela and Moshe Ma'oz, 1997
All rights reserved. Printed in the United States of America. No part of this book may be used or reproduced in any manner whatsoever without written permission except in the case of brief quotations embodied in critical articles or reviews. For information, address St. Martin's Press, Scholarly and Reference Division, 175 Fifth Avenue, New York, N.Y. 10010
ISBN 0-312-12906-8

Library of Congress Cataloging-in-Publication Data

Sela, Avraham and Moshe Ma'oz
The PLO and Israel: from armed conflict to political solution,
 1964-1994 / edited by Avraham Sela and Moshe Ma'oz.
  p. cm.
 Includes bibliographical references and index.
 ISBN 0-312-12906-8
  1. Jewish-Arab relations—1973—Congresses. 2. Israel—Politics and government—Congresses. 3. Munazzamat al-Tahrir al-Filastiniyah—History—Congresses. 4. Intifada, 1987- --Congresses. 5. Palestinian National Authority—History—Congresses. I. Sela, Avraham. II. Ma'oz, Moshe.
DS119.7.P5534 1997
956.9405'4—dc21
                                                                97-10190
                                                                    CIP
                                                                    r97

Design: Acme Art, Inc.
First St. Martin's edition: November, 1997
10 9 8 7 6 5 4 3 2 1

Contents

Acknowledgments v

Introduction: The PLO and Israel: From Armed Conflict
to Political Settlement, 1964-1994
AVRAHAM SELA vi

PART I:
THE MAKING OF A PALESTINIAN NATIONAL MOVEMENT

1. The PLO and the Politics of Ethnonational Mobilization
   EMILE SAHLIYEH 3

2. The Armed Struggle and Palestinian Nationalism
   YEZID SAYIGH 23

3. A Study of PLO Peace Initiatives, 1974-1988
   MUHAMMAD MUSLIH 37

4. From Palestine Liberation Organization to Palestinian Authority:
   The Territorialization of "Neopatriarchy"
   HILLEL FRISCH 55

5. Policy and Attitude Changes in the Palestine Liberation Organization,
   1965-1994: A Democracy in the Making
   MANUEL S. HASSASSIAN 73

PART II:
REGIONAL AND INTERNATIONAL ARENAS

6. The PLO in Regional Arab Politics: Taming a Non-State Actor
   AVRAHAM SELA AND MOSHE MA'OZ 97

7. Moscow and the PLO: The Ups and Downs of a Complex Relationship
   GALIA GOLAN 121

8. Misperceptions and Perfect Understanding: The United States
   and the PLO
   BARRY RUBIN 141

PART III: THE RISE AND INFLUENCE OF LOCAL ACTIVISTS

9. Mental Health Challenges for the Palestinian Authority: The Psycho-Political Legacy of the Intifada
   EYAD EL SARRAJ 163

10. Inside Versus Outside: The Challenge of the Local Leadership, 1967-1994
    MEIR LITVAK 171

11. Intifada Discourse: The Hamas and UNL Leaflets
    SHAUL MISHAL 197

12. The Role of Women and Female Leadership in the Intifada and the Peace Process
    NAOMI CHAZAN 213

PART IV: ISRAELI AND PALESTINIAN RELATIONS— BETWEEN PAST AND FUTURE

13. The Power-Oriented Settlement: PLO-Israel—The Road to the Oslo Agreement and Back?
    BARUCH KIMMERLING 223

14. Israel's Policy Toward the PLO: From Rejection to Recognition
    SUSAN HATTIS ROLEF 253

15. Strategic Reciprocity: The PLO and Israel
    LEONARD BINDER 273

Index 301

Biographies 309

Acknowledgments

The book's editors wish to thank the Truman Institute's staff who helped in organizing the conference "The PLO and Israel: From Armed Conflict to Political Settlement 1964-1994," especially Dan Bitan, Idit Avidan, and Francine Hazan. We would also like to thank the participants. Many could not be included in this volume, but all contributed to the conference's success. We are especially indebted to Chaia Beckerman for saving no effort in handling the reviewed papers, which she, Evelyn Katrak, and Steven V. Mazie edited. We also apprciate the efforts of Donna Cherry, Michael Flamini, Elizabeth Pautkis, and, in particular, Wendy Kraus of St. Martin's Press.

Introduction

THE PLO AND ISRAEL
FROM ARMED CONFLICT TO POLITICAL SETTLEMENT, 1964-1994

Avraham Sela

ANNIVERSARIES TYPICALLY CALL FOR AN HISTORICAL REVIEW of past experience, achievements and failures, as well as for an evaluation of future developments. On rare occasions, however, anniversaries coincide with groundbreaking events that impose a different retrospective view. Such was the case with the Israel-PLO Oslo Accord of 13 September 1993. The Oslo Accord came just as the Harry S Truman Research Institute for the Advancement of Peace at the Hebrew University of Jerusalem was preparing an international conference on the thirtieth anniversary of the PLO's founding. Hence, the conference's topic and program were reshaped in accordance with the new questions that the sudden turning point in the Israel-PLO relations evoked.

Although the conference's program focused on historical processes, the final sessions took note of realpolitik and future opportunities and constraints. The conclusion drawn by the late Yehoshafat Harkabi—to whom this volume is dedicated and whose pioneering studies on the Israeli-Arab conflict were eye-opening for Israelis and Palestinians alike—was characteristically penetrating. Israeli-Palestinian relations, he observed, were no longer a "zero-sum game" but rather an interdependence that had become fully recognized by the mainstream of both parties concerned. While the Oslo process would not automatically lead to paradise, its collapse would certainly lead to hell, for both sides concerned. Thus, each party would have to pay whatever price necessary to adhere to the process of political dialogue and to meet the other side's essential needs.

The Oslo Accord indeed opened the door to a substantial change in the relations between Israelis and Palestinians, stated participant Yezid Sayigh. Yet these relations would have to be more egalitarian and mutual in future negotiations if the Oslo process were to survive. The conflict, it was widely agreed, was far from being over and there would be a long way for the two parties to go before they would be able to reach a final settlement, to overcome the uncertainties, fears, and objections within the two communities. In the path toward a final settlement, both sides are bound to resort to both political leverage and controlled violence. And yet, despite all the difficulties and crises that lay ahead, the participants shared a strong view that the Israeli-PLO Oslo process was irreversible.

For many of the Israeli and Palestinian participants this was not the first opportunity to meet in an academic or public forum. The Truman Institute itself has, since the late 1980s, cosponsored research projects with Palestinian academic and research institutes in East Jerusalem, the West Bank, and the Gaza Strip. The Oslo Accord enabled bringing together Israeli and Palestinian scholars and practitioners for a joint public discourse in a congenial academic atmosphere, and this indicated a new era of cooperation between their respective political communities. Yet what rendered the conference a landmark in the development of relations between Israeli and Palestinian academics was its venue and its agenda: namely, Israeli-Palestinian relations in a historical perspective.

The ability of any society to critically regard its past is an indispensable step toward openness of mind, mutual tolerance, and human relationships within and between nations. It is especially crucial in the case of Israeli and Palestinian societies. The hundred-year-long dispute has left residues of bitterness and shaped mutual perceptions and beliefs, adding a formidable psychological barrier to their intractable historic conflict. If, as is commonly believed, intellectual discourse is a step ahead of political process, this conference certainly advanced some necessary principles for future Israeli-Palestinian mutual relations.

The structure of this book reflects the four main concerns of the conference. A majority of the papers are included here, with a few additions to bring the story of PLO-Israel relations up to the present. Part one discusses the making of a Palestinian national movement, primarily in Palestinian perspective. Part two examines the PLO's history in inter-Arab and international perspectives. Part three focuses on the dialectic of the Intifada—the uprising in the Palestinian occupied territories—and the impact on diaspora PLO politics. Part four is concerned with the politics of change in Israeli-Palestinian relations and their prospective development.

The founding of the Palestine Liberation Organization (PLO) in May 1964 was a result of a specific constellation of inter-Arab detente embodied by the Arab summit conference held in Cairo in January of that year. That it took more than fifteen years after the 1948 war until this seminal organization came into being was due to regional as well as Palestinian constraints. Yet what initially seemed to be nothing but an instrument in inter-Arab quarrels and bids for legitimacy in fact coincided with the emergence of authentic Palestinian nationalist groups whose revolutionary agenda contradicted the state of oblivion of the Arab-Palestinian national cause since 1948. After 1967 the PLO underwent a radical transformation, socially and institutionally, that turned it into an authentic Palestinian national organization representing a wide spectrum of communities as well as political and military groups. Despite the diversity, fragmentation, and dispersion of the Palestinians in various countries, the PLO managed to reshape a Palestinian national identity, to conduct a comprehensive mobilization of the community, and to build an institutional infrastructure, with diplomatic and civic attributes, that functioned as a state-in-the-making. Moreover, the PLO managed to gain the recognition of the major part of the Palestinian people, and to maintain its moral and political authority as the overall political center of the Palestinian people.

Both the inception of the PLO and its post-1967 transformation represented radical social and political changes among the Palestinians in the diaspora as well as in historic Palestine. Foremost among these changes was the development of education and the rise of a new professional middle class, especially among the refugees. It was primarily this group that experienced the suspicion and rejection with which Arab states and societies treated the Palestinian refugees. This often translated into a policy of isolation and tight restrictions on labor, business, and political activity. Against this backdrop of a growing sense of group deprivation among the Palestinians in the diaspora, amplified by a sense of Arab abandonment of the Palestinian cause, the seeds of Palestinian nationalism budded.

The advent of the PLO boosted the development of specific Palestinian national characteristics—historical and cultural symbols of identity, especially the bonds between people and territory—and their definition on a narrow national basis. At the same time, the PLO adhered to the principles of pan-Arab nationalism, reflecting the claim they made for unreserved Arab support for the Palestinian national struggle. In the absence of an autonomous territorial base, the PLO had to conduct a tenacious struggle for survival against ongoing disruptive efforts by Arab regimes and intransigent Israeli hostility. Not only did the principle of popular armed struggle against Israel, launched from Arab states' territories, entangle these states in undesired military confrontation with the Jewish state; by virtue of constituting the core issue of pan-Arabism, Palestinian nationalism was synonymous with a strong revisionist outcry that threatened the existing social and political order, primarily in the Arab states neighboring Israel. The Palestinian revolution often clashed with the Arab state system's basic premises and commitments to established international norms. Thus, Arab states, both individually and collectively, had continually sought to convert the Palestinian resistance into an internationally recognized national movement with limited territorial goals based on the U.N. Security Council Resolution 242.

Any peace agreement between parties to a long-lived dispute is likely to be the result of a tortuous process of frustrated aspirations, disillusion, and consequent psychological growth, and the Israeli-Palestinian accords are no exception. The Palestinian national movement came a long way from the disaster of the 1948 war to the historic mutual Israel-PLO agreement, signed on the White House lawn on 13 September 1993. The sea change that the Palestinian issue has undergone in that period is best told by the scope of the 1948 disaster for the Palestinian cause and the nadir from which it was revitalized and promoted. It has reinstated itself as an inalienable national problem and the key issue of the Middle East conflict.

Yet the practical Palestinian armed and diplomatic struggle against Israel also manifested the limitations of this thrust in view of the regional and international constraints, exacerbated by Israel's strategic magnitude. While the PLO gradually adapted to new realities, for example, following the 1973 war and the consequent American-mediated peace process, it was the Intifada, the Palestinian uprising that erupted in the West Bank and Gaza Strip in December 1987, that brought dramatic change to the official PLO political platform, with the declaration in November 1988 of the establishment of a Palestinian state based on UN Resolution 181 of 29 November 1947, which called for partition of Mandatory Palestine.

The Intifada indicated the growing role of the local Palestinian leadership in Palestinian politics at large, though most of this leadership was identified with Fatah, the largest Palestinian faction. Its success was best indicated by the United States' and Israel's official recognition of the Palestinians as a primary partner to a settlement in the West Bank and Gaza Strip. The Islamic Resistance Movement also had a considerable impact during the Intifada, intensifying the threats to both Israel and the PLO. The tension between the inside (local) leadership with its swelling ranks of grassroots activists, and the outside (diaspora) leadership was evident in the policy of institution building by the Palestinian Authority, established in Gaza under Yasir Arafat's leadership in June 1994. Still, it was only following the collapse of the Soviet Union and the Gulf War, with their detrimental consequences for the Palestinians, that the PLO agreed to participate in the Madrid Peace Conference in late October 1991, deferring to Israel's conditions.

The development of the PLO's political program on the issue of peaceful settlement, which often seemed reluctant and indecisive, is presented in historical context in part one. Underlying factors were the PLO's complicated decision-making process, reflecting its political and economic weakness, and its institutional and ideological fragmentation that mirrored the disputed inter-Arab arena—all this at a time when Israel and the United States adhered to their objection to recognizing the PLO or its claims.

Israel has shifted perceptions and policies toward the Palestinian issue, especially during the uprising in the occupied West Bank and Gaza Strip. Even then, however, the change was discerned more within the center-left body politic than on the nationalist right, remaining the main bone of contention between them. The changing Israeli attitude to the Palestinian issue is examined in part three against the historical backdrop of persistent denial of Palestinian nationalism and preference for a settlement with neighboring Arab states. The Israeli-Palestinian settlement is explained from two different perspectives: a power-oriented one versus an incremental, pragmatic one with a final settlement shaped by domestic political constraints.

PART I

The Making of a Palestinian National Movement

ONE

The PLO and the Politics of Ethnonational Mobilization

Emile Sahliyeh

The post-World War II era has witnessed waves of political action by numerous communal, ethnic, and nationalist groups. Such political action has been motivated by many grievances, including the denial of the opportunity to build a state, loss of the homeland, economic exploitation, and loss of individual and collective rights. Thus, the yearning to establish a state and recover lost territory and the desire to protect the group's identity, culture, language, religion, territory, and lifestyles against the intrusive demands of others have been behind these political movements.

Among these groups, the PLO has been the most active in evoking a distinct Palestinian national identity and in mobilizing resources for the creation of an independent Palestinian state. There are, however, no ethnocultural, religious, demographic, economic, or political traits that differentiate the Palestinians from the rest of the Arabs. In addition, the Palestinians were scattered. While a small minority continued to live inside Israel, others resided in the West Bank and the Gaza Strip; a third group lived in refugee camps in Lebanon, Syria, and Jordan; and a fourth group had emigrated to the rich Arab oil countries, Western Europe, and the United States. Yet, despite the physical dispersal of the

Palestinians and the common language, race, religion, and collective political aspirations they share with the rest of the Arabs, a discernible Palestinian national identity appeared. The Palestinians do not deny belonging to the Arab world; they nevertheless see themselves as a distinct national group. Given the complexities, how can one account for the rise of Palestinian nationalism in the 1960s and after?

Explaining Ethnonationalism: Primordialism vs. Instrumentalism

The literature on ethnicity reveals the presence of two competing perspectives to explain the phenomenon of group ethnic identity—the primordialist and the instrumentalist. The first conceives of ethnic nationalism as an indication of an enduring cultural tradition based on a primordial sense of ethnic identity.[1] It posits that the presence of a common culture and a distinct social origin, race, and region are essential for the rise of communal identity and the differentiation among assorted social collectivities.[2] Language and religion are additional requirements for ethnic awareness. Language, as a communication device, discriminates against the non-natives, while religion serves as an important foundation for communal identification and the emergence of a separate tradition. Religion also suggests to its adherents a world perspective and an encompassing social character.

The definition of ethnic identity also includes the presence of territory and a sovereign state. A territorial homeland provides the group with a reference point and draws the boundaries between it and other ethnic communities. The nation-state, however, reflects the collective will of the group and its common heritage, and furnishes the institutional framework within which the interests of an ethnic community are protected.

Although a combination of these variables and attributes lessens the anxieties and uncertainties of the individual and the social collectivity, they are not always relevant or sufficient to explain how communal identity is formed. For instance, while language and religion are pertinent to the formulation of the ethnic identity of some groups, class, race, social origin, or region may be more salient in other cases. In still other instances, ethnicity requirements may go beyond the primordial attributes mentioned here.

These shortcomings in the primordial perspective allowed for the rise of the instrumentalist approach,[3] which attributes the emergence of ethnic feelings to instrumental considerations and regards ethnicity as "an exercise in boundary maintenance." This viewpoint assumes that ethnic identity serves the practical needs and interests of the members of the community and that ethnicity is an effectual response to differential treatment.

The durability of the ethnic identity is contingent on its ability to provide more security, social status, and economic benefits for its members than other existing alternatives do. The presence of appealing opportunities outside the native circle for an individual's economic and social advancement can lead to the decline of ethnic solidarity. Members of the ethnic group would modify their identity to suit the new conditions. In view of the functional nature of this perspective, ethnic identity is not a closed system, as outsiders can be incorporated into the ethnic group.

The theoretical pronouncements of the primordial and the instrumentalist perspectives do not accurately and completely explain the rise of modern Palestinian nationalism. Both perspectives ignore the role of common historical experience as well as a group belief in a shared destiny and the presence of common symbols and grievances, elements that unite the members of that social collectivity. Some of the core features of the primordial perspective on ethnicity do not fully qualify the Palestinians to be a separate communal group. For instance, race and social origin do not entitle them to a discrete national identity. After all, the Palestinians share these features with the rest of the Arabs.[4] In their social mores, practices, customs, and conventions, the Palestinians also are like the rest of the Arabs. And religion and language are insufficient factors to account for the rise of a separate Palestinian identity. With the exception of a small Christian minority, Islam is the religion of the Palestinians, but it is not exclusive to the Palestinians. Arabic is the language of all the Arabs; it is not a differentiating feature of the Palestinian people. Moreover, many of the Palestinians converse in the local dialect of their country of residence. The dispersal of the Palestinians presents another challenge to the primordial perspective. The Palestinians do not live in a single country; they reside in different regions including the Middle East, Europe, and the United States.

The instrumentalist model is no more useful than the primordial perspective in explaining the emergence of Palestinian nationalism. It is difficult to imagine how the instrumentalist perspective could provide a justification for the rise of Palestinian nationalism. Despite the presence of opportunities for some of the Palestinians to assimilate into other societies, many of them did not abandon the quest for a distinct national identity and the formation of an independent state. Some of the Palestinians benefited from expanding economic opportunities in their place of residence, such as in the Gulf states. Others overcame some of the barriers that restricted their access to power in countries such as Jordan, and still others carved out, for a time, spheres of local influence and autonomy, as in Lebanon. Despite these opportunities, the Palestinians were not deflected from developing their own ethnic national identity and from seeking to build their own state.

Alternative Explanations

The literature on communal conflict analysis introduces two other theoretical perspectives for explaining the rise of ethnonationalism: relative deprivation and resource mobilization. The deprivation and grievances model ascribes the rise of ethnic nationalism to the multifaceted crises and the socioeconomic, psychological, and political grievances and frustrations that an ethnic group experiences collectively. The primary motivational force for a communal group's political action lies in its discontent about deprivation and the presence of deep-seated grievances about group status. The suffering of the group may also result from discriminatory treatment in its place of residence. Communal passions and self-esteem may also arise from the interaction of a certain group with other, rival people.[5] In this connection, external dangers to the security and survival of the group will reinforce feelings of ethnic solidarity among the members of that community.

In explaining the rise of a separate Palestinian identity, the deprivation model offers several advantages over the primordial and instrumentalist perspectives, as will be illustrated below. By itself, however, it is insufficient to provide a comprehensive understanding of the phenomenon of ethnonationalism. Weak and aggrieved individuals feel powerless to rebel.

The political activism of ethnic and communal groups can also be explained by employing a resource mobilization model.[6] This model assumes that the group is the focus of political mobilization and action by leaders who formulate the group's political interests and express the group's grievances and political aspirations.[7] It emphasizes the calculated mobilization of group resources in response to changing political opportunities. The resource mobilization model contains three components. First, a communal group's activism is not possible without the presence of political space and opportunities. External encouragement plays a major role in indigenous activism. In order to legitimize their rule, some of the power holders may manipulate communal groups and provide a congenial and receptive environment for their mobilization.

Second, the political vigor of a communal group also depends on the presence of an assortment of resources including political leadership, organizational structures, communication networks, labor force, funds, and ideology. These assets will determine the nature and the degree of the reaction of the aggrieved persons. Third, such ethnic groups cannot be mobilized without the presence of motives and incentives, including the desire to alleviate the widespread social, economic, and political inequities among the members of the group.

The relative deprivation and resource mobilization models are treated in the literature as competing and separate perspectives. But each on its own presents only a partial explanation for the rise of ethnonationalism. For the purposes of this study, the two are incorporated to bring about an ethnic communal mobilizational model. This model, which was developed by historian Ted R. Gurr, delineates four group traits.[8]

The first trait involves the presence of a gap between the aggrieved population and the governing groups. This gap is generated by policies that discriminate against the deprived group by limiting their material well-being and their admission to political power. Gurr hypothesizes that the greater the discrimination experienced by a group, the more it would feel the grievances, and the greater would be its potential for political mobilization.

The strength of group identity is the second condition for facilitating political mobilization. The identity of the group rests on shared historical experiences and on the presence of one or more of the following attributes: ethnic origin, common language and religion, and region of residence. Group identity is also a function of cultural and social variations between the afflicted group and the dominant or enemy groups. Such differences allow for the political mobilization of the communal group and enable the leaders to articulate the demands and the interests of the aggrieved group. Little prospect exists for political mobilization if grievances and group identity are weak. Conversely, strong group identity advances the chances for group political action.

The third factor involves the interconnectedness of the group, which is a function of its political organization and convergence in one region. The higher the degree of cohesion among the members of a communal group, the greater the potential for political activism.

The degree of repression by the dominant group is the fourth factor impelling political action. Though subjugated groups harbor profound grievances, they are reluctant to respond with open violence. The potential for political mobilization varies inversely with the intensity and level of government oppression.

The above four attributes explain how groups endure grievances and configure their responses to mobilization. Gurr outlined three additional factors that would increase the opportunities and incentives for political action by aggrieved ethnic and communal groups.[9]

First, a disadvantaged communal group's potential for political action is increased by the dispersion of its members among a number of neighboring countries, providing political activists in one country with a safe sanctuary among their fellow nationals in adjoining states. Whether these transnational kindred are disadvantaged minorities or a favored group, the activists usually can count on their diplomatic, political, economic, and military support.

Second, the communal group can benefit from the widespread presence of international networks. Many of these network groups share traits and similar conditions. The groups that are part of such networks have access to a myriad of resources, including ideology, leadership, organizational skills, and material inducements. Networks also provide publicity for the group's grievances and political demands. They try to do so through exchanging visits and meetings, newsletter coverage, and the supply of strategies and tactics for action and political organization.

Third, the lack of democracy hinders the process of assimilation and the accommodation of the interests of the ethnic group. The absence of democracy keeps the group's grievances alive and amenable to mobilization.

The ethnopolitical mobilizational model outlined above circumvents many of the shortcomings of the other perspectives discussed in this chapter. Because it incorporates the deprivation and resource mobilization perspectives, it offers a more appropriate analytical device for the explanation of the growth of modern Palestinian nationalism. In the following pages, I will utilize the relative deprivation, resource mobilization, and ethnopolitical mobilizational models to explain the rise of Palestinian nationalism.

THE REEMERGENCE OF PALESTINIAN NATIONALISM

Palestinian nationalism, as we know it today, has passed through a number of phases. The first phase began before World War I and ended with the outbreak of the first Arab-Israeli war in 1948. This phase witnessed the emergence of early Palestinian nationalism.[10] The second phase, 1948-67, was marked by the primacy of Arab nationalism, where the Palestinians relegated the task of reconstructing Arab Palestine to the Arab armies. The third phase began in the mid-1960s and especially after the 1967 Arab-Israeli war, when the defeat of the collective Arab armies allowed for the emergence of a distinct modern Palestinian nationalism. It is the third phase that is the focus of this chapter.

The rise of Palestinian nationalism in the 1960s is partly attributed to the crisis milieu that the Palestinians experienced. The crisis milieu refers to the Palestinians' deep sense of deprivation and grievance that resulted from Israel's occupation of all of Palestine and the Palestinians' subsequent physical dispersal among several states in the Middle East.

Since the early days of the twentieth century, the Palestinians have experienced an ongoing atmosphere of crisis. After World War I, Britain extended its mandate over Palestine and pledged to form a state for the Jews in Palestine. In an effort to realize this goal, Britain facilitated Jewish immigration to Palestine and the transfer of land to the new immigrants. The establishment of Israel in 1948, the subsequent dispersal of the Palestinians, and Israel's 1967 occupation of the West Bank and Gaza further compounded Palestinian grievances.

The harsh living conditions inside the refugee camps is another source for the anguish of the Palestinians.[11] Palestinian nationalism among the refugee dwellers appeared against a background of social and economic denial. These conditions are manifested by the widespread unemployment and the scarcity of social, educational, and health services. The prevalence of such harsh conditions aroused national militancy among the residents of the refugee camps.

The memories of the massacres of Palestinian civilians at Dir Yasin, Sabra, Shatilla, and Tal al-Za'tar are also at the core of the Palestinians' collective agony. The Palestinians have endured pain and discrimination at the hands of some of their fellow Arabs. They recall with pain the 1970 civil war in Jordan, Syria's repressive measures against the Palestinians in 1976 and 1983, and the Palestinians' mass exodus from Kuwait following the 1990-91 Gulf War. Such grievances reinforced the Palestinians' collective identity and perpetuated their continual responsiveness to the mobilizational efforts of PLO activists.

With regard to the Palestinians inside the West Bank and Gaza, the repressive measures associated with Israel's military occupation are in part responsible for the rise of Palestinian national identity. The intensification of such national sentiments also occurred as a result of Jewish extremist attacks on Palestinian institutions and personalities and on the Islamic holy places in Jerusalem and Hebron.

Israel's economic policies have also been responsible for the decline in Palestinian economic fortunes. Since its occupation of the West Bank and the Gaza Strip in 1967, Israel expropriated 52 percent of the West Bank land and 40 percent of the Gaza Strip, thus reducing the available land for cultivation.[12] By the mid-1980s, the proportion of Palestinians working in agriculture had dropped to 28 percent in the West Bank and 17 percent in Gaza.[13] Many of these peasants sought employment inside the Jewish state.

During the second half of the 1980s and the early 1990s, the economic conditions inside the occupied territories deteriorated further. The economic recession in Jordan and the Gulf region caused additional unemployment among the Palestinians. It was partly because of these gloomy economic conditions that on 7 December 1987, a popular nationalist uprising, the Intifada, broke out in the West Bank and the Gaza Strip.

The net effects of these historical experiences as well as the prevailing political economy explain the rise of an exclusive Palestinian nationalism and the development of communal solidarity even more than the central features of the primordial and instrumental perspectives. Yet these grievances alone cannot explain the intensification of Palestinian nationalism. Political and contextual factors also have a bearing on the rise of Palestinian nationalism. The Palestinians' common cultural identity, cohesiveness, and concentration in the Middle East region facilitated their recruitment at the hands of several mobilizing agents. As will be explained below, the Palestinians' traditional elite, militant counterelite, mass organizations, and the PLO, with its various factions, were all active in the process of the political recruitment of the Palestinians.[14]

The Ethnonational Mobilization of the Palestinians

The 1960s did not provide the political space for the rise of Palestinian ethnonationalism. The rivalries among the Arab countries and the political territorial ambitions of the Arab leaders hindered the development of separate Palestinian political institutions. In this connection, the Arab Higher Committee's request to the Arab League in 1948 to form a Palestinian government was foiled by the internal splits within the ranks of the Palestinians and the rivalry between Egypt and Jordan for the custodianship of the Palestinian cause.[15]

The advancement of Palestinian nationalism in the 1950s was also hindered by the primacy of the ideology of pan-Arabism. Following their political and physical dispersal, the Palestinians entrusted the task of liberating their land to the Arab armies. Arab unity was seen as sine qua non for the liberation of Palestine. The Arabization of the Palestinian question was facilitated by the emergence of Gamal 'Abd al-Nasir, the charismatic leader of Egypt. Nasir's espousal of pan-Arabism, as evidenced in the merger with Syria in 1958, lessened the appeal of nascent local Palestinian nationalism.

During the 1960s, five factors muted the allure of Arab nationalism and made available numerous resources and opportunities for the ascendance of a separate Palestinian national identity. First, the failure of the Arab countries to redress Palestinian grievances created a political vacuum. In addition to the inter-Arab divisions and rivalries, the collapse of the unity between Syria and Egypt in September 1961 brought into question the ability of the Arabs to liberate Palestine. These doubts were confirmed when the Arab heads of state failed to carry out a divergence of the waters of the Jordan River in the mid-1960s. The Arab armies' defeat in 1967 lent further substance to the Palestinian perceptions of the inefficacy of the joint Arab approach to the resolution of the Palestinian question. The insolvency of the collective Arab approach thus altered the Palestinians' outlook regarding their own role. After the 1967 defeat, the ideology of Palestinian nationalism replaced pan-Arabism as a rallying point and as an important resource for political mobilization.

Second, the presence of transnational networks, actors, and groups furnished the Palestinians with numerous resources and opportunities. The Algerians' attainment of their independence in 1962 through the strategy of national liberation warfare gave the Palestinians an alternative to the Arab collective approach. Likewise, outside governmental and private help were crucial in sustaining the PLO, which gained the financial, political, and military support of neighboring countries, movements, and individuals.

Outside private financial contributions enabled the PLO to provide social services, to initiate economic projects, and to give financial assistance to the families whose sons and daughters were in Israeli jails or had been killed in encounters with the Israeli army. The sources of such support were both international and regional network groups and transnational kindred or private citizens. In particular, the PLO received financial assistance from Palestinians working in Saudi Arabia and other Gulf states. This assistance took the form of a 4-percent tax on their salaries, levied on a monthly basis.

The Palestinians also exploited inter-Arab rivalries and hostilities to advance their national goals. In an effort to bolster their domestic legitimacy, neutralize the opposition, and consolidate their rule, Arab rulers extended political, diplomatic, economic, and military support to the Palestinian nationalist movement. This support was not confined to the progressive secular authoritarian elite; traditional regimes like Morocco, Saudi Arabia, and Jordan offered diplomatic and economic backing to the Palestinians. Oppositional groups in many Arab countries gave added impetus to the Palestinian movement. The promotion of the Palestinian cause had become a vehicle for the articulation of popular grievances and a potent force against incumbent Arab regimes.

In addition to the regional support, the Palestinians received political, military, economic, and moral support from the Soviet Union, China, North Korea, Eastern Europe, nonaligned countries, and several national liberation movements. Many of these countries trained military cadres of the PLO and supplied them with arms and funds. Such multifaceted support sharply increased Palestinian activism and gave the political leaders the space and opportunity to mobilize their followers.

Third, the reemergence of Palestinian nationalism was also a function of political space: the existence of internal and external opportunities. This political space has encompassed the tolerance of the powerholders; governmental permission or denial of the space has heavily influenced the ability of the PLO's leaders to operate. The cooptation of several Arab governments—Syria, Iraq, Libya after 1969, and Algeria—of the activities of the Palestinian commando groups created a highly favorable atmosphere for the ascension of Palestinian nationalism and allowed it to operate with few political limitations.[16]

Lebanon, for instance, furnished the PLO activists with the political space needed to build up mass support in different parts of the country. In the mid-1960s, Syria condoned the activities of the PLO, with the aim of checking the influence of Jordan. It encouraged Fatah to carry out military operations against Israel from Jordanian territory. The PLO also benefitted from the financial support of Kuwait and Saudi Arabia, which sought to restrain the influence of the Palestinian radical groups by offering the moderate leadership of the PLO financial rewards.

Fourth, the transnational presence of Palestinians in a number of Arab countries—Lebanon, Syria, Jordan, Kuwait, and the West Bank and Gaza Strip—provided a climate for the crystallization of Palestinian nationalism.

The split of Palestinian society after 1948 into four main clusters (Israeli Palestinians, West Bank and Gaza Palestinians, Palestinians living in refugee camps in the neighboring Arab states, and Palestinians residing in the Arab world and the West) initially complicated the task of ethnopolitical mobilization and nation building. Yet the presence of the Palestinians across national boundaries in the Middle East provided the PLO's political activists with numerous resources, including political and economic support as well as a sanctuary for recruitment and training of a military force. Many of the Palestinians who were living in refugee camps in Lebanon, Syria, Jordan, the West Bank, and Gaza provided the PLO with a population to recruit and mobilize. This force was used to carry out military operations against Israel, challenge the legitimacy of some Arab regimes, and police and administer the refugee camps. In contrast, the Palestinians residing in the Arab Persian Gulf region, especially in Kuwait, extended financial assistance to the mobilizational efforts of the PLO.

The relative degree of openness of the political system in Lebanon, Kuwait, and, to a lesser degree, Jordan, facilitated the recruitment efforts of the PLO. In these three states, trade unions, voluntary associations, and, in the case of Lebanon, political parties and movements existed in one form or another. This situation provided the opportunity for the PLO to operate openly and to recruit the Palestinians.

The nonassimilation of the Palestinians in their various places of residence kept their grievances alive. With the exception of Jordan, which granted Jordanian citizenship to the Palestinians living in the country, the rest of the Arab states did not integrate the Palestinians. The absence of pluralism and institutionalized democracies in the Arab world deprived the politically aware Palestinians of the democratic norms of equal rights and opportunities.

Fifth, the availability of organizational structures and political resources enhanced the process of mobilizing the Palestinian community. Without minimizing the significance of the political space and the transnational kindred, networks, and groups, the political mobilization of the Palestinians was also the result of the availability of certain assets and resources. The presence of a charismatic leadership, organizational structures, communication networks, labor force, economic assets, and political opportunities are other resources that facilitated the mobilization of the Palestinians.[17]

The concentration of the Palestinians in refugee camps proved to be another valuable resource for political mobilization. The camps provide a vehicle for close contacts between the leadership and the rank and file. A vast network of day-care agencies, schools, youth and sports clubs, clinics, and cottage industries was established. In addition, the post-World War II period experienced the rapid modernization of Palestinian society. This was evidenced by the spread of education and the exposure of the Palestinians to the mass media. The expansion of education was the driving force behind the emergence of a class of modern intelligentsia that broke away from the traditional order and eroded the dominance of the conservative elite.

The 1967 war accelerated the demise of the traditional elite. The change in the leadership was completed in 1969, when the leaders of the Palestinian commando groups took over the PLO. Since that time, such figures as Yasir Arafat, George Habash, and Na'if Hawatmah, among others, have facilitated the process of political indoctrination, recruitment, and organization of the discontented. The access of those leaders to television, radio, printed material, communal associations, and the refugee camps enabled them to disseminate their ideas among their followers and to take their message to the urban poor, the refugee camp dwellers, and the inhabitants of the rural areas.

While questioning the legitimacy and the authority of the older politicians, the new political entrepreneurs started to address issues relating to Palestinian nationalism and became instrumental in the acceleration of the growth of a Palestinian separate identity. Unlike the traditional leaders, who were passive and status quo oriented, the new leaders did not hesitate to use violence and to defy their enemies. The lifestyles of those leaders contrasted sharply with the luxuries enjoyed by Arab kings and presidents. Through daily contacts with their followers and the appeal of their message, those nationalist leaders gave hope to their adherents for a better future, when lost homes in Palestine would be restored.

THE ROLE OF MOBILIZING AGENTS

The combination of these five factors provided the Palestinian political entrepreneurs with the opportunity to launch modern Palestinian nationalism. The process of mobilizing the Palestinians occurred at different rates. After the breakup of Palestinian society in 1948, the political organization of the Palestinians was slow to occur. The provision of food, shelter, employment, and education were the immediate concerns for the Palestinians. Labor and professional unions were formed alongside cooperative health and child-care centers to provide services to the refugee camp dwellers. The organizations established in the 1950s and early 1960s included the General Union of Palestine Students, the General Union of Palestine Workers, the General Union of Palestine Women, the General Union of Palestine Teachers, and the Palestine Red Crescent Society.[18] In addition to serving the socioeconomic needs of the Palestinians, such mass organizations provided a communication channel between the national leadership and the masses and provided the Palestinians with the opportunity for political participation in their place of residence. The net effect of the rise of these organizations was to accelerate the process of identity renewal.

In addition to these mass organizations, four political groups were active in mobilizing the Palestinians.[19] Fatah—established by Arafat and his associates in the early 1960s—was the first of these groups. Its main preoccupation was the nurturing of a distinct Palestinian national awareness and the mobilization of the Palestinian masses.[20] In December 1964 Fatah's leaders used military struggle as a vehicle to liberate Palestine. The aim of Fatah's military activities was to force the "irresolute" Arab armies to engage Israel. After the defeat of 1967, Fatah espoused self-reliance as a new strategy to liberate Palestine, rather than relying on Arab conventional forces.

Two new Palestinian commando groups were formed in the aftermath of the 1967 war: the Popular Front for the Liberation of Palestine (PFLP) and the Democratic Front for the Liberation of Palestine (DFLP). The two organizations advocated guerrilla warfare and class struggle as tools to liberate Palestine. They believed that pursuing the road to Palestine was an integral part of a social revolution in the Arab world. The DFLP was engaged in international terrorism. Their radical Marxist orientation confined their support to a small circle of students and intellectuals.

The growing popularity of the resistance groups prompted some Arab regimes to sponsor commando groups. In order to influence the direction of Palestinian politics, Syria and Iraq each advanced organizations emphasizing the pan-Arab nature of the Palestinian struggle: al-Sa'iqa and the Arab Liberation Front (ALF) respectively.

The PLO was another mobilizational group. Its formation in 1964 came in response to growing Palestinian national sentiment and military activity. Until 1968, the PLO was dominated by traditional Palestinian notables. Prior to the 1967 war, the PLO had viewed its role in the liberation of Palestine as a corollary to that of the Arab armies. But, the Arab military defeat discredited the PLO. In July 1968, the Palestinian commando groups led by Arafat took over the PLO, and the new organization assumed a more vigorous role in mass mobilization and the articulation of a separate Palestinian national identity. In the late 1960s and the 1970s, the radical factions of the PLO used violence and terrorism to publicize their cause.

To enlist additional support for the Palestinian problem, the PLO established close contacts with various national liberation movements and groups that had similar ideological stands. It viewed the Palestinian struggle as part of a third world anti-colonial drive. The PLO also derived political support from international organizations and movements and from friendly countries. As a result of these efforts, Arab heads of state recognized the PLO as the sole legitimate representative of the Palestinians in October 1974. During the same month, the United Nations granted the PLO observer status, and many third world and communist countries recognized the organization.

In its efforts to mobilize the Palestinians, the PLO developed an impressive organizational, political, and economic apparatus. Its institutions and mass organizations became more energetic in rendering social, educational, and health services to the refugees. The organization possessed many attributes of the nation-state, including a cabinet, a parliament, and various social, economic, and cultural departments and agencies.[21] The Palestine National Council (PNC) has functioned as a parliament in exile. Its members represent the interests of the various Palestinian constituents, including the PLO factions, the popular organizations, prominent Palestinian individuals, and the Palestinian communities in different geographic regions.

In addition to the PNC, there is the fifteen-member PLO executive committee, which has several cabinet portfolios, including the departments of military, planning, information, foreign policy, the occupied homeland, education, social affairs, popular organizations, and the Palestine National Fund. The composition of the executive committee reflects the political weight of the differing PLO factions including Fatah, the PFLP, the DFLP, al-Sa'iqa, the communists, and the independents. There is also the Palestine Red Crescent Society, which serves as the department of health. It offers humanitarian and medical services to the Palestinians in the refugee camps and operates a number of hospitals and clinics in several Arab countries.[22] The various PLO departments provide numerous employment opportunities for hundreds of Palestinians.[23]

The PLO offices in various Arab and third world capitals function as Palestinian embassies, issuing travel documents and marriage certificates, and extending financial aid to students and needy families. These offices also provide a meeting ground for Palestinian political activities and for the celebration of national days.

The PLO military factions operate as political parties representing different ideological and political interests within the Palestinian nationalist movement. The competition among these factions has often been violent and intense. By the early 1980s there were approximately thirty Palestinian newspapers and magazines, attesting to the vigor of the political debate among these groups. The outcome of this competition was an increase in the political awareness of their constituents.

Inclusion of the Inside

The PLO's early mobilizational efforts took place in the refugee camps, whereas the Palestinians inside the occupied territories, in Israel, and outside the Arab world were mobilized at a later stage. Beginning in 1973, the PLO began to mobilize the Palestinians within the West Bank and Gaza. As a result of these efforts, the influence of the pro-Jordanian elite over West Bank local politics diminished.[24]

Palestinian national awakening was illustrated by the rise of West Bank/Gaza-wide political structures. In the summer of 1973, the Palestine National Front (PNF) was formed to check Jordan's influence and promote allegiance to the PLO. The PNF called for the formation of an independent Palestinian state in the occupied territories and advocated that the PLO should represent the interests of the Palestinians in any political talks. The 1976 municipal elections brought to power new leaders who espoused Palestinian nationalism. In October 1978, the National Guidance Committee (NGC) was created to oppose the self-autonomy plan of the Camp David accords and to assert the Palestinian right to self-determination. These structures advanced the mobilization of the Palestinian community.[25]

The efforts of these internal mobilizing agents were significantly enhanced when, in June 1974, the PNC endorsed the concept of an independent Palestinian state on any liberated part of Palestine and when the Arab heads of state convening in Baghdad in November 1978 appropriated $150 million annually for the West Bank and Gaza, to be distributed by the PLO and Jordan.

Palestinian ethnonational mobilization reached a new level when the Intifada erupted in December 1987. During the Intifada, numerous popular committees formed to render voluntary services and promote communal solidarity. A process of indigenous, independent institution building in areas of legislation, justice, trade, education, health, social welfare, and economic infrastructure was initiated. The Intifada constituted a turning point in Palestinian modern history, as it increased national awareness among the Palestinians. It also advanced their political weight and legitimized their role in the larger Palestinian nationalist movement. The experience that the Palestinians gained from the Intifada reinforced their sense of communal solidarity.

The PLO and the Mobilization of the Israeli Arabs

The growth of national consciousness among the Palestinians who live inside Israel was a slow and gradual process. The PLO did not engage seriously in their political mobilization and recruitment as it had done with the Palestinians in the occupied territories and in Lebanon and Syria. During the first three decades following the establishment of Israel, the PLO did not develop an articulate policy toward the Israeli Arabs. Its attitude toward them can be described as one of benign neglect. The interests of this segment of the Palestinian people did not figure prominently in the PLO's strategy and political calculations.

The political support of the PLO among the Israeli Arabs is useful and desirable, but not essential. Even after the 1970s, when the PLO began to recognize the political importance of the Israeli Arabs in the larger Palestinian struggle, its political statements toward them remained primarily reactive rather than purposeful and initiatory.[26] The PLO, after all, derives legitimacy basically from Palestinians within and beyond the occupied territories.

One can therefore attribute the rise of Palestinian nationalism among aggrieved Israeli Arabs to the exclusive nature of Israel's Jewish culture, the state's political identification with Zionism, and the fact that the Arabs have not been fully integrated into Israeli society. They have suffered from the confiscation of their land and a lack of employment opportunities. They have also experienced shortages in housing, classrooms, teachers, and municipal services and funds.

The national mobilization of the Israeli Arabs resulted also from the presence of political opportunities. With Israel's occupation of the West Bank and Gaza in the 1967 war, the geographic isolation of the Israeli Arabs ended. The opening of the borders allowed for the rise of political, economic, social, and cultural ties between the Palestinian community in the occupied territories and inside Israel—a situation that led many Israeli Palestinians to identify with the politics of Palestinian nationalism.[27]

Conclusion

I have sought to establish that the ethnopolitical mobilization model, which combines the grievances and resource mobilization perspectives, is a more appropriate theoretical device to explain the rise of Palestinian ethnonationalism than either the primordial or the instrumentalist approach. I have pointed to several factors that have facilitated ethnocommunal mobilization of the Palestinians: the transnational presence of the Palestinians in the Middle East; the political, economic, and diplomatic backing of regional and international networks and groups; and the alienation of the Palestinians in their places of residence.

Other conditions that increased the Palestinians' potential for mobilization were their regional concentration, cohesion, and political exclusion, the intensity of discrimination and grievances they experienced, and the presence of a leadership class. The exposure of the Palestinians to advanced education and to the mobilizational efforts of the PLO and other mobilizing agents have also had a significant effect on the crystallization of Palestinian nationalism. The often conflictual relationships among the Arab countries have provided the Palestinians with needed political space and enabled them to enlist political support by playing one state against another.

In addition, Palestinian national solidarity has intensified over the years due to a deep sense of deprivation. The grievances of the Palestinians resulted from Israel's military occupation of their lands and its threats to their physical and national existence. Unemployment and demographic stress are additional factors that have accelerated the growth of Palestinian ethnic national identity. Finally, the presence of a common language, religion, and history, the belief in the just nature of their cause, and the shared vision of a desired future are elements that have strengthened Palestinian cultural and ethnic identity. As a result, the Palestinians have become politically organized, acquired their own group identity, and pursued political independence. These factors separate Palestinian nationalism from pan-Arabism.

The net effect of all these factors is that the vast majority of the Palestinians envisage the formation of a state of their own as a requisite framework for the attainment of their political, social, cultural, and economic identity and existence. The establishment of a West Bank/ Gaza state, where Palestinian traditions and cultural heritage can be preserved, is the core objective for the Palestinians. Political independence is the highest end of Palestinian nationalism.

Notes

1. See Charles F. Keyes, ed., *Ethnic Change* (Seattle: University of Washington Press, 1981); Fouad Ajami, *The Arab Predicament* (New York: Cambridge University Press, 1981); Joseph Rothschild, *Ethnopolitics: A Conceptual Framework* (New York: Columbia University Press, 1981); Richard A. Schermerhorn, *Comparative Ethnic Relations: A Framework for Theory and Research* (New York: Random House, 1970); James McKay, "An Exploratory Synthesis of Primordial and Mobilizational Approaches to Ethnic Phenomena," in *Ethnic and Race Relations* 5 (October 1982): 395-420; and Jeffrey A. Ross, ed., *The Mobilization of Collective Identity: Comparative Perspectives* (Lanham, Md.: University Press of America, 1981).
2. For more on this topic, see Crawford Young, *The Politics of Cultural Pluralism* (Madison: University of Wisconsin Press, 1976), 23-55.
3. For the instrumental perspective, see Abner Cohen, "Introduction: The Lesson of Ethnicity," in *Urban Ethnicity,* Abner Cohen, ed., ix-xxiv (London: Tavistock Publications, 1974).
4. Laurie A. Brand, *The Palestinians in the Arab World: Institution-Building and the Search for State* (New York: Columbia University Press, 1988), 10-12.
5. See Dov Ronen, *The Quest for Self-Determination* (New Haven: Yale University Press, 1979), 53.
6. This model was applied by Brand to study institution building among the Palestinians in her pioneering study, *The Palestinians in the Arab World.*
7. For an explanation of the resource mobilization model, see Charles Tilly, *From Mobilization to Revolution* (Reading, Mass.: Addison-Wesley, 1978); Louise A. Tilly and Charles Tilly, eds., *Class Conflict and Collective Action* (Beverly Hills,

Calif.: Sage, 1981); and R. Aya, "Theories of Revolution Reconsidered: Contrasting Models of Collective Violence," *Theory and Society* 8 (1979): 39-99.
8. Ted R. Gurr, "Ethnopolitical Mobilization: Minorities at Risk" (paper presented at the annual meeting of the International Studies Association, Vancouver, British Columbia, 22 March 1991), 7.
9. Ibid., 16-18.
10. For a very useful analysis of the rise of early Palestinian nationalism, see Muhammad Y. Muslih, *The Origins of Palestinian Nationalism* (New York: Columbia University Press, 1988). See also William B. Quandt, Fuad Jabber, and Ann Lesch, *The Politics of Palestinian Nationalism* (Berkeley: University of California Press, 1973); David Gilmour, *Dispossessed: The Ordeal of the Palestinians, 1917-1980* (London: Sphere Books, 1982).
11. For an assessment of the impact of refugee camp life, see Rosemary Sayigh, "The Palestinian Identity among Camp Residents," *Journal of Palestine Studies* 6 (spring 1977): 3-22; idem, "Sources of Palestinian Nationalism: A Study of a Palestinian Camp in Lebanon," *Journal of Palestinian Studies* 6 (summer 1977): 17-40; and Bassem Sirhan, "A Refugee Camp Life in Lebanon," *Journal of Palestinian Studies* 4 (winter 1975): 91-107.
12. Cheryl A. Rubenberg, "Twenty Years of Israeli Economic Policies in the West Bank and Gaza: Prologue to the Intifada," *Journal of Arab Affairs* 8 (spring 1989): 35.
13. Meron Benvenisti, *West Bank Data Report* (Boulder, Colo.: Westview, 1987), 19.
14. For a comprehensive treatment of these mobilizing efforts, see Brand, *Palestinians in the Arab World*.
15. Ibid., 22-24.
16. Theda Skocpol, *States and Social Revolutions: A Comparative Study of France, Russia, and China* (Cambridge, Mass.: Harvard University Press, 1971), 19-24.
17. For a general discussion of the significance of these factors, see Rod Aya, "Theories of Revolution Reconsidered: Contrasting Models of Collective Violence," *Theory and Society* 8 (July 1979): 39-99; Louise A. Tilly and Charles Tilly, *Class Conflict and Collective Action*; Barrington Moore, Jr., *Injustice: The Social Basis of Obedience and Revolt* (White Plains, N.Y.: M. E. Sharpe, 1978); Mancur Olson, *The Logic of Collective Action: Public Goods and the Theory of Groups* (Cambridge, Mass.: Harvard University Press, 1971), esp. 19-24.
18. Brand's *Palestinians in the Arab World* is an authoritative source for these unions and associations.
19. For additional information, see Quandt, Jabber, and Lesch, *The Politics of Palestinian Nationalism,* part 2; and Kemal Kirisci, *The PLO and World Politics: A Study of the Mobilization of Support for the Palestinian Cause* (New York: St. Martin's Press, 1986), chap. 4.

20. See Abdallah Frangi, *The PLO and Palestine,* trans. Paul Knight (London: Zed Books, 1983), 94-96; and Quandt, Jabber, and Lesch, *Politics of Palestinian Nationalism,* 55-56.
21. For more information, see Rashid Hamid, "What Is the PLO?" *Journal of Palestine Studies* 4 (summer 1975): 90-109.
22. Brand, *Palestinians in the Arab World,* 39-40.
23. For additional information on the PLO, see Kirisci, *The PLO and World Politics,* chap. 4; and Helena Cobban, *The Palestinian Liberation Organization: People, Power, and Politics* (New York: Cambridge University Press, 1984).
24. Kirisci, *The PLO and World Politics,* chaps. 5-8.
25. Ibid., chap. 4.
26. For a detailed treatment of this subject, see Emile Sahliyeh, "The PLO and the Israeli Arabs" (paper presented at the Arab Minority Conference, Tel Aviv University, 1-3 June 1991).
27. Mark A. Tessler, "Ethnic Change and Non-Assimilating Minority Status: The Case of Jews in Tunisia and Morocco and Arabs in Israel," in *Ethnic Change,* Charles Keyes, ed. (Seattle: University of Washington Press, 1981).

TWO

THE ARMED STRUGGLE AND PALESTINIAN NATIONALISM

Yezid Sayigh

UNTIL THE SIGNING OF THE DECLARATION OF PRINCIPLES between the PLO and Israel in September 1993, most Palestinians consistently portrayed military action as the primary means of struggle against Israel. Carrying the banner of armed struggle began with the small bands of self-styled avengers and liberators who appeared in the refugee camps soon after the establishment of the State of Israel in 1948, over what had until then been Palestine, and of the state-sponsored *fida'iyyoun* ("self-sacrificers") of the mid-1950s. It was also true of the guerrilla groups that emerged among the scattered Palestinian communities over the following decade, and of the Palestine Liberation Organization (PLO). After 1964, and especially after the guerrilla groups took leadership of the PLO in 1968, the PLO transformed the call for military action into a full-fledged doctrine and instrument of policy.

Why did the Palestinians continue to emphasize the need for military action so vehemently and consistently, and for so long? And what were the primary achievements of the Palestinian armed struggle in the decades following its formal launch by Fatah, the dominant Palestinian group, in 1965? Since Palestinian military action had failed to dislodge Israeli control of any part of pre-1948 Palestine through direct, physical force, how can we understand the enduring function of Palestinian military action in historical perspective?

Setting the Context

There can be little doubt that the war surrounding the 1948 establishment of the State of Israel has been the foremost determinant of Palestinian politics ever since. In the course of the year after November 1947, 60 percent or more of all Palestinian Arabs became refugees, concentrated in the West Bank and Gaza Strip or in neighboring Arab states. The conflict had deprived a largely agrarian society of land, its main source of economic livelihood, and of social identity. The collapse of existing political and military organizations—rudimentary and factionalized as they were—and the precipitate flight of many in the rising middle class and educated elites during 1948 similarly removed the social strata that might otherwise have asserted their leadership in the wake of the destruction of the "old elite."

That Palestinian society could not speedily reconstitute itself and rebuild national political institutions in the wake of 1948 was also due to the dichotomous relationship with the Arab states under whose authority the scattered communities now came. The Palestinians had strong cultural and social links with surrounding Arab societies, an affinity that drew many into the domestic politics of the host countries. Palestinians provided much of the rank and file of the whole range of opposition parties in Jordan—the Ba'th party, Arab nationalist movement, Communist party, and Muslim Brotherhood Society, to mention the most important—and were active too in Syria and Lebanon.

The introduction of large numbers of Palestinian refugees posed a special challenge for newly independent Arab host countries. For the ruling elites in these countries, who were engaged in asserting their legitimacy and in building their separate nation-states, the refugees were a threat to domestic stability. This was especially the case because rival Arab governments could manipulate the Palestine conflict to undermine domestic stability. Infiltration by Palestinian refugees anxious to return home in what was now Israel, harvest crops, retrieve property, or simply wreak vengeance presented an additional security problem: increasing the risk of war with Israel. Whether in the Gaza Strip and West Bank or in neighboring places of refuge, Arab governments generally sought to both seal off their borders with Israel and to keep Palestinian nationalism firmly under control.

What the Palestinians knew as *al-nakba* (the catastrophe), severely impeded the revival of their national movement after 1948. It could no longer operate within a single, contiguous territory, nor draw on a single, integrated social base. The absence of representative political institutions enjoying both grassroots credibility and official Arab recognition was another major impediment; Hajj Amin al-Husaini's Higher Arab Committee and Ahmad Hilmi's All-Palestine Government now existed only in name and gradually faded into obscurity. Individuals or organized groups hoping to rebuild the national movement had to contend with physical dispersal, social disarticulation, and loss of the sources of autonomous economic income.

Not that the Palestinians resigned themselves to their fate, even amid the wretched conditions of the refugee camps. Former *mujahidoun* (combatants of holy war) and younger recruits organized themselves into small, locally based bands; thousands took part in economically and politically motivated infiltration into Israel in the next few years. Yet this was a scattered and largely uncoordinated effort, despite the efforts of Husaini and newly founded groups such as the Arab Nationalist Movement. The Egyptian and Syrian military intelligence services were to direct organized *fida'iyoun* activity against Israel in 1955–56, but this too subsided after the Suez war of 1956.

Nation Building

It is against this background that the relationship between Palestinian nation building and the armed struggle needs to be understood. No political force grasped this better than Fatah, the Palestinian guerrilla movement founded in 1959. It regarded the link between national identity and the practice of armed struggle as fundamental, and it was upon this core understanding that it proceeded to construct a broad constituency and assert its dominance in Palestinian national politics in the following years and decades.

Looking back many years later, Fatah cofounder Khalil al-Wazir (Abu Jihad) described his movement's belief that what the Palestinians faced after 1948 was "the elimination of Palestine, suppression of Palestinian identity, eradication of the Palestinian character, and the merging and dissolving of the Palestinian decision and Palestinian will."[1] This perception was a constant refrain in *Filastinuna* (Our Palestine), the monthly magazine produced between 1959 and 1964 by

Fatah, in which Wazir also played a major editorial part. In the words of one typical editorial, the Palestinians were the "children of the Catastrophe" who had been reduced to "nothing but jetsam and flotsam . . . dispersed in every corner."[2] What the Palestinians needed, Fatah concluded, was to escape dependence (*taba'iyyah*) on the Arab governments, achieve national unity, and reestablish their political entity.[3]

The solution that Fatah proposed was "revolution." This, even more than the slogan of armed struggle, predominated in the pages of *Filastinuna*. However, it had little connection with notions of social revolution to transform economic relations. Instead, it embodied the call to revolt against an intolerable and degrading reality, a rebellion of the psyche and soul. Fatah also reflected this clearly in its emphasis on the "cleansing" effect of violence on the psychology of the oppressed. This outlook was directly drawn from the writings of Frantz Fanon, the Mauritian-born thinker who witnessed the Algerian war of independence against French rule, which itself was a source of inspiration and lessons, both positive and negative, for the Fatah founders. According to Fanon, it was possible for a colonized or subjugated people to break the mental shackles of despair, quiescence, or humiliation only through armed struggle—active self-assertion.[4]

A direct and natural extension of this logic, for Fatah, was the stress in what came to be mainstream Palestinian thinking on the "event" or "act" (*al-fi'l*). The fact that an armed attack had taken place was in and of itself more important than the specific methods used or the quantifiable outcome of human losses or material damage. In effect, this was the concept of "armed propaganda" pure and simple, in which an example was set and an alternative offered to the mass of the population. This revealed another parallel, this time with the Cuban-Guevarist notion of the *foco* or armed revolutionary nucleus.[5] At a deeper level, each "act" represented a reassertion of Palestinian existence and independent will, and thus carried great psychological and political significance. So fundamental to Fatah thinking was this outlook that even as late as 1985, the purpose of continuing raids against Israel was still, Wazir explained, to demonstrate "our determination to pursue our course."[6]

Another comment by Wazir on the same occasion was even more revealing about the close, even symbiotic, relationship between armed struggle and nation-building in Fatah thinking. Reviewing the two decades of military action since 1965, he described the Palestinian version of "people's war" as a

> central, comprehensive and multi-dimensional process. Its sum total embodies the various facets and activities of the Palestinian people as a whole, whether those facets and activities are political, social, economic, military, or cultural. This is how we understand the armed struggle. This is also how we have proceeded to rebuild our people and reassert its national identity, in order to achieve its aims of return and liberation of the land. We understand it [the armed struggle] as an integrated process involving three dimensions: organization, production, and combat.[7]

In brief, raising the slogan of "armed struggle" in the 1950s and 1960s provided a specific program of action for Palestinians everywhere. It therefore played the central part in driving the process of national reassertion forward, and acted as a unifying theme. The appearance of the PLO's military wing in 1964 and the start of separate military action by the autonomous guerrilla groups in the next few years also allowed Palestinians to portray their recent history as an unbroken struggle against foreign domination since World War I. In this sequence the infiltrator *mujahidoun* and the state-sponsored *fida'iyoun* of the 1950s provided a link between 1948 and 1964. In each case, moreover, it was the call for armed struggle that allowed the various Palestinian organizations to act as mobilizing agents, to translate "potential politicization into political action" and so bestir and unite their scattered constituency.[8]

The dramatic arrival on the scene of the guerrillas after the June 1967 war therefore confirmed the self-perception of Palestinians as strugglers. Military action confirmed that the Palestinians, to themselves above all, were active participants in shaping their own destiny, rather than passive victims. True, Palestinian armed struggle had a negligible physical impact on Israel and was afflicted by wild exaggeration and jealous rivalries on the part of the guerrilla groups. Yet the excessive hyperbole and symbolism only went to show that military action served a different function entirely: to consolidate a national myth and imagined community.

At the same time the practice of military action—which also required the acquisition of arms, training, camps and depots, and organization—asserted the independence of Palestinian decision making from Arab "hegemony, tutelage, and containment." This was fundamental in the thinking of Fatah in particular; but even the guerrilla groups professing pan-Arabism, such as the Popular Front for the Liberation of Palestine (PFLP) understood that the armed struggle helped to demarcate an autonomous Palestinian identity in the Arab milieu. That the Palestinians were actually able to escape the government controls imposed since 1948 and assert their national and regional stature so rapidly and effectively after 1967 was entirely due to the shattering political and military defeat of the Arab armies in June 1967.

STATE BUILDING

The importance of the June 1967 war and of the subsequent assertion of armed struggle in the evolution of the Palestinian national movement cannot be exaggerated. This is not least because they provided the opportunity for the second, crucial component of nation building—namely, state building.

A note of clarification is necessary. The guerrilla groups were firmly opposed after June 1967 to the establishment of a Palestinian "ministate" in the West Bank and Gaza Strip, as part of a comprehensive peace settlement with Israel (regardless of whether or not this was an actual option). Conversely, the underlying nature of their political and social institutions and of the diplomatic recognition they sought was congruent with the processes commonly identified with state building.

The notion of statehood was not new for the Palestinians; they had demanded independence from British rule throughout the Mandate. The Palestinian leadership rejected the United Nations Partition Plan of November 1947 (General Assembly Resolution 181), as did the Arab states; but it also sought to set up its own national administration and state unilaterally in the course of 1948. Its attempts were blocked by the League of Arab States, despite the formation toward the end of the war of the ill-fated All-Palestine Government; the Arab governments subsequently made no attempt to establish a Palestinian state in the Gaza Strip and West Bank (including East Jerusalem).[9] Only in 1959 did Egypt's Gamal 'Abd al-Nasir and Iraq's 'Abd al-Karim Qasim reopen the issue, calling, respectively, for the establishment of a Palestinian "entity" or "republic."[10]

The apparent revival of interest was primarily the result of inter-Arab rivalries, however, and subsided with the escalation of the Arab "cold war" in 1961-62. The same motivation lay behind renewed Iraqi and Syrian calls for setting up a Palestinian quasi state in the Gaza Strip and West Bank in September 1963 and January 1964. All the Arab states could agree on, in contrast, was to hold further consultations on the forms of organization of the Palestinians. That this led to the formation of the PLO was due to the energy and ambition of the

Palestinian representative to the League of Arab States, Ahmad al-Shuqairi, and to the support of Nasir.

Despite the ambivalence or outright opposition of certain Arab governments, Shuqairi founded the PLO firmly in the image of a state. It had a constitution, executive committee, legislative assembly, "government" departments, army, audited budget, and internal statutes. Before 1967 it imposed limited taxes and conscription on the Palestinian civilian population, with the assistance of some Arab host governments, and attempted to establish a single, all-embracing "mass" organization as its political vehicle. The PLO defined itself as the Palestinian "entity," the embodiment of Palestinian nationalism, and at the same time was formed very much in the image of prevalent Arab state structures, especially Nasir's Egypt.

The PLO enjoyed the material attributes and diplomatic status of a state, albeit to a very modest degree, but its scope for independent political or military action remained severely constrained. The founding generation proved unable to transform its potential into a serious challenge to the status quo and finally fell victim to the debacle of June 1967. It was in this context that the guerrilla groups operating outside the PLO framework were able to assert themselves, through the conduct and promotion of the "armed struggle." Their ascendancy was completed with the election of Yasir Arafat as PLO chairman in February 1969.

From 1969 onward, the PLO "state" was imbued with the ethos and legitimacy of armed struggle, allowing it in turn to absorb and incorporate the various guerrilla groups, trade and professional unions, and other political organizations and social associations of the Palestinian people. Not all Palestinians or guerrilla leaders were happy with what they saw as the threat of bureaucratization, but some saw such institutionalization as "an ambition of all revolutions." For Fatah in particular, "the general Palestinian institution [was] the organized expression of Palestinian national identity."[11]

Nonetheless, the new Palestinian leadership was compelled to conduct both the armed struggle and the state-building exercise from outside its national territory. Fatah, joined belatedly by the PFLP and other groups, sought to organize an armed insurrection in the West Bank and establish a national authority in the latter half of 1967, but the failure of its attempt compelled the movement subsequently to operate from sanctuaries in often unwilling Arab host countries.[12] It was in this context, therefore, that the political appeal and military capability of the PLO gained importance in defending the nascent national institution and its growing social base from the reassertion of Arab government controls. By the same token, the center of gravity of Palestinian nationalism was to be mainly located in exile until the eruption of the Intifada in December 1987.[13]

THE ARMED STRUGGLE IN TRANSITION

The reassertion of Palestinian national identity had effectively been achieved by the outbreak of the Jordanian civil war in September 1970. Ironically, the defeat of the PLO by July 1971 actually assisted the second component of nation building—that is, state building. The hopes and ambitions born of the "armed struggle," embodied in the myth of "guerrilla war" and "people's war," were shattered, as were the calls by leftist guerrilla groups for social and political revolution in the Arab countries. The episode also revealed the resilience of the Arab states, reflected in their ability to ride out the crisis of and potential internal challenges exacerbated by the Palestinian issue.

The Jordanian civil war did more than mark the end of the armed Palestinian presence in the Hashemite kingdom, however. It also allowed the dominant guerrilla group, Fatah, to confirm the PLO as the central body for Palestinian decision making and policy formation, against the opposition of the enfeebled Left. The significance of this development soon became clear as Arafat and his colleagues in Fatah sought to translate Palestinian sacrifices into political gains, above all into Arab and international recognition. This effort was given a major boost by the Arab-Israeli war of October 1973, following which the PLO was recognized by the Arab states, the Non-Aligned Movement and similar third world groupings, and the socialist and Soviet-bloc countries as the sole legitimate representative of the Palestinian people.

Underlying this progression was a basic shift in the thinking of the Palestinian leadership. The 1973 war had been waged with the aim of revitalizing the peace process, and the Arab states sought to regain their territory with the aid of the regional and international balance of forces. It was from this point onward that the core of PLO strategy was to pave the way for a negotiated settlement leading to the creation of a small Palestinian state alongside Israel.[14]

The Palestinian mainstream was to engage in a bitter political dispute, occasionally accompanied by outbursts of violence, with its opponents within the PLO (and even within Fatah) over the next eight years. During this period the PLO pursued three main, practical objectives: to ensure its physical self-defense in Lebanon, to safeguard its political gains and enhance its diplomatic status, and to induce the United States to place the establishment of a Palestinian state on the negotiating agenda.[15] Toward the latter two ends, the exiled leadership in Beirut saw the Palestinians of the occupied territories as a major ally in the quest to assert the legitimacy and political predominance of the PLO. Yet although the "insiders" played an increasingly important role in the national movement and became principal beneficiaries of the Arab-funded patronage operated by the PLO from 1978 onward, they did not have commensurate influence within overall policymaking.[16]

The PLO continued to act militarily throughout this period, but its purposes had changed. In the first instance, PLO forces defended the headquarters, national institutions, and civilian population in Lebanon from the protracted onslaught mounted against them by various foes between 1975 and 1982. The expansion of the Palestinian military, accompanied by the acquisition of heavy weapons and adoption of quasi regular formations, was also seen to enhance the credibility of the PLO and its statelike character. In contrast to these defensive or symbolic purposes, guerrilla raids against Israel were conducted to assert the PLO's presence and impose its participation in the U.S.-sponsored peace process. The constant attempt to organize attacks by clandestine operatives in the occupied territories also served these demonstrative ends and enabled the PLO to "spoil" diplomatic initiatives that excluded it.

PLO strategy was beset by difficulties, not least of which were the impact of inter-Arab rivalries, internal factionalism, and disorganization. These factors severely constrained the mainstream, preventing it from taking the political steps necessary to secure a formal dialogue with the United States, let alone engage in direct negotiations with Israel. It also became obvious by 1982 that there was a strict ceiling, beyond which limited military action, grassroots support in the occupied territories, and international diplomatic support simply could not secure attainment of Palestinian goals. It was at this point of stalemate that Israel invaded Lebanon, dismantling the PLO's military infrastructure and compelling the PLO leadership to leave Beirut.

THE OCCUPIED TERRITORIES: A POSTSCRIPT

A central Israeli aim in 1982 was to undermine Palestinian nationalism in the occupied territories, by destroying the PLO's base in Lebanon.

The Palestinian state-within-a-state was indeed dismantled, and to that extent the process of state building in exile was halted, effectively reducing the PLO to a system of political management run from its new headquarters in distant Tunis. Yet the principal stages of Palestinian nation building had already been achieved, and the assertion of the PLO as the central institution and arena of Palestinian national politics despite its difficult straits and internal malaise, was not to be reversed.

Evidence of this came not only from the mere survival of the PLO and its main leaders but from the role played by the Palestinians of the occupied territories. The Palestinian national movement had experienced an implicit tension since 1967, when East Jerusalem, the West Bank, and the Gaza Strip came under Israeli occupation. The military forces, national institutions, and central leadership were all based in exile—"outside"—with the result that the political and material influence of the "inside" on decision making was marginalized to a significant degree. Only after 1974, with the prospect of a negotiated settlement leading to the establishment of a Palestinian state in the Palestinian territories occupied by Israel in June 1967, did the "inside" gain some influence.

What the inside-outside dichotomy also revealed was a divergence over the status and function of military action. For Palestinians inside, merely remaining on their land was an act of resistance, giving rise to the notion of "steadfastness" *(sumoud)* as a political strategy. Social and political organization—dubbed "mass action"—was an important embodiment of national identity and will in these circumstances. In contrast, Palestinian refugees in exile could do little to impede Israeli policy, let alone reverse occupation or liberate territory, except through military action.[17] It was no accident that the driving force behind the single-minded emphasis on armed struggle and the near obsession with autonomy from Arab-state control after 1948 came from Palestinians who had been made refugees by the establishment of Israel.

This is not to suggest that the Palestinians of the occupied territories believed less strongly than the PLO in the primacy of the armed struggle as a means of national liberation. The fact that the some 350,000-400,000 Palestinians had been interrogated or detained and 100,000 sentenced for security offenses by 1985 proves the opposite. The ceaseless, if unsuccessful, attempt to construct clandestine networks and organize armed attacks on Israeli targets ultimately produced the thousands of veteran activists who quickly gave the Intifada of December 1987 its organization and staying power. In this sense, especially, the uprising represented a complementary and natural evolution from the earlier tradition of armed struggle rather than a break with it.

THE ARMED STRUGGLE IN PERSPECTIVE

In retrospect, the armed struggle formed an integral part of the process of Palestinian nation building. It revived and reinforced national identity, defined common goals, made possible the mobilization of human and material resources, and provided the context for the conduct of internal politics and for the emergence of new leaders and organizational structures. By much the same token, the struggle enabled the Palestinians to distinguish themselves from their Arab environment and to gradually assert the concept of a separate Palestinian entity.

Viewed from this perspective, the contemporary Palestinian national movement that emerged in the mid-1960s performed credibly in building a national consensus around a central political institution, the PLO. Only a nationalist ideology constructed around the theme of armed struggle was able to galvanize and unite such a far-flung constituency. This still left the movement chronically vulnerable to the pressures of Arab host states, which sponsored rival Palestinian guerrilla groups, and riven by internal factionalism and disorganization; but the mainstream leadership succeeded in retaining its position and containing challenges, in large measure by engaging in state building.

For these reasons, the function of the occupied territories within the historical processes of nation building and state formation was distinct from that of the armed struggle directed from the "outside." Resistance to Israeli occupation and *sumoud* played a part in consolidating national consciousness but did not contribute directly to the formation of the state-in-exile. Quite the contrary. The PLO strove to coopt various sectors of the "inside" population through the parallel use of nationalism and rent-based patronage, and therefore asserted its own statelike autonomy. Israel assisted this effort, ironically, by preventing local social forces from translating their status and economic position into autonomous political assets. The Intifada created the opportunity to end this dichotomy and produce a local leadership that could challenge, or influence, the PLO's protostate. However, the success of the Tunis-based leadership, in reasserting its control over the grassroots movement in the occupied territories, limited the influence that local subelites may have had. More to the point, it allowed an extension of the PLO system of political management into the occupied territories, resolving the implicit duality by preempting and coopting potential social contenders.

This pattern is familiar from the experience of many third world societies that gained independence from Western colonialism; but in the Palestinian case it unfolded in relatively unique circumstances of statelessness, dispersal, and exile. Military action—and the militarization of society—played an even more important function in the process than elsewhere, by helping to rebuild societal structure and reconstitute the body politic. The mark of the success of the Palestinian armed struggle in this sense was the degree to which it enabled other dimensions of nation building—above all, the creation of national institutions—to evolve, in other words, to enable the Palestinians to move from nation building to state building.

Notes

1. al-Wazir, quoted in interview with Ahmad Sayf, *Shu'un Filastiniyyah* 152/153 (November-December 1985), 17.
2. *Filastinuna* 2:4 (January 1960), 3.
3. *Filastinuna* 2:2, 13.
4. Fanon's influence was considerable, and Fatah issued a summary of his work in Arabic: *"al-Thawrah wa al-'Unf Tariq al-Nasr"* (Revolution and violence are the path to victory), Fateh, *Revolutionary Studies and Experiences* 3 (n.d.).
5. The Cuban experience was summarized by Fateh in: *"al-Tajribah al-Siniyyah, al-Tajribah al-Vietnamiyyah, al-Tajribah al-Kubiyyah"* (The Chinese, Vietnamese, and Cuban Experiences) (Kuwait: Dar al-Qabas, for Fateh, n.d.).
6. al-Wazir, quoted in interview with Ahmad Sayf, *Filastiniyyah,* 14.
7. Ibid.
8. Discussed in a different context by Augustus Norton, *Amal and the Shi'a: Struggle for the Soul of Lebanon* (Austin: University of Texas Press, 1987), 34-35.
9. A useful history of the All-Palestine Government is Samih Shbib, *Hukumat 'Umum Filastin: Muqaddimat wa Nata'ij* (The All-Palestine Government: Introductions and Results) (Nicosia: Sharq Press, 1988).
10. One of the best accounts of this issue is Moshe Shemesh, *The Palestinian Entity, 1959-1974: Arab Politics and the PLO* (London: Frank Cass, 1988).
11. Mahjub 'Umar, *"Harb Ramadan al-Filistiniyyah: al-Mawqif wal-Nata'ij"* (The Palestinian Ramadan War: Position and Results), *Shu'un Filastiniyyah* 119 (October 1981): 78-79.

12. This attempt is discussed in Yezid Sayigh, "Turning Defeat into Opportunity: The Palestinian Guerrillas after the June 1967 War," *Middle East Journal* 46:2 (spring 1992): 244-65.
13. The consequences of the Intifada are discussed in Yezid Sayigh, "The Politics of Palestinian Exile," *Third World Quarterly* 9:1 (January 1987).
14. The evolution of PLO political strategy is discussed in Alain Gresh, *The PLO: The Struggle Within* (London: Zed Books, 1985).
15. PLO strategy and some of its contradictions are discussed in Yezid Sayigh, "Armed Struggle: Means and Ends," *Journal of Palestine Studies* 16:1 (autumn 1986): 61.
16. On the nature and role of patronage, see Rex Brynen, "The Neo-Patrimonial Dimension of Palestinian Politics," *Journal of Palestine Studies* 24:4 (summer 1995): 601-614.
17. These notions are developed in Yezid Sayigh, *"Dawr al-Kifah al-Musallah wa al-Intifada fi al-Nidal al-Watani al-Filastini"* (The role of the armed struggle and the uprising in the Palestinian national struggle), *Shu'un 'Arabiyyah* (Cairo), 67 (September 1991): 65-79.

THREE

A Study of PLO Peace Initiatives, 1974–1988

Muhammad Muslih

More than three years after the signing of the Oslo Agreement (September 1993), there are many, inside and outside Israel, who are still highly suspicious of the Palestine Liberation Organization (PLO) and of the commitment of the Palestinian leadership to the principle of peace with Israel. The skeptics believe, or pretend to believe, that the PLO opted to enter into an agreement with Israel in 1993 because it was weakened and isolated after the 1991 Gulf War. To survive, argue the skeptics, the PLO had no choice but to make the big concessions necessary for its return to the mainstream of regional and international politics. This required, they maintain, a deal with Israel because such a deal would open the door to good relations with Washington and, subsequently, good relations with Washington's Arab allies in the region.

This is not a convincing argument. During the 1970s and 1980s the PLO launched numerous peace initiatives, all intended to reach a peaceful accommodation with Israel within a framework that would accommodate the legitimate national rights of the Palestinian people. This chapter provides a history and analysis of the evolution of PLO positions toward peace with Israel. The story of the evolution is traced on the basis of the collective decisions of the PLO as expressed sequentially in the political programs adopted by the Palestine National Council (PNC), the highest policymaking body within the PLO.

I shall focus on the peace strategy of the PLO as it evolved between 1974 and 1988. During those critical years, the PLO reformulated Palestinian national objectives, affirming in the process its readiness to open a direct dialogue with the Israeli government and demonstrating its increasing readiness to rely on diplomatic means for achieving Palestinian national goals. The process of change was not erratic. It was consistent and it represented a profound evolution toward pragmatism in the PLO's policies toward Israel. The Oslo process, as defined by the Declaration of Principles (DOP), follows directly from this evolution. What happened between 1974 and 1988 played a crucial role in preparing the ground for a commonly defined path of peace between Israel and the PLO.

The Twelfth PNC and its Historical Import

I shall start the discussion with an analysis of the program of the twelfth PNC meeting which was held in Cairo from 1-9 June 1974. The main purpose of the meeting was to devise a strategy for coping with the unprecedented dilemmas created by the October war of 1973. Having made the war costly for Israel, the key Arab states, most notably Egypt and Syria, saw for the first time real possibilities for a peaceful settlement of the Arab-Israeli conflict. The U.S. government gave the conflict top priority status, with Secretary of State and national security advisor Henry Kissinger introducing his bilateral approach to peace. Egypt and Israel were the centerpiece of this approach. Both subscribed to it. Kissinger's prescription promised Egypt the return of its occupied territories. For Israel, the approach had the strategic advantage of neutralizing Egypt, the preponderant power in the Arab world.

On other fronts, Syria reiterated its acceptance of Resolution 242 and the principle of a peace process. It rejected the bilateral approach and opted for a multilateral framework.[1] So did Jordan and Saudi Arabia. Iraq and Libya, on the other hand, adopted a rejectionist position of no peace with Israel. As for the Soviet Union, it encouraged moderation, and even impressed upon the PLO the virtue of taking a realistic stand. The Kremlin publicly advocated the idea of a Middle East peace conference.[2]

Among the Palestinians themselves, there were those who favored a compromise settlement (mainly Fatah, al-Sa'iqa, and the Democratic Front for the Liberation of Palestine [DFLP]) and those who insisted upon total liberation (the Popular Front for the Liberation of Palestine [PFLP], and the Popular Front for the Liberation of Palestine-General Command [PFLP-GC]). Under the leadership of Arafat, a meeting was held in May 1974. Attending the meeting was a committee comprising the major Palestinian organizations, including the Palestine National Front (PNF), a West Bank/Gaza political body that came into existence during the summer of 1973 primarily for the purpose of giving an organizational expression to the Palestinians inside the occupied territories. These Palestinians, usually referred to as the "inside Palestinians" (filastiniyyu al-dakhil), came to play an ever greater role in PLO politics beginning in the early 1970s when Fatah started to recognize their significance for its peace strategy, including its desire to establish contacts, through proxies, with Israeli individuals and groups that favored a dialogue with the organization.[3] After meeting several times to deliberate, the participants concluded an agreement known as the "transitional" or "ten-point" program. This agreement won the unanimous approval of the PNC.

The twelfth PNC meeting was perhaps the most significant Palestinian meeting since the 1948 Palestine War. When it was held, the general atmosphere in the Arab world favored a political solution and an overall settlement of the Arab-Israeli conflict. This was the avowed aim of Egypt and Syria and of other Arab countries, with the exception of Iraq and Libya. Both Egypt and Syria had already accepted UN Security Council Resolution 242 and had entered into disengagement-of-forces agreements with Israel.

In the broadest of terms, the importance of the twelfth PNC lies in the fact that the PLO adopted a program that broke away from the previous programs that it had endorsed during 1964-1974. In general, those earlier programs envisioned a totally liberated Palestine as a secular democratic state shared by all citizens, whether Jewish, Christian, or Muslim. They also stressed armed struggle as the favored means for achieving this goal. Moreover, they rejected the idea of a Palestinian "mini-state" in the West Bank and Gaza.[4]

On the high-policy level, a number of major features make the twelfth PNC program particularly significant. First, a careful reading of the program reveals a disposition to accept rather than reject the idea of a Palestinian state in parts of Palestine. This new approach is illustrated in the totally new goal outlined in the second point of the program which calls for the establishment of the "people's national, independent, and fighting authority on every part of Palestinian land to be liberated."[5]

The vagueness surrounding the concept "authority" is striking. Indeed, PNC programs 12-18 can be described as the programs of creative ambiguity, because of the degree of vagueness concerning ultimate objectives that diminishes gradually, but does not disappear altogether until the nineteenth PNC program (November 1988). The main reason for the ambiguity can be found, on the one hand, in the absence of a consensus within the PLO on the idea of a Palestinian mini-state,[6] and on the other hand, in the fact that the Palestinians were not yet ready to accept the existence of Israel. Precisely for these reasons, the hawkish term "fighting" is used to describe the proposed authority. This was intended to address the concerns of those PLO hardliners who were not ready to concede even a square inch of Palestinian territory. Meanwhile, the mini-state idea was endorsed in the twelfth PNC program to fulfill the wishes of the West Bank and Gaza Palestinians who strongly supported the idea and who were becoming an increasingly important part of the PLO constituency.[7]

A second major feature of the twelfth PNC program is that its language reflects a tendency on the part of the PLO to accept diplomatic activities, rather than focus exclusively on armed struggle. A clear example of this propensity was the PLO's readiness to "struggle by every means," which suggests the recognition of diplomacy as an option. Another example was the PLO's rejection of Resolution 242, not because it embodied the principle of pacific settlement or because it recognized Israel, but because it did not accommodate the political aspirations of the Palestinians.

Third, this program also demonstrates a tendency on the part of the PLO to formulate a strategy of stages; a strategy that seeks to realize the dream of a secular, democratic state over a protracted period of time, rather than seeking to attain every goal at once. A demonstration of this approach was apparent in the fourth and eighth clauses of the twelfth program. These clauses stressed that the proposed "national authority" to be established in any part of Palestine would be just one stage along the path of the total national liberation of Palestine. However, although the goal of total liberation was retained, the adoption of the interim goal in 1974 represented a remarkable break with the past. This was partly because no Palestinian leadership had ever accepted the principle of partition, even as a transitional step, and partly because the new formulation stimulated, for the first time in the post-1948 period, a public Palestinian debate over the question of a peaceful settlement with Israel, and put this question firmly on the PLO agenda.[8]

Toward Consolidating the PLO Peace Strategy

The new ideas contained in the twelfth PNC program were reiterated and further elucidated in subsequent PNC programs, in addition to proposals made to Israel by prominent Palestinians who were close to Arafat and who made their proposals with his endorsement. The most notable of these proposals was articulated by Sa'id Hammami, a Fatah veteran, Walid Khalidi, head of the Institute for Palestine Studies in Beirut, Khalid al-Hasan, a senior Fatah leader, and Dr. 'Isam Sirtawi, a foreign affairs adviser to Arafat. The gist of the proposals by these Palestinians revolved around the idea of a two-state solution with mutual recognition and mutual security guarantees for both Israel and the proposed Palestinian state.[9]

As to subsequent PNC programs, three phases can be identified: (a) the phase that represents the ideas of the thirteenth, fourteenth, and fifteenth programs adopted in 1977, 1979, and 1981 respectively; (b) the phase that incorporates the ideas of the sixteenth, seventeenth, and eighteenth PNC programs adopted in 1983, 1984, and 1987 respectively; and (c) the phase that incorporates the ideas of the nineteenth PNC program which was adopted in November 1988.

Phase A: PLO Programs 13-15

The PLO faced a number of major challenges after the twelfth PNC. The most far reaching in effect was the Lebanese civil war, and in particular the Syrian crackdown against the PLO and its ally, the Lebanese National Movement, in June 1976. Israel, too, launched its relentless and incessant attacks. But despite these attacks, and despite the consolidation of Syria's military presence in Lebanon, the PLO managed to survive, somewhat restrained, but by no means totally fettered, in Lebanon. The Riyadh minisummit of October 1976, and the subsequent Cairo summit of heads of Arab states, both held to end the civil war in Lebanon, legitimized Syria's presence and brought about a tenuous understanding between the PLO leadership and the Syrian government.[10]

Another development was the Egyptian-Israeli peace treaty of March 1979 and the stepped-up pace of U.S. pressure-by-proxy on the PLO, mainly through Egypt and Saudi Arabia, to accept Resolution 242. The memoirs of Zbigniew Brezezinski, national security adviser to

President Jimmy Carter, clearly indicate the U.S. government's desire to "get the PLO under control."[11]

The third development was seen in the political achievements of the PLO. In October 1974, the Seventh Arab Summit Conference, which was convened in Rabat, Morocco, recognized the PLO as the sole, legitimate representative of the Palestinian people. In November of the same year Arafat addressed the UN General Assembly. By 1977 the PLO also had made significant diplomatic advances in Western Europe and many third world countries. Moreover, highly-placed PLO officials had contacts with Israeli and other Jewish groups and individuals.[12]

A fourth development was the split within the PLO following the twelfth PNC—a number of leftist groups led by the PFLP withdrew from the executive committee and formed the Rejection Front. They were disinclined toward a compromise settlement, and they favored the establishment of a democratic secular state in all of historic Palestine.[13]

The three PNC programs under review reveal a three-tiered PLO strategy that can be summarized as follows: First, there was the explicit endorsement, for the first time in the post-1948 period, of the principle of establishing an "independent national state" (stipulated in the eleventh clause of the thirteenth program [March 1977]). This new formulation had two aspects. On the one hand, there was no clear delineation of the boundaries of the proposed state. On the other hand, the absence of any reference to total liberation and to the concept of a secular, democratic state, together with the explicit endorsement of UN resolutions relevant to the Palestine question (clause 15 of the thirteenth program and the reference to same in the fourteenth program [January 1979] and to "international legitimacy" in the fifteenth program [April 1981]) suggest a willingness to accept an independent Palestinian state in parts of Palestine. At another level, there was a description of the nature of the proposed state. The modifying adjective "national" says it all. Whereas in the past, the suggestion of such a Palestinian state precipitated a PLO tirade of condemnation, now setting up such a state became an honorable national objective.

Second, there was in these three programs a clear and strong preference for diplomacy. Armed struggle was maintained not as the guiding strategy, but as an equal partner of diplomatic activity. This was vividly manifested in clauses 2 and 3 of the thirteenth and fourteenth programs, as well as in the final political statement of the fifteenth.

Practically speaking, and at a more strategic level, the following observations can be made: (a) there was in these programs an unequivocal emphasis on the "PLO's right to participate, independently and on an equal footing, in all international conferences, forums, and efforts related to the Palestine question and the Arab-Zionist conflict. . . ." (clause 15 of the thirteenth program); (b) there was a positive attitude toward peace plans that recognized Israel and provided for its security, as was evidenced in the Council's "welcoming" of Soviet president Brezhnev's peace proposals[14] of February 1981; (c) there was, for the first time in an official PLO document, a clearcut endorsement of the idea of establishing ties and relations of coordination with "Jewish democratic and progressive forces . . . which are struggling against the ideology and practice of Zionism" (clause 14 of the thirteenth program); and (d) there was an emphasis greater and more detailed than ever before on the West Bank and Gaza as the central component in the PLO strategy (illustrated in all three political programs).

Third, as the fourteenth and fifteenth programs amply demonstrate, the PLO had in this phase considerably scaled down its level of hostility to the Jordanian government. On the one hand, this was part of a larger PLO strategy designed to keep Jordan out of the Camp David process and its autonomy formula. On the other hand, a rapprochement with Jordan had the advantage of facilitating the PLO's access to the Palestinians in the West Bank and Gaza, in addition to making the PLO an acceptable peace partner in the eyes of the American government. Obviously this approach also promised to promote Jordan's West Bank strategy, a central aspect of which was to undertake negotiations with Israel about the future of the West Bank and Gaza. The King of Jordan knew that the Palestinians of the West Bank and Gaza would not accept his role without the PLO's endorsement.

Phase B: PLO Programs 16–18

The PNC meetings from 1983 to 1987 at which these three programs were adopted represented a decisive period for the PLO. All were held after the Israeli invasion of Lebanon, that ravaging assault that, ironically, brought in its wake several peace proposals for the Israeli-Palestinian conflict, most notably the plan outlined by U.S. President Ronald Reagan on 1 September 1982, and the Fez Arab Summit plan of 8 September of the same year. The Reagan plan was anchored in UN Resolution 242 and in the principle of full autonomy for the Palestinians in the West Bank and Gaza à la Camp David formula, for a five-year transitional period. In typical official U.S. fashion, the Reagan plan explicitly ruled out the establishment of a Palestinian state. It also excluded the PLO. The Palestinian reaction to the plan was ambivalent. The PLO leadership simply criticized the plan's exclusion of the principle of an independent Palestinian state and its failure to recognize the PLO. But it neither rejected nor endorsed the Reagan plan outright.

The Fez plan, on the other hand, was an elaboration on Crown Prince Fahd's proposal of 7 August 1981; it envisaged a permanent peaceful settlement, an independent Palestinian state, and the recognition of all the states in the region. This Arab plan rekindled old PLO disagreements over the value and modality of a peaceful accommodation with Israel. Arafat and the traditional leadership of Fatah supported the Fez plan. Neither al-Sa'iqa, the PFLP, the PFLP-GC, the Palestinian Popular Struggle Front (PPSF), nor the renegade Nimr Salih (Abu Salih) of Fatah were ready to endorse a plan that implicitly recognized Israel. Syria and Libya, each for its own reasons, threw their weight behind the opponents of the plan. A contest ensued between Syria's Asad and Arafat. Asad was able to swing the DFLP to his side. One of Asad's principal goals was to put the PLO under Syria's wing.

The Asad-Arafat rift, though not new, played a major role in causing the Fatah rebellion of May 1983. Other factors were also at play, most notably sharp Palestinian disagreements over the allocation of power within the PLO and over the goals and means that the organization should adopt in order to further the cause of Palestinian nationalism.

The upshot of the Fatah rebellion was to encourage Arafat to move closer to Egypt and Jordan. The rapprochement angered the PFLP and the DFLP, whose leaders feared that it might lead to a new Camp David. They therefore condemned Arafat's strategy, even though they maintained their original opposition to the rebellious leaders of Fatah. Later, however, both Habash and Hawatmah realigned themselves with Arafat, thanks to the Aden-Algiers agreement of June 1984.

This agreement was opposed by the Syrian-backed National Alliance of Abu Musa (the leader of the Fatah rebellion), the PFLP-GC, and al-Sa'iqa. There were also serious differences with regard to its interpretation. These differences, coupled with Syria's pressure on its proteges, prompted the PFLP and DFLP to renege on the agreement. Internal Palestinian differences encouraged the PLO leadership to accept, for the first time, the principles of unanimity and consensus at the expense of the principle of majority rule. This has become a distinguishing feature of PLO decision making, especially since the holding of the seventeenth PNC meeting in Amman in November 1984.

This was the background against which these three PNC programs were adopted between 1983 and 1987. A careful and sequential reading of these programs reveals that the PLO had made important new compromises, some implicit and some explicit, on a number of key issues. First, the paragraphs devoted to the Brezhnev plan in the programs of the sixteenth and seventeenth meetings represented a marked change from the earlier formulation of the fifteenth program. Whereas the PNC "welcomed" Soviet peace proposals in its fifteenth program, in subsequent programs it expressed unmistakable "appreciation and support" for these proposals. It should be noted that the former Soviet Union had encouraged the PLO to pursue a peaceful settlement with Israel. On the question of borders, the Soviets explicitly spoke of Israel's frontiers as those of the 1949-1967 armistice lines.[15] This suggests that the PLO's "support" for the Brezhnev plan represented an acceptance of these borders.

Second, the PLO's progress toward accepting the Fez peace plan of September 1982 was gradual but clear. The relevant paragraph in the sixteenth program considered the Fez Summit resolutions to be the "minimum for the political activity of the Arab states." Meanwhile, the eighteenth program elevated the status of the Fez plan to that of a "framework for Arab action on the international level to reach a solution to the Palestine question and to regain the occupied Arab territories."

Third, a striking and strategically significant change was the new attitude toward Jordan. This was illustrated, in all three programs, in the endorsement of the idea of an independent Palestinian state confederated with Jordan.

Neither the exact meaning nor the modalities of implementing this idea were spelled out. But the belief was clearly that a confederation, unlike a federation, would preserve the independence and sovereignty of a future Palestinian state. There were, however, other Palestinian calculations in opting for a confederation with Jordan. Most notable was the fact that King Husain was an acceptable partner to Israel and the United States. Thus, in an important sense, the suggestion of a confederation can be viewed as a concession to Tel Aviv and Washington. It can also be regarded as a gesture of deference to Egypt that encouraged the PLO to move in this direction and become, in the wake of the Israeli invasion of Lebanon, a strategic ally.

A second factor was the fact that some 1.2 million Palestinians resided on the East Bank, thus constituting the second largest Palestinian population after the West Bank and Gaza. Many of these Palestinians have relatives and property in the occupied Palestinian areas. Moreover, the PLO has always considered the Palestinians to be one indivisible community, irrespective of the fact of their geographical dispersal. A third factor, however, was tactical: King Husain, by virtue of his long relationship with Washington and his numerous secret contacts with the top Israeli leadership, was in a position to get a better feel "on the ground" for opinions among broad sections of Israeli and American policymakers. He could, therefore, negotiate, convey political messages, and accurately gauge what was politically possible in the eyes of the American and Israeli governments.

Fourth, two other features related to the methods of political action were also apparent in this phase of the PLO peace strategy. In concise, accurate, and unequivocal language, the eighteenth program called for "enhancing relations with Israeli democratic forces" (emphasis added), and not simply with Jewish forces as was the case in previous programs. This formulation further underlined the PLO's readiness to enter into direct negotiations with Israel. Moreover, the highlighting of diplomacy can be readily gleaned from expressions of a stronger interest in negotiation, and in a shift away from armed struggle. Consider, for example, the use of the word "struggle" without the adjective "armed" in the fourth clause of the eighteenth program, under the first subheading: "On the Palestinian Level." Some Palestinian critics, because of their discomfiture with this deemphasis on armed struggle, spoke sarcastically about what they called "unarmed struggle" *(al-kifah alla-musahllah)*. The gradual exposition of these ideas, with less and less ambiguity, was a precursor to the explicitly articulated strategy of the nineteenth program.

Phase C: The Nineteenth PLO Program

This program was adopted in the context of three major developments. The first was the Intifada that began on a mass scale in the West Bank and Gaza on 9 December 1987. There is no doubt that the Intifada imposed on the PLO the urgent need for new, decisive, and clearcut choices. The overriding concern of West Bank and Gaza Palestinians with ending the Israeli occupation and with reaching a settlement with Israel along the lines of Israel's borders of 4 June 1967 forced the PLO, following the uprising, to choose between two strategies: (a) to adopt unequivocally a partition-oriented strategy, of which the recognition of Israel was a central part, and in that context put Israel on the defensive, or (b) to continue the past policy of offering vague proposals and wait, thus keeping the initiative in Israel's hand and risking loss of influence in the occupied territories. The PLO came down in favor of the first choice. Largely because of the uprising, the priorities of the Palestinians in the West Bank and Gaza were put at the top of the PLO agenda.

The second development was Jordan's disengagement from the West Bank. This disengagement created a political vacuum in the occupied territories. Although the PLO welcomed King Husain's step, it nonetheless saw a threat of an Israeli counter-move in the form of outright annexation. Thus, before Israel could avail itself of the chance, the PLO stepped in and declared the establishment of a Palestinian state.

The third development was the failure of the Arab states to shoulder their responsibilities toward the Palestine question. This played an essential part in convincing the Palestinian leadership of the urgent need for an innovative Palestinian diplomatic initiative. A clear indication of Arab inaction was the extraordinary Arab Summit conference held in Amman on 8-11 November 1987. This was the first summit to focus primarily on inter-Arab problems rather than on the Arab-Israeli conflict. The two agenda items for the summit were: (a) the isolation of Iran from the international community as part of a larger strategy to forestall an Iranian victory in the Iran-Iraq war; and (b) the reopening of diplomatic relations with Egypt, which most Arab states had severed nine years earlier, in the aftermath of Sadat's peace treaty with Israel.

The Summit conference, which was called by the Arab governments the "conference of reconciliation and accord" *(mu'tamar al wifaq wal ittifaq)* was dubbed by many Palestinians as the "conference of hypocrisy and spending" *(mu'tamar al-nifaq wal-infaq)*. The official Arab designation was in reference to the need for Arab solidarity in confronting Iran. The popular Palestinian appellation was in reference to Saudi attempts at the conference to use financial aid as an instrument to secure wider Arab support for the Gulf-first policy of Egypt, Jordan, Iraq and the Arab Gulf states.[16]

Against this background, the nineteenth PNC convened in November 1988 in Algiers and adopted two documents—the Political Program and the Declaration of Independence—which, together with Arafat's statements in Geneva a month later, finalized the evolution of the PLO's peace strategy. In terms of ends and means these three documents are clear, concise, and to the point. They contain important departures from the norm, and variations from preceding programs.

A few words about the reason for the inclusion of the Declaration of Independence and Arafat's statement. The Declaration and the program constitute one indivisible unit. While the program outlines objectives and the means suggested for their attainment, the Declaration formally announces them in the idiom that befits the occasion. Arafat's statement is significant because it clarified the points considered ambiguous by the United States government. Their elucidation, or to be accurate, their over-elucidation, led to the initiation of a "substantive dialogue" between the PLO and the United States government. Thus the three documents represent the culmination of the process that started with the twelfth PNC program of June 1974.

The main ideas of these documents can be summarized as follows: (1) The most novel point in the political program was the PLO's acceptance of Resolutions 242 and 338 as the "basis" for convening an international peace conference on the Middle East problem and the Palestine question. In deference to Washington's wishes, and out of a desire to send a clear signal to Israel, Arafat's statement did stress, with even more clarity, the PLO's acceptance of "Resolutions 242 and 338 as the basis for negotiations with Israel within the framework of the international conference" (emphasis added); (2) The most significant aspect of the Declaration of Independence was the PLO's endorsement of General Assembly Partition Resolution 181 (11) of 1947. An equally important aspect was the declaration on the basis of this resolution of the establishment of the state of Palestine, with its capital in Jerusalem. Although the boundaries of the state were not spelled out explicitly, one can deduce from a careful reading of the political program that the Palestinian state would be confined to the West Bank and Gaza. This was evident in section 2, clause b, which called for "Israel's withdrawal from all the Palestinian and Arab territories which it has occupied since 1967, including Arab Jerusalem" (emphasis added). This suggests that the PLO had adopted the political, rather than the geographical aspect of the partition plan of 1947. In other words, the borders of the Palestinian state would simply include the West Bank and Gaza, about 23 percent of Mandatory Palestine. As was evident in the thematic content of the program and in Arafat's statement, partition along these geographic lines was meant to be a final settlement; (3) The phrasing, tone, and general political position of the program pointed to the PLO's acceptance and recognition of Israel. The Declaration, which constituted the basis of the program, was unmistakably clear on this issue, since Resolution 181 (as the Declaration stressed) partitioned Palestine into an Arab and a Jewish state. Arafat's statement went a step further in clarifying previously adopted positions. It affirmed the "right of all parties concerned in the Middle East conflict to exist in peace and security . . . including the state of Palestine, Israel and other neighbors, according to the Resolution [sic] 242 and 338" (emphasis added); (4) All three documents show a clearcut preference for diplomacy and a peaceful settlement with Israel. The references to Resolutions 181, 242, 338 among others, together with the emphasis on an international peace conference, were clear indications of the further ascendence of diplomacy over armed struggle. Another indication of this was the emphatic renunciation of all forms of terrorism, including individual, group, and state terrorism. This renunciation, affirmed earlier in the Cairo Declaration of 7 November 1985, was explicitly stated in the political program and in Arafat's statement. However, there was an affirmation in the program of the "right of peoples to resist foreign occupation, colonialism, and racial discrimination, and their right to struggle for their independence." A similar affirmation existed in Arafat's statement. The statement stressed that "neither Arafat, nor any [sic] for that matter, can stop the Intifada, the uprising"; that it would come to an end only when the national aims of the Palestinians were realized.

Altogether, then, the political program of the nineteenth PNC, the Declaration of Independence, and Arafat's statement, comprised a single political platform. The ideas enshrined in them did not only represent the culmination of the Palestinian peace strategy, nor did they only symbolize the departure from the old tactic of creative ambiguity. Equally significant, they reflected with unprecedented clarity, the consistency and continuity of the overall policy of the PLO since it started to move toward peaceful accommodation with an Israel that would be contained within its pre-1967 borders. In addition to the content, one has to consider the tone, which was low-key and conciliatory. One must also consider the recurrence of earlier principles of reconciliation, foremost among which was the idea of a confederacy with Jordan, and the PNC's "appreciation of the courageous role played by the Israeli forces of peace," as well as the PLO's strong interest in strengthening relations with these forces.

Conclusion

The path to Oslo began in 1974, when the PLO adopted the twelfth PNC program. The implications of this program were far reaching. It initiated a process of attitudinal change on the part of the Palestinian leadership that moved gradually but consistently from the rejection of the principle of Jewish sovereignty in parts of Palestine to an acceptance of this principle, and from the endorsement of armed struggle as the means of resolving the Palestine problem to the adoption of diplomacy as the preferred means of dealing with this problem. Once Arafat had at his disposal PNC decisions supporting a compromise solution, he was able to move forward to outmaneuver the Palestinian rejectionists who opposed compromise, and even to make his own proposals within the framework of the PNC programs. As outlined in this chapter, between 1974 and September 1993, when the Declaration of Principles between Israel and the PLO was signed, there had been no change in the PLO's peace strategy, although there had been a consistent Israeli refusal to respond positively to this strategy, and there had also been internal Palestinian opposition to the policy of the PLO leadership.[17]

In a real sense, this peace strategy remained consistent and constant for nearly two decades. Only after Oslo was Arafat seriously challenged, even by members of his own movement. He was challenged, first, because his critics believed that he had abandoned the general Palestinian consensus contained in PNC programs and that he was following a path that would not lead to real independence for the Palestinians in parts of their historic homeland. Second, he was challenged because he did not involve PLO institutions in the secret talks that led to Oslo. Third, Arafat's critics believed, and for good reason, that he had embarked on a process of consolidating all means of control and decision making in his hands. In a profound sense, therefore, many of those who opposed Arafat opposed him because he deviated from the PLO peace strategy that evolved between 1974 and 1988.[18]

This strategy neither envisioned nor created the Oslo agreement, but it did help make it possible by introducing fundamental changes in Palestinian thinking on two levels—that of policy and that of attitudes. On the policy level, the cumulative impact of the PLO's political programs was to make it perfectly acceptable and legitimate for the Palestinian leadership to speak publicly of the legitimacy of Jewish sovereignty in roughly 78 percent of historic Palestine, and to endorse the principle of a West Bank and Gaza Palestinian state that would live in peace with Israel, not as an interim solution, but as a final settlement for the Palestine problem.

The change on the second level, that of attitudes, brought with it a reorientation in the way the Palestinians view Israel within the wider Middle Eastern system. Israel is now accepted as a legitimate regional actor and as a nation entitled to live in peace and security. True, there are Palestinians who still reject Israel, but rejectionism is not a general trend of thought that shapes the world view of the majority of Palestinians. By making peace with Israel the central pillar of the PLO's strategy, the Palestinian political programs endorsed between 1974 and 1988 played a crucial role in bringing about this attitudinal change, thus setting in motion a peace strategy that greatly facilitated the accomplishment of the September 1993 breakthrough. This breakthrough was also made possible by the coming to power in Israel in 1992 of a Labor party led by Yitzhak Rabin, the first Israeli government willing to respond positively to the PLO peace strategy that had been evolving since 1974.

NOTES

1. For details, see Muhammad Muslih, "Dateline Damascus: Asad Is Ready," *Foreign Policy* 96 (fall 1994): 145-65; Moshe Ma'oz, *Asad: The Sphinx of Damascus, A Political Biography* (New York: Weidenfeld & Nicolson, 1988), 74-83; 123-135.
2. See Galia Golan, *The Soviet Union and the Palestine Liberation Organization* (New York: Praeger, 1980), 50-112; and her "Gorbachev's Middle East Strategy," *Foreign Affairs* 66: 1 (fall 1987): 45-46.
3. Shaul Mishal, *The PLO Under Arafat: Between Gun and Olive Branch.* (New Haven: Yale University Press, 1986), 97-107; Abraham Sela, "The PLO, the West Bank and Gaza Strip," *The Jerusalem Quarterly* 8 (summer 1978): 73-74.
4. For details, see Muhammad Muslih, *Toward Coexistence: An Analysis of the Resolutions of the Palestine National Council* (Washington, D.C.: The Institute for Palestine Studies, 1990).
5. All quotations from the political programs of the PLO as endorsed by the PNC are the author's own translation from the original Arabic documents. To the author's best knowledge, there is not a single volume in Arabic or in any foreign language that contains all of these programs. This author has collected and translated all these programs, adding introductions and notations. The interested reader may consult the relevant issues of the *Journal of Palestine Studies*

for translations of these programs, either in part or in full. The reader may also consult *International Documents on Palestine* (Beirut, Institute for Palestine Studies), published annually since 1967. Also recommended is Rashid Hamid's *Muqarrarat al-majlis al-watani al-filastini, 1964-1974* (The resolutions of the Palestine National Council, 1964-1974) (Beirut: PLO Research Center, 1975).

6. For studies on this subject, see Helena Cobban, *The Palestinian Liberation Organization: People, Power and Politics* (Cambridge: Cambridge University Press), 21-34, 139-165; Muhammad Y. Muslih, "Moderates & Rejectionists Within the Palestine Liberation Organization," *Middle East Journal* 30:2 (spring 1976).

7. See Abu Iyad with Eric Rouleau, *My Home, My Land.* (New York: Times Books, 1981; Helena Cobban, "Palestinian Peace Plans," in Willard A. Beling, ed., *Middle East Peace Plans* (New York: St. Martin's Press, 1986), 43-44; Saadia Touval, *The Peace Brokers: Mediators in the Arab-Israeli Conflict, 1948-1979* (Princeton: Princeton Unversity Press, 1982), 238-248.

8. For more details on the twelfth PNC and its political context see Faysal Hourani, *al-Fikr al-siyasi al-filastini 1964-1974* (Palestinian political thought, 1964-1974), (Beirut: PLO Research Center, 1980).

9. See Walid Khalidi, "Thinking the Unthinkable: A Sovereign Palestinian State," *Foreign Affairs* 56:4 (1978), 695-713; Khalid al-Hasan's interview in *Shu'un Filastiniyya* 104 (July 1980), 50-52, and 'Isam Sirtawi's interviews with Eric Rouleau, *Le Monde* (22 January 1982), and Anthony Lewis, *New York Times* (4 March 1982). For discussions of these proposals, see Mishal, *The PLO under Arafat*, 64-72; Alain Gresh, *The PLO, The Struggle Within: Towards an Independent Palestinian State* (London: Zed Books, 1985), 143-50; 195-202. For Palestinian reflections on the context in which this new thinking emerged, see *Palestinian Leaders Discuss the New Challenges for the Resistance* (Beirut, PLO Research Center, 1974); Sabri Jiryis, *"Qimmat al-Rabat wa-ihtimalat al-mawqif al-israeli"* (The Rabat summit and probable changes in the Israeli position), *Shu'un Filastiniyya* 40 (Dec. 1974), 32-40; Dr. Said Hammud, *"al-Taswiyya al-siyasiyya, khalfiyyat wa-nata'ij"* (The political settlement, background and results), *Shu'un Filastiniyya* 55 (March 1976), 46-52; Dr. Muhammad Rabi', *"Ihtimalat 'al-hall al-silmi' wa mawqif al-muqawama al-filastiniyya minhu"* (The prospects for a "peaceful settlement" and the position of the Palestinian resistance toward it"), *Shu'un Filastiniyya* 62, 31-51; Majid Abu Sharar, *"al-Sira' al-'arabi al-sahyuni fi marhalatihi al-rahina"* (The Arab-Zionist struggle in its current stage), *Shu'un Filastiniyya* 77 (April 1978), 66-80.

10. See Walid Khalidi, *Conflict and Violence in Lebanon: Confrontation in the Middle East* (Cambridge: Harvard Center for International Affairs, 1984), 56-65.

11. Zbigniew Brzezinski, *Power and Principle: Memoirs of the National Security Adviser 1977-1981* (New York: Farrar, Straus & Giroux, 1983), 87, 95, 102-105.
12. For an account of these contacts, which produced nothing, mainly as a result of the Israeli government's intransigence and the debilitating effect of the Lebanese civil war on the PLO, see Gresh, *The PLO, The Struggle Within*, 195-199, and the monthly Paris journal *Israel et Palestine* from December 1977 to February 1978, as well as the French daily *Le Monde* of 6 and 11 January 1977. More detailed accounts can be found in Seth Tillman, *The United States in the Middle East* (Bloomington: Indiana University Press, 1982), 213ff., and Noam Chomsky's articles in *New Politics* (winter 1975-76, winter 1978-79) and his book, *Towards a New Cold War* (New York: Pantheon, 1982), chap. 9.
13. M. Muslih, "Moderates and Rejectionists Within the PLO," *Middle East Journal*.
14. These were the proposals offered by the Soviet leader, President Leonid Brezhnev in February 1981. Brezhnev called for an all-party framework for a Middle East peace conference, and for the establishment of a Palestinian state. The Brezhnev proposal stressed the need to "ensure the security and sovereignty of all states in the region, *including Israel*" (emphasis added).
15. Robert O. Freedman, *Moscow and The Middle East: Soviet Policy Since the Invasion of Afghanistan* (Cambridge: Cambridge University Press, 1991), 105-47.
16. For a perceptive account of the complex relationships between the Palestinians and the Arab confrontation states, see Aaron David Miller, *The Arab States and the Palestine Question: Between Ideology and Self-Interest* (New York: Praeger, 1986); for a study focused on Egypt, see Ann Mosely Lesch and Mark Tessler, *Israel, Egypt, and the Palestinians: From Camp David to Intifada* (Bloomington: Indiana University Press, 1989). For a detailed study of the relations between the Palestinians and different Arab states, see Laurie A. Brand, *Palestinians in the Arab World: Institution Building and the Search for State* (New York: Columbia University Press, 1988).
17. For a discussion of Palestinian thinking on peace with Israel after the nineteenth PNC, see Muhammad Muslih, "The Shift in Palestinian Thinking," *Current History* (January 1992): 22-29, and "Jericho and Its Meaning: A New Strategy for the Palestinians," *Current History* (February 1994): 72-78.
18. For details, see Riyad al-Malki, *al-Mu'arada al-wataniyya: tahlil al-bada'il* (The Palestinian opposition: An examination of the alternatives) (Nablus: Center for Palestine Research and Studies, 1993). For a discussion of the dilemmas facing the Palestinians after Oslo, see Ahmad S. Khalidi, "Current Dilemmas, Future Challenges," *Journal of Palestine Studies* 94 (winter 1995): 5-14.

FOUR

From Palestine Liberation Organization to Palestinian Authority:
The Territorialization of "Neopatriarchy"

Hillel Frisch

In one of his major works, Palestinian scholar Hisham Sharabi describes neopatriarchy as follows:

> A central psychological feature of this type of society, whether it is conservative or progressive, is the dominance of the father (patriarch), around whom the national and natural family are organized. Thus between ruler and ruled, between father and child, there exist only vertical relations: in both settings, paternal will is the absolute will mediated in both the society and the family by a forced consensus based on ritual and coercion. Significantly, the most advanced and functional aspect of the neopatriarchal state (in both conservative and "progressive" regimes) is its internal security apparatus, the *mukhabarat*. A two-state system prevails in all neopartiarachal regimes, a military-bureaucratic structure alongside a secret police structure, and the latter dominates everyday life, serving as the ultimate regulator of civil and political existence.[1]

Ironically, soon after Sharabi, the distinguished Georgetown University man of letters and Palestinian activist, returned to his homeland in 1993 for the first time since 1947, Yasir Arafat was transforming neopatriarchy—one of Sharabi's most significant theoretical concepts in the study of the Arab world—into reality in Gaza and Jericho. This essay analyzes some of the most distinguishing characteristics of the Palestinian Authority (PA) and its transformation into a neopatriarchy—or what Hassan Naji 'Amr, the paramount chief of the Hebron district *(shaykh al-mashayikh lil Mukhafazat al-Khalil)* and a noted figure in customary law, described as "soon to be another Arab state."[2]

THE BIRTH OF THE PALESTINIAN NATION: A MILITARY TAKEOVER

The institutionalization of neopatriarchy begins with the birth of the PA. Sharabi's concept of neopatriarchy, which explains the hybrid mix of "tradition" with modernity, was designed above all to explain the deviation from modernization of such radical military regimes as Syria and Iraq and their slide into authoritarianism. The PA at birth followed a similar pattern. To be sure, it was not in the form of a putsch; it was a takeover by the PLO "outside" of the "inside."

As an interim government, the PA's emergence was unaccompanied by a constitution, a bill of rights, the swearing in of a government, or the modalities of elections, preparations for which a year and a half after the emergence of the PA, were still being ironed out. Instead, as the media meticulously documented, convoy after convoy of "policemen" (1,500 in number) dressed in the military uniform of the Palestine Liberation Army, crossed the bridges that link Jordan with the West Bank or passed through the Rafah border crossing that links Gaza with Egypt. Atop the front windshields of the lorries towered portraits of Yasir Arafat in military uniform. While the long-familiar photograph showed him from the chest up, it took little imagination to conjure up his holster and gun as well. By the end of May, the soldiers-turned-policemen, who had poured in from the diaspora, numbered 6,000. By April 1995 the numbers had swelled to 17,000, as local inhabitants were recruited into the ranks of the police and the various arms of the security network.[3] Even the civilians arriving from the diaspora did little to dispel the concentration of political-military power that descended on Gaza soon after Israeli soldiers had evacuated the area. Most of those who arrived in early and mid-May were designated to hold top positions in the emerging internal security network—a network that soon encompassed five agencies in an area of control one-third the size of Long Island. The foundation of government, then, resembled a military takeover.⁴ The first sign of civilian government appeared on 1 July, when the initial meeting of the PA Executive took place with Arafat, still in uniform, presiding as chairman. It was his first day in Gaza. He has yet to be seen in public in Gaza without the uniform, and only when abroad has he been photographed without his gun and holster. He has, in fact, explained that he will continue to wear the uniform as long as the process of liberation remains incomplete.

The same has been true of the PA expansion into the West Bank following the Oslo 2 Accord of 28 September 1995, which transferred authority over the major towns in the West Bank from Israel to the PA and gave the PA civilian control over approximately one-third of the villages. On the eve of the Israeli withdrawal from the town of Jenin, Colonel Fa'iz 'Arafat, in charge of the transfer of power declared: "We will enter Jenin in our military uniforms and armed."⁵ 'Arafat, it is important to note, was the designated commander of the National Security Forces *(quwwat al-amn al-watani),* the military branch of the security apparatus, whose members wear khaki. They are an army in all but name, so called only because the Oslo Accords, and later the Cairo agreement, forbade the establishment of an army.

The importance of the military was reflected also in the expenditures of the PA. In 1995, the PA's budget amounted to $440 million, approximately one-third of the GNP of the area it controls. By Western—although not Middle Eastern—standards, it is a big government, being the largest employer in Gaza and the source of most new jobs as the state bureaucracy and security apparatus rapidly expanded. The international aid regime originally set up to aid the Palestinians had conceived of a much smaller Authority. The Emergency Assistance Plan (EAP), drafted by the World Bank in cooperation with Palestinians from the PLO and the occupied territories earmarked $100 million of a $1.3 billion total—less than 10 percent of the total aid package—for the initial costs of the PA.⁶ The reality was strikingly different. In the latter half of 1994 alone, budget support amounted to $154 million, compared to a projected $100 million for the first year of government operations. The propensity to subvert government expenditure became much more marked in the first five months of 1995, when $123 of $154 million—80 percent of the total—was disbursed to pay the salaries of the growing bureaucracy and security complex.⁷

Judging by this trend it seems that the EAP will primarily become a framework for the setting up of the state, rather than for promoting economic development. The number of salaried civil employees grew from 20,000 in June 1994 to 27,000 ten months later, and that of security personnel from 6,000 to 17,000. Thirty million dollars were spent on these salaries alone.[8] By October 1995 the number of salaried security personnel had almost doubled, reaching 30,000.[9] A special multilateral fund, the Holst Fund—named after the Norwegian Minister of Foreign Affairs who had hosted the secret negotiations that led to the Oslo agreement—was set up by six of the major state EAP donors to finance the operating costs of the PA, especially the salaries of the police force. Increasingly, international aid is being negotiated bilaterally between the donor states and the PA, giving the PA greater freedom in utilizing the funds.

The large-scale failure to instill democracy in new states during the wave of decolonization in the 1950s and 1960s raises the question of how important or feasible the creation of democratic institutions is in fledgling states—as Samuel Huntington's research on state formation since decolonization has so persuasively demonstrated.[10] The problem has been that the neopatriarchal, absolutist, or one-party states that were supposed to be the preferred alternative to the anarchy of implanting democracy[11] in the third world have not done much better, as demonstrated by the economic and bureaucratic failures of the absolutist communist states and personal rule in Africa and elsewhere.[12]

The failure of both the democratic and the autocratic models has led to "third-wave" thinking about state formation by scholars converging from the two different perspectives.[13] Prominent political economists from the strong state/weak society school have pointed to the importance of the state in achieving sustainable growth-particularly the development of autonomous state capacity. But they have also recognized that the state must place limits on its penetration of society. The birth of the PA hardly conforms to the third-wave paradigm, though it has not been nearly as brutal as most other Arab regimes.

Strengthening Extended-Family Structures as a Form of Depoliticization

Neopatriarchal regimes cultivate family structures and personal-hierarchical ties rather than functionally based organizations; this is true even of those spheres that are the PLO's very own creation and is best reflected in the relationship between the PA and customary law. On 29 September 1995, a notice in the East Jerusalem daily *Al-Quds* reported:

"After Friday prayers an honorable procession composed of notables from the Bethlehem district and notables from the Hebron district proceeded to the Diwan of Ahl al-Halaika in the village of Shuyukh in order to complete the rites of tribal conciliation *(sulh 'asha'iri)* in the wake of a sorrowful car accident." One of those mentioned as participating in the *jaha,* the procession of important dignitaries invited to participate by the family of the deceased, was Colonel Abu Khalid al-Lahham, a former officer in the Palestine Liberation Army, presently the adviser to President Arafat. Al-Lahham, a recent returnee from exile and originally from Bethlehem, is designated to be the district governor of Bethlehem once the Oslo 2 Accord takes effect in the area.

He is by no means, however, the only official to be involved in customary law. On 30 September 1995 customary law reconciliation took place in the headquarters of Force 17, one of the five security agencies of the PA, in the presence of leading security personnel and personalities.[14] At the end of the meeting the two Jericho families, the Qaysia and the Nisann, concluded the *sulh* ceremony "with the blessing of the Authority and Force 17." On 1 November, the lawyer Ibrahim Qandalaft, the PA official for Christian religious affairs, represented the PA in the procession of notables in a customary truce between the Taha Abu Sneineh family and the Christian Habash family, concerning a fight that had broken out two months previously in the Old City of Jerusalem.[15] Indeed, the PA has established the Office of the President for Tribal Affairs *(maktab al-ra'is li-idarat shu'un al-'asha'ir)* to adjudicate problems between families. In early November, for example, some members of the Da'ud family, who are refugees from Majdal/Asqalan, thanked the PA for refraining from registering the family council whose legitimacy they contested.[16]

Neopatriarchal rule has also permeated Islamic law *(shari'a)* in the PA. A *shari'a* ruling by an arbitration committee headed by the Mufti of Gaza "under the sponsorship of the honorable President, the leader and symbol Abu 'Ammar [Arafat], may God keep him" indicates tolerance of a legal system that competes on the turf of the state-directed legal system. This is especially true as the matter involved homicide—in this case the killing of a member of the 'Abid family in October 1995.[17] Jurisdiction over homicide is very much a part of the monopoly over violence and thus, should be under the sole jurisdiction of the civil courts who formally possess that monopoly.

While the subject matter of the ruling indicates just how little the PA has been striving to assert the supremacy of the civil system, the flowery reference to Abu 'Ammar highlights the close connection between legal pluralism and neopatriarchy. In neopatriarchy, personal fealty is often achieved by the absence, and therefore expense, of formal jurisdictional division of labor. It is in fact the very competition among individuals and organizations generated by institutional pluralism that serves as a means of ensuring loyalty. Arafat in a sense prefers personal loyalty at the expense of state building. It is no coincidence that the newly appointed attorney general in the PA, Khalid Al-Qidra, in an interview four months before the ruling of the Mufti, had excluded the possibility that such a ruling could ever take place.[18] He claimed that the state-run civil court system monopolized adjudication over penal matters.

Of course, neopartriarchy could scarcely have been possible had there been no social basis for it. The political announcements that appeared in the Jerusalem Arab press after the Oslo Accords were remarkably similar to those gracing the pages of Jordanian newspapers in honor of special occasions associated with King Husain and his family. It is interesting to note that of the 87 announcements, only 11 referred to such collective and institutional concepts as the Palestinian people and the PLO in their main headings; 65 congratulated President Arafat, employing his official title; and 11 congratulated Abu 'Ammar, "the commander and symbol" *(al-qa'id al-ramz)* without any reference to his formal title. In 40 of these announcements, the traditional word "homage" *(mubaya'a)* appeared in the major headlines.[19] The announcements were made by both kinship and corporate groups. The findings indicate just how prevalent feelings of personal fealty and traditional stratification of society continue to be and, as a result, the extent to which Arafat can effectively employ strategies based on kin-based patronage. And just as the return of Arafat evoked familial cohesion, so did the return of relatives active in the various organs of the PLO after long years of exile.[20] Nevertheless, one might expect an emerging political entity such as the PA to attempt, in Weberian fashion, if not to monopolize law and conflict resolution altogether, at least to assert the superiority of the civil-public domain over other systems of conflict resolution. But the PA—both its officials and the corporate groups within it—have instead become integrated into the customary law framework, and have thus blurred the lines between state and society in typically neopatriarchical fashion.

Depoliticizing Fatah

Official involvement in customary law is one facet of neopatriarchy; thwarting the institutionalization of Fatah as a political party and weakening the remaining factions is another. Depoliticization is taking place on two levels: (1) in the allocation of positions within the PA in a way that ensures the dominance of the "outside" over the "inside"; and (2) in the efforts to weaken all political parties, especially Fatah, relative to the power of kin-based corporate groups. The two processes are interrelated, because PLO officials from the outside are characterized by longstanding personal ties to Arafat, whereas the "inside" by and large has had to operate clandestinely and in a more organized fashion.

It is important to realize that the categorization of officials and activists within Fatah as "inside" or "outside" is organizational rather than geographic. Cadres belonging to the "inside" are those who possess a power base in the front organizations of Fatah that they helped set up in the late 1970s and early 1980s, even if they were later exiled.[21] Obversely, a person like Jibril Rajub, head of the *al-amn al-wiqa'i* (the preventive security forces) in the West Bank, who does not have such a background, can be regarded as an outsider, even though he was incarcerated inside. Those who originate from the outside, however, can never be insiders. Nonetheless, there is no doubt that it was the outside that received the key posts in the PA, especially at the higher levels of the bureaucracy and the security forces, and in the designation of district governors. At the ministerial level, officials from the outside head the three major ministries in the PA: Nabil Sha'th serves as Minister of Planning and Cooperation, Ahmad Quray' (Abu al-'Ala) as Minister of Economy, Trade, and Industry, and Muhammad Zuhdi Nashashibi as Minister of Finance. Another veteran PLO official Al-Tayyib 'Abd al-Rahim is Secretary General of the PA. Even in Jenin, where the PA tried to be more evenhanded and appointed major figures from the Fatah organization "inside," it was Hikmat al-Kaylani, a former exile who was appointed to the key position of governor.[22] With the exception of Faisal al-Husaini, the highly placed officials such as Sa'ib 'Ariqat (Minister of Local Government Affairs) and Jamil Tarifi (Head of the Liaison Committee with Israel) did not emerge from the middle command of Fatah, to whom the distinction between inside and outside is relevant.

No less important has been Arafat's success at thwarting district-level organization building through primaries and elections within Fatah. The only district-level elections took place in Ramallah in November 1994. They were initiated by Marwan al-Barghuthi, the Secretary of the Higher Movement Committee of Fatah. Al-Barghuthi was one of the founders of the Shabiba movement in the West Bank,[23] head of the student Shabiba faction in Birzeit University in the early

1980s, and former president of the student council. He was deported by the Israeli authorities in 1987 and was the only member of the middle command to become a member of the Fatah Revolutionary Council. His biography is typical of a generation of activists who joined Fatah in the late 1970s, formed guerrilla cells, were apprehended, and later developed the popular arms of Fatah in the occupied territories. If he was accorded membership of the Revolutionary Council in the Fifth Fatah Assembly in August 1989 in order to coopt or placate him, he has hardly been playing his assigned role. Since the Oslo agreement Barghuthi has been highly critical of the outside leadership, particularly Yasir Arafat, for monopolizing power:

> There is no doubt that the Madrid Conference and the composition of the delegation from the "inside" gave a big and important push to the role of the inside, but now part of the leadership has returned. In other words, the leadership has returned to the homeland, because the leadership essentially is Yasir Arafat. Wherever Yasir Arafat is to be found, the Palestinian leadership is to be found, because it is clear historically and in the last few years that the power of Yasir Arafat makes him the sole leader and the sole decision maker regarding the Palestinian people.[24]

The omnipotence of one leader and the absence of any role for the most important collective bodies in the PLO are exacerbated by the way PA officials have been chosen.[25] Baghruthi directly links these developments with the strengthening of the role of families and extended clans. Both Sufian Abu Zaidah, a fellow Fatah activist from Gaza, and Nabil 'Amr, a member of the Revolutionary Council from the outside and presently editor of the daily *al-Hayat al-Jadida,* generally concur with Barghuthi. Even though 'Amru is editor of the semi-official newspaper of the PA, he nevertheless censures the "Fatah base" for "making a big mistake when it did not continue, despite the leadership [meaning Arafat], the process of holding elections that began in Ramallah."[26]

The possibility of democratization in Fatah has become even more remote since the above interviews were conducted in February 1995, for at least two reasons. First, Fatah officials from the outside have been taking the lead in reorganizing Fatah without holding district-wide elections, principally in Gaza. Second, key Fatah personalities on the inside who championed the cause of elections are being effectively coopted into the PA. An excellent example is Na'if Suwaytat, a founder of the Shabiba movement in the north and president of the student council at al-Najah University in 1984, who has been appointed general political adviser to the governor of Jenin.[27]

Once again, Arafat is making the most of an existing phenomenon rather than inventing it. Both Abu Zaidah and Marwan al-Barghuthi sharply criticize the opportunism and factionalism that characterize Fatah politics. Al-Barghuthi hoped, however, that elections throughout Fatah would help contain processes that are weakening political organization in favor of family-based politics. The growing strength of the latter is well captured in an *Al-Quds* article entitled "The Heat of Elections Invades the Palestinian Street," by Muhammad Zahayka, who notes the growing importance of "the tribal factor in the absence of any activity of the political and factional forces in acknowledging the innovations that occurred on the Arab and international planes in the last couple of years."[28]

There is however, one point on which both inside and outside concur. Neither side perceives the need to transform Fatah into a political party before the elections scheduled to be held in January 1996. The implications are not only ominous for democracy but also seriously undermine the inside. Fatah independents and coalitions of extended family representatives will in time replace Fatah itself. Ironically, the belittlement and depoliticization of Fatah is taking place under the guise of preserving its revolutionary nature—with very neopatriarchal outcomes.

The Weakening of the Civil Society

In the contest between the PA and the Palestinian nongovernmental organizations (PNGOs), Palestinian civil society has been weakened over three central issues: funding, licensing, and participation in policy formulation. The funding issue is probably the most crucial. The emerging PA has decided that the only conditions under which PNGOs can receive financial support either from government or from international donors (the European Community, the UN agencies and the international nongovernment organizations [INGOs]) are (1) that the state approves such aid and (2) that the aid be coordinated with the relevant state agencies. It is perhaps ironic that Anis Al-Qaq, the Deputy Minister for International Cooperation, who explained this position to the PNGOs, held a totally different view before the emergence of the PA.[29] As founder and former chairman of the largest nongovernmental provider of public health services in the West Bank, he had written a detailed article in the Jerusalem daily *al-Quds* defending a decentralized public health service and opposing the role of the state as the major health service provider.[30] As a senior government official he is now marginalizing the role of the civil society.

Licensing has also become an important issue. On 24 September 1994, the PA called on all private voluntary organizations to register with the authorities by 2 November or else be considered "nonoperational." With considerable foresight, the PNGOs had anticipated state encroachment, and one month after the signing of the Declaration of Principles (DOP), twenty of them formed the Network of PNGOs, stressing their right to international funding, immunity from any form of licensing, and opposition to registration until a law is promulgated that defines the relationship between PNGOs and the PA. Members of the Network feared that the outside PLO, influenced by Arab politics around it, would impose its political culture on the more democratic inside in the West Bank and Gaza.[31] They little realized, however, that the outside would find support for the centralization of public services, at the PNGOs' expense, from former colleagues in Palestinian civil society now well placed in the PA bureaucracy.

To gain legitimacy in contesting the state, the Network commissioned a local lawyer to make a comparative study of legislation regulating NGO work in six states: Denmark, Egypt, India, Israel, Jordan, and the United States. The study, completed in May 1995,[32] revealed that only Jordan required licensing, that Egypt required many more procedures of registration than the other states, and that both of these Arab states accorded officials considerable latitude to interfere in the workings of the NGOs. None of the six states specifically addressed the issue of international aid. The upshot of the paper is clear. First, it established a clear correlation between the democratic nature of a state and noninterference in the affairs of NGOs beyond ensuring these organizations' financial accountability to their respective members and donors. The PA would therefore have to decide whether to adopt the democratic mode and join the ranks of the United States and Denmark, or to adopt the mode that characterizes such states as Egypt, Brazil, and, to a lesser extent, India. Second, the paper suggested that by placing limitations on international funding to PNGOs, the PA would place itself in the unenviable position of being in a class of its own in its treatment of NGOs. The PNGO Network was thus challenging the PA regarding one of its most basic failings—the almost total absence since its inception of any lawmaking, even in the form of ordinances. By the end of 1995 only twelve laws had been put into effect, as compared with the Israeli experience, when nearly one hundred laws (formally called ordinances) were issued between its declaration of independence on 14 May 1948 and the convening of its first parliament, the Knesset, nine months later.

In the year since its establishment, the PA has succeeded in attracting to its ranks only 62 out of a total of 1,200 voluntary organizations operating in the occupied territories. Though some of these organizations rank among the biggest in the occupied territories, they represent but a small fraction of total voluntary activity[33] and are not evenly spread throughout the area. Only 16 of the 62 organizations are based in Gaza, though Gaza represents over 40 percent of the total Palestinian population. The general profile of these organizations is highly urban, elitist, and secular.

The PNGOs, moreover, operate in a political environment where the only possible support for their activity comes from weak opposition parties. Polls conducted in the occupied territories since the establishment of the PA indicate the extreme weakness of non-Islamic opposition groups.[34] This is why international aid is so crucial in enabling the Network to challenge the state.[35]

That such aid is not forthcoming in sufficient quantity is attested to by the proposed law governing voluntary organizations unveiled by the PA's Ministry of Social Affairs in August 1995. The proposed law, which was drafted without consultation with the PNGOs, requires the PNGOs to register and receive permits, and empowers either the Minister of Social Affairs or the Minister of the Interior, or both, to suspend organizational activity without recourse to judicial review, and places restrictions on foreign funding. The PNGOs have especially highlighted the proposed involvement of the Ministry of the Interior—the ministry that in most Arab states is closely linked to public security matters.[36]

THE PROPOSED ELECTION SYSTEM

Neopatriarchy, as a hybrid product of modernity and tradition, is also linked to the preference of a particular electoral system over others. One of the most problematic and intricate aspects of the interim peace process between Israel and the Palestinians was related to the holding of elections and the creation of an elected government. For both sides the issue of elections, even regarding aspects that could be considered procedural, was in fact subsumed under the more immediate issue of sovereignty. And the issue of sovereignty was closely related to both the size of the proposed Legislative Council and to the powers it would wield. Israel wished to limit the number and powers of the council to a level of an autonomy.[37] In contrast, the Palestinians proposed a 100-member council with extensive legislative powers that would bring the Palestinians closer to de facto statehood. The PLO insisted that the elections for the PA take place in East Jerusalem and that its Arab inhabitants should have the right to both elect and to be elected.[38] Israel was prepared to allow them to vote only outside of Jerusalem, which it has formally annexed, and would not allow East Jerusalemites to present themselves as candidates to the Council. Finally, the elections were held up because Israel insisted that the candidates and parties running for election support the peace process and renounce violence. Palestinian acceptance of these conditions would probably have led to the exclusion of the Hamas and Islamic Jihad groups, which according to recent opinion polls, have the support of approximately one-sixth of the population.[39]

The Oslo 2 Agreement, concluded on 28 September 1995, finally resolved the issue of elections in Jerusalem and set the size of the Palestinian assembly at 89 members.[40] The elections took place on 20 January 1996, based on a proposed electoral law circulated in the West Bank and Gaza in late October 1995.[41] The continual postponement of elections, more than a year and a half behind the original schedule, presented a problem in its own right. Taking a cue once again from the relevant literature, one can safely assume that a lengthy institutionalization of nondemocratic practices is bound to make it more difficult for any future government to undo them.

Moreover, the electoral system that was adopted is unlikely to provide a panacea for the centralization of power and its attendant abuses. The PA has drawn up a law for elections to its Council that adopts the multiseat, multidistrict system. Accordingly, voters choose among individual candidates (though they might belong to a party), and the number of voting choices equals the number of seats allotted to that district.[42] This system, used in Jordan in the past, tends to maximize the power of the largest political formation, strengthen independents affiliated to the largest political formation, and generally weaken party organization. This last effect is particularly strong in Arab societies, including the Palestinian, where clans remain important and can be coopted by the government. It is not surprising then that the Independent Palestinian Group for Elections, composed of leading figures in

Palestinian civil society and headed by Hanan 'Ashrawi, the former member and spokeswoman of the Palestinian delegation to the Washington talks, proposed instead a single-district proportional representation system.[43]

THE ACHIEVEMENTS OF NEOPATRIARCHY

According to Sharabi, to speak of "the achievements of neopatriarchy" is almost a contradiction in terms. To a student of transitions from national movement to territorial state and modern state formation, however, neopatriarchy does have its virtues, one of the greatest being public security—assurance of the personal safety and property of the population. For a population that has borne the brunt of an increasingly onerous military occupation and the lawlessness of the Intifada, this is no mean achievement. Preventing the deterioration of existing services is another. Most people in precarious, unsettled conditions are averse to risk; they want first and foremost to ensure that conditions do not deteriorate further before they seek to improve them. Arafat might have succeeded where the local society and the Israeli authorities failed—at least according to the research data collected by the Nablus-based Center for Palestine Research and Studies.[44] The preference for Arafat as head of the Palestinian Authority has been increasing steadily from the time that the organization began administering Gaza and Jericho, and it is significantly higher there than in the areas of the West Bank that will soon come under its rule. The problem lies in the trade-off between present stability and the future costs of instutionalizing neopatriarchy. As the experience in many third world states demonstrates, such regimes are usually characterized by a long-term decline in the capacity to govern due in part to the increasingly stringent control and cooptation of the civil society. The vicious cycle of conflict between state and society that ensues is extremely difficult to break.

CONCLUSION

It is impossible to discuss the phenomenon of neopatriarchy and the birth of the PA without anchoring its internal dynamics to its wider setting. After all, Palestinian state formation is only one aspect of the peace process. In Sharabi's terms, the dependent relationship of the

PLO and the Palestinians on Israel and the United States will reflect the dynamics of peripheral and hybrid information in a system characterized by core, semiperipheral, and peripheral states. Arafat may be the patriarch of the PA, but he is a child to the forces that surround him; and the PA, if it achieves statehood, will, like other neopatriarchal regimes, join the ranks of the peripheral states. To those Palestinians who fought on the ground for something different, this might seem a tragedy; but the conduct of the factions and personalities that have historically constituted the PLO portended no different trajectory—as this volume and many other writings attest. The Palestinians fighting for a truly democratic Palestine are precious few, as is attested to by the mostly fundamentalist inmates who are presently incarcerated in the PA's detention centers. Palestinian state building is therefore unlikely to disprove the general rule regarding fledgling states in the third world, namely, that there are no shortcuts to democracy.

NOTES

1. Hisham Sharabi, *Neopatriarchy: A Theory of Distorted Change in Arab Society* (Oxford: Oxford University Press, 1988), 7.
2. Hassan Naji 'Amr, interview by author, Dura, Hebron, 25 October 1995.
3. *Al-Quds* 21 May 1995.
4. This revolutionary military image also extends to structural arrangements. Arafat effectively stopped a process of holding district elections in Fatah that was meant to transform the faction he controls within the PLO into a political party. Author's interview with Marwan al-Barghuthi, Chairman of the Fatah Central Political Committee in the West Bank, 23 November 1994.
5. *Al-Quds* 25 October 1995.
6. On the EAP, see Prem C. Garg and Samir el-Khouri, "Aiding the Development Effort for the West Bank and Gaza," *Finance and Development* (September 1994): 7-9.
7. Data provided by Dina Abu-Ghaida, consultant to the World Bank, and various World Bank materials.
8. George T. Abed, Assistant Director of General Finance in the IMF, as reported in *Al-Quds* 31 May 1995.
9. 'Imad Qutayna, *"Al-Tadhakhum al-Wazhifi wa-In'ikasatihi 'ala al-Majal al-Mali wal-Dhara'ibi"* (The inflation of positions and its ramifications on the fiscal and tax spheres), *Al-Quds* 31 October 1995.

10. Samuel P. Huntington, *Political Order in Changing Societies* (New Haven, Conn.: Yale University Press, 1968).
11. On the virtues of absolute rule, at least in the long run, see Lisa Anderson, "Absolutism and the Resilience of Monarchy in the Middle East," *Political Science Quarterly* 106:1 (spring 1991): 1-16. On one-party rule see Huntington, *Political Order,* 54.
12. The literature on the failure of personal rule is voluminous. Some of the best examples are Victor Azarya and Naomi Chazan, "Disengagment from the State in Africa: Reflections on the Experience of Ghana and Guinea," *Comparative Studies in Society and History* 29:1 (1987): 107; James S. Wunsch and Dele Olowu, eds., *The Failure of the Centralized State: Institutions and Self-Governance in Africa* (Boulder, Colo.: Westview, 1990); and Robert Jackson and C. G. Rosberg, "Why African Weak States Persist: The Empirical and Juridical in Statehood," *World Politics* 35:1 (1982): 1-24, which explains the difficulties of taking a model from the past to explain the present.
13. Peter Evans, "State as Problem and Solution: Predation, Embedded Autonomy and Structural Change," in R. Kaufmann and S. Haggard, eds., *The Politics of Structural Adjustment* (Princeton University Press, 1992). From the civil society perspective, see John W. Haberson, "Civil Society and Political Renaissance in Africa," in John W. Haberson, Donald Rothchild, and Naomi Chazan, eds., *Civil Society and the State in Africa* (Boulder, Colo: Lynne Rienner, 1994), and "The Comparative Study of Clientelism and the Changing Nature of Civil Society in the Contemporary World," in *Democracy, Clientelism, and Civil Society,* Luis Roniger and Ayse Günes Ayata, eds. (Boulder, Colo.: Lynne Rienner, 1994).
14. *Al-Quds* 1 October 1995.
15. *Al-Quds* 2 November 1995.
16. *Al-Quds* 5 November 1995.
17. *Al-Quds* 26 October 1995.
18. Author's interview with Khalid al-Kidra, Attorney General of the Palestinian Authority, Gaza City, 25 May 1995.
19. *Al-Quds* 14-16 September 1993.
20. Three announcements that appeared in *al-Quds* on 26 June 1994, one month after the establishment of the PA, vividly reflect the durability of embedded social groups in local Palestinian society. In the first, the family council of the al-Dajani family congratulated Mundhir 'Izz al-Din al-Dajani, PLO ambassador to Algeria, on his arrival in the country; in the second, the Bandak family of Bethlehem, which owns one of the biggest manufacturing plants in the West Bank, condemned the attack on two members of the family relating to a land

feud, and asked that the PA intervene "with an iron hand" on its behalf; a third thanked Nabil Sha'ath for his attendance at the *diwan* of Mukhtar Fuad Sha'th of Khan Yunis. The killing in Gaza of Nasr Ishaq Sawalha, a 22-year-old Hamas activist, reflects this reality from a different perspective; presumably this was a revenge killing by the family members of a man whom the Hamas had suspected of collaboration and killed during the Intifada. See *Al-Quds*, 24 June 1994.

21. Hillel Frisch, "The Palestinian Movement in the Territories: The Middle Command," *Middle East Studies* 29:2: 254-274.
22. *Al-Quds* 29 October 1995.
23. The Shabiba movement, founded in the late 1970s by released Fatah prisoners on the model of the communist front organization, became the major vehicle of political mobilization in the West Bank and Gaza during the ensuing decade. For a detailed analysis of its genesis and development, see Hillel Frisch, *"Binuy Mosdot Falestinai baShtachim, 1967-1985"* (Palestinian institution-building in the territories, 1976-1985), Ph.D. diss., The Hebrew University, 1989, chap. 7.
24. *Majallat al-Dirasat al-Filastiniyya* 21 (winter 1995), 66.
25. Ibid., 65.
26. Ibid., 78.
27. *Al-Quds* 29 October 1995.
28. *Al-Quds* 26 October 1995.
29. *Wizarat al-Takhtit wal-Ta'awun al-Dawli, Waraqat 'Amal Lil- Ta'ammul ma'a al-Munazamat Ghair al-Hukumiyya, Muqaddama min al-Duktur Anis al-Qaq, Wakil Wizarat al-Ta'awaun al-Dawli* (Ministry of Planning and International Cooperation, working paper regarding relations with the nongovernmental organizations, presented by Anis al-Qaq, Deputy Minister for International Cooperation), n.p., n.d.
30. *Al-Quds* 16 February 1994.
31. Naseer Aruri, "Oslo and the Crisis in Palestinian Politics," *Middle East International* 467 (January 1994): 17.
32. Hiba Husseini, "A Comparative Analysis of Legislation Regulating NGO Work in Various Country Contexts," May 1995. Unpublished manuscript.
33. Author's interview with Rana Bishara, Coordinator of the PNGO Network, 22 June 1995.
34. In the monthly polls conducted by the Center for Palestine Research and Studies in Nablus between November 1993 and February 1995, support for the DFLP and PFLP ranged from 9 to 11 percent. See Lauren G. Ross and Nader Izzat Sa'id, "Palestinians: Yes to Negotiations, Yes to Violence," *Middle East Quarterly* 2:2 (June 1995): 16, table 1. For a qualititative analysis that

draws the same conclusion, see Isama 'Abd al-Sitar al-Fara, *"Al-Intikhabat al-Muqbila Satua'di al-Kharita al-Siyasiyya al-Muqbila"* (The coming elections will prepare the coming political map), *Al-Quds* 2 November 1995.
35. *Newsletter-Perspectives on the PNGO Network* May 1995, 2.
36. For an extensive analysis of this law, see the two-part article by Tahir al-Nimri, *"Al-Qira'a fi Mashru' al-Jam'iyyat al-Khairiyya wal-Hai'at al-Ijtima'iyya wal-Mu'assasat al-Khassa," Al-Quds* 1 and 2 November 1995.
37. *Ha'aretz* 13 July 1994.
38. *Ha'aretz* 3 May 1995.
39. Lauren G. Ross and Nader Izzat Sa'id, "Yes to Negotiations," 16, table 1.
40. *Jerusalem Post* 29 September 1995; *Al-Yawm* 10 October 1995 (FBIS-NES-95-200).
41. *Al-Quds* 29 and 30 October 1995.
42. *Al-Intikhabat wal-Nizam al-Siyasi al-Filastini* (Nablus: Center for Palestine Research and Studies, February 1995), 172-73.
43. *Al-Intikhabat wal-Nizam al-Siyasi al-Filastini,* 199.
44. *Results of Public Opinion Poll #19* (Nablus: Center for Palestine Research and Studies, August/September, 1995).

FIVE

Policy and Attitude Changes in the Palestine Liberation Organization, 1965–1994:

A Democracy in the Making

Manuel S. Hassassian

History demonstrates that territorial conflicts pose a great threat to peace, harmony, and interdependence. In spite of dramatic global transformations in technology, economics, and politics, regional conflicts based on territoriality continue to command attention in the international arena. Of course, avenues other than war have been opened to settle territorial disputes—for instance, the use of bargaining and negotiation as tools of diplomacy. In such processes, perceptions, beliefs, and cognitions enter into the calculus of pragmatism, of "making choices within constraints."

The essential stakes in the Israeli-Palestinian conflict are the core value systems by which nation-states and peoples define their existence, sovereignty, territory, and, above all, security. For Israel, a basic dilemma is the relationship of territory to security and survival, and the question of "secure boundaries" has run deep through its history as a modern state.[1] Israel's acquisition of territory after the 1967 war collided head-on with Palestinian territorial claims and neighboring Arab states' concerns about their territorial integrity.

The Palestinians, for their part, have been deprived of territory and denied the status of a sovereign state, two important factors that mold their political identity. The Palestinian concept of how much territory is required for a viable sovereign state has changed over the years.[2] From an early policy laying claim to all of Mandatory Palestine, Palestinians today are settling for the West Bank and Gaza Strip. Even with this change of attitude, Palestinian-Israeli positions still collide over the same contested territory.

Since its inception, the PLO has considered several alternatives in defining the Palestinian emotive and practical arguments. Its earlier mode of thinking revolved around arguments that rejuvenated Palestinian historic rights in Palestine. At the Palestine National Council (PNC) of 1988, the PLO endorsed a two-state solution, and at the Madrid Peace Conference in 1992 it dramatically shifted its political discourse into pragmatic arguments based on political accommodation. Of course, Palestinian politics in the 1980s witnessed a volatile transformation in the positions, attitudes, and practices of the PLO, a change that made its political development nonlinear.

During the 1980s, the PLO moved its political center of gravity from periphery—the neighboring Arab countries—to center—the Palestinian homeland—giving more weight to the politics of the occupied territories. One therefore cannot overlook the role of the Intifada in shaping PLO policy. Furthermore, the intelligentsia had already embarked upon the process of democratization and it was taking root in the institutions of the occupied territories as well, paving the way for the PLO to consider political reconciliation as a bargaining tool in the negotiation process with Israel. Thus, it is fair to conclude that the pragmatic position of the PLO has been tremendously affected by political developments inherent in the transformation of Palestinian civil society. Undoubtedly, the democratic trends in West Bank and Gaza politics have been crucial in opening new avenues for the PLO to negotiate peace with Israel.

The purpose of this chapter is to trace the evolution of Palestinian politics through a historic survey of the PLO's Palestine National Council and its various resolutions. I will emphasize the impact of West Bank politics on the PLO, and its influence on the PLO's political behavior, especially in the areas of pluralism and democracy.

This chapter consists, for the most part, of two interrelated parts, one dealing with the historic evolution of PLO politics and the other with the evolution of democratic trends in the occupied territories and their impact on the PLO.

THE FORMATION OF THE PLO

The Palestinians established the PLO in 1964, against a background of inter-Arab rivalries. President Nasir of Egypt, at that stage the champion of the Arab cause, backed the idea in order to coopt the new organization into the Arab League,[3] and provide a means of preventing any Palestinian action against Israel that might draw Egypt into confrontation with Israel.[4] The PLO was headed by Ahmad al-Shuqairi, known for his close relationship with Nasir, and the Palestinian Liberation Army (PLA) was directly under the Arab Unified Command, headed by an Egyptian. The inaugural conference of the PLO was held in May 1964, and its chairman spared no effort in raising material and public support from the various Arab capitals.

From the moment of its inception the PLO was embroiled in factional bickering because its decision-making processes were subject to inter-Arab rivalries, particularly those involving Syria and Egypt and, to a certain degree, Jordan. But Fatah, the leading faction within the PLO, emphasized military action against Israel and managed to rise above the old Arab feuding.[5]

The 1967 war was a disaster for the Arab states as well as for the Palestinians. Another cohort of Palestinian refugees who went to Jordan and to other Arab states, such as Syria and Lebanon, were denied the right to return to their homes, while the rest of the Palestinians were destined to remain on their land and suffer Israeli occupation. Arab military might was shattered, its leadership disoriented and destroyed, while the international community was more sympathetic toward Israel than toward the regimes that the international press and world public opinion presented as intransigent. The Palestinian leadership became disenchanted with the Arab regimes, even when they were supportive, and began to call for Palestinian organizations to be independent of Arab control. They turned from the cause of pan-Arabism and Arab unity to Palestinian nationalism, and the struggle for independence became their main concern.

After the 1967 War, there appeared an urgent need for the reconstruction of Palestinian life. Ideology, armed struggle, and diplomatic posture were secondary to the building of an organization that could act on behalf of all Palestinians. The Palestinian leadership concentrated its efforts on gaining legitimacy and credibility—not only from Palestinians but also from the international community. This involved purchasing arms, raising funds, and developing a territorial base that could help in maintaining close contact with the Palestinians on the West Bank and in Gaza, as well as launching military activities against Israel.

Building such an organizational structure was difficult and required strenuous efforts. Struggling to consolidate their power, the leading Palestinian organizations could not afford open confrontation with the small organizations that proliferated during that time. However, the large commando groups contrived, more by persuasion than by sheer force, to coopt these small groups. A tolerance of division and diversity therefore characterized the Palestinian nationalist movement, and a sense of pluralism thrived, to become almost a tradition, though social divisions and fragmented authority could not be completely avoided. By February 1969, however, Fatah had succeeded in gaining control of the PLO and in uniting the fragmented commando movement to a considerable degree.[6]

The PLO has managed to maintain and operate a remarkable infrastructure against all odds, thus catering to the political and social needs of the dispersed Palestinians.[7] According to scholar Cheryl Rubenberg:

> The PLO's role goes beyond the traditional roles of national liberation movements, for it not only struggles for the attainment of the national political rights of the Palestinian people, but it is the only instrument for the reconstitution of Palestinian, shattered society.... The PLO has to rehabilitate a nation as well as to struggle for its liberation.[8]

Despite the preponderance of militant elements in its organizational structure, the PLO succeeded in building a civilian-institutional infrastructure that took care of the needs of the Palestinian nation in exile. The myriad social institutions and their institutionalization have been crucial in the development of a framework to deal with internal political processes and strategy formulations.[9] This infrastructure has provided the PLO with the means and mechanisms for containing factionalism and divisiveness among the resistance groups, and for representing the Palestinians abroad—not to mention the rendering of medical and social care to the refugee communities in Lebanon and elsewhere.[10]

Though Fatah was the largest, wealthiest, and most influential group within the PLO, it could not arbitrarily set PLO policies without coordinating with the other smaller groups. It feared fragmentation and could not risk losing its representative and democratic image, or its support from the Arab states, which prompted it to afford the smaller groups a political leverage disproportionate to their size and capabilities. Fatah always managed, however, to set objectives geared to promote unity and avoid factionalization.[11]

This institutionalization of the PLO reflects a certain political maturity that legitimizes the quest for statehood. Hence, it is important to consider the political institutions of the PLO.

The Institutional Structure of the PLO

According to the PLO's fundamental law, the most important political institutions of the PLO are the PNC, the Central Council, and the Executive Committee.[12]

In addition to its political organs, the PLO was able to develop a militia and an active military police force in Lebanon. A closer look at the formal structure of the major political organs of the PLO prompts several inferences about the nature of the political process in the PLO and the extent of power sharing and collective decision making. The PLO as an umbrella organization subsumes all the various elements of the Palestinian nationalist movement, thus curbing the likelihood of authoritarianism as a modus operandi.[13]

Further, the PLO has succeeded in maintaining its legitimacy by integrating the complex positions and attitudes of the various Palestinian social strata. The high level of literacy among Palestinians and their political consciousness, deepened by dispersion, occupation, and repression by Israel as well as by authoritarian Arab regimes, have furnished them with a unique identity.

In terms of decision making, the PLO strives toward consensus, although constitutionally, a simple majority will do. Unlike in Arab states, the chief executive of the PLO cannot make independent arbitrations or unilateral decisions; he must use the tools of persuasion and bargaining in order to arrive at a balance among the diverse political trends in the PLO. It is fairly clear that authoritarianism could exacerbate factionalism and divisiveness, a trend that could threaten the PLO and deprive it of its legitimacy. In fact, the history of the PLO is replete with dissidence, and it has often been on the verge of collapse. Arafat's practicality and pragmatism, however, has pulled the PLO together. Of course, one cannot entirely overlook the elements of factionalism in the PLO, based not only on tactics but on ideology; and since Fatah is the predominant faction it can often act unilaterally without causing serious confrontations and outright contradictions. Chairman Arafat has proved a master of diplomacy in containing Palestinian factionalism and has successfully contrived to use the PLO's political structure to promote his ideas and institute his pragmatic moves. Of course, he could not have survived critical periods if he had not enjoyed widespread popular support, in particular from the Palestinians living in the occupied territories. This leads to the conclusion that certain democratic practices are embedded in the pragmatic policies of the PLO. In particular, the PLO's survival has depended heavily on a full synchronization between the "exterior" and "interior" Palestinians, and the Intifada illustrates this phenomenon best.[14]

PLO Politics in the 1980s

In the light of present political realities, one detects a clear transformation in Palestinian politics, especially after the Israeli invasion of Lebanon in 1982—notwithstanding that with the invasion, the military and civilian infrastructures of the Palestinians were almost shattered. It is evident that three major internal changes within the Palestinian national movement have been major catalysts in changing the strategy of the PLO in its political struggle against Israel. One of those changes has been in the role and status of the formal political organizations—that is, the commando groups that make up the PLO. A second major shift has been the concentration of power in Arafat's hands as the undisputed leader of the PLO. A third major shift has been the switch in focus of the national struggle from the periphery to the center—meaning to the occupied territories.[15]

Naturally, the dramatic shifts in PLO politics were not made in a vacuum but were the outcome of a particular period of inter-Arab politics involving especially Jordan and Syria. The focus of the political struggle shifted to the West Bank and Gaza because the PLO's formal institutions and infrastructure had been partially shattered. The single trump card left for Arafat to play was the West Bank card, and he played it brilliantly. His trip to Egypt after the PLO's expulsion from Tripoli in 1988 added a major component to the success of PLO diplomacy, although there was a clear demarcation between the Arafat mainstream and the "rejectionist" opposition composed of the PFLP-General Command (PFLP-GC) and other groups, which in March of 1985 came together and formed the Syrian-based Palestine National Salvation Front.[16] But in the end its impact was marginal because it failed to advocate a viable alternative to the diplomatic posture advocated by Arafat and Fatah.

On the other hand, after Fatah split in 1983, the PFLP and the Democratic Front for the Liberation of Palestine (DFLP) formed a "loyal" opposition camp, critical of Arafat, yet loyal to the PLO framework. Unlike the National Salvation Front, the two groups were successful in mobilizing support through the building of organizational structures in the occupied territories and in exile. The opposition to Arafat hammered on political issues, mainly the diplomatic strategy of Fatah and the closer relations with Jordan and Egypt after a catastrophic military failure to crush Arafat's political power during the Battle of the Camps in 1985. It was not until the eighteenth PNC, held in Amman in 1985, that the traditional veto power held by the smaller factions was undermined in the decision-making process. Subsequently, Fatah has dominated the PLO and consolidated its central role in the PLO's decision-making process.[17] According to Palestinian scholar Emile Sahliyeh:

> Although Fatah's moderate leadership demonstrated some willingness to give the floating peace plans a chance, it simultaneously continued to pay lip service to the relevance of the strategy of military struggle. The moderate leadership was unwilling to gamble with too many odds working against it. With such mixed feelings and sentiments, the leadership of the PLO moderates approached the Reagan initiative, coordination with Jordan and contact with Egypt, Syria and Israeli peace groups.[18]

The moderates inside the PLO realized that the participation of the United States was indispensable for a Middle East settlement in view of that country's massive assistance to Israel in all areas; they therefore accepted American conditions for opening a dialogue[19] and tried to improve their situation vis-à-vis the United States. In December 1988, a United States-PLO dialogue was initiated, but was later disrupted due to the American conviction that Arafat had not explicitly renounced terrorism. However, a closer look at the PNC resolutions will be helpful in tracing the transformation of the PLO's "armed struggle" policy to one of "peaceful coexistence."

The PNC Resolutions

A close analysis of the PNC resolutions sheds light on the Palestinians' democratic and pluralistic thinking, which had been developing since the time of the twelfth PNC session, in June 1974. In fact, since 1974, the Palestinians had been moving steadily toward accommodation and compromise. By the eighteenth PNC, convened in Algiers in April 1987, most of the elements of the peaceful strategy and acceptance of the two-state solution on the basis of United Nations resolutions were in place.

To illustrate the transition in the PLO's political thought, the PNC sessions can be divided into three distinctive phases:

1. *Liberation and return* (the first four PNCs: 1964-1968). Since Israel's victory in the partial destruction of Palestine in 1948, Palestinians have suffered homelessness and exile; it is incumbent upon them to redress these injustices through the liberation of their occupied homeland and the repatriation of their exiled community.[20] However, the Palestinian National Charter of 1964 and the amended National Charter of 1968 drawn up at the fourth PNC—as well as the resolutions of the second and third PNCs—all emphasized the total liberation of Palestine.[21] Self-reliance along with armed struggle were stipulated in Article 9 of the 1968 National Charter. Moreover, the concept of national unity was reiterated to draw together the different commando groups within the PLO. As a result of the fourth PNC, the newly emerged PLO vigorously stressed the building of sociopolitical and economic institutions that could cater to the needs of a shattered society.[22] Above all, the PLO managed to define its national identity, goals and aspirations a coherent national movement.

2. *The secular democratic state* (5th-11th PNCs: 1969-1974). During this phase, the Palestinians encountered the problem

of how to reconcile their maximalist demands with the political and demographic realities that had been created after the defeat in the 1948 war.[23] This phase was characterized by a further dramatic shift in Palestinian objectives, from total liberation to a democratic secular state in which Christians, Jews, and Muslims could live harmoniously together. The emphasis was put on the right of return of the refugees, as stipulated in the UN General Assembly's Article 194.

Thus the fifth PNC, in 1969, introduced the idea of establishing a "free democratic state in Palestine." At the sixth PNC the same concept was reiterated, substituting, however, the word "society" for "state."[24] In fact, at the eleventh PNC, the establishment of a "democratic society where all citizens can live in equality, justice, and fraternity" that would be "opposed to all forms of prejudice on the basis of race, creed and color" was emphasized. This proposal represented a historic compromise in which a framework for peace was presented, although Israel perceived this as a threat to its sovereignty. This official policy of the PLO remained the basic objective until 1974, when the organization made the first gesture toward a two-state solution, at the twelfth PNC.[25]

3. *The two-state solution* (12th-19th PNC: 1974-1988). In July 1974, after the October war, new prospects seemed to emerge in the Middle East and hopes for a comprehensive settlement were high. This induced the PLO to embark on the road to a political settlement through pragmatism that culminated in the declaration of a Palestinian state in the occupied territories and the ultimate acceptance of a two-state solution. This historic decision was a response to an accumulation of important events such as the Lebanese civil war, Sadat's visit to Jerusalem, the Camp David Accords, the Egyptian-Israeli peace treaty, the 1982 Israeli invasion of Lebanon, and the Intifada in the occupied territories. In the time span between the twelfth and nineteenth PNCs, the PLO managed to respond to all the political developments in the Middle East.

In fact, during these crucial years, the PLO also witnessed internal changes and such dramatic events as the temporary withdrawal of the PFLP from the PLO's Executive Committee, the splitting off of the Abu

Musa faction in 1983, and Arafat's controversial trip to Cairo after the PLO's expulsion from Lebanon. All these incidents were crucial blows to the fortunes of the Palestinian national movement; yet the Palestinians survived them and the PLO managed to stabilize its profound commitment to the concept of a two-state solution.

One can safely assert that the twelfth PNC was the turning point in Palestinian political decision making and could be considered the earnest beginning of the search for peaceful coexistence and political accommodation. It was in this council that the "ten-point" program was drafted, calling for the establishment of the "people's national, independent, and fighting authority on every part of liberated Palestinian land."[26]

Subsequent PNCs, the thirteenth, fourteenth and fifteenth, emphasized repeatedly the right of the Palestinians to establish their independent state under the leadership of the PLO in any part of Palestine.[27] During this period, a broadly based international consensus emerged for the creation of an independent Palestinian state in parts of Palestine as the basis for resolving the Arab-Israeli conflict. The PLO endorsed the resolutions of the 1982 Fez Conference, which laid down a practical vision for the resolution of the Arab-Israeli conflict.[28]

After a rapprochement with Egypt, Arafat managed to ease relations with Jordan, and in the sixteenth PNC there was a decision for a direct and open dialogue with Jordan, including on the formation of a confederation. At all events, the confederation plan was repeatedly raised in subsequent PNCs, despite the formal abrogation of this strategy.[29]

From the twelfth PNC on, the concept of "armed struggle" became secondary to political diplomacy, but it was never ruled out as an option. The strategy set was a political course toward a peaceful resolution of the conflict.

It was at the seventeenth PNC, in Amman in 1984, that the consensus in PLO debate came to represent the majority, since the Damascus-based opposition to the mainstream within the PLO did not have popular support. The Amman PNC explicitly consecrated the paramountcy of Palestinian aspirations and wishes in the occupied territories,[30] and emphasized negotiations with Israel in the context of an international conference.[31]

The eighteenth PNC, which was convened in Algiers in April 1987, represented a major PLO triumph over a threat to its unity, national cohesion and legitimacy. According to Muhammad Hallaj, the PNC was significant because:

The return of the opposition to the parliamentary and constitutional structure of the PLO was an admission of the failure of extra-constitutional confrontation and the triumph of democratic dissent within the Palestinian political process. The importance of the reinforcement of the PLO's democratic traditions by the PNC cannot be overestimated.[32]

The strategy of Palestinian leadership during this third phase comprised three substantial elements that emphasized previous decisions: (a) mobilizing and politicizing the Palestinian people behind an organization representing them; (b) maintaining the unity of the Palestinian movement through very difficult times; and (c) achieving a political program based on consensus.[33]

In November 1988, the nineteenth PNC met in Algiers to adopt a declaration of independence and a political statement. In these documents a clear and concise peace strategy was laid down based on UN Resolutions 242 and 338. This PNC constituted a clear formulation of PLO objectives in achieving political compromise with Israel.[34]

Undoubtedly, the nineteenth PNC irrevocably changed the commitment of the PLO from former claims for a state in all Palestine to a limited one in the West Bank and Gaza. Regardless of the PFLP's and DFLP's opposition to the mainstream Fatah in the PLO, they never withdrew from the PLO institutions.[35]

The mainstream of Palestinian thinking came to accept a clear, unequivocal yet flexible strategy, rejecting past tendencies to adopt the familiar all-or-nothing position. The "no" of the Palestinians with regard to negotiations with Israel and the restoration of their rights in Palestine has been altered by two important developments: (a) the PLO's adoption of a two-state solution and acceptance of the relevant UN resolutions, and (b) the reluctance of the Palestinians in the occupied territories to play a leading role in the negotiation process.[36]

In sum, one can infer that the Palestinian national movement had encountered dramatic shifts in objective, strategy, and political achievements due to changes in the political realities and to the pragmatic approach of its leadership, which compromised basic principles to reach a political settlement with Israel. The radical change from emotive arguments to practical ones involved a rather complicated process, culminating in the acceptance of the PLO-Israel accord of 1993. That accord is divided into two stages: an interim phase and a permanent phase for Palestinian political empowerment.

The path toward full normalization of relations is complex and requires perseverance and stamina from both sides. But regardless of the opposition to the Palestinian peace camp, the mainstream has shown flexibility in an ingenious political scheme, containing the opposition in a democratic process that emphasizes the rule of the majority in the decision-making process.

Certain democratic trends in the political behavior of the Palestinians are also reflected in the civil society, especially in the West Bank and Gaza. A closer look at the Palestinian socioeconomic infrastructure will shed more light on the process of democratization that has affected the political attitudes of the PLO.

Major Trends and Forces in Palestinian Society Today

The Palestinian political arena can be divided into four main forces: (a) *The mainstream,* comprising Fatah and its allies; Feda (Palestinian Democratic Union); and Hizbal-Sha'b (People's Party); (b) *The Left* (opposition to the mainstream), comprising the PFLP (Habash faction), and the DFLP (Hawatmah faction); (c) *The Islamists* (opposition to the mainstream), comprising Hamas (the Islamic resistance movement), the Islamic Jihad, and independent Islamists; and (d) *The Independent Nationalists* and the undecided.

Of course, Palestinian politics witnessed sharp divisions with the Madrid Peace Conference in 1992, where the opposition, secular, and religious practically joined forces against Fatah and the mainstream in trying to abort the peace process. However, by using the back channel—an unofficial negotiation track—in Oslo between the mainstream of the PLO and Israel, Arafat curbed all efforts by the opposition to reverse the political trend toward forging peace. Despite the opposition's attitude toward the Oslo accords, it failed to consolidate its power and position because of the lack of viable alternatives and options at a time when the Palestinian people were suffering tremendously from occupation.

Since the establishment of the Palestianian Authority (PA) in May 1994, the opposition camp has advocated democracy because it fears suppression by the PA during the interim phase and early empowerment. In this context, the question of elections to the PA's legislative council was at the core of Palestinian politics, perceived by most Palestinians as a useful instrument in the process of nation building and democratization. Many Palestinians also deemed elections useful for unification of the West Bank and Gaza Strip, for the inclusion of Jerusalem Palestinians into the process of building a nation and national institutions, and for the creation of a legitimate and accountable system of government that will respect individual civil liberties and human rights. But for the many Palestinians who identify with the opposition, the elections had negative repercussions: providing legitimacy to Arafat's and Fatah's dominance and to the negotiated agreements.

By and large, the debate over Oslo's provisions has divided the Palestinian national movement. Those in opposition to the Oslo process believe that this is not the time for diplomatic moves and that the military struggle against occupation must be continued until Palestine is totally liberated. Both the Islamic opposition groups and the PFLP have taken this stance.

Israel was not instrumental in helping Arafat to consolidate his power among the various Palestinian constituencies. In fact, Israel made it even more difficult for him by not honoring the deadlines agreed upon in the accords and continuing the policy of closures that deny the Palestinians of the occupied territories access to jobs and markets in Israel—devastating Palestinian hopes for improvement as a result of the Oslo process.

In spite of these circumstances, Arafat has to embolden Palestinian political culture by incorporating various trends of democracy in the institution-building process of a nascent civil society. He has made a discernable effort to coopt Hamas and the secular opposition groups through pluralism in the electoral process, with limited success.

DEMOCRATIC TRENDS IN THE OCCUPIED TERRITORIES

The quest for democracy is emerging as a global phenomenon. In the post-World War II era, democracy has developed into a universal political norm. In fact, the philosophical tenets of democracy that led to the rise of nationalism are a prelude to independence and a prime factor in "the democratization of the peripheralized society." For democracy to be entrenched in a society, it must be strengthened not only on the institutional level but also on the sociopolitical level.[37] World recognition of the principle of national self-determination has culminated in the globalization of democracy, a principle that most third world societies are struggling to realize.

The Palestinians are no exception; as actors on the world political stage, they could not evade the new global trends of democratization even if they wished to—hence the new Palestinian political realism and pragmatism. In fact, for democracy to succeed it must be institutionalized in a way that mediates the multiple and conflicting interests that will emerge once statehood is achieved. This process of transition is difficult as well as critical for developing societies because they lack experience in dealing with methods that may hamper their legitimacy and performance.[38]

Pluralism—a democratic trend—in Palestinian politics has always been assessed in the context of the erosion evident in Arab politics, resulting from fragmentation, repressive conditions, economic discrepancies, and lack of legitimacy and credibility. It is no wonder that the basic tenets of democracy—political participation, power sharing and public accountability—are nonexistent in the Arab states. Furthermore, the lack of self-sustaining institutions embedded in consolidated communities is a serious impediment to the emergence of democracy. Consequently, the Arab Middle East suffers from inadequate industrial growth and heavily militarized, bureaucratized, and centralized governments.[39] Nonetheless, its people are striving to achieve political freedom, justice, and a decent life. It is therefore imperative to emphasize the human elements that transcend all geopolitical boundaries when analyzing the Middle East.

As noted earlier, Palestinian nationalism—an offshoot of Arab nationalism—has over the years developed a secular ideology committed to democracy. The process of democratization has been facilitated by the high level of education and literacy achieved by Palestinians, along with the emergence of their institutions and professional societies.

The PLO has portrayed itself as the institutional expression of Palestinian nationalism—a framework into which all Palestinian cultural, social, educational, political, and military activities are integrated.[40] By providing an array of services to the Palestinians, it gained legitimacy in the past and shouldered the burden of integrating Palestinians of various attitudes and status—refugees living in camps, intellectuals, middle-class merchants, and resistance fighters.

In recent years, the PLO has managed to emphasize certain democratic pragmatic trends in its political program; and undoubtedly the Intifada has been a catalyst in changing its perceptions, attitudes, and even political strategies, laying the groundwork for negotiations, political settlement, and accommodation. Implementation of the Oslo Accords is a culmination of the PLO's evolutionary political development.

By and large, Western democratic values are accepted everywhere in the world, and the discussion of democracy is carried on in a liberal democratic framework. Of course, there is quite a discrepancy between support for the rhetoric and support for the reality of democracy. Many intellectuals among the Palestinians genuinely support democracy, and many of the masses support it because it signifies to them dramatic change and prosperity. The ruling elites, however, are at best unwilling converts.

The procedural definition of democracy is still inadequate among the Palestinians, because one cannot presume the existence of a culture of accommodation that will make democracy work. An alert political observer cannot deny that the Palestinians in the occupied territories have developed certain trends of democratic behavior that are relatively inferior to those evinced by Western liberal democracies. The democratic trends among the Palestinians are embedded in the sociopolitical culture of a nascent civic society that was initiated during the 1980s and 1990s by building institutions and grass-roots organizations. But today these organizations are threatened by disintegration because of Israeli closures of the territories and their impact on the Palestinian economy.

By and large, Palestinian cultural expression has been organically interwoven with political developments and political realities. In the course of their political struggle, Palestinians have succeeded in embodying within their national ethos a culture of resistance and a momentum of sociopolitical transformation. In fact, Palestinians have always defined democracy in the context of human rights, civil rights, and self-determination. They have made some headway in developing their socioeconomic infrastructure and have prioritized changes in their educational system. Undoubtedly, the Intifada was instrumental in inducing the Palestinians to build civic institutions, thus expanding the democratization process among the grassroots of the Palestinian community through the growing number of and membership in trade unions, professional associations, women's organizations, student and youth movements and the like. A great number of Palestinians regarded their participation in these organizations as an important way to defy Israeli occupation and establish democratic institutions. Consequently, the notion of democracy grew alongside ideas of national solidarity and struggle against occupation, a major ethos among Palestinians. And throughout the 1980s, democracy was perceived as the basis of Palestinian solidarity, popular mobilization and steadfastness *(sumoud)*.[41] This democratic process gained momentum as a result of substructural changes, the expansion of education and a growing political awareness among the lower strata of Palestinians, urban and rural alike.

The lessons of the past five decades or so—indeed, the lessons of this century, marked by conquest, occupation, and colonization—have taught the Palestinians that unless democratic practices are implemented at every level of daily life—in the home, in schools, in offices, and in factories—the new state of Palestine will emerge as a replica of the surrounding authoritarian Arab regimes. A large number of Palestinian intellectuals, including proponents of the fundamentalist wing, consider freedom and political pluralism to be basic ingredients of the future Palestinian polity. Hence, a multiparty system is upheld as the most desirable model.

To illustrate the process of democratization already in progress, it is necessary to shed some light on the labor unions, professional associations, and popular organizations. Because political activity was banned under occupation, Palestinian political factions were operating clandestinely. Nevertheless, all elections held in these organizations were based on partisanship.

The Labor Unions

The Palestinian work force has undergone dramatic changes in the occupied territories. Reportedly, of about 160,000 workers in 1968, only 6 percent were organized in labor unions. By the late 1970s, the total Palestinian labor force in the occupied territories and Israel had increased to 230,000 with 20 percent registered as members of trade unions.

Since the early 1980s the Palestinians claim to have more than one hundred labor unions with a total of 40,000 members, organized into three federations affiliated to the various PLO factions.[42] Regardless of their objectives, they run their internal affairs along bureaucratic and democratic lines, holding regular elections and maintaining checks and balances.

The Student Movement

Unlike the labor unions, the student movement has been vociferously political owing to its politicized nature and its assumption of a leading role in fighting the occupation. Because of its high level of education and exposure to Western liberal concepts, the student movement is definitely considered avant-garde in applying democratic practices.

The student movement is structurally and ideologically spread along a political spectrum that encompasses the PLO, the Islamists, and Hamas. Twenty-thousand students are enrolled in the six universities in the occupied territories, and elections for the student senates have been conducted in a democratic fashion with a high percentage of student participation.

THE WOMEN'S MOVEMENT

In the early 1980s, a variety of new social organizations emerged, reflecting a wide range of political participation, the women's movement being a prime example. Comprising some 15,000 members, the women's movement draws its membership from the lower strata of society and is affiliated politically with the main factions of the PLO. Here, too, the members have held democratic elections; and they have been highly active in sociocultural, vocational, and paramedical work, as well as in national political activities against occupation.

PROFESSIONAL ASSOCIATIONS

Other organizations established during the 1980s include associations of merchants, artisans, lawyers, physicians, engineers, writers, and journalists. These associations have provided the intellectual and ideological guidance for mass political participation in the national struggle against occupation. Democratic elections based on pluralism have marked the activities of these associations and have reflected a structural hierarchy that is based on decentralized and delegated authority.

THE CRAFTING OF DEMOCRACY AND THE FUTURE OF PALESTINE

The Palestinian Declaration of Independence addresses the question of the type of regime that will exist in the future independent Palestinian state. In fact, the last paragraph of the Declaration is emphatic about full equality of rights among its citizens, and that Palestinians will be able to enjoy their national and cultural identity. Further, the Palestinian state will safeguard "their political and religious convictions and their human dignity by means of a parliamentary democratic system of governance, itself based on freedom of expression and the freedom to form parties."[43] In the area of authority and representation the Declaration makes clear that "the right of minorities will be duly respected by the majority, as minorities must abide by decisions of the majority. Governance will be based on principles of social justice, equality and non-discrimination in race, religion, color, sex under the aegis of a constitution which ensures the rule of law and an independent judiciary."[44] In principle, then, the language of the Declaration reflects a philosophical commitment to the development of democratic institutions.[45]

On the basis of the above observations, one might be justified in asserting that the evolving democratic Palestinian society augurs well for future relations with democratic neighbors. But it should be borne in mind that Palestinian democracy has not yet taken root, it is still in the process and could be considered at best a fledgling democracy. Giovanni Sartori explained it well when he warned that

> new states and developing nations cannot pretend to start from the level of achievement at which the Western democracies have arrived. In fact, no democracy would ever have materialized if it had set for itself the advanced goals that a number of modernizing states currently claim to be pursuing. In a world-wide perspective, the problem is to minimize arbitrary and tyrannical rule and to maximize a pattern of civility rooted in respect and justice for each man . . . in short, to achieve a humane polity. Undue haste and overly ambitious goals are likely to lead to opposite results.[46]

This warning is definitely applicable to the Palestinian political culture; because the Palestinians have never experienced their own state, it is unrealistic to expect them to adopt Western democratic values and incorporate them overnight. Notwithstanding the many hurdles, there are good indications that Palestinian society will develop along democratic lines and will establish a democratic political entity. According to Hisham Sharabi, a leading Palestinian scholar

> Only a free and democratic Palestinian entity alongside Israel will guarantee a genuine and lasting peace. An autocratic regime, such as exists today

in many Arab countries, would not last but would inevitably lead to economic and political disintegration, with unpredictable consequences.[47]

Democracy cannot survive in Palestine if it offers merely elections and multipartisanship. It must restore faith in the civic society and provide self-fulfillment and national pride. Furthermore, democracy cannot develop without a viable economic infrastructure. Stimulating economic development in the occupied territories is an urgent need and an essential precondition for political stability in the area.

There is no doubt that over the past three decades of Israeli rule serious structural problems in the economy of the occupied territories have emerged and require immediate attention. Among them are:

1. A heavy dependence of the labor force on outside sources of employment;
2. A low degree of industrialization;
3. A trade structure heavily dominated by trading links with Israel, with large trade deficits;
4. Inadequate public infrastructure and services;
5. A need for economic assistance from the World Bank and donor countries to build Palestinian institutional capacity;
6. A need to promote the private sector of the economy with public sector involvement;
7. A need for foreign aid to support:

    a. Infrastructure projects;
    b. Training and education;
    c. Technical assistance;
    d. Welfare programs.

A three-phased strategy for economic development in the occupied territories has been espoused by the Palestinian National Authority:

Phase One: Moving from dependence to independence and its substrategies;
Phase Two: Moving from independence to interdependence;
Phase Three: The involvement of Israel and Palestine in other blocs; interdependence with the Arab world; and building bridges with the United States, Europe, Russia, and Japan.

Such a strategy would ensure an infrastructure that would synchronize with democratic ideals, a society based on freedom and rights of the individual. Democracy should evolve to be the supreme political value, prevailing over ideological and factional adherence.

Conclusion

The formation of the PLO has been the major achievement of the contemporary Palestinian national movement. It has also been essential for preserving and developing the political unity and national identity of the Palestinian people. However, a reconstructed and reformed PLO could boost its bargaining power and give impetus to the building of institutions of Palestinian civil society. Moreover, Arafat and the PA should address the concerns of the Palestinians by establishing a system of government, maintaining security and order, and improving economic conditions. The high expectations of Palestinians have not yet been realized. Many Palestinians are concerned about what they perceive to be the inability of the PA to institutionalize government, because the infrastructures of government are not being established. In addition, economic conditions have not yet improved in any significant way. International donors are still arguing over accountability and transparency, and Palestinian investors are in a wait-and-see situation. All these factors deprive the PA of sources of legitimacy. The Palestinians therefore, need the support of the international community in helping to make the peace process succeed and bear fruit for a just and lasting peace. A comprehensive political settlement alongside a sustained socio-economic infrastructure would lead to meaningful economic development and regional cooperation. That very development would consolidate the peace that made it possible in the first place.

Notes

1. United States National Conference of Catholic Bishops, Statement on the Middle East. "Toward Peace in the Middle East: Perspectives, Principles and Hopes," adopted 6 November 1989, Baltimore, Md., 4.
2. Ibid., 5.
3. Charles D. Smith, *Palestine and the Arab-Israeli Conflict* (New York: St. Martin's Press, 1988): 188-89.

4. Ibid.
5. Helena Cobban, *The Palestinian Liberation Organization: People, Power and Politics* (London: Cambridge University Press, 1984): 35.
6. For the historic evolution of the PLO, see Quandt, Jaber and Lesch, *The Politics of the Palestinian Nationalism* (Berkeley: University of California Press, 1973).
7. Yezid Sayigh, "The Politics of Palestinian Exile," *Third World Quarterly* 9:1 (January 1987): 57.
8. Cheryl Rubenberg, *The PLO: Its Institutional Infrastructure* (Belmont, Mass.: Institute of Arab Studies, 1983): 1.
9. Sayigh, "The Politics of Palestinian Exile," 59.
10. Aaron David Miller, "The PLO and the Politics of Survival," *The Washington Papers* 99 (1983): 56.
11. Ibid., 57-59.
12. Sami Musallam, *"Al-Bunya al-Tahtiya wa al-Haikal al Mouassassati li Munathamat al-Tahrir al-Filatiniyya," Shu'un Filastinniya* 166-67 (December-January 1987): 103.
13. Rubenberg, *The PLO,* 14.
14. See Emile Sahliyeh, *In Search of Leadership: West Bank Politics since 1967* (Washington, D.C.: The Brookings Institution, 1988).
15. Yezid Sayigh, "Struggle Within, Struggle Without: The Transformation of PLO Politics since 1982," *International Affairs* 65:2 (1989): 248.
16. Ibid., 249-50.
17. Ibid., 255; see also Cobban, *The Palestinian Liberation Organization,* 5-17.
18. Emile F. Sahliyeh, *The PLO after the Lebanon War* (Boulder and London: Westview Press, 1986): 93.
19. Ibid.
20. Muhammad Hallaj, "The Arab-Israeli Conflict: A Palestinian View," *Vierljahtesberichte* (Problems of international cooperation), 99 (March 1985): 32.
21. Muhammad Y. Muslih, "Toward Coexistence: An Analysis of the Resolutions of the Palestine National Council, *Journal of Palestine Studies* 20:2 (spring 1990): 8.
22. Ibid., 10.
23. Sa'id Hammoud, *"Al-Majalis al-Wataniyya al-Filastiniyya wa al Wihda Al-Wataniyya," Shu'un Filastiniyya* 18 (February 1973): 80.
24. Hallaj, "The Arab-Israeli Conflict," 32.
25. For the historical background and PLO deliberations on the concept of a "democratic secular state," see Alain Gresh, *"Shi'ar al-Dawla Al-Dimocratiya"* (February 1982): 142-68.
26. Hamid, "Munathamat al-Tahrir," 525-526.

27. Faysal Hourani, *"Munathamat al-Tahrir al-Filastiniyya wa al-Itijah Nahwa al-Taswiya,"* Shu'un Filastiniyya 99 (February 1980): 52-66; Bilal al-Hassan, *"Al-Dawra Al-Khamisa 'Ashar Lil Majlis al-Watani al-Filastini: Dawrat al-Tadqiq Fi al-Qarar al-Siyasi,"* Shu'un Filastiniyya 115 (June 1981).
28. al-Hassan.
29. Hallaj, "The Arab-Israeli Conflict," 33.
30. Rashid Khalidi, "The Palestinian Dilemma: PLO Policy after Lebanon," *Journal of Palestine Studies* 15:1 (autumn 1985): 88-91.
31. Khalidi, "The Palestinian Dilemma," 101.
32. Hallaj, "The Arab Israeli Conflict," 33.
33. Nadia Hijab, "The Strategy of the Powerless," *Middle East International* 12 May 1989, 17-18.
34. Rashid Khalidi, "The Resolutions of the Nineteenth PNC," *Journal of Palestine Studies* 19:2 (winter 1990): 29-32. See also Matti Steinberg, "Change Despite Duality," *New Outlook* 32:1 (1989): 15-17.
35. Maxim Ghilan, "The Palestinians: What Has Changed in the PLO," *Israel/Palestine* (November 1988): 2-3.
36. Fouad Moughrabi, Elia T. Zureik, Manuel Hassassian and Aziz Haidar, "Palestinians on the Peace Process," *Journal of Palestine Studies* 21:1 (autumn 1991): 37.
37. Yashikazou Sakamuto, "Introduction: The Global Context of Democratization," *Alternatives* 16 (1991): 119.
38. Giuseppe Di Palma, "Transition in Eastern Europe," *Journal of Democracy* (1991), as cited in *Dialogue* 4 (1991): 25.
39. M. Muslih and August R. Norton, "The Need for Arab Democracy," *Foreign Policy* 83 (summer 1991): 5.
40. Cheryl A. Rubenberg, "The Civilian Infrastructure of the Palestinian Liberation Organization: An Analysis of the PLO in Lebanon until June 1982," *Journal of Palestine Studies* 12:3 (spring 1983): 54.
41. Moshe Ma'oz, "Democratization among West Bank Palestinians and Palestinian-Israeli Relations," in E. Kaufman, S. B. Abed and R. L. Rothstein, eds., *Democracy, Peace, and the Israeli-Palestinian Conflict* (Boulder, Colo.: Lynne Rienner, 1993): 231.
42. Ibid.
43. Palestinian Declaration of Independence.
44. Ibid.
45. Sari Nusseibeh, *Ha'aretz* (supplement), 7 September 1989.
46. Giovanni Sartori, "Democracy," in David L. Sills, ed., *The International Encyclopedia of the Social Sciences* 4 (Macmillan, Free Press, 1968): 120-22.
47. Hisham Sharabi, "Only a Democratic Palestine Can Survive," *Washington Post*, July 1994.

PART II

Regional and International Arenas

SIX

THE PLO IN REGIONAL ARAB POLITICS

TAMING A NON-STATE ACTOR

AVRAHAM SELA AND MOSHE MA'OZ

THE RESHAPING OF THE POST-OTTOMAN FERTILE CRESCENT by the European powers after World War I sowed the seeds of future ethnopolitical and intercommunal disputes in and between the newly established entities. Fertile Crescent politics were particularly affected by the intensive interplay between domestic and regional politics, high degree of permeability of the state, and salience of suprastate revisionist movements.[1] Nowhere was this more evident than in the case of historic Palestine, where the British Mandate (1920-1948) in effect created two new political entities competing for hegemony over this territory. In the late 1920s, the growing Jewish-Arab dispute in Palestine increasingly became a matter of public and then official concern for the neighboring countries. In fact, the Palestine conflict turned into a focal issue in the ensuing regional system of Arab entities, along with inter-Arab competition for regional hegemony, national liberation, and the rise of pan-Arab nationalism.

The interplay of these foci since the interwar period shaped a concentric regional system, revolving around struggle for power among the core actors as well as cultural issues rooted in the shared symbols and beliefs of Arab-Islamic societies. The emergence of a Jewish state in the heart of the Arab homeland and House of Islam *(dar al-islam),* in conjunction with sociopolitical changes, played a central role in the formation of pan-Arab nationalism and crystallization of the Arab regional system. The idea of liberating Palestine has remained pivotal in all Arab political discourses—including Arab nationalism, social revolution, and Muslim fundamentalism—as the essence of the ethos of struggle against the foreign invader.[2]

During the Mandate the Palestinian national movement was marked by institutional weakness and severe fragmentation that forced it to seek external Muslim and Arab material and political support. Unlike the *Yishuv* (the Jewish community in Palestine), which by the mid-1930s had become the center of gravity of the world Zionist movement, the Arab-Palestinian cause moved constantly outward into the Arab-Muslim arena.[3] The confrontation with the British Mandate and the *Yishuv* escalated toward the late 1930s. By the end of the 1936-39 revolt, the Palestinian political center was in disarray; its hard core, represented by al-Haj Amin al-Husaini, was forced to seek refuge in the neighboring Arab countries, while the Palestinian political community was itself torn by serious social and political cleavages. Palestinian structural weakness drew the new Arab entities of Jordan, Lebanon, Syria and Iraq, along with Egypt, into growing involvement in the Arab-Jewish conflict in Palestine, culminating in the invasion of Palestine by their regular armies on 15 May 1948.

The results and implications of the 1948 war for the Palestinians—succinctly expressed as "catastrophe" *(nakba)*—reached beyond the loss of human lives, land, and material possessions; it resulted in the uprooting of more than half of the Arab population and their dispersion as refugees in historic Palestine and the neighboring Arab states, social disintegration, and a death blow to the national leadership. The crisis also led to the blurring and dissolution of the concept of Palestinian identity for more than a decade. Since the late 1950s even the term "Palestinians" has undergone a fundamental change in international public discourse, reflecting a claim for recognition of their national rights.

The founding of the PLO in May 1964 represented a renewal of Arab recognition of the unique Palestinian national identity, after a period of oblivion as a result of the 1948 war and suppression by regional actors. Since then, the PLO's history in regional dynamics has witnessed two main interactive trends:

    1. A thrust to consolidate its status as the exclusive political center of the Palestinian people, rebuild Palestinian national identity,

and restore Palestine. This effort was conducted primarily within the Israeli-Jordanian-Palestinian triangle, amid tireless efforts to mobilize the Arab states' capabilities for the Palestine cause.

2. Constant efforts by the Arab regimes to use the Palestinian issue as a "trump card" in their regional struggle for power through the imposition of patronage over the PLO, or part of it, and interference in its decision making. Syria's location and role in the conflict with Israel made it the most assertive and outspoken of all the Arab states in this regard.

Apart from the PLO's authentic efforts toward realization of Palestinian national goals, its international status as well as its practical strategic choices have been shaped primarily by the Arab states, both individually and collectively. The Arab states, acting collectively, not only facilitated the establishment of the PLO, but also operated—violently when necessary—to control, contain, and subordinate this organization to their norms and rules and, primarily, to instill respect for their individual sovereignties. The quest of the Arab states for exclusive and effective sovereignty within their territories led to the elimination, or "nationalization," of such supra-state movements as the Arab Ba'th Socialist party, the Arab Nationalist Movement, and the Muslim Brotherhood.

Against this backdrop the PLO, in the three decades of its existence, witnessed shrinking opportunities in the Arab regional arena and growing threats to its autonomous survival. As a consequence, it was obliged to reduce its national goals and adhere to norms of international legitimacy. This historical process found its best expression in the redefining of the practical territorial goal on which the Palestinian state was to be founded—from a state on the whole territory of Mandatory Palestine to the occupied West Bank, the Gaza Strip, and East Jerusalem. The PLO's diminishing power base in the Arab world, especially following Israel's Lebanon war, coincided with an incremental shift of the center of gravity of Palestinian national action from the "Republic of Fakahani"[4] in Beirut to the occupied territories, culminating in their uprising in late 1987 and the proclamation of an independent Palestinian state a year later.

THE DIALECTIC OF THE PALESTINE CONFLICT

The Palestinian conflict was an essential instrument of inter-Arab relations, epitomized by its primacy in the dominant political discourse as well as in collective institutions such as the Arab League and Arab summit conferences. Arab regimes made extensive use of the conflict in order to bolster their own legitimacy, compensating for interstate divisions and failure to meet the social and economic expectations and needs of the masses. The common Arab commitment to the cause of Palestine represented both a substitute for the frustrated vision of pan-Arab unity and an incarnation of the myth of Arab struggle for national liberation from Western domination.[5]

This, however, was of primarily ideological significance, linked to state-society relations and representing an essential component of Arab nationalist rhetoric. In practical terms, the Arab commitment to Palestine meant a head-on collision with Israel, which most Arab states were both reluctant and unprepared to undertake prior to the 1967 war. Articulating total hostility to Israel was a useful pretext to justify repressive measures at home and a compulsive style of pan-Arab conformity, often defined as a prerequisite for the liberation of Palestine. It is precisely this manipulative formula that the Palestinian Resistance (PR) came to alter, suggesting armed struggle against Israel as a means to realize Arab unity but in fact representing a strong claim for recognition of the Palestinians' identity and right to self-determination within a separate Palestinian state, in line with the processes of state formation in the region as a whole.

The reemergence of Palestinian nationalism was a result of social and political radicalization processes that affected the Arab societies in the decade following the 1948 defeat. These processes, which ripened toward the mid-1960s, gave rise to Palestinian radical groups with nationalist revolutionary ideologies that challenged the political status quo in the Arab-Israeli conflict and, by definition, questioned the legitimacy of Arab regimes, especially that of Gamal 'Abd al-Nasir of Egypt. The vicious inter-Arab power struggle in the late 1950s and most of the 1960s, revolving around Nasir's quest for regional Arab hegemony in the name of pan-Arabism, could hardly conceal the low priority to which the Palestinian problem had been relegated on the Arab political agenda. This was a reflection of the preoccupation of most Arab regimes with social and political upheavals and inter-Arab struggle to define the boundaries of the sovereign state vis-à-vis collective Arab identity. Thus the establishment of the PLO in May 1964—at the initiative of Nasir with King Husain's acquiescence—as an institutional expression of the "Palestinian entity," was intended in fact to coopt Palestinian nationalism into the regional Arab system and shape its development in accordance with Nasir's Arab policies.[6]

Nasir's policy of indefinite delay of the confrontation with Israel dictated the prevention of Palestinian guerrilla operations against Israel, which represented a rebellion against his *raison d'état* and pan-Arab leadership. That his arch rival Syrian Ba'th regime supported the "popular armed struggle" made the Palestinian challenge all the more dangerous for Nasir. Indeed, whereas Damascus's main thrust in the years 1963-67 was to force Nasir to recognize its militant regime, the armed Palestinian groups led by Fatah sought to entangle the Arab regimes in an early war against Israel, both through the latter's retaliations and through domestic pressures.[7]

The advent of the PLO was indeed a product of temporary inter-Arab detente in which the Palestinian problem came to play a growing role. It is doubtful, however, that the PLO, which was meant to organize the Palestinians politically and to preserve their collective identity, would have lasted and developed into what it eventually became, from the late 1960s on, had the necessary sociopolitical conditions not existed in both the Palestinian and the Arab societies. Palestinian nationalism was catalyzed enormously by the 1967 Arab defeat, which enhanced the PLO's autonomy in the inter-Arab arena and led to its growing military and political impact on the Arab-Israeli conflict. The combined impact of Palestinian armed struggle inside Israel and across its borders, Israeli retaliations, and prolonged military occupation of the West Bank and Gaza Strip by Israel underlay a growing process of Palestinization of the Arab-Israeli conflict. It witnessed the adoption of Palestinian assumptions and symbols by widening circles among the Palestinians, increasingly enhancing specific Palestinian national identity at the expense of pan-Arabism. Nonetheless, the PLO adhered to the principle of pan-Arabism, portraying itself as the "beating heart" and raison d'être of the Arab nation at large, hence claiming the Arab world's full support for its specific national cause.[8]

The Arab states manifested growing involvement in the conflict with Israel and, given the growing prestige of the PR, also in the latter's political and military affairs. Indeed, with the loss of Arab territories to Israel in 1967, Israel could no more be regarded as a nonentity—the so-called *(al-maz'uuma)*. In fact, the war's outcome turned Israel into a tacitly recognized actor in regional politics with growing influence over inter-Arab alignments.[9] Clearly, the 1967 war marked the beginning of a shift in the conflict's essence from the issue of Israel's legitimacy to the question of its boundaries. In other words, the conflict began to change from the paradigmatic—that is, the cultural, religious, and ideological—to a "normal"—and thus more manageable—political dispute. This became possible when Arab states could relate to the conflict with Israel as states rather than as parts of a supra-state nation or religion.[10]

The Arab states' attitudes toward the PLO were shaped primarily by direct individual interests in Palestine, but no less by regional, inter-Arab considerations. Egypt has traditionally perceived the Palestine cause as a pivotal element in its effort to attain regional Arab leadership. Egypt's regional Arab policy was marked by a constant attempt to support the Palestinian national right to self-determination and the PLO's drive for political independence, which collided head on with Hashemite Jordan and weakened the grip of both Amman and Damascus on the organization. In practical terms, however, Egypt led the political effort to tame the PLO's revolutionary fervor and coopt it into the Arab states system's rules of the game, along with their fluctuations and recurrent reinterpretations by Egypt. Historically, no other Arab state has affected the PLO more than Egypt, which ever since the late 1960s has represented increasing "stateness" in its regional foreign policy.[11] Even when excluded from the Arab League, Egypt was, as of 1983, an indispensable ally to the PLO, especially in view of Syria's brutal efforts to subordinate the organization to its own political needs.

Unlike the radical states that extended military support to the PR but also collided with it violently on grounds of political disagreement, Egypt's crises with the PLO were short and assumed only a political form. Egypt backed the PR's efforts to secure its military and political existence on Lebanese and Jordanian soil but refrained from offering its own territory for guerrilla operations against Israel. Yet Egypt, particularly under Sadat, played a primary role in prompting the PLO's mainstream leadership to adopt pragmatism and limit its strategic goal to the establishment of an independent Palestinian state in the West Bank and Gaza Strip, instead of seeking Israel's destruction and recovery of historic Palestine in its entirety. Especially in the years 1974-77, Sadat repeatedly suggested to the PLO that it establish a government in exile that would lead to wider international recognition, weaken the organization's image as a terrorist movement, and increase its dependence on Egypt.[12]

The role of the PLO and its national cause in Arab politics changed along with the historical development of regional Arab order. The late 1950s and early 1960s were marked by domestic turmoil in the Fertile Crescent states and regional struggle for power, as well as strong social and cultural links and political permeability. The tumultuous nature of

Arab politics encouraged the emergence of militant Palestinian nationalism as a source of legitimacy in domestic and regional political struggles. Yet the Palestinian revolutionary approach and social bases in the Arab states soon became a threat to the Arab social and political order. This, in turn, obliged the Arab states to undertake separate or collective measures—in effect complementing Israeli repressive policy—to contain the PLO's revolutionary threat or eliminate its capacity for autonomous violence. As of the late 1960s, the Arab states system's main impact on the Palestinian issue was the persistent effort to tame the PR's revolutionary activity and reshape its strategy toward statehood in part of Palestine. By encouraging the institutionalization of the PLO and acknowledging it as the sole legitimate representative of the Palestinian people, the Arab states virtually associated the PLO with the international rules and constraints, admitting their own limitations. Arab financial aid, contributed mainly by the oil-rich monarchies of the Gulf—served inter alia as a security measure against possible sabotage and terrorism.

The institutionalization of the PLO was motivated both by its growing prestige and political capabilities, and by the Arab states' jealousy of their own sovereignty and regime security. As a national structure with control of resources, political institutions, military power, media, and international relations, the PLO became a full—albeit non-territorial—actor in the Arab region's political web. Moreover, the PLO often appealed directly to popular sentiments and opposition groups in an attempt to impose its own political agenda on the Arab regimes, which further alienated the latter.[13] The PR's military presence and vehement interference in Jordan's and Lebanon's domestic affairs were viewed with ambivalence by most Arab regimes, which explains the constant tension between the state and the revolution, and its intermittent culmination in armed confrontation, with detrimental consequences for the PR.

The PLO's relationship with the Arab states, from its establishment to the Oslo accords, was marked by mutual suspicion and antagonism. From its advent, the PLO strove for full Arab political backing for its national struggle, yet insisted on the principle of "independent Palestinian decision making" *(istiqlaliyyat al-qarar al-filastini)*. This insistence tended to be exacerbated under pressure of assertive Arab regimes—Syria in particular—to subordinate the PLO to their own individual interests.[14] Despite the PLO's self-proclaimed status as the Arab world's standard-bearer, by virtue of the identity of its national cause and Arab nationalism, the organization had been repeatedly frustrated by the Arab states' individual priorities and strict protection of their individual sovereignties. Hence the PLO's lament that the Arab regimes have betrayed it: "The territorial [state] *(iqlimi)* defeated the pan-national *(qawmi)*" and "regime security superseded pan-Arab national security."[15]

The schism between the PLO and Arab regimes has been evidenced by the former's shrinking opportunities in the Arab countries since the early 1970s. This derived primarily from the processes of state formation, which were dialectically linked to structural and normative changes in the regional Arab system. Among these processes were the state centralization and control of the economy, the growth of state bureaucracy and armed forces, and the enhanced capability of the regime to enforce authority within its sovereign territory by coercive means—all of which led to the declining power of domestic opposition and relative stability of the regime. The consolidation of power in the Arab states also witnessed a growing capability to withstand external Arab political pressures in the form of propaganda and subversion. On the regional level these processes have been matched by growing mutual recognition of the Arab state sovereignty and equality. The 1958-67 "Arab Cold War," identified with Nasir, represented the defeat of the idea of Arab political unity, and led to the acceptance of the notion of a regional Arab system comprised of discrete and sovereign Arab states regardless of their ideology or regime. This process was cemented by Arab institutions—mainly the Arab League and the Arab summit conferences—that remained strictly bound to collective Arab decision making concerning the Palestine conflict.[16]

A major factor contributing to this trend was the post-1967 war impetus to retrieve particular occupied Arab territories from Israel, a thrust that brought individual state interests—most conspicuously manifested in the case of Egypt—into growing conflict with pan-Arab conformity on the Palestinian conflict. This trend was accelerated by the post-1973 Arab-Israeli diplomatic process which provided core Arab states with varying degrees of opportunities and constraints regarding collective versus individual action in the conflict with Israel, further enhancing their sense of *raison d'état*. This trend encompassed the PLO as well, resulting in a growing drive on the part of the PLO's mainstream leadership toward self-reliance and the localization of national goals, focusing on political mobilization of the population in the occupied West Bank and Gaza Strip.[17] The growth of state-owned oil wealth also contributed to the weakening of Arab solidarity despite the inter-Arab financial aid, mainly to the confrontation states. The emergence of a new Arab regional center of power, comprising Saudi Arabia and other Gulf monarchies, eroded the centrality of the Palestine conflict and its immediately involved Arab actors.[18]

The increasing disintegration of the regional Arab system in the 1980s indicated a further decline of the Arab-Israeli conflict as a core issue. Whereas Egypt's peace treaty with Israel practically eliminated the Arab military option, the Shi'i revolution in Iran and the Iran-Iraq war shifted the Gulf Arab states' concern, as well as a substantial segment of their financial resources away from the Palestinian conflict front. Furthermore, growing threats to states' national security by regional disputes and socioeconomic constraints underlaid the Arab world's return to subregional geography. The emergence of separate cooperation councils to meet the needs of specific states marked a further growth in the autonomy of the Arab states and a departure from obligatory pan-Arab conformity.[19]

Israel's peace treaty with Egypt and Syria's alliance with Iran against Iraq attested more than anything else to the erosion of the "[pan-]Arab national security" *(al-amn qawmi al-'arabi)* concept, a synonymous appeal for Arab conformity against the foreigner.[20] This concept was finally proven bankrupt in the Kuwait crisis when major Arab actors joined the international coalition against Iraq. The Kuwait crisis and the Gulf War dealt a severe political and economic blow to the PLO and to the Palestinians as a whole. The Iraqi invasion of Kuwait had already eliminated the steadiest and most significant source of financial aid to the PLO and the Palestinians in the occupied territories, both from the Kuwaiti government and from the large Palestinian community in this emirate. Moreover, the PLO's explicit support of Saddam Husain led to the cessation of financial aid and expulsion of Palestinian labor migrants from the Gulf Arab monarchies, including Saudi Arabia.[21]

But the worst was yet to come, with the return of the Sabbah ruling family to Kuwait, following its reconquest from Iraq. Within months, the presence of a large Palestinian community in Kuwait, one of the PLO's strongest political and economic levers in the Arab world, came to an end. The Kuwaitis apparently took advantage of the PLO's support for Saddam to rid themselves of the large Palestinian presence on their soil, which had long been perceived as a political and social threat to the regime. Of the 350,000 Palestinians who had lived in Kuwait before the Iraqi invasion, only 15,000-20,000 remained.[22] As in previous cases of Palestinian mass displacement in 1948 and 1967, the majority of the third wave of displaced Palestinians found refuge in Jordan, which had little choice but to absorb them. All this occurred at a time when the Intifada had reached a political dead end and intra-Palestinian social and political tensions and use of violence had intensified. This was a clear indication that the PLO had lost control of the Intifada. In addition, the deterioration of economic conditions and collapse of social order proved fertile ground for the rapid development of the Islamic Resistance Movement (Hamas), which increased its power at the expense of its political adversaries—primarily Fatah.

Besides the direct economic repercussions of the Kuwait crisis and the Gulf War on the Palestinian political community, other regional and global political developments had motivated the PLO's inclination toward the diplomatic option in the conflict. The return of Egypt to the Arab League in 1989 reflected the revitalization of the Egypt-Saudi axis in regional politics, in view of the Iranian threat to the Gulf Arab monarchies. The loss of Soviet strategic backing and end of the Iran-Iraq war diminished Syria's veto power in regional Arab politics, which had been effective against the PLO and other non-state actors in Lebanon in the immediate aftermath of the Israeli invasion in 1982. Yet it also deprived the PLO of its global ally. The PLO's predicament was aggravated by the resumption of diplomatic relations between Moscow and Jerusalem and the massive wave of Jewish immigration from the USSR to Israel, which raised the specter of a large-scale Jewish settlement in the occupied territories. These developments enhanced Arab inclinations toward pragmatism and cooperation with Washington, culminating in the active participation of leading Arab states, such as Saudi Arabia, Egypt, and Syria, in the American-led international coalition against Iraq, and heralding the onset of a new regional and world order based on the termination of the Cold War and its bipolar global framework.

The prolonged Intifada—and the passivity of Arab states in terms of financial and political support—underlined the return of the Arab-Israeli conflict to its initial pattern as a predominantly local intercommunal struggle within historic Palestine. In retrospect, the "Palestinization of the Arab-Israeli conflict" that began in the mid-1960s reflected a continuous attempt on the part of the Arab states to disengage from the Palestinian cause.[23]

Indeed, regardless of the PLO's political position, both internationally and regionally, since the late-1970s the Palestinian issue has increasingly been the main driving force for American peacemaking efforts in the Middle East. This has been the case from the Reagan peace plan of 1 September 1982, through Secretary of State George Shultz's efforts to renew the peace process following the eruption of the Intifada in late 1987, to Secretary James Baker's post-"Desert Storm" diplomacy that led to the convening of the Madrid peace conference in October 1991.

The October 1991 Madrid conference and consequent peace talks, encompassing Israel, Syria, Lebanon, and a Jordanian-Palestinian delegation under international auspices, witnessed a further decline of previously core attributes of regional Arab politics. The renewed peace process clearly reflected Syria's failure to impose its own priorities and interests on its minor Arab partners, as witnessed in the latter's participation in the multilateral talks in disregard of Syria's decision to boycott this channel of negotiations. Especially following the advent of the Rabin government in June 1992, the diplomatic process following the Madrid conference was marked by mutual suspicion and competition among Syria, Jordan, and the PLO, lest any of them be outflanked by a separate agreement of another, which would diminish their bargaining positions.[24] The PLO in particular demonstrated an unprecedented autonomy by taking part in the Oslo secret talks as of early 1993 which culminated in September of that year in an official agreement with Israel on mutual recognition and the beginning of a PLO-led interim self-government in the West Bank and Gaza Strip. That the Oslo accords were discussed and concluded independently and in disregard of the other Arab parties underlined the autonomous nature of the PLO's decision making. Moreover, despite Syria's and Lebanon's reservations, the Arab League Council approved the Oslo accords.[25]

JORDAN AND THE PLO: CONFRONTATION AND POLITICAL DISENGAGEMENT

In the aftermath of 1948, even when the Palestinian national movement seemed to have been decimated, the narrowly recognized status of the West Bank as an integral part of Jordan and the temporary military government in the Gaza Strip under Egypt were living evidence of the unfinished nature of the Palestinian issue. Accordingly, the borders of these two areas with Israel, demarcated by armistice "green lines," denoted their lesser, temporary status compared to internationally recognized borders.

Already before 1967 the PLO and Jordan had engaged in a political dispute over the former's claim for freedom of action in the West Bank. Given the tight linkage between the two banks of the kingdom and the massive presence of Palestinians east of the River Jordan, the dispute had direct repercussions for the existence of the Hashemite regime itself. In the aftermath of the 1967 war, this dispute intensified when the PR managed—with Syrian, Iraqi, and Egyptian moral and military support—to entrench itself in Jordan's territory as a "state within a state." Indeed, what eventually paved the way for an all-out war between the Hashemite regime and the PR in 1970-71 was the latter's direct threat to Hashemite sovereignty in Jordan.

The Arab regimes' support for the PR represented a quest for legitimacy following the June 1967 military defeat, a response to domestic frustration, and in the case of Syria and Iraq, a substitute for their military inaction along Israel's eastern front. Jordan's and Lebanon's proximity to Israel and their large Palestinian populations rendered them preferable to the PR as territorial bases for guerrilla warfare against Israel. Yet it was primarily their fragile domestic systems and strategic vulnerability that subjected these states to pressures by stronger Arab neighbors to allow the PR to operate on their soil and pay the heavy price entailed in terms of Israeli retaliations.

The September 1970 crisis in Jordan demonstrated the vast gap in capabilities and level of institutionalization between the Hashemite regime and the PR. This was saliently manifested by the passive behavior of most of the Palestinian population in Jordan during the crisis. The crisis marked a domestic as well as an international showdown between the state and the revolution that ended with the latter's victory over both Palestinian and Syrian revolutionary movements. Damascus's military intervention by an armored attack in support of the PR was defeated by Jordan—with American and Israeli strategic backing. The Arab summit, convened by Nasir to manage the crisis and save the PR from total demise, proved the Arab state system's inadequacy in imposing a return to the previous status quo or preventing the Hashemite regime from further violent enforcement of its exclusive sovereignty within its territory.[26]

The Hashemite military success in 1970-71 proved politically detrimental to the regime's claim for exclusive representation of the West Bank as far as the Palestinians and the Arab regimes were concerned. Challenges to the legitimacy of new Arab regimes in Egypt, Syria, Libya, and Sudan motivated their harsh political reactions toward Jordan and political support for the PR, resulting in ever inhibiting the king's posture and freedom of diplomatic maneuver regarding the West Bank. Yet the September crisis also ushered in a new era for Jordan—an era of political stability, economic prosperity, and discernible progress in state formation. Another consequence was the emergence of a new school of thought within Jordan's political elite that supported separation from the West Bank and making do with the East Bank of the Jordan. Although the king adhered to his claim to represent the West Bank, a psychological and institutional adjustment of the regime to its eroded claim for the West Bank was rendered inevitable. It was best represented by King Husain's "Jordanian-Palestinian Federation Plan" announced in March 1972.

The post-1973 peace process marked a growing Arab political and financial support for the PLO. Egypt's and Syria's common interest in recovering their lost territories from Israel by diplomatic means—no less than their disagreements on the appropriate strategy to realize this goal—underlay the Arab states system's efforts to boost the PLO's political status at the expense of Jordan and turn a blind eye to the PR's blunt violation of Lebanon's sovereignty. An immediate result of this trend was the acceleration of the PLO-Jordan competition for representation of the Palestinians in the West Bank and Gaza, which ended in proclaiming the PLO the sole legitimate representative of the Palestinian people at the October 1974 Arab summit conference in Rabat. In spite of this resolution, Arafat confidently appealed to King Husain to continue exercising his practical responsibilities toward the Palestinian population in the West Bank, due to the PLO's lack of administrative means to function as a political authority.[27]

In addition to the PLO's inability to exercise its political role in the West Bank, there was an unbridgeable contradiction between the PLO's growing international recognition as the sole representative of the Palestinians and its rejection by Israel and the American administration. This contradiction explains the impasse concerning Palestinian representation in the post-1973 peace diplomacy in the Middle East, that provided the Hashemite regime with a potential role in that diplomacy, despite all odds. Moreover, however dim the king's prospects to realizing his claim to represent the West Bank or of recovering his sovereignty over this territory, he had little choice but to adhere to this policy despite the general Arab tendency to support the PLO and Israel's objection to returning to the 4 June 1967 border.

In fact, the king's struggle on this matter represented crucial strategic considerations of political survival, both domestically and regionally. Adherence to the policy of recovering the West Bank from Israeli occupation served as a source of legitimacy for the Hashemite regime in a historically hostile and contemptuous regional Arab environment. Given the large Palestinian population in Jordan and its close links with the Palestinians west of the Jordan River, the regime had little choice but to adhere to its self-imposed role as the savior of and legitimate successor to what had been left of Palestine. The king's policy also justified Arab financial aid to Jordan as a confrontation state and, despite fierce PLO objection, as an instrument for channeling "steadfastness" *(sumoud)* funds to the Palestinian inhabitants of the West Bank and Gaza Strip. In this context, the king showed consistent willingness to come to terms with the PLO—despite their continued struggle for representation of the West Bank issue—on an instrumental and temporary level, and as long as the PLO refrained from challenging Hashemite sovereignty in Jordan per se. His resilience, accompanied by intermittent cooperation and crises with the PLO, was meant to contain the latter's political challenge rather than to collide with it, thus mitigating domestic threats to his throne.

In retrospect, King Husain had been forced to conduct a rearguard battle in the course of which he acquiesced to the loss of his formal status as the representative of the West Bank for the sake of preserving his political standing in this area through extending practical services that the PLO could not offer to the population. The king's last line of defense was his willingness to sacrifice his official status in the West Bank for the sake of survival of his sovereignty over Jordan east of the river. Thus, on 31 July 1988, following eight months of Palestinian uprising in the occupied territories—which was strongly identified with the PLO and threatened to spill over into the king's own domain—and growing Arab pressures, he proclaimed Jordan's legal and administrative disengagement from the West Bank.

The armed struggle served as a rallying force and main instrument of Palestinian nation building. It was also the main vehicle for enlisting the Arab world's political support for the PLO's revisionist effort to force Hashemite Jordan to abdicate the role it had forged for itself in 1948 as the legitimate heir of Arab Palestine. The PLO's political struggle was aimed at both Jordan and Israel. Yet while Israel was the ultimate enemy and the permanent target of the Palestinian armed struggle, Jordan was considered an enemy only as long as it remained an obstacle to the PLO's quest for political and diplomatic recognition as the legitimate representative of the Palestinians in the West Bank and Gaza Strip.

Nevertheless, reasserting Palestinian sovereignty over the West Bank and Gaza has never represented the PLO's full political aspirations vis-à-vis Jordan. This can be seen in the PLO's fluctuating—and at times ambiguous—claim to represent the Palestinian people, including those in Jordan proper, and—following the showdown of 1970—its even calling for the Hashemite regime to be deposed. The claim, which has always been upheld by the militant leftist Palestinian groups such as the PFLP and the DFLP, remained one of the PLO's most powerful bargaining chips in its competition with Hashemite Jordan over the West Bank. Hence, in spite of Fatah's official policy of avoiding confrontation with Arab regimes, it was dragged into the fray as an active participant in the strife fueled by the Palestinian militant groups—as later occurred in the Lebanon civil war.[28]

A turning point in the relations between the Hashemite regime and the PLO was the establishment of a Joint Jordanian-Palestinian Committee to administer the distribution of $100 million in annual aid—allocated by the Arab summit conference held in Baghdad in November 1978—to the Palestinian residents of the occupied territories. The Israeli-Egyptian agreement on establishing Palestinian autonomy in the West Bank and Gaza Strip heightened the interest of both Amman and the PLO in reinforcing their positions in the occupied territories so as to prevent circumvention by other actors. In 1984, Arafat was willing to risk a split with the PFLP and DFLP for the sake of closing ranks with King Husain. This approach derived from the PLO's stressful conditions of expulsion from Lebanon; President Reagan's peace plan which designated Jordan as Israel's main partner in negotiations over the Palestinian occupied territories; and Syrian hostility, which inspired a mutiny of Fatah splinters against Arafat and caused his expulsion from Tripoli in November 1983, after weeks of Palestinian and Syrian artillery attacks on his last foothold in Lebanon.[29]

Under these constraints, the PLO's mainstream was willing to shift its strategy toward diplomacy, aiming to break the American ban on contacts with the organization and using Egypt's and Jordan's good offices as mediating partners. Yet the PLO-Jordan dialogue, which culminated in the February 1985 Amman accord on joint political action, fell short of realizing its aims, and, with its collapse a year later, the parties reverted to political competition over the occupied territories. The fall of the Amman accord led to the king's overt attempt to restore his leading position in the occupied territories—through, among other things, an ambitious five-year development program. It also revived Israel's moribund "Jordanian option," as attested to by the Peres-Husain London agreement of April 1987—according to which Husain was to take part in an international peace conference on the Middle East as the representative of the Palestinian territories, regardless of the PLO's position. At the Arab summit convened in Amman in November 1987, Husain made an attempt to overlook Arafat and undermine the PLO's official standing as the sole legitimate representative of the Palestinian people.[30]

Neither of the king's attempts could diminish the strong adherence of the Palestinian population to the PLO that was demonstrated by the Intifada, as a result of processes of penetration and institutionalization by the PLO in the occupied territories. Husain's acquiescence to the new reality by proclaiming Jordan's disengagement from the West Bank was a turning point in the history of the Palestine conflict. What rendered his move irreversible was the PLO's decision to translate it into a political gain by declaring the Independent Palestinian State four months later, and consequent worldwide recognition of the state, including by Jordan. Furthermore, the decision signaled a new policy of "Jordanization" of the Hashemite kingdom, and its consolidation as a sovereign state with defined boundaries and citizenship. This policy was implemented amid a media campaign against the PLO and the Palestinians' "dual loyalty," and attempts to downplay the proportion of Palestinians in Jordan's population. Hence, contrary to the conventional wisdom that Palestinians constitute more than half the population, estimates were revised by almost half—to 34.6 percent—by Prime Minister Badran.[31]

Husain's retreat from competition over the West Bank paved the way for improvement of his relations with the PLO, and in January 1989 the embassy of the State of Palestine was opened in Amman, marking a new era in Jordanian-PLO relations. Mutual interests and anxieties, as well as existential dependency, came to underpin the new alliance between yesterday's contenders, for whom the new political situation meant opportunities as well as uncertainties. The PLO's new freedom of action on Jordan's soil enabled Arafat to enhance his capacity for inspiring political action among the Palestinians in the West Bank and Gaza, providing him with increased control of the Intifada. This proved crucial in view of the growing power of Hamas in the occupied territories since the beginning of the Intifada, and the challenge it posed to the PLO's political authority.

The PLO came to serve essentially as King Husain's agent in the process of state building in the East Bank, sending a message to Jordan's

Palestinians, particularly in the refugee camps, that they were to accept Jordanian nationality. The PLO proved instrumental in smoothing King Husain's domestic hardships, which originated partly in the new definitions and implications of his "Jordanization" policy, and partly in the deteriorating economy. During the April 1989 riots that stemmed from economic strains, the PLO played a pacifying role among the Palestinians in Jordan, preventing their participation in the unrest. The transfer of the headquarters of the PLO's National Fund and financial assets to Amman in August 1989 helped stabilize Jordan's economy and halt the dangerous devaluation of its currency, the dinar, which had severely affected West Bankers and Jordanians alike.[32]

The Jordan-PLO cooperation culminated in the latter's policy of "noninterference" during Jordan's parliamentary elections in November 1989, the first to be held in the kingdom since 1967. The Jordanian decision to hold elections, which had been on the agenda for a few years, became crucial for the process of consolidating the Jordanian state in the wake of Husain's disengagement from the West Bank. Arafat instructed Fatah activists to refrain from allying themselves with any of the opposition parties, though some of those parties were in fact offshoots of Palestinian radical factions.[33]

The Iraqi invasion of Kuwait marked a watershed in the relationships of both Jordan and the PLO with the Arab world, which further solidified the Jordanian-PLO alignment. Their support of Saddam Husain, albeit more explicit on the PLO's part, was a reflection of political constraints and limited opportunities. The rising tide of hostile feelings toward the West and Israel, and Jordan's renewed political life following the parliamentary elections of November 1989, resulting in the considerable success of the Muslim Brotherhood movement, severely limited the king's freedom of maneuver in his inter-Arab policy, rendering him the captive of his inflamed Palestinian public.

Fading Syrian Veto Power

Since the late 1930s, Syrian nationalists had perceived themselves as the standard bearers and protectors of the Palestinian cause. Under the Ba'th regime from the mid-1960s, Syria manifested an interest in attaining patronage over activist Palestinian groups and identity of interests with them as part of its struggle for Nasir's recognition. Syria's main means to win the PR over to its side was through intensive military and political support. Apart from offering arms, money, training bases and headquarters on its soil, Syria also appeared, especially in the years 1968-73, as an active opponent to Jordan's and Lebanon's efforts to impose their authority on the PR or restrict PR activities. After 1970, under Hafiz al-Asad's regime, the thrust to secure Syrian patronage over the PLO had become a cornerstone in Damascus's regional Arab policy. Thenceforth, Syria's motivation to interfere in Lebanon was on the rise, along with the development of the PR's autonomous territorial base in this country after the expulsion from Jordan in 1970-71.

By assuming control of the PR, the Syrians sought to use the PLO as an instrument for advancing their strategic interests in both inter-Arab and Arab-Israeli spheres. Syria's grip on the PLO became ever more important after 1973, against the backdrop of Sadat's overt inclination to conduct independent peace diplomacy under American auspices in disregard of Syria's interests. Hence the adoption by the regime of the "Greater Syria" vision to encompass the PLO, Lebanon, and Jordan. This would enhance Syria's bargaining position vis-à-vis Egypt and the Gulf oil monarchies and force Sadat to reckon with Damascus's constraints and strategic needs in the conflict with Israel. Alternatively, this Syrian-led coalition would isolate Sadat if he adhered to independent diplomacy with Israel.

Asad's policy toward the PLO was a reflection of the high stakes with regard to Syria's national security and the PLO mainstream's willingness to adjust itself to Damascus's strategic priorities. Whereas Asad, in 1974, had proposed to the PLO a political unity with Syria, defining Palestine as "Southern Syria," in the early 1980s Damascus adopted the argument that the PLO was not the only representative of the Palestinian cause, claiming that Syria had no less right to be such. But Syria's efforts to impose patronage over the PLO only made the latter increasingly adamant about preserving its political independence. The growing Syria-PLO rift underlay the PR's entrenchment in Lebanon and alliance with the Lebanese left, which resulted in Syria's invasion of Lebanon in June 1976 and consequent military confrontation with the Palestinian and Lebanese leftist forces. This confrontation represented a watershed in Syrian-PLO relations, which were to deteriorate to an overt crisis in the wake of Israel's invasion of Lebanon.[34]

Syria failed to force the PLO to abide by the October 1976 Riyadh minisummit, which had stipulated strict adherence to the 1969 Cairo agreement between the PLO and Lebanon and legitimized Syria's military presence in Lebanon. That the PR managed to maintain its semi-independent military and civilian activities in Lebanon despite the Syrian and Lebanese pressures was due partly to the PR's deployment in southern Lebanon, to which Syria had no military access, but due mainly to Syria's rift with Egypt following Sadat's visit to Jerusalem. Syria's response to Sadat's peace policy strove to isolate Egypt by forging a regional Arab alliance whose hard core was comprised of radical forces. Obviously, the PLO, as the living symbol of the Arab world's core issue, had an essential role in the anti-Sadat alliance.

Syria's strategic constraints following Egypt's defection from the Arab confrontation with Israel, and the renewed rift between Damascus and Baghdad thereafter, provided the PLO further freedom of political maneuver internationally. The failure of the Israeli-Egyptian negotiations on Palestinian autonomy in the occupied territories triggered a new thrust of European leaders—such as Austrian Prime Minister Bruno Kreisky and former German chancellor Willy Brandt—to come to terms with the PLO mainstream, opening new opportunities for the PLO to advance its interests in the international arena. Syria responded with overt discontent at the PLO's growing diplomatic independence—including contacts with Israeli leftist leaders—which peaked in the Syrian-Saudi controversy at the November 1981 Fez summit over Crown Prince Fahd's peace plan, to which Arafat had apparently agreed.[35]

Israel's siege of Beirut and the consequent withdrawal of the PLO's institutions and armed personnel from Lebanon was effectively a result of tacit inter-Arab collaboration with Israel through American mediation efforts. The long siege resulted in Saudi Arabia's attempt to forge inter-Arab agreement on withdrawal of the Palestinian military establishment from Beirut, in which Lebanese, Syrian, and Jordanian leaders fully cooperated. It was the most salient evidence of a tacit collaboration of sovereign Arab governments, including Syria, with Israel in eliminating the PLO's independent military base in Lebanon. Damascus's cooperation was strongly motivated by expectations for rapprochement with the United States and possible American support in evicting Israel from Lebanon and recognizing Syria's role in this country.[36]

Syria's frustrated expectations from Washington—stemming from the absence of any reference to its requirements in Reagan's peace plan and continued U.S. support of Israel's aspirations in Lebanon—further exacerbated the rift with the PLO. Not only did the PLO leadership prefer exile in Tunis to asylum in Syria, bluntly demonstrating their mistrust of Syria, but Arafat and King Husain began shortly thereafter an unprecedented political dialogue that threatened to isolate Syria in the context of the conflict with Israel. It is against this backdrop that Syria attempted to bring about Arafat's replacement by a more compliant figure (through encouraging a revolt within Fatah's forces in the Biqa' in May 1983); employed the splinter group of Abu Nidal to murder Palestinian and Jordanian figures; orchestrated the expulsion of Arafat from Tripoli in November of that year; and gave its full backing to the Shi'i militia's siege and violent attacks on the refugee camps in the Beirut-Tyre area that lasted until the beginning of the Intifada, although even then Syrian intermittent shelling on the Palestinian refugee camps continued. Of all the Arab states, only Syria refused to recognize the Independent State of Palestine proclaimed in November 1988 in Tunis.[37]

Syria's excessive use of violence against the PLO in the wake of Israel's invasion of Lebanon proved militarily successful, leading to the elimination of the autonomous Palestinian presence in that country. Politically, however, Syria overplayed its veto power to the point of losing control over the PLO, forcing the latter's leadership to seek alliance with Egypt and Jordan, despite repeated efforts to heal the "bleeding open wound"[38] in relations with Damascus. The PLO's loss of its Lebanese base, and effectively, the loss of its military option against Israel, entailed far-reaching implications for its strategy, primarily its growing involvement in the American peacemaking diplomacy.

The PLO's diplomatic role grew ever more significant, coinciding with the difficulties of Israel, Jordan, and the United States in finding a qualified substitute for the PLO. This trend had been repeatedly manifested since the mid-1980s despite recurrent American, Israeli and Egyptian efforts to find a formula that would satisfy both Israel and the PLO. Cutting the Gordian knot of the Palestinian representation indeed proved to be a matter of necessity rather than choice for the Israeli government under Rabin, proving the PLO's indispensability in settling the historic Israeli-Palestinian dispute.

NOTES

1. Albert Hourani, *A History of the Arab Peoples* (Cambridge, Mass.: Harvard University Press, 1991), 310; Lisa Anderson, "The State in the Middle East and North Africa," *Comparative Politics* 20 (1987): 5.

2. This is discussed at length in Avraham Sela, *The Decline of the Arab-Israeli Conflict: Middle East Politics and the Quest for Regional Order* (Albany: State University of New York Press), ch. 1-2. Forthcoming.
3. Avraham Sela, "The Wailing Wall Riots (1929) as a Watershed in the Palestine Conflict," *The Muslim World* 84 (1994): 60-94.
4. This trend is astutely analyzed by Sabri Jiryis, "'Ishrun Sana Min al-Kifah al-Musallah: Nahw Nizam Filastiniti Jadid," *Shu'un Filastiniyya* (January-February 1985): 19-20. See also his "Hiwar Min Naw' Aakhar Hawl al-Hiwar wal-Wahda al-Wataniyya," *Shu'un Filastiniyya* (May-June 1987): 21-29.
5. Jamil Matar and 'Ali al-Din Hilal, *Al-Nizam al-Iqlimi al-'Arabi* (Cairo: Center for Arab Unity Studies, 3rd edition, 1983), 122; Sela, *The Decline of the Arab-Israeli Conflict,* ch. 2.
6. Charles D. Smith, *Palestine and the Arab-Israeli Conflict* (London: Macmillan, 1988), 188-189; Mohamed E. Selim, "The Survival of a Non-State Actor: The Foreign Policy of the Palestine Liberation Organization," in B. Korany and A. E. H. Dessouki, eds., *The Foreign Policies of Arab States* (Boulder, Colo.: Westview Press, 1984), 198-99.
7. Yehoshafat Harkabi, *Fatah Ba'astrategia Ha'Arvit* (Tel Aviv: Ma'arakhot, 1969), 27-47; Helena Cobban, *The Palestinian Liberation Organization: People, Power, and Politics* (Cambridge: Cambridge University Press, 1984), 22-23.
8. See for example the Palestinian Charter, articles 12-15, Leila S. Kadi, *Basic Political Documents of the Armed Palestinian Resistance Movement* (Beirut: PLO Research Center, 1969), 137-42.
9. Especially after accepting UNSC Resolution 242. Anwar al-Sadat to *al-Ahram,* July 3, 1975.
10. Gabriel Ben-Dor, *State and Conflict in the Middle East* (New York: Praeger, 1983), 186-201.
11. Gabriel Ben-Dor, "Stateness and Ideology in Contemporary Middle Eastern Politics," *The Jerusalem Journal of International Relations* 9:3 (1988): 10-37.
12. Moshe Shemesh, *The Palestinian Entity 1959-1974: Arab Politics and the PLO* (London: Frank Cass, 1988), 196-98.
13. Selim, 197; Ahmad al-Shuqairi, "Dhikrayat 'An Mu'tamar al-Qimma fil-Khartoum," *Shu'un Filastiniyya* 4 (September 1971): 91-92; text of final announcement of the 18th PNC, April 26, 1987 in Algiers, distinguishing between Egypt's people and regime, *Journal of Palestine Studies* 16:4 (summer 1987): 201-4; 'Arafat to *al-Watan al-'Arabi,* 30 November 1984.
14. Eric Rouleau, "The Future of the PLO," *Foreign Affairs* 62:1 (fall 1983): 145.
15. Editorial in *Filastin al-Thawra,* January 5, 1985; Jiryis, 16-21; Fouad Mughrabi, "The Palestinians After Lebanon," *Arab Studies Quarterly* 5:3 (summer

1983): 211; Yezid Sayigh, "Fatah: The First Twenty Years," *Journal of Palestine Studies* 13:4 (summer 1984): 115.
16. This is thoroughly discussed in Sela, *The Decline of the Arab-Israeli Conflict.*
17. Hillel Frisch, *Palestinian Institution-Building in the Territories, 1967-1985,* Ph.D. diss., The Hebrew University of Jerusalem, 1989.
18. Fouad Ajami, *The Arab Predicament: Arab Political Thought and Practice since 1967* (Cambridge: Cambridge University Press, 1981), 126; Ali E. D. Dessouki, "The New Arab Political Order," in M. Kerr and Yassin, eds., *Rich and Poor States in the Middle East* (Boulder: Westview Press, 1982); 319-47; Hisham Sharabi, "Arab Policy and the Prospects for Peace," *American-Arab Affairs* 1:104 (summer 1982): 108.
19. A. M. Al-Mashat, "Arab National Security in the 1980s. Threats and Strategies," *International Interactions* 12:3 (1986): 245-65; Ghassan Salame, "Inter-Arab Politics: The Return to Geography," in William B. Quandt, ed., *The Middle East: Ten Years after Camp David* (Washington, D.C.: The Brookings Institute, 1988), 319-53.
20. For a conservative Arab perception of this notion, see Mahmud Riyad, *Mudhakkirat, 1948-1978,* part 2 (Beirut: 1987), 256-259. See also Mashat, 261-64.
21. The total annual loss to the PLO and residents of the territories was estimated at $400 million, *Middle East Monitor,* 31 August 1990: 14-15; *al-Hayat,* 21 August 1990; *International Herald Tribune,* 23 October 1990.
22. Muhammad Muslih, "The Shift in Palestinian Thinking," *Current History* (January 1992): 22-27.
23. Herbert C. Kelman, "The Palestinization of the Arab-Israeli Conflict," *The Jerusalem Quarterly* 46 (spring 1988): 3-15.
24. Ami Ayalon, ed., *Middle East Contemporary Survey* XVI, 1992 (Boulder, Colo.: Westview Press, 1995), 552-53; Robert Satloff, "Assad and Arafat: Trying to Control the Process," in M. Feverweger, M. Indyk, R. Satloff, eds., *Peacewatch: Analysis of the Arab-Israeli Peace Process* (Washington, D.C.: The Washington Institute, 1993), 5-6.
25. Ami Ayalon, ed., *Middle East Contemporary Survey* XVII, 1993 (Boulder: Westview Press, 1995), 77, 653.
26. On the September 1970 crisis and its consequences, see Shemesh, 140-148; William B. Quandt, *Decade of Decisions: American Policy Toward the Arab-Israeli Conflict 1967-1976* (Berkeley: University of California Press, 1977), 113-19. On the Cairo Arab summit, see Mohammed H. Heikal, *The Road to Ramadan* (London: Collins, '1975), 98-99; Musa Sabri, *Watha'iq Harb October* (Cairo: 1975), 167-206.

27. Khalid al-Hasan, *Al-Ittifaq al-Urduni al-Filastini* (Amman: Dar al-Jalil lil-Nashr, 1985), 86.
28. Shemesh, 148-51; Cobban, 68-74.
29. Rouleau, 138-54; Bruce Hoffman, "The Plight of the Phoenix: The PLO Since Lebanon," *Conflict Quarterly* 5:2: 5-17.
30. Al-Hasan, 104-15, 158-59; *Shu'un Filastiniyya* (July-August 1985): 109. Avraham Sela, "The Changing Focus of the Arab States System," *Middle East Review* 20:3 (spring 1988): 49-50.
31. *The Economist,* 12 November 1988; Lamis Andoni, "Jordan," in Rex Brynen, ed., *Echoes of the Intifada* (Boulder, Colo.: Westview Press, 1991), 173-76.
32. Andoni, 178-81; Gregory Gause, "The Arab World and the Intifada," in Robert O. Freedman, ed., *The Intifada: Its Impact on Israel, the Arab World, and the Superpowers* (Miami: Florida International University Press, 1991), 204; Laurie Brand, "The Intifada and the Arab World," *International Journal* 45 (summer 1990): 510-12.
33. Schirin H. Fathi, *al-'Aamil al-Filastini fi al-Intikhabat al-Barlamaniyya al-Urduniyya lil-'Aam 1989* (Jerusalem: PASSIA [Palestinian Academic Society for the Study of International Affairs], 1990), 8-11; Ami Ayalon, ed., *Middle East Contemporary Survey* XIII, 1989 (Boulder: Westview Press, 1991), 463.
34. Moshe Ma'oz, *Asad: The Sphinx of Damascus* (New York: Grove Weidenfeld, 1988), 119-22; Patrick Seale, *Asad: The Struggle for the Middle East* (Berkeley: University of California Press, 1988), 280-88.
35. Uri Avnery, *My Friend the Enemy* (London: Zed Books, 1986), 172-83; *Filastin al-Thawra,* July 10, 1979. For Arafat's attitude to the "Fahd plan" see the Fez summit proceedings, *al-Mustaqbal,* 5 December 1981.
36. Elie Chalala, "Syrian Policy in Lebanon 1976-1984: Moderate Goals and Pragmatic Means," *Journal of Arab Affairs* 4:1 (1985): 80; Adeed Dawisha, "The Motives of Syria's Involvement in Lebanon," *The Middle East Journal* 38:2 (spring 1984): 228-36.
37. Ma'oz, 167-69; On the siege of the camps, see *Shu'un Filastiniyya* (September-October 1985): 113-18; *al-Jazira,* 1, 3 November 1987, *The London Times,* 18 January 1988.
38. Rashid Khalidi, "The Assad Regime and the Palestinian Resistance," *Arab Studies Quarterly* 6:4 (1984): 259-66; Dawisha, 228-36.

SEVEN

Moscow and the PLO
The Ups and Downs of a Complex Relationship

Galia Golan

The Soviet attitude toward the PLO, and any national liberation movement for that matter, was determined primarily by Moscow's global and regional policy objectives, rather than from characteristics or matters intrinsic to the movement itself.[1] Thus the Soviets were relatively late in taking up the Palestinian cause, hesitatingly beginning to support the PLO only four years after its creation in 1964, and then apparently only in response to the urgings of Moscow's state clients in the Arab world. Having viewed the Arab-Israeli conflict as one involving states only (the Palestinian issue perceived solely in terms of a refugee problem), the Soviets only gradually in the late 1960s acknowledged that the Palestinians constituted a people and, later still (after the 1973 Yom Kippur War), a people with national rights. In 1974 the Soviets finally abandoned their opposition to the idea of a Palestinian state, provided such a state were next to the state of Israel (that is, in the West Bank and the Gaza Strip) rather than instead of Israel—ruling out the PLO's original idea of a democratic secular state in all of what had been Palestine under the British Mandate.

The emergence of this Soviet position and other refinements that appeared over the years were the result of Soviet considerations in connection with their Arab allies and, increasingly, in competition with the United States. The Palestinian issue was the Achilles' heel of the American position and therefore the vehicle through which Moscow apparently hoped to halt the steadily progressing inroads the United States was making in the region in the 1970s. Thus the Soviet leadership adopted what appeared to be a greater commitment to the PLO as a tactical asset in the regional competition between the two superpowers.

Despite this tactical support of and growing involvement with the movement, which included training and arming as well as political support, there were numerous problems in the Soviet-PLO relationship. Aside from the delay in Soviet interest altogether, that is, the early failure to recognize the Palestinians as a people and the opposition to their aspirations for a state—both of which were gradually abandoned—disagreements between the two persisted in a number of areas. For years the Soviets pressed the PLO to moderate its positions and methods, specifically with regard to the existence of the state of Israel and the idea of armed struggle. Moscow maintained that the objective of destroying Israel was totally unrealistic and dangerous to the point of risking superpower confrontation in an escalating Middle East war. Similarly, armed struggle, including (particularly) the use of terrorism, was disdained because of its inherent dangers and also because it was deemed on the whole counterproductive.[2]

Neither objection, however, was sufficient to alter Soviet support for the organization over the years. Indeed Moscow trained and aided the PLO in its armed struggle, although the Soviets did seek to limit the use of force and its targets. Moreover, they sought to direct it along the lines of conventional warfare (which entailed the protracted rebuilding of PLO guerrilla forces into a regular army), much the way the Soviets sought to influence the struggles of other national liberation forces such as those in Africa in the 1970s. At the same time, they advocated PLO acceptance of UN Resolution 242 in an effort to moderate the organization. For Resolution 242 opened the way to negotiations (it was the basis for the convening of an international conference) and this was in keeping with Moscow's preference for a political, rather than the more dangerous armed, solution to the conflict. It also contained the more realistic, less dangerous recognition of Israel's right to exist within its generally accepted 1949-67 borders.

Even when the Soviets were willing to add the Palestinians' rights to self-determination and statehood to the more limited formulation of Resolution 242, Soviet positions remained problematic for the PLO. There were even open polemics between one of the major PLO factions, George Habash's Popular Front for the Liberation of Palestine (PFLP), and Moscow on these very issues. This highlighted another set of complications for Soviet-PLO relations: the lack of unity within the PLO, the linkage between most PLO factions and various, often rival, Arab states, as well as the variety of ideologies and policies advocated by the component factions.

Habash's PFLP and Nayif Hawatmah's Democratic Front for the Liberation of Palestine (DFLP) were both Marxist and, therefore, at least theoretically, acceptable to Moscow. The PFLP, however, was a bit too radical for Moscow, both with regard to its chosen methods and its objectives. It generally adopted a "rejectionist" position and was often linked with the rejectionist Arab states. The DFLP also adopted rejectionist positions, though less frequently, thus posing problems in spite of the closer affinity to Soviet Marxism.[3] In any case, both groups were too small to provide a channel for Soviet control of the PLO, and their positions often impeded rather than promoted some of Moscow's broader political objectives.

There were some attempts by Moscow, through the Arab communist parties, to create their own Palestinian group within the PLO. Al-Ansar was created in 1970 and sought representation in the PLO executive committee. It was rejected by the PLO, both because the organization sought to protect its independence from Moscow, and because of the group's advocacy of a political settlement rather than armed struggle and acceptance of Israel's right to exist (including Resolution 242). Following its demise in 1972, a new group was created in 1973, according to Soviet sources, by the Jordanian Communist Party. This was the Palestine National Front (PNF), a moderate coalition of groups within the West Bank, dominated by communists and independents advocating what was in fact the Soviet position, that is, a two-state solution to be achieved by political means. By the end of the 1970s the PNF had been virtually destroyed by Israeli deportations of its leading figures; it also ended in dispute with the PLO leadership outside the occupied territories.

The successor to the PNF in the territories, the National Guidance Committee, was a much more radical body in which the communists had no power. In the meantime, however, the decision to strive for a Palestinian state in the West Bank and Gaza led to the beginning of the separation of West Bank communists from the Jordanian Communist Party. The West Bank branch of the party formed the Palestine Communist Organization in 1975 and finally broke away altogether in 1981, creating the Palestine Communist Party in February 1982. This body also sought membership in the PLO executive, unsuccessfully until 1987.[4]

Although the Soviets drew quite close to the Marxist DFLP and had their own communist channel, Arafat's faction, Fatah, was the major beneficiary of Soviet support. The bourgeois, nationalist Fatah was at best "nonideological" in Soviet terms; the large contributions it received from Saudi Arabia created further complications. Yet Fatah was by far the largest, most powerful faction within the PLO, leaving Moscow little alternative but to deal with it. Moreover, Arafat's positions deviated little from those of Moscow with regard to the political option, the two-state solution, talks with Israelis, and other issues.

Arafat's relative moderation facilitated his relationship with the Soviet Union, despite the Palestinians' periodic complaints over the limited nature of Soviet aid[5] and various other matters. Yet it was this very moderation which finally, indirectly precipitated a rift between the two in 1985-86. The Israeli invasion of Lebanon in 1982 had strengthened the radicals within the PLO and even inside Fatah who argued that Arafat's political path was senseless in the face of Israel's use of force. Fortified by internal opposition to Arafat's personal leadership methods, and Syrian efforts to take over the PLO, the anti-Arafat forces launched a campaign to topple the leader. Ostensibly neutral, Moscow backed Arafat in this struggle up to a point. The point was reached when Arafat took decisive steps in the direction of Jordan, which culminated in the Arafat-Hussein agreement of early 1985. This led to a split in the already badly divided PLO and a break in Soviet-Fatah relations, including the suspension of Soviet arming and training of Arafat's people.

The Soviet Union was opposed to a formal split in the movement and the creation of a competing Palestinian organization; it also opposed a Syrian takeover of the movement. Such measures would have crippled if not totally eliminated the Palestinian movement as an effective, independent actor in the Middle East scene. They also would have strengthened rejectionist positions that had little to offer the Soviet Union while augmenting Syria's power to maintain its independence from Moscow. Yet the Soviets were unwilling to tolerate Arafat's move to King Husain because it was clearly designed to pave the PLO's way to Washington. Moscow's competition with Washington far outweighed the substantive issues and even the possibility of an Arab-Israeli settlement. Therefore, without supporting a formal split, the Soviet Union suspended relations with Arafat's Fatah and, reportedly, sought an alternative to the problematic leader. More fruitfully, it campaigned against the Arafat-Husain agreement—privately and publicly—until the accord itself was abandoned in the spring of 1986. While this occurred for reasons basically unassociated with the Soviet Union, it eliminated the major source of the rift. The Soviets then proceeded to mediate a reunification of the PLO, under Arafat, with the provision that this be accompanied by formal abrogation of the Arafat-Husain agreement by the Palestine National Council (PNC). All of this was achieved by the PNC meeting of April 1987. Having given the Palestinian communists a role in the mediation process, Moscow was also able to gain acceptance of one communist and one fellow traveler in the PLO executive at that PNC meeting. A long-sought achievement, this did not, however, create a significant change in either communist or Soviet influence over the organization.

THE GORBACHEV ERA

In the meantime, a new leader, and new policies, had come to power in Moscow. Gorbachev's "new thinking," the foreign policy aspect of perestroika, was rooted in a set of theoretical principles, the most important of which was the idea of the interdependence of the nations of the world and, therefore, the need to seek a balance of interests between them, ruling out anything but political solutions to conflict. The balance-of-interests idea was meant to replace the old ideologically motivated "zero-sum-game" approach or competitive model of superpower relations and opposing camps. The end of this competition, according to the new line of thinking, would remove the superpowers from regional conflicts, reducing these conflicts to their local elements. These then could be resolved on the basis of balance of interests, with outside powers serving only to facilitate or mediate between the local parties rather than assuming a competitive advocacy position. Application of this approach to the Middle East would mean superpower cooperation and relations with all the actors in the region—rather than the zero-sum-game competition between "radical" or "progressive" (pro-Soviet) elements versus "conservative" or "reactionary" (pro-Western) elements. It would also mean reduction of the Arab-Israeli conflict to its local, core issues: Israel's relations with its Arab neighbors and the even more central underlying issue of Israeli-Palestinian relations.[6]

The PLO could, therefore, under the new thinking, expect a substantial change in the Soviet attitude on two accounts. At the more general level, an end to the zero-sum-game approach and de-ideologization of foreign policy (as it was called in Moscow) spelled a reduction of support for national liberation movements, including that rendered for the conduct of armed struggle and terrorism. In view of the fact that Soviet support for the PLO was directly related to the competition with the United States, the context of the Soviet interest in the regional conflict (which itself was linked to the superpower competition), there was little hope that support would continue. In theory, at least, disengagement from the Arab-Israeli conflict would mean total disengagement from the Palestinians. Yet, there was also the possibility that Soviet interest in resolution of the conflict might also lead Moscow to maintain, rather than abandon, its involvement with the Palestinian issue in a new manner, out of a conviction that a lasting settlement would be impossible without resolution of this issue. In 1987 Gorbachev announced the application of new thinking to the Arab-Israeli conflict, explaining publicly to the visiting Syrian president Hafiz al-Asad in Moscow that there could be no military solution to the conflict, and that there should be a normalization of Soviet-Israeli relations. Indeed both Israel and Syria were beginning to get a taste of new thinking at this time, which was gradually to be applied to the PLO. The first public sign of the change regarding the PLO occurred during Arafat's visit to Moscow in April 1988, when Gorbachev counseled the PLO leader to accept Israel's right to recognition and security, along with the Palestinians' right to self-determination.[7] This was in keeping with the newly adopted principle of balance of interests; it became the thrust of a subsequent concerted effort on the part of the Soviet Union to persuade the PLO to officially recognize Israel's right to exist. Both Habash and Hawatmah were invited to Moscow in September and October 1988, where the Soviets prevailed upon them to agree to Resolution 242 in order to advance the possibility of a political solution to the Arab-Israeli conflict.[8] A Fatah delegation also visited Moscow in October following a visit to PLO headquarters in Tunis by Foreign Ministry Middle East director Vladimir Poliakov.

This flurry of activity was designed to moderate PLO positions prior to the November 1988 meeting of the PNC in Algeria. Indeed, despite Palestinian denials of Soviet pressures at the time, Moscow was later to admit, and even proudly claim, that it had played a role in the PNC's adoption of new, moderate positions regarding Israel.[9] While it was probably the impact of the Palestinian uprising (Intifada) in the occupied territories more than these Soviet pressures that prompted the historic new program adopted at the PNC, the PLO was subjected to a heavy dose of Soviet advice designed to generate a new peace process. What the Soviets were less enthusiastic about was the intention of the PLO to declare the creation of a Palestinian state at the same PNC session.[10] Moscow's motives were most likely connected with the desire to maintain a maximum of open and flexible options on the way to resolution of the conflict, so as to induce Israel to enter a negotiating process. Therefore the Soviets counseled the PLO to preserve the creation of a state as an objective, without seeking to create a *fait accompli*. This part of their advice ignored by the PNC, the Soviets were a bit slow in recognizing the newly declared state, merely acknowledging the declaration and only belatedly—and quietly—officially changing the status of the PLO office in Moscow to that of a full-fledged embassy in January 1990.[11] To avoid the complications that the proclamation of the state created, Moscow cooperated in the effort to prevent this new entity from joining the UN or the World Health Organization in 1989.[12]

The Soviets were satisfied, however, with the two major decisions adopted by the PNC and embodied in the PLO's new program: the acceptance of Resolution 242, that is, of Israel's right to exist within secure borders, and the condemnation of the use of force or terror. The latter suited the shift that had occurred in Soviet policy, from a mere preference for political means rather than armed struggle, toward an exclusive reliance on political means alone. And with this came outright Soviet condemnation of armed PLO operations, "whatever the motivation," and labeling of them as clearly acts of terrorism. Palestinian "extremists," as they were now called by Soviet media, and Palestinians who still advocated violence and terrorism were increasingly criticized. More importantly, the Soviet Union began to cooperate with international efforts to curb terrorism, in part out of their desire to present themselves as a responsible part of the international community.[13] Moscow not only sought to play such a role, but it also began to limit its own support to armed movements, ordering the closing of Abu Nidal's offices in Eastern Europe, for example, and gradually reducing, if not actually terminating, its own training and arming of even mainstream PLO groups. Thus armed incursions into Israel from Palestinian groups in Lebanon, including groups close to Moscow, such as the DFLP (both before and after the split within that organization), were discouraged.

The Soviets were also careful to make a distinction between armed struggle and the Intifada that began in the occupied territories in December 1987. Indeed the Intifada was praised by Soviet media for its restraint and rejection of the use of arms, and the use of strikes, demonstrations and stone-throwing rather than the more dangerous "Molotov cocktails" or stabbings. Yet the increasingly free Soviet press also carried negative evaluations of the efficacy of the Intifada, and official pronouncements accorded surprisingly little attention to the uprising. Such treatment, or lack of treatment, lent credence to the conclusion that under Gorbachev Moscow valued even unarmed rebellion in the occupied territories less than the use of political measures in the broader arena.

It was to facilitate these political measures that the Soviet Union showed itself particularly satisfied with (and instrumental in achieving) the other major aspect of the PLO's 1988 program: acceptance of Resolutions 242 and 181. These resolutions embodied the principle of partition (181), that is, the two-state solution and the explicit recognition of Israel's right to exist within secure borders (242). This was the balance of interests Gorbachev had been advocating and the key, presumably, to the initiation of Israeli-Palestinian negotiations. It was also the key to engaging not only Israel in negotiations but also the United States. PLO acceptance of Resolution 242, along with the renunciation of terrorism, had been a condition set by the United States in the past; with the PNC decisions Washington agreed to open a dialogue with the PLO. The Soviet response to the American-PLO dialogue was a clear sign of just how far the new thinking had come. Attempts by Arafat to open talks with the Americans in 1985 had led to a major rift between Moscow and the Palestinian leader; in 1988 the move towards Washington was welcomed and supported by the Soviet Union. Indeed when the dialogue was suspended by Washington following the June 1990 terrorist attempt against Israel by the forces of PLO executive member Abu al-Abbas, Soviet media expressed regret over the suspension. Moscow even implicitly justified Washington's response in a letter to Arafat reportedly urging "a rational policy" on the grounds that terrorist operations would be harmful to the peace process.[14] Similarly, the Soviets sought to persuade the PLO to accept the various ideas raised for the convening of Israeli-Palestinian talks, including proposals by U.S. Secretary of State James Baker, which allowed for only indirect PLO participation in talks to be held in Cairo between Israel and Palestinians from the occupied territories (unofficially chosen by the PLO). These talks never took place, because of Israeli Prime Minister Yitzhak Shamir's opposition to the participation of Palestinians from East Jerusalem. There were numerous comments and hints, particularly after the Gulf War, that Moscow favored a solution to PLO participation in peace talks in the form of a joint Arab or even joint Jordanian-Palestinian delegation, and it urged the organization to be flexible.

The Gulf crisis, with the PLO supporting Saddam Husain, did little to alter the generally cooling relationship between Moscow and the PLO in the Gorbachev period. There were numerous trips to Moscow by PLO figures during the crisis, and Soviet media barely mentioned Arafat's support for Saddam. Indeed those in the media associated with the more conservative position regarding Gorbachev's budding rapprochement with Israel and those generally opposed to perestroika actually sought to defend the PLO's stance, themselves urging direct linkage of the Gulf and Palestinian conflicts as demanded by Saddam Husain. Such a sympathetic attitude, however, was generally absent from official pronouncements, explaining, perhaps, why Arafat refused to meet with Soviet Foreign Minister Edward Shevardnadze in Turkey when the latter was on his way home from meetings in Washington (including one with Shamir) in December 1990. Nonetheless, primarily to demonstrate that relations were back to normal, Arafat did meet in Geneva with Shevardnadze's successor Aleksander Bessmertnykh following the war, at the close of Bessmertnykh's visit to the Middle East in May 1991.

Relations did not, however, return to normal after the Gulf war. The Soviet media carried reports of demands for Arafat's replacement, including comments from senior Soviet commentators critical of Arafat's decisions to support Saddam and encourage attacks on Israel. Not only was Arafat's leadership questioned but, for the first time, Soviet media carried comments challenging the PLO's position as the sole legitimate representative of the Palestinians.[15] This did not necessarily reflect an official decision on the Soviets' part, and conservative elements continued to defend the PLO as such, but there were increasing signs that Moscow might be seeking some diversification of its contacts with the Palestinians. Aleksei Chistyakov, Soviet consul-general in Israel, told an interviewer: "We have found that there is room and possibilities for cooperation between us and the Palestinians in the occupied territories. We have just started this cooperation now and we intend to pursue it."[16] Such an approach was in keeping with American contacts with Palestinians (approved by the PLO albeit after some initial reluctance) from the occupied territories, and the increasing likelihood of a joint Jordanian-Palestinian delegation for peace talks.

The Palestinians were not particularly pleased with the changes that occurred in their relationship with Moscow. Even more than the

Syrians, they suffered from the loss of such important East European supporters as Czechoslovakia and East Germany. It is difficult to know at what point these losses began to affect the PLO's operational capability, but even at the political level East European and Soviet assistance could no longer be counted on. Even the day-to-day nature of the relationship with Moscow changed, as perestroika reduced the involvement of the Soviet Communist Party in foreign affairs, shifting treatment of the PLO from the sympathetic care of the (now greatly reduced) International Department of the Central Committee to the more formal, businesslike treatment of the Foreign Ministry. While the PLO maintained its access to leading circles, the nature of these Soviet contacts went from supportive, to demanding, to virtually neutral—at least as viewed from the Palestinian side. And the increasingly free Soviet media presented startlingly frank, often negative or critical portrayals of the PLO.[17]

Despite denials by some Palestinian leaders, concern was expressed by Palestinians and other Arabs over what was viewed as a contraction of the Soviet commitment to the Palestinians' cause, to the benefit of Israel, and the warming Soviet-Israeli relationship during the Gorbachev period. The Council of Arab Ambassadors in Moscow apparently raised the issue with Poliakov, who assured them in January 1989 that the "Soviet Union [continued] to support the Arab causes, foremost the Palestinian cause."[18] Ahmad Jibril, for example, openly called upon Moscow to return to its former positions and reconsider its new policy, which, he said, "worries [them]."[19] Soviet officials and commentators also indicated that there were Palestinian complaints, and, as a *Pravda* correspondent explained the situation: "the new ideas in Soviet foreign policy have confused some of our traditional close friends," adding the fact that Arab and Soviet positions simply did not fully coincide.[20] Intending to dismiss rumors of difficulties, Foreign Ministry spokesman Gennadii Gerasimov actually revealed that Arafat's annual trip to Moscow had been "skipped" in 1989 (it likewise did not take place in 1990), when he said that "despite the lack of a recent visit to Moscow by Mr. Yasir Arafat . . . " full support was still being given the PLO.[21] Such denials, on both sides, disappeared during the Gulf War, when Gorbachev himself alluded to the dissatisfaction in some Arab quarters, and PLO executive member 'Abdallah Hourani characterized Moscow's behavior as "an attempt to please the Zionist movement and obtain American money," concluding that "it [was] no longer possible to regard Moscow as a friend and ally of world forces of liberation, including the

Arab world and the Palestinian people and cause."[22] PLO ambassador in Moscow Nabil 'Amr took the Soviet media to task for what he termed its "one-sided . . . biased . . . misrepresentation" of the Palestinians.[23] Even Arafat, generally cautious about even implying criticism of Moscow or admitting the existence of a problem, told an interviewer that, with regard to the Soviet attitude towards the Palestinian question, one must "understand that there are international changes that must be taken into consideration."[24]

The openly acknowledged bone of contention was over the emigration of Soviet Jews to Israel. An issue raised by various Arab countries, the massive immigration of Soviet Jews to Israel was of particular importance and concern to the Palestinians, who believed this population influx would strengthen both the Israeli will and ability to hold on to the occupied territories. This fear was not diminished by Shamir's comments on one occasion that Israel needed the territories in order to absorb the large influx of immigrants.[25] A Palestinian delegation, including figures from the occupied territories, discussed the issue with Soviet Jews in Moscow as well as with Soviet authorities, in the spring of 1990, and the PLO sent an official memorandum on the subject to Shevardnadze in June 1990. The memorandum warned Moscow not to accept Israeli promises that the immigrants would not be settled in the territories; it called for a "neutral international supervisory committee to implement the international resolutions to halt settlement in the occupied territories and to suspend intensive Jewish emigration from the Soviet Union to the occupied territories."[26] Thus they urged Moscow to link emigration to the broader issues of the Israeli-Palestinian conflict and Palestinian rights, such as the end of Israeli settlements in the territories (including the expropriation of houses, lands, and water resources), the lifting of heavy taxes, granting of freedom of movement and expression, reopening of the universities, and other demands.

Despite the fact that Palestinian complaints were taken up by most Arab states and domestic Soviet opponents to the Soviet rapprochement with Israel, the most Moscow was willing to do was delay implementation of an agreement for direct Moscow-Tel Aviv flights. The Soviets also joined the campaign of countries, including the United States, to demand assurances from Israel that the immigrants would not be settled in the occupied territories. Gorbachev did threaten delays, even suspension of the emigration if Israel were not to comply, but it was most unlikely that such threats were anything more than gestures to the complaining Arabs.[27] Emigration was an issue intimately connected with sorely needed American trade benefits, specifically the granting of Most Favored Nation (MFN) status which Washington had promised only on condition of free emigration. The passage in May 1991 of the long-awaited Soviet bill on emigration was a clear sign that Soviet priorities would not be altered by Palestinian or Arab complaints.

The Break-Up of the USSR and Russian Policy

The break-up of the Soviet Union in December 1991 was not likely to bring about any change in the new Soviet attitude toward the PLO, particularly since leading PLO figures such as Farouq Qaddoumi expressed support for the coup attempt of August 1991 (though once the coup failed Arafat sent congratulatory wishes to Gorbachev).[28] The Palestinians' attitude toward Gorbachev was probably most accurately reflected in an editorial published in East Jerusalem several months after Gorbachev's fall from power and during his visit to Israel in June 1992:

> Gorbachev's visit to Israel and his remarks about the Palestinian problem and the Palestinian leadership have revealed the degree of his contempt for the fate of our people and showed how for many decades we were deceived by delusive friendships that were, in fact, one-sided, that is from the Arab and Palestinian side. . . . The reason for the Palestinian people's disappointment with the old 'friend' is that they were hoping that Gorbachev would alleviate their suffering and ease the hard conditions under which they are living . . . There is no doubt that Gorbachev played an important role in all the crises that hit the Middle East in the past eight years. Soviet immigrants are being settled now on Palestinian lands. After those lands are planted by these immigrants, the original inhabitants will be expelled to Jordan, from where they will be dispersed all over the Arab world. All this is thanks to Gorbachev's policy. That is what you have done to the Palestinian people. If the Israelis are welcoming you today, our people will never welcome you because you have contributed to their suffering and pain . . . You have sold us very cheaply. . . . [29]

Yeltsin and his foreign minister, Andrei Kozyrev, continued the policy adopted by Gorbachev even with regard to the language employed regarding a settlement of the conflict that would respond to the interests of both Israel and the Palestinians. Like their predecessors, the new leaders of Russian foreign policy sought to maintain a role for Russia in the peace process without jeopardizing their close relationship with the United States by adopting anything but the positions advocated by Washington. They maintained contacts with the PLO, even conducting meetings designed to demonstrate Moscow's continued importance in the world and influence in the region. These moves, however, were little more than exhortations to support the policies originating in Washington, such as PLO acceptance of Israeli-Palestinian negotiations that would exclude official PLO representatives (or even Palestinians from East Jerusalem).[30] The post-Soviet leadership went so far as to agree to American-Israeli demands to exclude the PLO from the multilateral negotiations that took place in Moscow in January 1992.

The official attitude of the Yeltsin government was by no means accepted by all in Moscow. There was quite outspoken criticism of the policy toward Israel and the Arab-Israeli peace process in general, as well as condemnation of Russia's virtual abandonment of the Palestinians, in particular.[31] Following the PLO-Israeli accords of September 1993, which brought the organization into the peace process, Russian critics began to accord attention to the rejectionists, indirectly (though not directly) challenging Moscow's cooperation with the official PLO-Israeli-American agenda, or at the least, expressing pessimism as to its potential for success.[32] Some critics went so far as to champion an anti-Arafat group of Palestinians who had set up a so-called Palestinian government-in-exile in Moscow.[33] What gave this criticism a certain weight, however, was the fact that it was increasingly part of the much broader policy debate and political struggle developing around post-Soviet Russia and the Yeltsin government.

Beginning in the late Gorbachev period, and especially after the Gulf War, voices were increasingly raised against Moscow's becoming a mere appendage to Washington and abdicating its superpower status altogether. After the breakup of the Soviet Union, the extreme right wing and communists' complaints of this type were joined by those of many moderate centrists, including the influential ambassador to the United States—later chair of the International Affairs Committee of the new Russian Duma—Vladimir Lukin. The main argument of these forces was over what constituted Russia's national interest—a policy orientation based on the West or on the countries of the former Soviet Union and their neighbors. The last are known as the "near abroad." Disappointment over the paucity of economic assistance from the West, combined with the most serious domestic problems, apparently brought this debate to a close, with the near abroad winning, by 1993. Yeltsin, in his battle on the political scene with the center as well as the right wing and communists, increasingly adopted positions designed to demonstrate Moscow's independence and strength, with regard to the former Soviet republics (most recently Georgia) and on the world scene. These positions were manifested in a new assertiveness regarding Bosnia, NATO, Eastern Europe, the Baltics, and the Middle East. With regard to the Arab world, Russia's new policies had an economic justification as well. Aside from the need for investment in the desperate Russian economy, there was the matter of arms sales. The export of arms once accounted for 15 percent of Moscow's foreign currency earnings, and the military industries provided the most important export item after oil and gold. The military and military-industrial complex, badly hit by perestroika and the end of the Cold War, became deeply involved in the political struggles in the Kremlin, demanding not only a return of Russian pride and influence, but also the revenues sorely needed by the sagging Russian economy. They argued that American opposition to Russian arms sales was not only meddling in Moscow's affairs but also designed to protect American arms industries from competition. The alarmingly popular neofascist Vladimir Zhirinovskii claimed that participation in the American-dictated boycott of Iraq and Libya is costing Russia billions of dollars both in monies owed Moscow from the past and in potential contracts. His complaints were shared by more than a lunatic fringe. Even Russian Foreign Minister Kozyrev spoke of arms sales to the Arab world, as well as Arab investment in the Russian economy, as Russia's foreign policy interest in the Middle East for 1994, along with promoting Arab-Israeli peace and the "realization of Palestinian aspirations."[34]

Kozyrev's mention of the Palestinians, without a balancing reference to Israel, was an indication of the benefits the PLO might derive, almost as a by-product, from the change in Russian policy and Moscow's efforts to secure an independent role in the Arab-Israeli peace process. There was no economic gain as such to be sought by Moscow through improved relations with the PLO. Moreover, the original reasons for Soviet support of the PLO were no longer paramount, namely, the centrality of the Palestinian issue in the eyes of the Soviets' Arab allies and the weakness of American policy on the matter of the PLO. Nevertheless, as long as the Palestinian issue occupied center stage in the Arab-Israeli peace process, it could be of use once again to Moscow as a vehicle for playing a greater role. Thus, in connection with the White House signing of the PLO-Israeli accords in September 1993,

Kozyrev invoked Moscow's past credit with the PLO, noting disingenuously: "we have worked with Arafat earlier, too, and supported him. Today . . . he has been recognized in the West as well. . . . It should not be forgotten that, in the Arab world, relations with the United States have not always been positive and it is important for Moscow to also lend support to the new initiatives."[35]

Far more significant was a flurry of Russian activity following the February 1994 massacre of Palestinians at prayer in Hebron by an Israeli settler. Yeltsin dispatched a special envoy, first deputy foreign minister Igor Ivanov and then Foreign Minister Kozyrev himself to visit the region—going first to the PLO in Tunis and then to Israel. Ignoring the United States, these Russian emissaries sought to mediate the crisis that developed between Tunis and Jerusalem; Moscow even claimed credit for Arafat's agreement to resume peace talks, provided that the UN Security Council pass a resolution condemning the massacre and calling for international observers to be sent to the occupied territories.[36] The Russians not only supported the PLO demand for such observers immediately after the massacre, in a statement issued by the Foreign Ministry on 2 March; they also called for a reconvening of the Madrid conference, as distinct from the delayed Washington-based bilateral Israeli-PLO talks.[37] This proposal itself did not gain much attention, as both Washington and Jerusalem conveyed to the Russians their dissatisfaction with Moscow's independent actions. Nonetheless, it clearly marked an effort by the Russians to play a more important and independent role by championing the Palestinians' interests.

The same effort received further expression in the official visit to Moscow by Arafat—the first in many years—the following month, on 19-20 April, just days before a scheduled visit by Yitzhak Rabin. Arafat was warmly received and held meetings with Yeltsin as well as Kozyrev and speaker of the Duma Ivan Rybkin; he signed agreements with the Russians for cooperation in the area of culture and science. It was also agreed that a Palestinian delegation come to discuss economic matters. While it was unclear as to just what was meant, Arafat said that Russian assistance in the setting up of the Palestinian police force was also discussed.[38] Arafat was full of praise for Russia's diplomatic "success" and support at the UN in connection with the resolution of the problems in the negotiating process and the issue of an international force to be placed in the occupied territories.[39] He said that the PLO maintained its demand that Russian soldiers be included in such a force. Yeltsin responded to Arafat's praise by underlining Russian interest in the peace process, declaring that the region was "vitally important for Russia," a phrase long absent from Russian and even Soviet pronouncements.[40] Yeltsin did not go any further than that, however, and a few days later, on the eve of Rabin's visit, a senior Foreign Ministry official, Viktor Gorgitidze, said that Russia would not exert any pressure on Israel despite requests by Arafat to do so.[41] Moreover, Yeltsin appeared to respond to Rabin's (and President Clinton's) complaints by emphasizing repeatedly during the Rabin visit—the first visit to Moscow ever by an Israeli prime minister—Russia's commitment to work in coordination with the United States regarding the peace process. In retrospect, to a large degree, the Russians were taking advantage of a situation that had developed in the Palestinian-Israeli talks; they do not appear to have actually sought to initiate or encourage problems as a means of carving out a role for themselves. While there were persons in the Russian political arena who would prefer that they do so, in an all-out competition with the United States reminiscent of the Brezhnev period, there were also many who took the opposite view. Speaking of the broader foreign policy changes of recent months, Gorbachev's former political advisor Anatolii Chernaiev warned that "Kozyrev's [new] doctrine . . . reeks of Zhirinovskii," while Yurii Afanasyev claimed that the new policy was dictated mainly by the military-industrial complex.[42] Such criticism was yet to focus on Middle East policies, but there were signs, particularly during the Rabin visit, that Yeltsin was concerned over the damage that could occur to relations with Washington if he were to pursue an uncoordinated policy on this issue.

In evaluating, therefore, the importance and the future direction of the new relationship Moscow was seeking to establish with the PLO, the role of the United States as a restraining factor on Russia must clearly be taken into account. The effectiveness of this factor was itself a function of both the domestic political struggle in Moscow and of the broader Russian-American relationship. At the same time, the Russians have little to offer today in the way of political power. The chaos and conflict within the country, the ethnic and border disputes and actual fighting in various regions of the CIS, and the dire economic and social problems, all limit Moscow's ability to play much of a role outside. However, in terms of the full expanse of the Soviet-Russian relationship with the PLO from 1964 to the present, the graph that generally flowed upward and then sharply downward, reaching its lowest point in the 1988-91 period, has turned upward once again.

Notes

1. For the history of the Soviet-PLO relationship, see Galia Golan, *The Soviet Union and the Palestine Liberation Organization: An Uneasy Alliance* (New York: Praeger Publishers, 1980).
2. The use of armed struggle and terrorism by the PLO are treated more thoroughly in Golan, *The Soviet Union and the Palestine Liberation Organization;* for a discussion of the Soviet attitude toward terrorism in general, see Galia Golan, *The Soviet Union and National Liberation Movements in the Third World* (London: Unwin-Hyman, 1988).
3. The DFLP was the first PLO faction to advocate the two-state solution as early as 1973, in accord with the position the Soviet Union was privately urging at the time. In Hawatmah's interpretation, however, this was to be but a first stage of the achievement of a democratic secular state in all of Palestine, while Moscow saw it as the final settlement. Moreover, there were disagreements between the DFLP over negotiations and armed struggle, talking with Israelis, and other issues over the years. Nevertheless, the DFLP pursued a close relationship with Moscow and, according to some reports, even suggested converting itself to a communist party.
4. For a detailed history of Palestinian communism, see Alain Gresh, *Communistes et nationalistes au Proche-Orient: le cas Palestinien depuis 1948* (Paris: Presses universitaires de France, 1983).
5. Particularly in Lebanon, during the civil war and the PLO-Syrian confrontation of 1976 as well as during the Israeli invasion of 1982. Other matters concerned PLO efforts to have Israel expelled from the UN and to have the Soviet Union withdraw its recognition of the country, its permission for Soviet Jews to emigrate to Israel, Soviet-Ethiopian suppression of the Fatah-supported Eritreans in Ethiopia, the Soviet invasion of Afghanistan, and so forth.
6. For Soviet policy in the Middle East under Gorbachev, see Galia Golan, *Moscow and the Middle East: New Thinking on Regional Conflict* (London: The Royal Institute of International Affairs, 1992).
7. *Pravda,* 10 April 1988.
8. *Pravda,* 10 September 1988; 12 October 1988; interview with deputy foreign minister Petrovskii *al-Hawadith* (London), 21 October 1988; and with Foreign Ministry Middle East Director Poliakov (*le Quotidien de Paris,* 13 October 1988); Moscow domestic radio, 23 October 1988 (FBIS-SOV, 25 October 1988).
9. *Al-Ittihad* (Abu Dhabi), 18 January 1989 quoted a Soviet Foreign Ministry official as revealing that "the intensive consultations conducted between Moscow and the PLO have helped in formulating the new PLO stand toward

the peace process in the region." See also Terasov in *al-Anba'* (Kuwait), 7 January 1989 and Abu Mazin interview to *Izvestiia*, 30 April 1989.
10. See, for example, *Pravda*'s senior commentator Pavel Demchenko, 10 September 1988 or Poliakov, *le Quotidienne de Paris*, 13 October 1988, or deputy foreign minister Petrovskii according to KUNA (Kuwait), 14 October 1988, citing *al-Qabas*.
11. The PLO office in Moscow had, in fact, held diplomatic status since 1981, so the significance of the 1990 change was not fully clear. It came at the time of a visit to the USSR by a member of the Israeli government, Science Minister Ezer Weizman, and therefore may have been intended to balance this gesture towards Israel. While the Soviets subsequently referred to the Embassy of Palestine, they did not take the commensurate step of naming an ambassador to Palestine, although there was a minister in the Soviet embassy in Tunis—Gromyko's former interpreter Robert Turgaiev—who dealt with the PLO there.
12. Reuters, 7 December 1989, carried U.S. State Department as well as Israeli Embassy praise for Moscow's cooperation on this.
13. See Galia Golan, *Gorbachev's New Thinking on Terrorism* (New York: Praeger, 1990).
14. TASS, 22 June 1990; Amman domestic radio, 7 July 1990 citing an Arab diplomat source in Tunis regarding a letter to Arafat (FBIS-NES, 9 July 1990). There were other Soviet media expressions against the U.S. suspension of the dialogue, mainly arguing that Arafat had dissociated himself from the Abu al-Abbas attempt.
15. Shishlin, Moscow television, 23 March 1991 (FBIS-SOV, 25 March 1991.); *Izvestiia*, (Bovin) 20 March 1991; *Izvestiia*, 16 (Skozyrev) 25 May 1991, to which PLO representative in Moscow, Nabil 'Amr, answered that PLO-Soviet relations had deepened as a result of the Bessmertnykh meeting with Arafat in Geneva ('Amr claimed that Arafat had authorized the Soviets to speak for the Palestinians). A Foreign Ministry source subsequently denied the according of such significance to the meeting.
16. Kol Israel (Voice of Israel) radio, 11 June 1991.
17. There had been criticism of the PLO in the past, usually signifying official grievances if not actual differences of opinion within the Soviet leadership. Under glasnost, however, such comments became more frequent, penetrating and comprehensive, as past Soviet support for the PLO was criticized and PLO policies and behavior—in Lebanon as well as vis-à-vis Israel—were attacked. See, for example, Moscow television ("International Panorama"), 20 November 1988 (FBIS-SOV, 22 November 1988); Vladimir Nosenko, "Sowing Fear is Not a Way of Building Peace," *New Times* 12 (1989): 9-11; Vladimir Nosenko, "A Gun or An Olive Branch?," *New Times* 39 (1989): 12-14; Leonid

Medvedko, "A Time to Throw Stones and a Time to Collect Them," *New Times* 36 (1988): 16; Dmitry Zgersky, "Yasser Arafat in Moscow," *New Times* 16 (1988): 9.

18. *Al-Ra'i* (Jordan), 1 February 1989.
19. *Al-Ittihad* (Abu Dhabi), 29 January 1989.
20. *Pravda,* 18 February 1989.
21. *Times* (London), 1 May 1989.
22. Moscow domestic radio, 31 August 1990 (Gorbachev in response to a question from a Palestinian journalist); Reuters, September 27, 1990 (Hourani).
23. Letter from the Palestinian Embassy to the Soviet radio, Radio Peace and Progress, 26 September 1990 (FBIS-SOV, 27 September 1990); Dmitry Zgersky interview with Nabil 'Amr, *New Times* 38 (1990): 6-7.
24. Arafat to *Sawt al-Sha'b* (Aman), 2 June 1991 (FBIS-NES, 3 June 1991).
25. The statement, according to the *Jerusalem Post* was: "'big immigration requires Israel be big as well.'" The paper continued: "The flood of immigrants made it imperative that Israel maintain its hold on the territories, he said, as 'we need the space to house all the people.'" (*Jerusalem Post,* 15 January 1990.
26. *Al-Dustour* (Jordan), 2 July 1990.
27. Israel radio news, 10 May 1991.
28. PLO ambassador to Moscow Nabil 'Amr publicly said that "the statements of these Palestinian figures were too hasty and they shocked Yasir Arafat somewhat." (*Komsomol'skaia pravda,* 7 September 1991.)
29. *Al-Nahar* (Jerusalem) 16 June 1992.
30. For example, the September 1991 trip to Tunis by deputy foreign minister Aleksandr Belonogov on the eve of the PNC session was crucial to PLO agreement for the convening of the Madrid conference the following month.
31. For criticism, see, for example, *Pravda*'s leading Arabist Yurii Glukhov, 12 January 1993 or Moscow Mayak Radio Network, 19 May 1993 (FBIS-SOV, 20 May 1993); *Pravda,* 28-29 July 1993.
32. *Pravda,* 11, 14 September; 5 November 1993; 21 December 1993; *Krasnaia zvezda,* 19, 28 October, 4 November 1993. Most critics did not go so far as to support the rejectionists, pointing out on one occasion rather, that the "Arab war party" played into the hands of the Israeli war party.(*Krasnaia zvezda,* 28 October 1993.)
33. The Palestinian group was headed by Shaaban Hafez, described as a businessman who published a newspaper in Moscow called "al Kods." (*Sovetskaia Rossiia,* 28 November 1992.)
34. *Rossiiskiye vesti,* 9 February 1994 on "The Tasks of Russia's Foreign Policy." This comment also referred to Arab investments in the Russian economy. A government representative (Yeltsin's adviser on military conversion, Mikhail

Malei) recommended to the Arab Business Club of Moscow that investment be made in the military industries (Udmort in the Urals was a suggested complex). Persons as varied in political views as Duma deputy Nikolai Stoliarov from Zhirinovskii's party, Arkadi Volskii's deputy Vasilii Lipitskii, and Khasbulatov have all been involved with this club (which resolved early in 1994 to set up an Arab lobby)(*Izvestiia,* 26 February 1992; *Pravda,* 29 May 1993; *Segodnia,* 29 January 1994). Khasbulatov was even head of the organizing committee of the group's May 1993 conference on Russia and the Arab world. Criticizing the decline in economic cooperation, Khasbulatov said that "right up to the beginning of 1993 the government adhered to certain criteria in the illusory hope that the country could be extricated from the crisis in a very short time with the help of Western aid."(*Rossiiskaia gazeta,* 25 May 1993.)

35. ITAR-TASS, 14 September 1993 (FBIS-SOV, 14 September 1993, p. 6).
36. Russian Foreign Ministry statement, ITAR-TASS, 12 March 1994 and comments by Middle East Department Chief Posovoluk, ITAR-TASS, 19 March 1994.
37. Moscow Radio Rossii, 2 March 1994 (FBIS-SOV, 4 March 1994, p. 9). The foreign ministry issued a statement, just a few hours after the massacre, in which it condemned the killings. This statement noted the condemnation expressed by the Israeli leadership and main political parties but added that this did "not absolve the Israeli leadership from full responsibility." (ITAR-TASS, 25 February 1994.)
38. Arafat press conference, INTERFAX, 20 April 1994.
39. INTERFAX, 20 April 1994.
40. Ibid.
41. INTERFAX, 22 April 1994.
42. Yurii Afanasiev, "Revanche," *Novoe vremia* 4 (January 1994): 10-13; Chernaiev to *Frankfurter Allgemeine Zeitung,* 14 April 1994. Aleksei Pushkov in *Moskovskiye novosti,* 23-30 January 1994 also criticized "Andrei Kozyrev's attempts to play Zhirinovskii."

EIGHT

Misperceptions and Perfect Understanding
The United States and the PLO

Barry Rubin

It may seem obvious that the historic relationship between the United States and the PLO has been one of mutual hostility. Yet this assessment conceals some fascinating elements. Prior to the Declaration Of Principles, the United States saw the PLO primarily as an extremist force opposed to U.S. interests, bent on destroying an American ally, Israel, and as a terrorist partner to the USSR and anti-American Arab states. The PLO considered the United States an imperialistic great power, opposed to Arab and Palestinian interests, and either (or, in a sense, both) Israel's master or puppet.

Beyond these perceptions were more complex considerations. First, the United States had several conflicting interests. It wished to keep good relations with various Arab states that supported the PLO, to limit Soviet influence and, moreover, to win away Moscow's clients, and to encourage an Arab-Israeli peace, even if this might require including the PLO as a partner. A minority view in the American policy debate thus favored a stand more accommodating to the PLO.

As for the PLO, it required U.S. recognition to achieve any negotiated settlement and sought to split the United States from Israel in order to force Israel to make major concessions. While the pro-PLO view in the United States lost the debate—largely because of the PLO's own actions—the PLO was eventually forced toward a rapprochement with U.S. interests that, in turn, enabled a change in U.S. policy as well. The PLO's image of the United States was an important element in its formulation of methods and goals: If the United States was inevitably at odds with Palestinian aspirations and Israel was a fascist state doomed to extinction, negotiating with either was futile and compromise was unthinkable.

The PLO's historic interpretation underestimated Israel's endurance and overestimated that country's dependence on the United States. Expecting that its power could compel a change in U.S. policy or force Israel's surrender made other options less attractive. Believing that Washington could be persuaded to abandon Israel or order it to yield territory led to miscalculations. The difficulty in seeing Israel as a viable and independent country caused the PLO to continue using radical means and rhetoric that hardened Israel's aversion to negotiating with it—much less yielding territory to it.

A spate of events that damaged the PLO's interests in the 1980s and early 1990s made a rejectionist analysis harder to maintain though it still served a useful function within the Palestinian political arena. If the PLO and its allies could not expel U.S. influence or defeat Israel on the battlefield, the diplomatic route became the only viable option. Whatever moral or historical arguments Palestinians might employ, the reality was that not one inch of land could be obtained without reaching some agreement with the only two countries that might materially affect the Palestinians' fate for the better.

The PLO was pushed toward tough decisions and irreversible choices as West Bank and Gaza Palestinians demanded action, Arab rulers reduced support for the PLO and involvement in the conflict, the USSR collapsed, U.S. power grew, and Israel became stronger and more deeply entrenched in the territories. The opening of direct Arab-Israeli and Israeli-Palestinian negotiations in 1991 further challenged PLO leaders to bridge the gap between opportunities to progress and limits imposed by internal politics or ideology, in order to move from being a revolutionary movement to being a governing authority. This situation made the PLO's view of its foes all the more central in determining its strategy and fortunes.

In the 1970s and into the 1980s, some U.S. policymakers were frustrated in their efforts to work with Arafat, for the apparent impossibility of finding an Israeli-Palestinian settlement, the PLO's hostility to U.S. interests, and the evidence that the PLO's power was limited all undermined the appeal of a changed policy. Failing either to endanger U.S. interests or to help in a diplomatic breakthrough, the PLO found U.S. policy largely ignoring its concerns. By the time the organization began moving toward a more flexible position both its psychological and material advantages had eroded.

THE HISTORICAL RECORD

United States policy, first formulated by Secretary of State Henry Kissinger in 1975, was to refuse to deal with the PLO until it accepted UN Resolution 242, abandoned terrorism, and recognized Israel's right to exist. These conditions were meant to ensure that the PLO had genuinely changed its position so as to make possible successful talks and a stable settlement. There were some secret contacts between U.S. embassy officials and the PLO in Lebanon for security purposes and indirect exchanges in which Washington tried to persuade the PLO to meet the conditions. Although the PLO's diplomatic contacts with West European and third world countries increased steadily in the mid-1970s, its terrorism and ideology prevented it from making headway with the U.S. government.

Those stressing the PLO's importance predicted that unless the Palestinian problem was solved as soon as possible, on its own terms, the Middle East would explode, U.S. interests and influence would be destroyed, and pro-U.S. regimes would be overthrown or decide to embrace Moscow or Islamic fundamentalism out of anger or self-preservation. Terrorism, anti-Americanism, radicalism, revolution, Islamic fundamentalism, and every other regional phenomenon was attributed to this single-cause explanation, appealing in its simplicity and its focus on the regional issue with which Americans were most familiar.

All the area's problems were said to be rooted in this dispute. Zbigniew Brzezinski expressed the belief that "it [was] impossible to seek a resolution to the energy problem without tackling head on—and doing so in an urgent fashion—the Arab-Israeli conflict." Otherwise, "any stable arrangement" was impossible. But, in fact, the oil crisis and related financial issues were handled successfully on their own. "Unless the United States makes a real concession to the Palestinians soon by recognizing the PLO," one critic wrote in 1979, "it may find it has burnt its bridges."[1] The next year the influential scholar Malcolm Kerr claimed that because the issue had "continuously been the number one preoccupation" of the area, "the decline in American prestige [hung] like a cloud over ... any other form of diplomatic initiative in the Middle East that Washington might wish to pursue."[2]

Others argued that the USSR's apparent losses and the United States' apparent gains were only a mirage. The Arabs, wrote Professor Edward Said in 1979, were "losing hope" in U.S. credibility and turning "to Moscow ... because they felt they had been left with no alternative. America [had] been paying heavily for the unresolved conflict in many large and small ways. These include[d] the radicalization of half a dozen Arab regimes, the strengthening of their ties with Moscow ... their hostility to the United States; [and] the destruction of Lebanon."[3] A leading regional expert, John Campbell, insisted in 1981 that "the Palestine question remain[ed] a formidable obstacle and burden to U.S. relations with the Arab world. It undermines the moderates and strengthens the wild men," he said. "It plays into the hands of the Soviet Union. It threatens to isolate the United States with Israel as the only friend in the region."[4]

In 1983, the journalist David Lamb wrote that U.S. policy had convinced most Arab governments, "that the Reagan Administration [could] not be an honest broker in the stalemated Arab-Israeli conflict." *Time* magazine opined in 1986: "On the Arab side, the sense of betrayal is deep. The Arabs feel that Washington has moved closer to Israel than ever before, thus endangering U.S. strategic interests and abandoning claims of being an honest broker."[5] Yet that was precisely the role Arab states repeatedly asked the United States to play.

Professor Udo Steinbach wrote in 1983 that until a settlement of the Palestine question was achieved "which [would] correspond approximately to [Arab] views of a 'just' solution—then close cooperation with the United States [could] not fail to operate in a destabilizing manner for the states of the [Persian Gulf] region." The Arabs of the Persian Gulf were supposedly obsessed about the Arab-Israeli conflict and mistrustful of the United States as a result. "We should not assume," warned author Robert Lacey in 1982, that the Saudi royal family "will continue to be as pro-Western as it is at present.... [It] could very easily shift itself in a more radical direction."[6]

Yet at that very moment, Saudi Arabia was cooperating with the United States, buying vast amounts of arms from it and overbuilding military facilities for U.S. use if American protection was ever needed.

In 1987, Kuwait put American flags on its tankers and asked the U.S. Navy to convoy them in order to stop Iranian attacks. An Arab summit meeting endorsed the arrangement although no progress had been made on resolving the Arab-Israeli conflict. Saudi Arabia did not hesitate—just a few months after the United States broke off its dialogue with the PLO—to invite U.S. troops to save it when Iraq invaded Kuwait in 1990. Egypt, Syria, and other Arab states aligned with Washington against Baghdad in a war.

By the same token, anti-Americanism was not merely a reaction to U.S. help for Israel or opposition to the PLO. A U.S. policy defending the regimes in Saudi Arabia, Jordan, Lebanon, Libya, and Iraq in the 1950s against radical forces—at a time when it had only minimal links with Israel—angered radicals seeking to overthrow incumbent rulers and expansionist states eager to take over neighbors. American power frightened pan-Arab nationalists and Muslims who thought a Western cultural and political invasion threatened to swamp their way of life, destroy their independence, and block their plans for unity. Radicals would have fomented revolution and regimes would have battled over regional hegemony even if Israel had never existed.

In short, while the Palestine issue was undoubtedly an important one for Arab states, it neither pushed them into the Soviet camp nor prevented them from cooperation with the United States when it was otherwise to their advantage. They were more preoccupied with their own problems and strife, including the search for identity in the aftermath of independence, and confronting traumas of development comparable to those elsewhere in the third world. These factors generated crises often having little or no relation to the Arab-Israeli one, constantly drawing attention and resources away from the PLO's cause and dragging it into costly diversions.

The "Arab Cold War" and frequent coups of the 1950s and 1960s were followed by such strife as Qadhafi's takeover in Libya and subversion of neighbors; instability in Sudan; Lebanon's civil war; the fall of Iran's shah, displaced by an Islamic republic; Kurdish revolts and the Iran-Iraq war; the Soviet invasion of Afghanistan, Islamic fundamentalism; the upward spiral of oil prices; and Iraq's invasion of Kuwait. In all these circumstances, Arab support for the PLO was limited or distorted by state interests.

Unwilling to fight Israel—as respect for its strength grew—and increasingly concerned by threats from Iran or Iraq, internal problems, and internecine quarrels, Arab states devoted diminishing resources to help the PLO. Pro-PLO statements did not stop Saudi Arabia and Egypt from strengthening ties with the United States, nor did Iraq let PLO interests stand in its way when it needed U.S. aid to defeat Iran during their war.[7] Apathy toward the PLO became antipathy: Arab rulers attacked the PLO in the name of the Palestinian cause, assassinating or jailing its leaders, helping anti-Arafat factions, and withholding aid. The PLO had to compete with Jordan's claim to represent the Palestinians and rule the West Bank, as well as Syria's claim to Palestine as "southern Syria" and demand for veto power over its policies. Arafat found no consistent champion in any Arab leader or government.

Instead, these regimes gradually came to accept Israel's existence. Egypt and Israel made peace. In practice—though not formally—Jordan and Israel settled into peaceful coexistence; Syria and Israel avoided strife. Competing with Israel for U.S. favor, many Arab rulers improved relations with the world's strongest state. The very anxiety that U.S. power might be used against them made radicals more cautious. Assistant Secretary of State Richard Murphy explained that close U.S. ties "to both Israel and Arab states [made it] the only superpower trusted by both." In contrast, "the Soviet Union, without diplomatic relations with Israel and with limited diplomatic ties and bilateral relations in the Arab world, [had] only a peripheral role to play."[8] Even Kerr conceded that alliance with Israel aided U.S. interests, "As long as the Arabs let the United States get away with . . . managing to befriend Israel without sacrificing important interests in the Arab world."[9]

Despite Moscow's role as the PLO's superpower patron, its influence declined in an Arab world that found the USSR to be an unreliable champion, a miser on aid, and ineffective in exerting diplomatic or military leverage. Egypt and Sudan expelled the Soviets; Iraq turned its back on them. Even South Yemen—whose close alignment with Moscow was hardly inspired by the Palestinian issue—gave up and merged with conservative North Yemen. Despite the many times when the U.S. position was said to be on the verge of ruin, it succeeded in limiting regional instability, defeating its Soviet rival, containing extremist regimes, protecting allies, maintaining influence, and ensuring access to oil. With superior technology, reliability, and power, the United States won the cold war in the Middle East several years earlier than elsewhere.[10]

Consequently, through the 1970s and 1980s, the PLO had only limited and declining Arab and Soviet backing, no capacity to defeat or destroy Israel, and little leverage in changing U.S. policy. While Arafat was aware of these general trends, he also continually overestimated his assets, banking on the PLO's centrality in the Arab-Israeli conflict and that issue's alleged primacy for the region. Thus he repeatedly threatened to unleash a volcano destroying U.S. interests unless Washington met his demands.

Yet history was moving in the opposite direction and the PLO, unable to force a U.S. retreat, needed a strategy inducing U.S. policy to be more favorable. The power balance meant that the more moderate the PLO's position, the greater its chance to enter negotiations and achieve some form of Palestinian self-determination; the more ambiguous or hardline the PLO's stand, the less likely that the United States would deal with it, endorse its direct inclusion in talks, or accede to a Palestinian state in the West Bank and Gaza. Since only the PLO and the Palestinians gained nothing from the status quo, the burden of proof for achieving any change was placed on them.[11]

If the PLO could not bring progress by force or revolution, only moderation and diplomacy could do so; if it was disinclined to change policy in order to alleviate current Palestinian suffering, the United States could hardly be expected to do so. As early as the mid-1970s, U.S. policy had provided Arafat with a way to involve the PLO in a diplomatic process. He could either show a readiness to change the conflict's terms by meeting three conditions—recognizing Israel, accepting UN Resolutions 242 and 338, and rejecting terrorism—or he could choose pro- but non-PLO delegates to represent Palestinian interests.

A moderate strategy's requirements, however, clashed with the PLO's goals, structure, tactics, and rhetoric. For the PLO, anti-Americanism encompassed both anti-imperialist ideology and a reaction to the U.S.-Israel alliance. In 1968, Arafat claimed that Israel was a U.S. or Western "military base" established to ensure the Middle East remained "disunited and backward."[12] Almost two decades later, in 1986, he called the United States "the controlling force of neo-colonialism, imperialism, and racism [that] employs Israel to spearhead its strategy of domination in the Middle East."[13] There could be no rapprochement with an America trying to dominate and exploit the Middle East, using Israel as a tool and inevitably opposing Palestinian rights.

According to the Palestinian-American Palestine National Council (PNC) member Edward Said, an advocate of this determinist view, "the United States, as a government and as a society, [was] hostile to us." It was not an arbiter but "a party to the conflict." He urged the PLO to turn military defeat into political victory by dealing "with the United States the same way the Vietnamese dealt with Henry Kissinger in Paris."[14] This stance implied that the PLO could subvert domestic U.S. support for the client-state; erode U.S. willpower by protracted struggle; and make agreements, only to break them as soon as possible. On the other hand, the PLO wanted to split the American patron from its Israeli client. How could this be achieved if the United States was so irredeemably hostile? Arafat's solution was to force the United States to bend by virtue of PLO strength and persistence rather than to entice it to bend by changing PLO policy.

Thus, the PLO rejected completely such U.S. initiatives as the Camp David accords of 1978 and the Reagan plan of 1982, rather than seeking to develop them in a direction more to its liking. Although the organization was understandably angry at the failure of U.S. guarantees for the safety of Palestinians in Lebanon in 1982, it did benefit from U.S. safe conduct for its own withdrawal in 1982 and 1983. Nonetheless, the PLO often identified the United States as its chief enemy. The PLO, Arafat said, had fought bravely against a U.S.-directed attack, held Beirut for over two months, and yielded only because of a lack of Arab support.[15]

Despite the rejection of the Reagan plan by Israel's government, the PLO refused a chance to enter a process in which it could have worked to take over power in the territories during the transition period, gain U.S. support, and then propose itself as their rightful ruler. George Habash, leader of the Democratic Front for the Liberation of Palestine (DFLP) faction, called the Reagan plan a "political bomb no different from the cluster bombs which our fighters confronted bravely in Beirut." Na'if Hawatmah, leader of the PFLP faction, called it an "imperialist American-Zionist plan." Arafat, too, scorned the proposal. "I have not heard a single Palestinian say that he accepted Reagan's plan," said his ally Abu Iyad. He closed the 1983 PNC meeting by claiming Israel's invasion of Lebanon was a U.S. plot "to destroy the PLO" and that U.S. warships had convoyed Israeli troops there.

Was U.S. opposition to Palestinian rights so deeply entrenched? Or did the PLO fail to exploit opportunities to influence U.S. policy?[16] The PLO view of America as hostile was, in part, a self-fulfilling prophecy. The main reason the United States became the PLO's enemy was due to that organization's behavior and professed goals. During the long cold war decades, a PLO policy aligned with Moscow, prioritizing on armed struggle, employing terrorism even against U.S. citizens, and seeking to destroy Israel gave the United States no compelling political or strategic incentive to change, take risks, or weaken its own ally.[17]

Even Said thought that "negligence, corruption, and incompetence" damaged the PLO's attempt to improve its image in the United States.[18] It failed to take advantage of such elements in American political culture as sympathy for "underdogs" and support for self-determination. Moreover, an American tendency to attribute conflicts to misunderstanding or poor communication, rather than to clashing interests, created an expectation that proof of good intentions and concessions might transform enemies into friends. Even those journalists, experts or officials eager to recognize or exaggerate moderation from the PLO were denied evidence of its predicted "pragmatism" in recognizing Israel or stopping terrorism.

The PLO's transparently cynical approach to handling these issues during much of its history had a counterproductive effect on its credibility in the United States. Examples include the organization's handling of the Achille Lauro affair and Arafat's subsequent declaration in Cairo against international terrorism. U.S. Secretary of State George Shultz rejected Arafat's renunciation of "all terrorism except in Israel or the West Bank." "The U.S. government," said Ambassador for Counterterrorism L. Paul Bremer III, "has always considered politically motivated attacks against noncombatants anywhere (including Israel and the occupied territories) to be terrorism."[19] After Abu Jihad's assassination by Israel in 1988, Arafat claimed the U.S. government was planning to kill more PLO leaders, and he ordered attacks on U.S. citizens and facilities.[20]

Viewing U.S. patronage of Israel as inevitable and innate encouraged PLO leaders to believe that any attempt at negotiation, compromise, or moderation was useless. The extent of U.S. support for Israel, of course, was no mere illusion. Aside from a large, politically active Jewish community, such factors as memory of the Holocaust, Israeli assistance to U.S. interests, mutual opposition to Soviet influence and radical Arab states, and greater cultural proximity created positive public opinion toward Israel. A PLO newspaper contended in 1991 that pro-Israel forces "terrified all U.S. presidents of the past 40 years and became so strong that any state wanting to move closer to the White House and to enjoy its care and loans had to obtain Israeli approval first." Abu Iyad claimed in 1989 that Israel "to a large extent controls the United States." Hani al-Hasan said in 1990, "It is regrettable that a superpower . . . the greatest one at present, is governed by the Zionist lobby."[21]

The PLO Charter had defined Israel not as the result of Jewish nationalism but as a "base for world imperialism placed strategically in the midst of the Arab homeland to combat Arab liberation, unity, and progress . . . to secure continued imperialist robbery and exploitation of our country."[22] One of the PLO's leaders, Khalid al-Hasan, admitted in 1989, "We don't consider ourselves as fighting Jews but the U.S. military. Israel itself cannot do anything. And if Israel is left alone without this kind of military support we could have solved the problem long ago."[23] In 1993, he quoted an old antisemitic forgery to make the point: "As George Washington said, [Jews] cannot live except by sucking the blood of others. The Israeli political leadership is like a coward seeking protection from a strong man. . . . Israel is the United States' slave."[24]

By the late 1980s, the PLO was exploring an approach based on its longstanding idea that the United States was Israel's master. Now the view of Israel as a U.S. puppet was deemed a factor that might be turned to the PLO's advantage. Concluding that "nothing can get done in the region without the United States," Arafat sought serious talks with Washington by meeting its conditions for a dialogue in December 1988.[25] Instead of trying to defeat America, the PLO sought to both pressure it and woo it as a substitute for making peace with Israel. If, as Arafat explained, Israel merely did what America said, "peace is not in Israel's hand, but in the hand of the United States, because Israeli decision making is in Washington and not in Tel Aviv."[26]

PLO Executive Committee member 'Abdallah Hourani said, "the party that decides . . . is neither us nor Israel. It is the two superpowers and the [UN] Security Council's permanent member states." Nabil Sha'ath, a leading PLO moderate, insisted, "the United States is a realistic country. The longer the uprising continues and the wider Palestinian peace movements spread or gain supporters in the world, the more the United States is forced to change its line."[27]

The PLO believed that several factors would impel U.S. policy to accommodate itself to them. Especially important was the Intifada, whose extensive coverage in the U.S. media brought more sympathy for the Palestinians. In speech after speech, Arafat assured the Palestinians that a few more months of steadfastness and struggle would bring total victory. Muhammad Milhem, the PLO's coordinator with the Intifada, asserted, "The maintenance of the current PLO policy and the continuation of the PLO's firm strategy will force Israel and the United States to accept the Palestinian peace initiative."[28]

The PLO also thought its hand was strengthened by the end of the Iran-Iraq war—Arafat claimed that it would allow Arabs to "devote more of their attention to supporting the Palestinian people's cause"— and by the end of the cold war. Khalid al-Hasan suggested the latter event would undermine U.S. support for Israel: "When the Zionist entity becomes an obstacle in the vital American interests, Washington will be the first to jettison Israel." Farouq Qaddoumi, a PLO Executive Committee member, asserted, "International detente has diminished Israel's strategic value."[29]

But rather than subverting U.S.-Israel relations, the cold war's finish ended any American need to woo the PLO or Arab states away from the Soviet camp, extinguishing the old argument that only concessions to the PLO could prevent a pro-Moscow Middle East. Furthermore, while the United States knew that only an Israeli-Palestinian agreement could bring a breakthrough, the PLO believed that internal weaknesses and U.S. pressure would force Israel's withdrawal without requiring a clear and major revision of PLO policy, tactics, or goals.

From the PLO's standpoint, diplomatic progress was impeded by the fact that the United States and Israel rejected an independent Palestinian state and preferred dealing directly with West Bank and Gaza Palestinians rather than with the organization. It feared a permanent Israeli occupation might be hidden behind an offer of local autonomy. Yet these problems were not so insuperable as they might appear at first glance. Whatever reluctance the PLO's two enemies had shown to a fully independent state, they were open to a Palestinian federation with Jordan, which the PLO had officially accepted. In addition, the peace process was designed with an interim stage of self-rule in the territories, which the PLO could use in order to consolidate control, creating, step by step, an infrastructure that would ensure its own future rule and make any loosening of Israeli control an irreversible process.

At the same time, the PLO could have developed a strategy to strengthen the opposition Labor party's position in Israel while trying to weaken U.S.-Israel ties, by putting forward a serious peace initiative. Moreover, if the Palestinian people were as united behind the PLO as it claimed, the organization could certainly have negotiated through a screen of West Bank and Gaza Palestinians. This arrangement arguably had advantages for the PLO, since it would not have to make the concessions—ceasing armed struggle, for example—that would be necessary if it were to enter negotiations directly.

But the PLO did not act to defuse U.S. and Israeli suspicions deriving from its own acts and goals nor, even while moderating its stand, did it develop any such comprehensive strategy for advancing the process. Instead, it remained enamored of the idea that the United States and Israel could be defeated or outmaneuvered with the minimal modification of its own policies. The PLO was more concerned with proving itself to be an indispensable negotiating partner than an acceptable one. Palestinians easily rationalized their stands on the basis of historical and current injustice, but the result was that the PLO's approach was ineffective.[30]

The round of diplomacy between the United States and the PLO between 1988 and 1990 is a classic demonstration of the PLO's mixture of misperception and deliberate strategy. The PLO by now understood that to obtain U.S. recognition it had to appear flexible and moderate. "The days of indirect contacts with the United States are over," said Khalid al-Hasan in 1988. "They took us nowhere in the past twenty years."[31]

Indeed, the 1988 PNC meeting was dedicated to changing U.S. policy. In sharp contrast to the past, anti-Americanism was largely absent. But the effort to meet U.S. preconditions for dealing with the PLO came up against the leaders' own hesitancy to change their policy and risk splitting the organization. Thus, the PNC tried to give the impression that it was recognizing Israel, while not recognizing Israel; accepting UN Resolution 242, albeit with major qualifications; condemning terrorism, but with loopholes; and seeking a Palestinian state in the West Bank and Gaza only, though never actually saying so.[32]

The U.S. government was unconvinced by the PNC meeting's results, calling its resolution a step forward that was not yet satisfactory. And, the State Department still refused Arafat a visa to speak at the UN General Assembly in New York, identifying twenty-two PLO terrorist acts—some of them against U.S. citizens—carried out between the time of its 1985 declaration promising to stop international terrorism and March 1988.[33] When the General Assembly voted to convene a special session in Geneva to hear Arafat speak, the State Department secretly told Arafat that it would open a dialogue if he met the U.S. conditions in that talk. Arafat pledged to do so.

Thus, as the PLO leader mounted the podium on 13 December 1988, the U.S. government expected a breakthrough. Shultz scheduled a press conference to announce a U.S.-PLO dialogue; State Department officials settled down in front of a television, copies of the agreed-upon language in hand, to watch the performance. But Arafat again broke his promise, making a polemical speech instead of a conciliatory one. While a discouraged State Department noted "some positive developments" in the speech, Shultz canceled his press conference. One more long diplomatic effort was on the brink of failure. The following day, however, Arafat gave a press conference in which he accepted the American conditions.[34]

The PLO's leaders did not take full advantage of this opportunity. Arab and Palestinian factors pressured them against concessions. Moreover, PLO leaders erroneously assumed that Israel was a U.S. puppet that would do what Washington ordered. They seized on the dialogue, which was renewed despite the shortcomings of Arafat's speech, as a triumph to show its constituents that the Intifada was forcing a change in U.S. policy. Since the United States was being forced to give the Palestinians a state, the PLO did not have to convince Israel to do so. The Palestinian uprising, Iraq's victory over Iran, and other factors, Nabil Sha'ath claimed, "changed the balance in favor of the Palestinian cause." PLO broadcasts to the territories boasted, "The U.S. Administration has . . . been forced to cooperate with the PLO as the Palestinian people's sole representative.[35]

While the PLO now expected that the United States would meet its demands, the United States saw the opening of dialogue as merely the start of a negotiating process in which the PLO would have to prove its moderation and convince Israel that a solution with Arafat was possible. The U.S. government defined the new stage not as negotiations but as a constructive dialogue that would endure only if the PLO was seen to live up to Arafat's pledge in Geneva.

Arafat disagreed, claiming that the PLO had great leverage over the United States and that the Arabs held "99 percent" of the cards. This was a carefully chosen image. A decade earlier, Anwar Sadat had justified making peace with Israel through U.S. mediation by commenting that the United States held "99 percent" of the cards.[36] Rather than try to persuade Israelis that they could achieve peace and security by dealing with the PLO, Arafat argued that only Washington counted. Israel's decisions, he insisted, were made "in Washington and not in Tel Aviv." He recalled the 1956 Suez crisis, when Britain, France and Israel invaded Egypt but pulled back at President Dwight Eisenhower's insistence. "What happened when he ordered them to withdraw? They immediately withdrew." He expected Israel to do the same now, quickly and simply, from the West Bank and Gaza.[37]

The PLO feared that U.S., Israeli, or even Egyptian plans might split people in the territories from the PLO. PLO leaders now began complaining. "The Americans haven't done anything for us" and claimed that Washington was merely "stalling while waiting for the Intifada to die." Occasional U.S.-PLO meetings in Tunis between United States Ambassador Robert Pelletreau and a PLO delegation, however, were far less important than the efforts being made in Washington.

President George Bush's new administration took office in January 1989. "We are concerned," explained Secretary of State James Baker, that if we act too precipitously we might preempt promising possibilities." He wanted to find a way to address both "Israel's legitimate security needs and . . . the legitimate political rights of the Palestinian people." This involved a delicate balancing act to avoid losing either side's cooperation.[38]

The U.S. argued that Israel's May 1989 offer was a serious one that could break the deadlock in the peace process. U.S. officials lobbied for the plan with the PLO and West Bank and Gaza Palestinians. But to balance this position, the United States made gestures toward Palestinian political rights and indicated support for an eventual Israeli withdrawal from the occupied territories. To respond to one of the PLO's criticisms, Baker called on Israel to help find a "creative solution . . . to enable the participation of Palestinians who do not currently reside in the West Bank and Gaza Strip," and he urged that country to give up "the unrealistic vision of a greater Israel."[39]

In order to maintain the U.S.-PLO dialogue, the State Department bent over backward to avoid acknowledging any terrorism: it minimized the PLO membership of the smaller groups carrying out terror attacks, ignored evidence of continued terrorism by Fatah, and refused to define attempted attacks across the Lebanon-Israel border as terrorist on the grounds that their targets "were unclear," since Israel killed or captured the infiltrators before they were able to carry out their mission. Abu Iyad explained that while the PLO rejected the idea that the Intifada itself use arms, it wanted to escalate "the armed struggle away from the Intifada's areas but in interaction with it." In other words, the PLO could continue cross-border attacks. "We did not promise the Americans or others that we would stop the armed struggle," he claimed, in total denial of the basis of the U.S.-PLO dialogue. Terrorism in this perception meant only international operations; armed operations inside the territories or against Israel were permitted, even if they "affect civilians by mistake."[40] This was, of course, at odds with the commitment the United States thought Arafat made in 1988 in Geneva, where he stated that any group engaging in terror "shall be expelled from the PLO ranks."[41]

U.S.-Israel tension presented the PLO with an opportunity to divide Washington and Jerusalem further. Washington was about to support a UN resolution condemning Israeli settlements in the occupied territories in April 1990, but when the PLO and some Arab states kept demanding tougher language, the deal fell through. Similarly, the State Department promised Arafat to raise the level of the U.S.-PLO dialogue if he gave a temperate speech to the May 1990 UN session in Geneva. Instead, his talk was hardline.[42]

Finally, the 30 May attack on Israel's coast by a PLO member group could not be ignored by the United States.[43] When the PLO refused to criticize or punish the act, despite U.S. efforts to salvage the dialogue, the Bush administration felt compelled to suspend it on 20 June.

The PLO, however, was already deeply involved with Saddam Husain's drive for Arab leadership, which would lead to Iraq's August 1990 invasion of Kuwait. At a January 1991 Baghdad rally, a few days before fighting began, Arafat said that if the United States wanted war, "then I say welcome, welcome, welcome to war." "Iraq and Palestine," he continued, would be together, "side by side" in battle. In February he proclaimed, "If they want to have o-i-l, then they have to also take P-L-O," and he called for military attacks on Israel.[44]

The result of this strategy was another debacle for the PLO, again demonstrating that it could get nowhere except through negotiations, mutual compromise, and an agreement with Israel. "The Palestinians," an Arab writer said, "do not accept the proposition that, in the age of the people's right to self-determination, they should be singled out for denial of this right."[45] Yet they could not achieve this goal while denying it to Israel. By maintaining a hard line in doctrine and tactics, the PLO ensured that U.S. and Israeli policy excluded it, and exclusion became a rationale for preserving a hard line. To decide that it was ready to redefine the conflict was the PLO's central task in the 1990s.

When the PLO finally did accept the Rabin/Kissinger conditions, U.S. policy was helpful—if not always to the PLO's liking—in advancing negotiations and a process that would make possible a West Bank and Gaza Palestinian state. But the breakthrough required direct talks with Israel and acknowledgement that only Israel could make peace for itself. The theory that Israel was either America's puppet or master had to be abandoned. The outcome was an agreement with Israel, signed on the White House lawn, with a U.S. president as host and facilitator.[46]

Notes

1. *The Middle East,* June 1979, 14.
2. Malcolm Kerr, "American Middle East Policy: Kissinger, Carter and the Future," *Institute for Palestine Studies Paper* 14 (1980): 7-8, 27.
3. Edward Said, *The Palestine Question and the American Context* (Beirut: Institute for Palestine Studies, 1979), 17.
4. John Campbell, "The Middle East: A House of Containment Built on Shifting Sands," *Foreign Affairs* 60:3 (1981): 626.
5. David Lamb, *Los Angeles Times,* 14 July 1985; William E. Smith, "Plight of the Moderates," *Time,* 16 June 1986, 19.
6. Udo Steinbach, "The Iranian-Iraqi Conflict and its Impact Upon the 'Arc of Crisis,'" *Journal of South Asian and Middle East Studies* (summer 1983), 15. Robert Lacey, "Saudi Arabia: A More Visible Role," *The World Today* (January 1982): 11.
7. For a broader discussion of these issues, see the author's *Cauldron of Turmoil: America in the Middle East* (New York, 1992).
8. U.S. House of Representatives Foreign Affairs Committee, testimony, 6 March 1986.
9. Kerr, *American Middle East Policy,* 11. Its worst setback came from the revolution in non-Arab Iran, where the Arab-Israeli conflict was—at most—a marginal concern.
10. The PLO and radical regimes saw the USSR as a model for development, an enemy of the rulers against whom they rebelled, and an ally in achieving their ambitions. Nasir's alliance with Moscow took place shortly after the United States saved his regime in 1956, preventing its own allies—Britain, France, and Israel—from overthrowing him. The Soviet regional position was strongest in the early 1960s, when the Arab-Israel conflict was quiescent. Syria and Iraq sided with the USSR in exchange for its support against neighbors and such huge material benefits as virtually free loans, military advisers, and large amounts of arms.
11. Presidents only risk prestige and spend political capital when sensing a reasonable chance for success on a problem, given the number of other pressing or promising issues. As long as the PLO sought to destroy Israel through a

terrorist, anti-American strategy, there could be no settlement with the PLO, just as there could be none without it. Before engaging in any effort, commented Secretary of State George Shultz, "I should have at least a 0.1 probability of accomplishing something" *(Washington Post,* 6 January 1989). Shultz spoke from experience. In his 1982 Senate confirmation hearings, he made resolution of the conflict his top priority. But the PLO, Israel, Jordan, and others were less cooperative than he had been led to expect. U.S. mediation efforts in 1982-83, 1985-85, and 1988-90 ended in failure as both sides pulled back from private promises or public hints of flexibility. Progress was possible only when the parties in the dispute were ready to take the necessary steps. Otherwise, the United States had neither the stake nor ability to break the deadlock. For a history of U.S. policymaking, see the author's *Secrets of State: The State Department and The Struggle Over U.S. Foreign Policy* (New York: Oxford University Press, 1985), and William Quandt, *Peace Process* (Washington, D.C.: Brookings Institution, 1993).

12. *International Documents on Palestine* 1968 (Beirut, 1969), 301, 379. When Senator Robert Kennedy was assassinated by a Palestinian in 1968, Fatah claimed the killer "must undoubtedly have been a tool employed by world Zionism, by persons having political, personal or capitalistic interests, and by the American CIA."
13. Interview with Yasir Arafat, *Third World Quarterly* 8:2 (April 1986).
14. Interview with Yasir Arafat, *al-Anba* (Foreign Broadcast Information Service [FBIS], 19 October 1989, 1-8). For the PLO's response, see 'Abd al-Rabbu, *al-Quds al-Arabi,* 13 October 1989 (FBIS, 19 October 1989, 6).
15. Interview with Yasir Arafat, *Middle East,* May 1983; Khalid al-Hasan, *al-Madina,* 31 August 1982 (FBIS, 9 September 1982); Yasir Arafat, speech, Voice of Palestine (Aden), 8 September 1982 (BBC, *Survey of World Broadcasts,* 11 September 1982).
16. There were some cooperative contacts but these were largely non-political. In November 1973, PLO leaders held a secret meeting with deputy CIA director Vernon Walters in Morocco and promised not to attack Americans. Ali Hasan Salama, one of Black September's leaders, was the organization's liaison to the CIA. After about 1975, the PLO helped protect U.S. diplomats in Beirut. David Ignatius, *Wall Street Journal,* 10 February 1983; Lally Weymouth, "Andy Young Wasn't Alone," *Washington Post,* 4 June 1989. There were reportedly 35 meetings between U.S. diplomats and the PLO between 1978 and 1981 to discuss embassy security and the release of U.S. hostages in Iran but not political issues. U.S. Ambassador John Gunther Dean coordinated his travels with the PLO and Abu Jihad may have helped release 13 hostages from Teheran. The PFLP had assassinated U.S. Ambassador Francis Meloy in 1976.

Salama reportedly visited the United States to meet with CIA officials in 1976, early in the relationship.

17. Terrorism was a particular cause of friction. Even on the eve of the U.S.-PLO dialogue in 1988, the PLO was blocking the extradition from Greece of Muhammad Rashid for bombing a U.S. airliner and killing a passenger. Rashid's boss, Colonel Hawari, a close associate of Arafat, had been convicted in court for attacking U.S. targets including another bombing that killed four Americans, including an infant. The State Department denied Arafat himself a visa based on his direct involvement in attacks on Americans. Two years later, a terrorist act by a PLO member group, which the organization refused to denounce, destroyed the dialogue. See, for example, *Washington Post,* 3 March 1988.
18. Interview with Yasir Arafat, *al-Anba.*
19. L. Paul Bremer Jr., "Countering Terrorism, U.S. Policy in the 1980s and 1990s," George Washington University, 22 November 1988, typescript, 10-11.
20. *New York Times,* 22 February 1988; *Washington Post,* 11 May 1988.
21. Abd al-Bari Atwan, "Counter Storm?" *al-Quds al-Arabi,* 16 September 1991 (FBIS, 19 September 1991, 4). On Abu Iyad, see *Al-Madina,* 7 July 1989 (FBIS, 19 July 1989, 1); *al-Anba,* 12 April 1990 (FBIS, 19 April 1990, 5).
22. Y. Harkabi, *The Palestinian Covenant and its Meaning* (London, 1979), 73.
23. Interview with author, Tunis, 13 August 1989.
24. *Al-Quds al-Arabi,* 7 January 1993 (FBIS, 12 January 1993, 10).
25. FBIS, 28 December 1988, 1.
26. Edward Said, *The Palestine Question and the American Context,* 12; "Year-Old Palestinian Uprising Will Continue—Arafat," Reuters, 9 December 1988.
27. Voice of the PLO (Baghdad), 26 January 1989 (FBIS, 30 January 1989, 6); *al-Siyasa,* 30 January 1989 (FBIS, 1 February 1989, 4); *al-Dustur,* 17 November 1988 (FBIS, 17 November 1988, 4).
28. *Al-Anba,* 19 September 1989 (FBIS, 22 September 1989, 7).
29. Matti Steinberg, "The Pragmatic Stream of Thought within the PLO According to Khalid al-Hasan," *Jerusalem Journal of International Relations* 11:1 (1989); *al-Qabas,* 3 October 1989 (FBIS, 5 October 1989, 2).
30. *Al-Akhbar,* 22 September 1989, 3 and 8 (FBIS, 25 September 1989, 1-5). *Al-Ra'y,* 10 October 1989, 1 and 16 (FBIS, 11 October 1989, 4-6).
31. *Le Monde,* 1 July 1988.
32. Key sources for the Palestinian National Council Resolution were the September 1982 Fez Arab summit resolution, printed in Walter Laqueur and Barry Rubin, *The Israel-Arab Reader* (New York: Viking-Penguin, 1990), 663-65; Yasir Arafat, speech to the June 1988 Arab summit, text, FBIS, 10 June 1988, 6.

33. *Washington Post,* 25 October 1988; Interview, Voice of Lebanon, 3 December 1987 (FBIS, 4 December 1987, 3-6); *Washington Post,* 4 and 5 January 1989 and 1 March 1989; Bremer speech, "Countering Terrorism," 10-11. On PLO attacks just prior to the PNC meeting, see also *Los Angeles Times,* 25 October and 14 November 1988.
34. Text, Voice of the PLO (Baghdad), 15 December 1988 (FBIS, 15 December 1988, 3); *New York Times,* 14 December 1988.
35. Voice of the PLO (Baghdad), 16 October 1989 (FBIS, 17 October 1989, 6).
36. FBIS, 25 January 1989, 4; *al-Musawwar,* 19 January 1990. Sadat's comment, 17 February 1977, *International Documents on Palestine,* 1977 (Beirut, 1978), 329.
37. Voice of Palestine (Algiers), 9 March 1989 (FBIS, 21 March 1989, 11).
38. *New York Times,* 12 and 22 February, 11, 14, and 16 March 1989; *Washington Times,* 16 February 1989; *Washington Post,* 24 February and 2 May 1989.
39. *New York Times,* 31 March and 7 April, 24 and 28 May, and 25 and 30 June 1989; *Washington Post,* 24 May and 29 June 1989; *Washington Times,* 8 June and 19 July 1989.
40. *Al-Tadamun,* 5 February 1990 (FBIS, 5, 1990, 5-6). For a similar statement by Abu Iyad, see *al-Thawra,* 22 April 1989, 2 (FBIS, 25 April 1989, 4).
41. Reuters, "Guerrillas Killed as Radicals Keep up Attacks on Israel," 2 March 1989.
42. See, for example, Algiers Television, 22 March 1990 (FBIS, 23 March 1990, 4, 6).
43. *Washington Post,* 28 August 1990.
44. *Jordan Times,* 23 February 1991; *New York Times,* 21 January 1991. See also Barry Rubin, "The United States and Iraq" and "The PLO and Iraq" in Amatzia Baram and Barry Rubin, *Iraq: Politics, History, Prospects* (New York: St. Martin's Press, 1994).
45. Muhammad al-Hallaj, director of the Institute of Arab Studies, cited in Cheryl Rubenberg, *The Palestine Liberation Organization, Its Institutional Infrastructure* (Belmont, Mass.: Institute of Arab Studies, 1983), 1-2.
46. *New York Times,* 15 September 1993; *Congressional Quarterly,* 18 September 1993, 2469-71.

PART III

The Rise and Influence of Local Activists

NINE

Mental Health Challenges for the Palestinian Authority:

The Psycho-Political Legacy of the Intifada

Eyad El Sarraj

The psycho-political or psycho-social aspects of the Intifada are a broad topic. I will try here to highlight some of the important points that I observed as a clinician in Gaza during the course of the Intifada and shortly thereafter, regarding the responses of the Palestinians in Gaza to the uprising and their responses to the changes of today.

My experience on 18 May 1994, when the last Israeli soldiers left Gaza, illustrates one dynamic. At three A.M. I was awakened by a hail of bullets that sounded like a hundred machine guns next to my house. The people were celebrating the withdrawal of the Israeli forces from the military headquarters of Gaza. I joined the celebration, but with skepticism because I was not very happy with the Cairo agreement myself. Yet in the middle of the crowds I felt the jubilation and it was very therapeutic. Everyone was hugging and kissing; everyone was enjoying the freedom of no more Israeli soldiers in Gaza town. Since then, for the first time in 27 years, the Gazans could go to the beach at night. People could now spread their blankets on the beaches and stay until the very early morning. People were enjoying this time and some could not believe their eyes and these hours. Some felt they should take advantage before the Israelis came back!

With the withdrawal of the Israeli forces from parts of Gaza and the West Bank, the people began to feel safe, gradually identifying themselves with the Palestinian police force. This is a significant phenomenon since many had expressed their concern that the Palestinian police force would adopt oppressive and brutal means to assert its authority. But on the contrary, what emerged was a situation in which the people have begun to assist the police force in protecting the public against thieves, robbers, and delinquents in the streets. These are hopeful signs that the Palestinian people will actively participate in the building of a Palestinian society. But the road ahead will not be easy.

The Palestinian community has been devastated as the result of twenty-seven years of occupation. Extremely stressful circumstances have characterized day-to-day life during the years under occupation. This was exacerbated during the six years of the Intifada. The chronic stress experienced by many has been caused not only by adverse economic factors but, more importantly, by the occupation and Israel's policies of humiliation, harassment, intimidation, and detention.

During the Intifada, these policies became widespread, putting the whole community, both individually and collectively, in an acute state of anxiety. Approximately 12 percent of the adult population of Gaza suffers from anxiety reactions that call for intervention, and approximately 15 percent suffer from anxiety requiring counselling.[1]

Palestinian society is patriarchal; it is dominated by the father and father figure and retains a strong tribal identity. We can even say that to some extent its political organizations, those that comprise the PLO as well as the Islamic movements, have been run according to tribal identity. Instead of promoting a kind of national identity, these political groups formed during the Intifada came to replace the tribes in the Palestinian society and the authority of the family. They held authority—any authority—in disdain and with total disregard. These groups took control of the streets and encouraged the people to defy all forms of authority, including their families and schools. Those who joined were encouraged to conform to the ideas and regulations of the groups, and no one was allowed to interfere—neither family nor any other party. Political organizations were spearheaded by armed groups such as Fatah's vigilante "Hawks" and people wanted and pursued by the Israeli forces.

The challenge of the Palestinian authority is to deal with these groups that now face difficulties. With the changing political situation, the groups have begun searching for a new role to play. The police force has attempted to integrate them by recruiting their members and providing them with training. Many, however, have found it difficult to conform to this new form of imposed discipline and have already deserted.

If they do not join the police force these groups look for other means to remain active. When they do join the police, other problems emerge. Most members of these organizations have been either victimized or traumatized. Once they are placed in a position of authority, they are highly likely to abuse in turn and exercise a type of authority that verges on the oppressive. This is an issue the Palestinian leadership must address.

The relationship between the Palestinians and the state authority has always been characterized by alienation. Palestinians have never had their own Palestinian rulers. They have, throughout history, always been alienated from the authority and the state; from the Turks to the British to the Egyptians, and finally to the Israelis. The situation in the West Bank before 1967 differed slightly from that in Gaza because most of the Jordanians were of Palestinian origin.

The Palestinians in the occupied territories could not identify themselves with public places or with anything that belonged to the government or the civil service. The prevalent feeling was that if it belonged to "them," then it didn't belong to "us"; my house belongs to me, but the streets do not. This feeling of alienation from state authority has meant that Palestinians have learned to excel in manipulating the system. The risk, however, is that this pattern will lead to corruption and further alienation from authority. Exploiting corruption within the Israeli system, common during the occupation, inevitably influenced Palestinian norms—there were many incidents in which Israeli officers were caught taking bribes offered by Palestinians.

The Palestinian people's relationship with the PLO differs quite markedly from that pattern of alienation from public authority. Yasir Arafat was always viewed as a father figure and major symbol for the Palestinians. However, the relationship was a skewed one, based more on romantic notions than on a sense of partnership.[2] Arafat was always that distant lover who could not be met or held. Such a relationship built on an illusion is, of course, abnormal. In becoming a local leader, Yasir Arafat has encountered the need to reassess and change his perception of the Palestinians. This is crucial if he is genuinely interested in state building and developing a political leadership based on democratic principles. Inevitably, as this process occurs, his relationship with the Palestinian people will be transformed.

The Palestinian people have always felt victimized; they view the outside world as the source and reason for their victimization. They feel helpless, and often this helplessness translates itself into despair, cycles of defiance, anger and despair again. It is a vicious circle. The fatalistic attitude toward justice that derives from a feeling of helplessness can lead to fanaticism, for once one becomes fatalistic, one begins to believe that a religious ideology is needed to help construct personal concepts of life and the hereafter. This fatalistic attitude often leads to extremism.[3] Despair and helplessness, widespread in Gaza, especially among the young, are important reasons for the increased strength of the Islamic movement there.

The Intifada was, to a certain degree, a defiant cry against all forms of authority. This included the authority of the family, the school, and most of all, that of the Israeli occupation. Many of the young identified this authority as the cause of their personal malaise, and they heeded the national call for liberation. In an attempt to liberate themselves on a personal level, they were assisting in liberating the nation and the country.

During the first two years of the Intifada, and after the initial confrontations with the Israelis, the Palestinians began to feel a kind of moral victory over the Israelis. This was a significant development in the history of the Palestinians. It produced a sort of ecstasy that helped prepare the psychological platform for Yasir Arafat to embark on his peace initiative in 1988. He recognized Israel and renounced violence, which, for the Palestinians, was a new kind of victory. It was the first time that they accepted recognition of the state of Israel. Only as a result of the initial triumph produced by the onset of the Intifada could the Palestinians feel that peace was now equal to victory. This was an important transformation; a decade earlier the Palestinians had rejected the Camp David accords because then peace had meant defeat to them.

The Israelis, on the other hand, rejected the PLO's offer in 1988 because they considered it a form of defeat for themselves. In contrast, after Israel's victory in 1967, Defense Minister Moshe Dayan said that he was prepared to relinquish all the land it had just occupied and sign a peace treaty with the neighboring states. He was victorious and was prepared to return all the land. The Israelis, who long felt that talking to the PLO was a form of treason, are now returning the occupied territories to the same PLO that for many years was an anathema to them. Now it is the Palestinians who are skeptical about the peace process. This is because they have lost their sense of victory.

When considering the victimization of the Palestinians, it is important to take into account the trauma experienced as a result of the state-organized violence that the Israeli forces perpetrated against them. This included a policy of systematic collective and individual punishment. A study conducted by the Gaza Community Mental Health Program on the children of Gaza (nearly 3,000 of them) found that 85 percent of the houses in Gaza were raided by the Israeli soldiers at one time or another. Nearly 55 percent of the children had witnessed the beating of their fathers and watched while they helplessly collapsed in front of their very eyes.[4]

The trauma intensified the Palestinians' sense of victimization. After the first two years of the Intifada, they began to feel dispirited. And in despair, they began using arms against the Israelis. But the Israelis had begun, for the first time, to view the Palestinians as the victims. The Israelis had always believed themselves to be the only and eternal victims, surrounded by an ocean of hatred and people wanting to kill them and throw them into the sea. And of course they have reasons for this belief. They also always viewed the Palestinians as the aggressors. Only during the early part of the Intifada did this perception begin to change. Palestinians were no longer the aggressors; now they were viewed as the victims as well. Many people within Israel (including members of Imut—the Israeli mental health workers for peace, who visited Gaza—and the Palestinian-Israeli Physicians for Human Rights) started to condemn the occupation as corrupt—as *morally* corrupting the Israelis—and harmful to the peace cause.

The adoption of armed struggle by the Palestinians transformed this image again and damaged the spirit of the Intifada. Armed, the Palestinians no longer presented an image of victim. The Intifada became a form of armed struggle dictated from above in which the general population did not have a role to play. A few armed people belonging to underground groups controlled the situation. The Intifada was in a sense taken away from the masses who helped the spontaneity of the uprising during its first years. Once it was transformed into a dictated form of calculated action, and people were forced to follow orders, those who did not obey found themselves at risk of punishment. In the last two years of the Intifada, many Palestinians became disillusioned and exasperated by it.

The future remains complicated. Beyond the economic factors and the challenging relationship between the people and the authority, the Palestinians lack many of the elements necessary for successful nation building. As I have described, this is a nation that is traumatized. A large sector of the population was imprisoned for many years, many of whom were systematically tortured. Their numbers reach tens of thousands. These people are expected to be the future generation of leaders, but they have suffered so much themselves that they require a long process of rehabilitation to prepare them for that role. Many of the children were deprived of a proper education or lost many years when they were unable to attend schools. They must be reeducated and rehabilitated.[5]

The civil servants, now numbering approximately seven thousand, were trained during the past twenty-seven years of occupation to perform as slaves. They were not allowed to make decisions because the Israeli officers were the ones in control of budgets and ultimate decision making powers. I speak here from experience because I was part of the administration for health services. That body is like a body without a head. Now they need heads; heads that are professional and able to make decisions.

Women have been the ultimate victims of violence, particularly in the male-dominated society of the Palestinians. They took on much of the burden, particularly with their husbands imprisoned. When their husbands are released, their wives are the perfect target for their anger and aggression.[6] And of course, other recipients of this rage are the children. In the process, the children are traumatized and subjected to new forms of abuse. Those abused children will in turn transmit their trauma to their own children in the future. Therefore, the trauma of the Palestinian people needs to be addressed first and foremost. Much preventive work is required to rehabilitate most of the population.

Finally, there is the question of the democratization of the Palestinian society. It will be a difficult process since people reached their lowest point. They were forced to think only of the basics of survival—food and security. They are not concerned with the question of democracy as an intellectual concept at the moment; they are preoccupied with more crucial issues. However, democracy is the next struggle in which they will need to engage in order to facilitate the rebuilding of society and to assist in the evolution of a new kind of leadership. Only through democracy can the Palestinians find the right track.

Notes

1. Qouta, S., El Sarraj, E. (1993). "Level of Anxiety in Gaza before and after the Intifada," *Journal of Psychological Studies,* 3:1 (1993): 1-11.
2. El Sarraj, E. "The Palestinian People Will Not Accept Anything Short of Freedom and True Democracy," *Al-Quds,* 21 June 1994.
3. El Sarraj, E. "The PLO-Israeli Handshake: A View from Gaza." *Mind and Human Interaction,* 5:2 (May 1994): 51-5.
4. Abu Hein, F., Qouta, S., Thabet, A., & El Sarraj, E. "Trauma and Mental Health of Children in Gaza," *British Medical Journal* (1993): 306, 1129.
5. Qouta, S., Punamaki, R. L., & El Sarraj, E. "The Relations between Traumatic Experiences, Activity and Cognitive and Emotional Responses among Palestinian Children," *International Journal of Psychology,* (1995): 30, 289-304.
6. Matar, S. "A Study of Women in the Gaza Strip Affected by Violence," Gaza Community Mental Health Programme (GCMHP), 1994.

TEN

INSIDE VERSUS OUTSIDE
THE CHALLENGE OF THE LOCAL LEADERSHIP, 1967-1994

MEIR LITVAK

THE RELATIONS BETWEEN THE PLO—"the Exterior" or "outside" *(al-kharij)* in Palestinian terminology—and local leadership groups in the West Bank and the Gaza Strip— "the Interior" or "inside" *(al-dakhil)*— has been characterized by mutual dependence and suspicion throughout most of the period since the 1967 war.[1] In analyzing these relations, I argue that although the importance of the Interior as a pressure group in Palestinian politics grew continuously, reaching its apex during the Intifada, and even though the Intifada was largely an expression of frustration with the PLO, the Interior could not endanger the supremacy of the Exterior due to persistent structural factors. A comparison of the Palestinian situation with similar cases of national liberation movements will shed further light on these factors.

The PLO's main constituency and power base was until the late 1980s the 1948 Palestinian diaspora. In contrast, the majority of the population in the territories, particularly in the West Bank, had not undergone the same social dislocation as the diaspora. Consequently, while the two communities shared a common national solidarity and long-term aspirations, they differed in their short-term priorities. The diaspora's main interest was to reverse the consequences of the 1948 war, while the first concern of the Interior was to reverse the effects of the 1967 war, even at the cost of postponing a solution to the 1948 problem. Localist allegiances and the desire of local elite groups to maintain a measure of autonomous decision making have added to this division.

As an organization based in the diaspora, it was of utmost importance for the PLO to achieve a position of decisive influence in the territories, where the fate of the Palestinian problem was to be decided after 1967, and in order to justify its claim to represent the entire Palestinian people. The PLO relied on Arab political and material support and legitimation, as well as on its own ideological appeal, to attain this goal. In addition, it channeled funds to the territories so as to acquire influence, and occasionally resorted to violence and assassinations against its opponents.

However, the failure of Fatah and other Palestinian guerrilla groups to shift their base of operations to the territories meant that the PLO remained an external factor to the territories. Since Fatah and most other Palestinian organizations stressed armed struggle, political initiatives were left to local elements, which set up the various leadership bodies in the territories, presenting the PLO with a fait accompli. For its part, the PLO could not allow the latter to emerge as an alternative leadership to the organization itself.[2] As Hillel Frisch has pointed out, it was essential for the PLO to maintain its status as the Palestinian political and spiritual center, and keep the territories in the status of political periphery, which should follow the center's cue.[3]

The emergence of an independent leadership in the territories after 1948 was impeded by internal and external factors. Both Jordan and Israel banned area-wide political institutions as well as open political party activity.[4] In addition, Israel often deported local elements who led active opposition to its rule. A growing sense of vulnerability to Israel and the region's economic dependence on outside forces had induced local leadership groups to turn to outsiders for political leadership. Equally important, the deep divisions in Palestinian society had a debilitating effect on the leadership structure.

The local leadership was always under suspicion that it might surrender the long-term national goals of the Palestinians in return for securing the narrower interests of the territories' inhabitants by getting rid of Israeli rule. Consequently, local leadership groups never considered themselves—nor were they ever regarded, either inside or outside the territories—as a national leadership entitled to make major political decisions or represent the Palestinian people on the national level.

The outcome of this constellation was that all major political decisions regarding the Palestinian position vis-à-vis Israel were taken by the Exterior. The leadership of the periphery could exert pressure on the center, but it could not take an independent political course of action opposed to that of the PLO. Concurrently, the PLO's ability to determine developments in the territories was limited, the most celebrated case being the Intifada, which broke out spontaneously.

During the period 1967-94, the PLO had to grapple with four leadership groups in the territories that presented different types of challenges to the organization: (1) the traditional, pro-Jordanian elite; (2) the nationalist, pro-PLO elite; (3) the PLO organizational leadership; and (4) the Hamas leadership.

The PLO and Traditional Leadership, 1967-1973

The aura of guerrilla warfare after the defeat of the Arab armies in the 1967 war launched the Palestinian organizations as major political players in the Palestinian arena, but the PLO's status in the territories was still disputed. The three leadership bodies that emerged in 1967—the Islamic Council (IC; *al-Hay'a al-Islamiyya)*, the Higher National Guidance Committee (HNGC) in the West Bank, and the Unified National Front (UNF) in Gaza—were all set up by local initiative and encompassed members from both the traditional pro-Jordanian urban elites and from the radical opposition.[5]

Although they did not openly challenge the PLO, these leadership bodies offered an alternative course to that of the organization by stressing political action rather than armed struggle. More important, they called for the restoration of the *status quo ante* rather than for the establishment of an independent Palestinian state. In other words, while the traditional elite maintained a pro-Jordanian line, even the radical elites had not internalized the PLO's ideology of particularist Palestinian nationalism but still adhered to previous pan-Arab ideas.[6]

The political activity of the IC and HNGC wound down after Israel had deported several of their most prominent activists in the course of 1968-69. Neither did the HNGC and the UNF control sufficient organizational resources to perpetuate their struggle. Jordan, for its part, transformed the IC by administrative means into a bureaucratic rather than a political institution.[7]

The proposals to establish an independent Palestinian state in the territories, which were raised separately by lawyer 'Aziz Shehadeh, physician Hamdi Taji al-Faruqi, and the mayor of Hebron, Shaykh

Muhammad ʿAli al-Jaʿbari, in July-September 1967, challenged basic Palestinian ideological tenets, and those of the PLO in particular, by focusing on the territories and, explicitly, on accepting a settlement with Israel.[8] While Israel was cool in its response, the proposals were rejected by the vast majority of the politically active public in the territories, let alone by Jordan and the PLO. Yet the Palestinian organizations felt so insecure at even the slightest challenge to their interests that they felt obliged to resort to open threats and intimidations against the three men.[9]

The PLO's weakness following its 1970-71 debacle in Jordan was manifested in its failure to prevent the 1972 municipal elections in the territories. PLO leaders attacked Israel's decision to hold elections as legitimizing Israeli occupation, and as an attempt to create "fraudulent representation" of the Palestinian people.[10] The elections took place in the spring of 1972, following strong Israeli pressure, with a relatively high voter turnout.[11] The PLO's resort to condemnations of and open threats against candidates indicated further that it did not have sufficient moral authority to impose its will.

Yet the traditional elite failed to pose a long-term challenge to the PLO due to a series of developments: (1) the PLO's rising fortunes following the 1973 war and the subsequent Algiers and Rabat summits, where it was recognized by the Arab states as the sole representative of the Palestinian people, boosted its status and seriously undermined Jordan's position in the territories; (2) the continued Israeli occupation intensified the politicization and radicalization of the Palestinian population, which enhanced Palestinian identity and strengthened the PLO's popularity at Jordan's expense; (3) land, capital, and patronage, the major sources of power of the traditional elite lost part of their importance in light of the economic changes in the territories;[12] (4) employing traditional modes of operation such as patronage and family links, the traditional elite failed to establish grassroots organizations or articulate any ideology or political platform that could mobilize substantial social groups behind them.

THE PLO AND THE NATIONALIST ELITE

The PLO's predicament during 1971-73 prompted it to focus its efforts on securing Arab recognition of its status as sole legitimate representative of the Palestinian people. This shift enhanced the importance of the territories, which were internationally perceived as the core area of the Palestinian problem. Hence it was essential for the PLO to secure the allegiance of the population in the territories behind the organization.[13] Reflecting this new policy, the tenth and eleventh sessions of the Palestine National Council (PNC) in April 1972 and January 1973 called on the organization to "mobilize" the masses in the territories and "set up a joint Palestinian-Jordanian national front to act as a PLO guided framework for all the nationalist forces operating in the territories."[14]

The establishment of the Palestinian National Front (PNF) in August 1973, on the initiative of the Palestinian Communist Organization of the Jordanian Communist Party (JCP), marked the emergence of the nationalist pro-PLO elite as the major force in the territories. Many members of this new elite owed their position to nationalist activity in municipalities or civilian associations, as well as to affilation with prominent families, and thus felt relatively self-assured in their dealings with the PLO. The nationalist elite actively supported the PLO as the national leadership, but the frictions that emerged between the elite and the organization reflected the overall problematic relations between these two sectors of the Palestinian people.

Fatah's main concern was that the PNF would develop into an independent or even an alternative leadership to the PLO. These fears were accentuated by the dominant role in the PNF played by the communists, who had not been part of the PLO and maintained primary loyalty to the Soviet Union, as well as by Soviet efforts to bolster the PNF at the PLO's expense.[15]

Consequently, whereas Fatah demanded the clear subordination of the PNF to the PLO Executive Committee (EC), the PNF desired a division of labor in which the PLO would carry out armed struggle and be responsible for the strategic and international spheres, while the PNF would be in charge of political activity and mobilization in the territories with a measure of autonomous decision making.[16] A corollary disagreement arose over the PNF's request to be the exclusive link between the PLO and the territories, whereas the PLO wanted it to be just one among several channels for its activity in the territories.[17] Fatah also objected to its inferior position inside the PNF vis-à-vis the communists.[18]

The PLO frowned on the PNF's calls to incorporate the Interior in the formulation of the general Palestinian strategy and in PLO leadership bodies. Israeli prohibitions, however, foiled the PNF's hopes for the participation of delegates from the territories in the PNC's discussion in 1974. But the PLO consented to include in the PNC the eight PNF leaders deported in December 1974. Once in exile, these leaders were deemed more dependent on the Exterior leadership and could be expected to share its views. Arafat agreed to include only nationalist PNF members in the EC, while excluding the independent-minded communists.[19]

The PNF also sought to influence the PLO to adopt a more pragmatic political approach vis-à-vis Israel, in line with the communist concept of the conflict, and possibly also reflecting the more urgent needs of the inhabitants of the territories.[20] It would be wrong, however, to attribute the PLO's 1974 endorsement of the phased plan primarily to such pressures. Rather, the PLO's fears of Jordan's gaining a foothold in the West Bank following an agreement with Israel, and the organization's awareness of the necessity to resort to political means of struggle under the changing political circumstances in the region, had been more important factors.

With its position enhanced after the 1974 Rabat summit, the PLO demanded that the PNF limit its activities to the signing of the memoranda in support of PLO policies and against anti-PLO activities. Moreover, in 1975, Fatah elements went so far as to call for the establishment of a new Palestinian front to be dominated by Fatah.[21]

The PNF suffered a serious setback following the deportation of eight of its leaders in December 1973 and the arrest of several hundred activists in May 1974. It was also weakened by the primary loyalty of its components, aside from the communists, to their external parent organizations rather than to the Front itself.[22] The 1976 municipal elections brought about the final demise of the traditional pro-Jordanian leadership in the territories and its replacement by the pro-PLO nationalist elite. Israel's decision to hold the elections and the consequent relaxation of its policy provided the PNF with the opportunity to recover and to set up "national blocs" in most West Bank towns, while the PLO maintained a cautious position in light of its previously held misgivings concerning the rise of a strong local leadership.[23]

The pro-PLO mayors repeatedly declared their allegiance to the PLO and their adamant refusal to emerge as an alternative to it. Concurrently, most of them did perceive their roles as political in addition to municipal, since they conveyed the position of the Palestinians in their support of the PLO and opposition to various Israeli measures, and their views were recognized by the Israeli military government and media. Several of the mayors exerted considerable efforts to solicit financial aid in the oil states, without resorting to the PLO's mediation.[24]

The 1978 Camp David accords, which threatened to exclude the PLO from a settlement of the Palestinian problem, compelled the organization to resort to the local leadership in order to thwart the accords. Concurrently, the PLO did not shy away from assassinations as a means to deter the limited support for the accords in the territories. As in past cases, however, local opposition to the Camp David accords did not require external prodding, taking advantage of greater Israeli tolerance toward political activity at the time. The National Guidance Committee (NGC) was established, following a conference in the West Bank village of Beit Hanina on 1 October 1978, as a coordinating and leadership body against the Camp David accords. It consisted of twenty-two members, including nine mayors and representatives of various organized corporate and regional interests. The NGC was, as researcher Hillel Frisch has pointed out, a charismatic body, since its authority was not based on an organizational infrastructure or on direct subordination to the PLO but on the prestige of its members.[25] That was also a source of weakness, since the NGC lacked a widespread institutional infrastructure and the resources to withstand Israeli suppressive measures against it. For such resources, it needed the Exterior's support.

Their common opposition to the Camp David accords notwithstanding, the frictions between the PLO and the PNF—which was reactivated in 1979—and NGC resembled those that had existed with the first PNF, namely: (1) the extent of the Exterior's control over internal affairs in the territories; (2) the power struggle between Fatah and the leftist factions, which dominated both bodies (unlike previous leadership bodies, the reactivated PNF resulted from a joint effort by the Exterior PFLP and DFLP factions in alliance with radical groupings in the territories to forge an instrument to limit Fatah's power in the territories);[26] (3) disagreement over the emphasis on political mobilization, which Fatah wanted, as opposed to combining it with grassroots institution building, as advocated by the Left.[27]

These tensions came into the open on several occasions during 1979-80, reflecting the limits of power of each side. The NGC shared the opposition of the PLO Left to the joint Jordanian-Palestinian committee, which had been established following the 1978 Baghdad summit, labeling it as a tool serving Jordan's interests at the expense of the PLO and accusing it of ignoring the real needs of the population. It demanded, therefore, that a new committee be set up under the sole chairmanship of the PLO that would establish clear guidelines for the distribution of funds.[28] Fatah joined hands with Jordan in appointing Anwar Nusseibeh as the chairman of the Jerusalem Electric Company in January 1979, despite protests from West Bank mayors. And, seeking to deter Israel from deporting mayor Shak'a of Nablus in November 1979, most mayors threatened to resign collectively, ignoring Fatah's directive to the contrary.[29] In other words, the Interior failed to change the PLO's positions or actions, but it could defy the PLO in matters it deemed crucial to itself.

As in previous cases, Israeli policy undercut the potential challenge the Interior could pose to the Exterior. Following the appointment of Ariel Sharon as defense minister in June 1981, Israel sought to forcibly uproot PLO influence in the territories. During 1982 twelve radical mayors were dismissed from their posts by the Israeli administration. On 11 March 1982 the NGC itself was officially banned. Sharon's attempt to cultivate a more malleable rural leadership in the form of the Village Leagues, as opposed to the pro-PLO urban leadership, failed when both Jordan and the PLO came out against them.[30] The suppression of the public pro-PLO leadership in 1982 created a political vacuum that enabled the youth and student organizations to become the dominant political factor in the territories.

The PLO and the "Organizational Leadership"

During the late 1970s Fatah sought to coopt various grassroots organizations and "national" institutions *(al-mu'assasat al-wataniyya)* in the territories. These institutions were designed to enhance the steadfastness of Palestinian society against Israel and to mobilize it behind the PLO, in addition to serving as an infrastructure for the future Palestinian state. After 1981 Fatah went further, setting up its own organizations, the most important of which was the youth movement *Lijan al-Shabiba lil-'Amal al-Ijtima'i* (youth committees for social action) known as *al-Shabiba.* Fatah also set up its own trade union, after splitting the communist-dominated movement. The Democratic Front for the Liberation of Palestine (DFLP), the Popular Front for the Liberation of Palestine (PFLP), and the Palestine Communist Party (PCP)[31] created their own parallel organizations. The top echelons of the national institutions were called "organizational leadership" *(qiyadat tanzimiyya).*[32]

Unlike the mayoral leadership, which represented the cities and large towns, this new leadership, which encompassed a large variety of organizations spread throughout the territories, represented diverse sectors of society and cut across all social classes. Moreover, the expansion of the national institutions, largely thanks to funds made available by the PLO, provided employment opportunities and a channel for upward social mobility to many high school and university graduates from the rural regions and the lower classes.[33] The new leadership was not structured hierarchically in the territories as a whole, nor did it function as a cohesive body like the PNF and NGC. Rather, it resembled a loose amalgamation of parallel organizations and cadres. This decentralized structure enabled it to weather arrests or deportations of individual members by the Israeli authorities, since it could replenish itself and thus enjoy organizational continuity. Concurrently, this leadership was less threatening to the PLO leadership than such charismatic bodies as the NGC, since it derived its influence and legitimacy from its affiliation with the external PLO factions. The only exception was the PCP, whose leadership and main source of power were inside the territories.[34]

The loss of the PLO's state-within-a-state in Lebanon following the 1982 Israeli invasion appeared to shift the balance of power away from the PLO to the territories. The dispersion of the PLO forces in several Arab countries marked the bankruptcy of the strategy of armed struggle and left the political option as the only viable one for the Palestinians. With the loss of effective control over almost all diaspora centers, the Interior remained the only constituency the PLO could hope to mobilize. In addition, the support of the Interior strengthened Arafat's claim to represent the Palestinian people against counterclaims by Fatah's rebels.

Frustration with the failure of the PLO's ethos of armed struggle and with Arafat's *la'am* (yes and no) policy, which appeared futile, led to a significant rise in acts of mass disorder and civil disobedience in the territories. More important, loss of hope that the PLO could liberate Palestine propelled the rise of the Islamic movement as a major force in the territories, particularly in the Gaza Strip. The PLO's predicament reached a symbolic apex during the 1987 Arab summit in Amman, when Arafat was personally humiliated by King Husain, and the Palestinian issue was relegated to second-place priority behind the Iran-Iraq war. Both events were among the immediate triggers for the Intifada.

The PLO and the Intifada Leadership

The outbreak of the Intifada on 9 December 1987 was a spontaneous event that was neither initiated nor led by the PLO. Moreover, it was partly an expression of frustration with respect to the PLO's failure to relieve the Interior from Israeli rule.[35] For the first time since 1948, the center of gravity of the Palestinian struggle against Israel had shifted from the Exterior to the Interior. Consequently, the Intifada seemed to free the Interior from a sense of marginality vis-à-vis the PLO, raising the possibility of a qualitative change in the relationship between the two parties.

Local DFLP activists took the initiative for setting up a leadership body, later called the Unified National Leadership of the Intifada (UNL, *al-Qiyada al-Wataniyya al-Muwahhada lil-Intifada*), in order to transform the spontaneous demonstrations into a permanent and organized mass uprising. The Exterior PLO leadership sanctioned its establishment only retroactively.

Unlike the PNF and NGC, the UNL was composed not of well known public figures, but of members of the "organizational leadership" on the basis of the coordinating committee of the four largest PLO factions in Jerusalem: Fatah, the DFLP, the PFLP, and the PCP. The representatives of the four factions in the UNL were mostly mid-level activists and not members of the decision-making echelon of the PLO factions.[36] The lower-class and even refugee origin of many of these activists, as well as the fact that most had served prison terms in the past, indicates that they owed their position to their political activity rather than to economic or family status. The new leadership reflected the leading role of the youth in the Intifada and a certain rebellion against the ineffectiveness of their elders.[37]

While the UNL enhanced the cooperation between the PLO factions during the first months of the Intifada, each maintained its separate organization. The UNL's main role was to provide guidance to the population by setting tactical goals and courses of action, and by coordinating the activities of the main factions.[38] Although regional leadership bodies based on the UNL's model were set up, they seemed to act not so much as a link between the UNL and the local committees but as regional coordinating bodies among the various factions. In other words, there was no formal hierarchical structure combining the UNL, the regional leadership, and the local committees. Rather, the UNL appealed directly to the local committees through its handbills *(nida'at)*, which were distributed as leaflets and broadcast by the PLO radio from Baghdad and San'a. Attempts to form sectorial bodies of leadership—such as higher judicial or educational councils—encompassing the entire territories met with only limited success.[39] The loose and decentralized structure of the Intifada leadership rendered it less vulnerable to the arrests of its members by the Israeli authorities. Yet in the long run this proved to be also a source of weakness, as indicated by the proliferation of interfactional fighting and by loss of control over the wanton killings of alleged collaborators with Israel.[40]

The UNL activists were subordinated to the external PLO leadership and were committed to the PLO as both a symbol and organizational expression of the Palestinian national movement. Yet many of them were not necessarily supportive of their factions' leadership and resented the inferior status of the Interior activists in the PLO.[41] Initially, the UNL did seem to uphold certain independent positions. Thus, in its second leaflet, issued in January 1988, it set the immediate political goals for the Intifada, which reflected the priorities of the Interior—such as the holding of municipal elections and abolition of the value added tax—rather than those of the Exterior.[42] However, even while disagreeing with the Exterior over various policies, the UNL neither could nor sought to supplant the PLO.

As with previous leadership bodies, Fatah demanded the strict subordination of the Interior to the Exterior under its own domination. The leftist factions, both inside and outside the territories, advocated greater power for the UNL in order to reduce Fatah's predominance. They urged the establishment of "democratic relations," rather than the "bureaucratic" approach that had characterized the relations of the PLO with the masses in the territories, and demanded greater autonomy for the UNL.[43] In view of the Interior's success in perpetuating the Intifada, a compromise was reached whereby the UNL was recognized as the sole leadership in the territories, which meant the relegation of pro-PLO public figures to a secondary position. The UNL, for its part, accepted its status as "the fighting arm of the PLO," indicating that it would not seek to be part of the decision-making echelon of the PLO.[44] Fatah supporters described the link between the two leaderships as dialectic. Tactical decisions were the responsibility of the UNL, while decisions on the strategic and political levels were taken by the PLO.[45] UNL activists affiliated with the Left, however, stressed the advantages it enjoyed over the Exterior, as the UNL was free of the interference from Arab states to which the PLO was often subjected.[46]

The success of the Intifada during its first year compared with the inability of the PLO establishment to rid the Palestinians of Israeli rule, seemed at first to have brought about a significant change in the Interior-Exterior equation. The numerical parity among its four components, as opposed to Fatah's domination of the external PLO institutions, also contributed to discrepancies between its position and those of the PLO. Consequently, the UNL defied the PLO on several issues, often determined by the changing alignments among its member factions. More important, pressure from the Interior activists, who regarded the Intifada as a lever for political ends, was a major factor prompting the PLO to adopt a more moderate political program on possible coexistence with Israel during the nineteenth session of the PNC in 1988.[47]

At the same time, the PLO did not allow the UNL to emerge as a body parallel or equal to the Exterior. Communications between the Interior and Exterior were maintained separately by each faction rather than by the UNL as a body with the PLO leadership.[48] Likewise, the PLO declined the UNL's request to distribute the PLO funds in the territories, which would have given the Interior, rather than the PLO, effective control over large sectors of Palestinian society. Thus the PLO continued to channel funds directly to various organizations and individuals in order to maintain their dependence on the Exterior. In addition, the UNL's leaflets were to be edited by the Exterior before being distributed in the territories, further limiting the UNL's autonomy.[49]

The arrests of experienced cadres during the Intifada weakened the organizational leadership vis-à-vis the PLO, leading to excessive interference of the PLO leadership in day-to-day decisions previously taken by the UNL. Palestinian analysts argued that these developments brought about a certain gap between the UNL and PLO on the one hand and the local population on the other, and to the Intifada's loss of momentum during 1990-91.[50]

The decline of mass participation in the Intifada—primarily due to growing economic hardships and the fatigue of the population, and paradoxically, the Intifada's main political achievement of launching a diplomatic process—all but eclipsed the UNL vis-à-vis the PLO. The Interior activists, bound by their own ideology, insisted on the PLO's exclusive role in any political process, thereby forfeiting the initiative they had previously gained.

THE ISLAMIC CHALLENGE TO THE PLO

The most serious challenge to the PLO in the territories came from the Islamic wing of the Palestinian national movement, primarily the Islamic Resistance movement (*Harakat al-Muqawama al-Islamiyya* or Hamas). In contrast to all the leadership groups surveyed above, Hamas presented itself as an alternative to the PLO leadership and possessed the organizational infrastructure needed to sustain its claim.

Rather than embark on a detailed discussion of Hamas here, I will focus on criteria concerning the leadership challenge. Whereas the PLO was a diaspora organization seeking to assert its authority on the territories, Hamas emerged as a local movement based on the Muslim Brotherhood, which had been active in the Gaza Strip since 1948.[51] The fact that Hamas leaders lived among their constituency, maintaining daily contact and sharing the same hardships with them, gave them a certain advantage over the aloof PLO leadership, whose lifestyle was sometimes resented in the territories as corrupt.[52]

Consequently, unlike the PLO-affiliated organizations, the leadership and power base of Hamas originated from the territories, with Gaza as its stronghold. In its covenant Hamas hardly refers to the Palestinian diaspora.[53] Various Hamas representatives stressed the fact that the Interior rather than the Exterior had carried the main burden of the struggle against Israel and consequently improved the Palestinians' position vis-à-vis the Arab states. The duty of the Palestinian Exterior, therefore, was simply to support and assist their brethren in the territories[54] In view of the Exterior's failures, Hamas argued, the Palestinians should formulate a new strategy based on the achievements of the Interior—that is, of Hamas. Such a proposal stands in sharp contradistinction to the more modest demands raised by UNL activists for greater equality between the Interior and Exterior.[55]

An important characteristic of Hamas leadership in the Gaza Strip has been the relatively large number of refugees among its numbers, in sharp distinction from the pro-PLO leadership in the West Bank— probably due to the much larger proportion of refugees in the population of the Gaza Strip than in that of the West Bank, and to the greater appeal for the refugees of Hamas' uncompromising position on the conflict. Hamas capitalized on this fact and on publicizing their resentment over the opulent lifestyle of certain PLO leaders by stressing that, unlike the PLO, it did not speak on behalf of the traditional elites in Palestinian society but on behalf of the ordinary masses.[56]

From the outset, the Palestinian Islamic movements had maintained an ambiguous position vis-à-vis the PLO's status as the sole legitimate representative of the Palestinians. Hamas had made a distinction between the official purpose of the PLO as a "national framework" representing all the Palestinian people and the PLO's current leadership and political course, which it rejected. Hamas argued that this distinction set it apart from the Israeli rejection of the PLO as a national movement.[57] Consequently, Hamas refused to join the UNL, since the latter was willing to seek a peaceful solution to the Arab-Israeli conflict. Another major reason for its detachment from the UNL was the UNL's subordination to the PLO's outside leadership, which would have required Hamas to give up its independence.[58]

The intensifying disagreement with the PLO over Palestinian participation in the peace process and its growing power led Hamas to explicitly declare itself as the proper movement to lead the Palestinians rather than the PLO. On various occasions Hamas leaders referred to the PLO as the representative of the Palestinians of the Exterior, and themselves as the genuine leadership of the Palestinians of the Interior. They also supported the holding of elections in the territories so that the population could choose its representative—hinting that the PLO did not fulfill that capacity, and expressing confidence in Hamas's victory. Younger activists spoke of the need to transform Hamas into a wide framework that would encompass not just the Islamic circles but the entire Palestinian people—in other words, a movement that would supplant the PLO as the umbrella organization of the Palestinian national movement.[59]

Hamas leveled a series of charges against the PLO that amounted to a denial of its legitimacy. It stated that only when the PLO announced the Islamization of its program would it become representative of all the Palestinian people. Hamas not only accused the PLO leadership of making unilateral concessions, it also charged it with subordinating PLO bodies to the rule of a single individual and his entourage; it claimed that neither the PNC nor any of the other PLO bodies represented the Palestinian people any longer, as they were not democratically elected.[60]

The early leadership groups in the territories, except for the communists, failed to build extensive grassroots organizations. The PLO-affiliated national institutions were often dependent on outside sustenance for their functioning. In contrast, the Islamic movement began with institution building before embarking on open political activity. In 1981 it set up "the Islamic community" *(al-mujamma' al-Islami),* as the umbrella organization of its communal activity. During the Intifada the *mujamma'* served as the logistical and human reservoir for Hamas. Whereas the PLO spent considerable funds on financing its apparatus in the territories, Hamas allocated greater resources to its social activity, taking advantage of the predicament of the national institutions caused by the PLO's financial difficulties following the 1991 Gulf War to expand its base of support.[61] Hamas was also unique as the only local leadership group to articulate a comprehensive ideology that could challenge the PLO by incorporating both religious and nationalist elements.[62]

Israeli measures against Hamas, particularly the arrest and deportation of its leading cadres, produced a certain shift from the Interior to the Exterior. Musa Abu Marzuq, head of the Hamas political bureau, and Ibrahim Ghawsha, the movement's spokesmen, like other bureau members resided outside the territories. The nature of the relationship between Hamas activists in the territories and in the diaspora, and particularly the leadership's control of the 'Izz al-Din al-Qassam armed units, was and is unclear. Hamas, then, may be undergoing a process similar to that undergone by the PLO.

Internal and External Leadership: A Comparative Perspective

A comparison of the various components of the Interior-Exterior equation in the Palestinian case and in the cases of Algeria, Vietnam, and South Yemen may provide an additional angle in explaining the continued subordination of the Interior to the Exterior leadership. In Algeria power shifted from the internal to the external leadership, whereas in Vietnam the external or northern leadership maintained its superiority and control throughout the war. In South Yemen, on the other hand, a second-echelon internal leadership of the National Liberation Front (NLF) overcame the established external leadership.[63]

The tensions between PLO/Fatah and local leadership groups in the territories reflected the divisions between the Palestinian diaspora and those who remained in their land, as well as the rivalry between opposing elites. In Algeria and South Yemen it was a conflict between rival elites espousing different ideologies. In Vietnam traditional cultural and regional differences had generated mutual antagonism between north and south, influencing the Communist Party itself. In both the Palestinian and Vietnamese cases, then, the Exterior relied on a major constituency that would not disappear even after a political settlement was achieved.

Leadership bodies of the Palestinian Interior were not always formally subordinated to the Exterior leadership institutions, but they were by and large committed ideologically to the political superiority of the Exterior. This limited their ability to challenge the Exterior's authority had they wished to do so. In Vietnam the Interior's subordination was complete— ideologically, formally, and in practice.

In the Palestinian, Vietnamese, and Algerian cases the Exterior enjoyed superiority in resources and in institutional infrastructure. All major leadership and decision-making bodies were controlled by the Exterior. In Vietnam the north had an entire state apparatus at its disposal. The PLO and FLN did manage to build an external protostate infrastructure; however, the ability of the Palestinian and Algerian Exterior to initiate or dictate developments in the Interior was more limited than in the Vietnamese case. In South Yemen, Interior NLF activists had built an institutional infrastructure which was equal to that of the Exterior.

The proportion of representatives from the Interior in PLO institutions was negligible. The number of deportees from the territories in the PLO Executive Committee declined from four in 1974 to one in 1993. Most of them were given secondary roles; and if they dared to challenge the PLO leadership, as did 'Abd al-Jawad Salih, they were ousted.

Several deportees were nominated to the PNC—most notably Shaykh 'Abd al-Hamid al-Sa'ih—to the largely ceremonial post of speaker. The PLO had always claimed that a large number of seats in the PNC was allocated to representatives from the territories. However, their names were kept secret, ostensibly to avoid arrest by Israel. Consequently, Palestinians from the territories did not take part in PNC discussions. Petitions, behind-the-scenes pressure, and PLO fears of losing the allegiance of the population in the territories were the most effective means by which the Interior could influence PLO policy.

One question that may be raised in this context is whether deported activists who spent many years abroad still felt themselves to be, or were regarded by others as, representatives of the Interior. 'Azmi Shu'aybi, a DFLP activist deported in 1986, recounted after returning to the West

Bank that he had always felt himself to be a spokesman for the Interior within the DFLP institutions; but it is unclear whether such persons as 'Abd al-Hamid al-Sa'ih or 'Abd al-Muhsin Abu Mayzar could still be regarded in that category.

Ideology was the domain of the Exterior in the Palestinian, Algerian, and Vietnamese cases, thereby consolidating the Exterior's legitimacy. The only exception was Hamas, whose own ideology challenged the nationalist one. The situation was different in South Yemen, where the Interior leadership advocated revolutionary Marxism to counter the pan-Arabism of the Exterior and offered, in addition, a model of a more socially active political party.[64] The Interior's power to influence strategies and policies of the Exterior, then, was limited only in the Palestinian, Vietnamese, and Algerian cases.

The attrition of the Interior's ranks during the struggle was a major factor that prevented it from preserving its supremacy in the Algerian case or from emerging as a rival to the Exterior leadership in the Palestinian and Vietnamese cases. The Israeli policy of deportations deprived the Palestinian Interior of some of its most vital elements and seriously undermined the ability of Palestinian society to replenish the ranks of local elites.[65] In contrast, the Interior in South Yemen did not experience the same attrition as in the three other cases.[66]

The Israeli attempt to foster an alternative leadership to the PLO—the abortive Village Leagues—failed because those involved were perceived as traitors to the Palestinian cause. Likewise, the Israeli attempt to circumvent the PLO following the Madrid peace conference by negotiating with a delegation from the territories proved unsuccessful. The legitimacy enjoyed by the PLO among the Arab states and internationally inhibited the emergence of any open challenge to its authority.

Although North Vietnam made every effort to win international recognition for its NLF (the South Vietnamese arm of the Vietnamese Communist Party) as an independent movement, the United States always sought to negotiate with the North Vietnamese government, since it held the key to any solution. In Algeria, the only attempt by the French to conduct negotiations with Interior leaders, in 1959, failed convincing de Gaulle of the need to negotiate with the exiled FLN leadership.[67]

In other words, attempts by the adversary to enhance an internal party by negotiating a settlement with it proved unsuccessful and insufficient to outweigh the organizational and ideological preponderance of the Exterior leadership. Moreover, this very attempt may have occasionally tarnished the nationalist credentials of the party it sought to enhance.

PLO armed activity across the borders of neighboring Arab countries played an important role in drawing international attention to the Palestinian case but had a smaller role in changing Israeli policies. In Algeria and South Yemen military activity of the Interior played the major role in persuading the imperial power to leave. In Vietnam the Interior initially played an important military role, but the final outcome was achieved by the regular military forces of the North. The Intifada brought the Palestinians their main political gains, by forcing Israel to recognize the high cost of continued rule over the territories. But it was the Exterior leadership that assumed the lead in the negotiations and in the nascent Palestinian entity. In other words, the Interior could not secure the fruits of its own achievement.

The PLO and the Interior: From the Gulf War to the Oslo Accords

The setback suffered by the PLO following the Gulf War brought the change in the relations between the Interior and Exterior to its furthest point since the beginning of the Intifada, but also reflected its limitations. Arafat's support for Saddam Husain was greatly influenced by popular pressure in the territories. The change was manifested in numerous calls in the territories to reassess the Palestinian national policy following the debacle of the war, implicitly pointing to the PLO's failures. Various memoranda submitted to the PLO demanded a greater role for the Interior in formulating Palestinian policies. Perhaps more important in the longer run were the calls to democratize the PLO, drawing explicitly on the Israeli model. The fact that some of these calls were made by Fatah activists with respectable nationalist credentials is also significant. Indicative of the new mood was the statement by Dr. Muhammad Jadallah, a DFLP activist from Jerusalem, that "the PLO should learn the rules of political conduct from the leadership inside the territories." It is the people of the Interior, he added, who would now determine whether or not the PLO would continue to exist, and both sides knew it. PLO supporters in the territories were more willing to criticize publicly inefficiencies and corruption in the PLO apparatus, calling for changes in the PLO leadership and institutions.[68] While reflecting a change, these calls indicate that the Interior did not challenge the PLO as the national leadership, but only advocated changes within it. Moreover, many of these proposals encountered opposition even inside the territories, on the grounds that to undermine the PLO's position served Israeli and American policies. The PLO official organs tended to ignore the proposals rather than openly reject them. In other words, the Exterior still had the final say in major decisions, and the Palestinians of the Interior were still unable, and many were unwilling, to change it.

Acting from a position of weakness in the aftermath of the 1991 Gulf War, the PLO succumbed to American and Israeli pressure and consented to a representation of the Palestinian case by a delegation from the territories. Not only did it (temporarily) concede one of its most cherished gains—exclusive representation of the Palestinians—but it faced the risk of exclusion from a settlement by an alternative leadership from the territories.

The Exterior however, proved sufficiently strong to be able to determine the composition of the delegation from the territories. It thus made sure that most of the delegation's members would lack any independent power base. Moreover, the delegation's only source of legitimacy in the Interior was its identification with the PLO, because of the circumstances of its formation under foreign pressure. Thus taking an independent line would have been perceived by the Palestinian public as serving Israel's goal of undermining the PLO. The delegation, however, did have some impact in internal PLO deliberations during 1992, when it sided with Arafat against critics of the peace process, thereby demonstrating the Interior's support for his leadership.

It was the PLO leadership in Tunis that decided whether the Palestinian delegation would take part in the talks or would suspend its participation, overruling protests or requests from the Interior. More important, the Exterior determined the Palestinian agenda and position in the talks. Consequently, by bringing the sensitive question of Jerusalem to the forefront of the talks, Arafat deprived the delegation, which lacked an independent power base or local legitimacy, of any room to maneuver, thereby effectively blocking any prospect of progress through this channel. Concurrently, he continuously conveyed to the Israelis that he could prove more flexible thanks to his broad-based legitimacy. The concern that the PLO's financial and organizational distress would elevate Hamas to a dominant position in the territories prompted Israel to opt for direct negotiations with the PLO. Similar fears compelled Arafat to make some of the concessions that made the Oslo Accords possible.[69] Previously, the PLO had suspected that the local leadership would seek a settlement while excluding the Exterior and compromising

Palestinian national goals. Now the threat of losing the Interior drove Arafat to do just that.

The signing of the Declaration of Principles between Israel and the PLO in September 1993 restored—at least temporarily—the PLO's decisive superiority. The Exterior leadership attained full control over the institutions of the autonomy, and Arafat's avowed intention to give most senior positions in the autonomy's power structure to cadres from the Exterior signified the relegation of the Interior to a subordinate position.

Yet this process did not totally eliminate the internal challenge to the PLO, as even members of the organizational leadership expressed discontent and resentment at the secondary role assigned to them. Similarly, criticism of the outdated structure of the PLO and of Arafat's autocratic style of leadership, as well as the persistent calls voiced by local Fatah activists and academics to conduct the elections as promised by the DOP, indicated a desire among important segments of the politically conscious public in the territories to curb the domination of the Exterior leadership and seek a process or a vehicle that would produce a legitimate local leadership.[70] Ironically, under the Oslo Accords, the very fate of the Exterior leadership could be determined inside the territories. Accordingly, the implementation of the autonomy and consequent state building would "dictate," in the words of various PLO supporters in the territories, "the alteration [of] the existing structure and content of the PLO."[71]

NOTES

1. For extensive studies on these relations until the 1980s, see Moshe Ma'oz, *Palestinian Leadership on the West Bank: The Changing Role of the Arab Mayors under Jordan and Israel* (London: Frank Cass, 1984); Emile Sahliyeh, *In Search of Leadership: West Bank Politics Since 1967* (Washington, D.C.: The Brookings Institution, 1988); Hillel Frisch, *Palestinian Institution Building in the Territories, 1967-1985* (Ph.D. diss., The Hebrew University of Jerusalem, 1989); Shaul Mishal, *The PLO under Arafat: Between Gun and Olive Branch* (New Haven: Yale University Press, 1986).

2. Avraham Sela, "The PLO, the West Bank and Gaza Strip," *Jerusalem Quarterly* 8 (summer 1978): 67-68; Rafik Halabi, *The West Bank Story* (New York: Harcourt, Brace, Jovanovich, 1981), 191-93; 'Issa Shu'aibi, "The Develop-

ment of Palestinian Entity-Consciousness," *Journal of Palestine Studies* 9:2 (winter 1980): 60.
3. Frisch, *Institution Building,* 13-16.
4. On the Jordanian period, see Shaul Mishal, *West Bank/East Bank: The Palestinians in Jordan, 1949-1967* (New Haven: Yale University Press, 1978); Clinton Bailey, *Jordan's Palestinian Challenge* (Boulder, Colo., 1990); Ma'oz, *Leadership,* 24-61.
5. David Farhi, "The Muslim Council in East Jerusalem and in Judea and Samaria since the Six-Day War," *Hamizrah Hehadash* 28:1-2 (1979): 6-7, 10; Ibrahim Dakkak, "Back to Square One: A Study in the Re-emergence of the Palestinian Identity in the West Bank, 1967-1980," in Alexander Scholch, ed., *Palestinians over the Green Line: Studies on the Relations between Palestinians on Both Sides of the 1949 Armistice Line Since 1967* (London, 1983), 71; "The United National Front in the Gaza Strip" (in Arabic), *The Palestinian Encyclopedia,* 2nd ed., vol. 2 (Acre: Dar al-Aswar, 1986), 28.
6. 'Issa Shu'aibi, *Palestinian Statism: Self Consciousness and Institutional Development, 1947-1977* (Beirut: PLO Research Center, 1979), 137-38, 147-48; Moshe Shemesh, "The West Bank: Rise and Decline of Traditional Leadership, June 1967 to October 1973," *Middle Eastern Studies* 20:3 (July 1984): 294; Dakkak, "Back to Square One," 72; Sahliyeh, *Leadership,* 23.
7. Dakkak, "Back to Square One," 72, Sahliyeh, *Leadership,* 23.
8. Shemesh, "The West Bank," 300-304; Shu'aibi, "Development," 64; Ma'oz, *Leadership,* 95-96.
9. Shu'aibi, "Development," 60, 63-64.
10. Text of the political committee's report in Yehoshafat Harkabi, *The Arabs and Israel* 3-4 (in Hebrew) (Tel Aviv: Am Oved, 1975), p. 193.
11. Shemesh, "The West Bank," 309-12; Sahliyeh, *Leadership,* 38-39.
12. Sahliyeh, *Leadership,* 42-45.
13. Shemesh, "The West Bank," 307-8; Frisch, *Institution Building,* 39-40.
14. Harkabi, *The Arabs and Israel,* nos. 3-4, 181, 211.
15. "Roundtable: The West Bank: Occupation, Resistance and a Look at the Future," *Shu'un Filastiniyya,* April 1974, 53-54; Dakkak, "Back to Square One," 79, 91; Galia Golan, *The Soviet Union and the Palestine Liberation Organization: An Uneasy Alliance* (New York: Praeger, 1980), 166-68.
16. "Program of the PNF," *al-Hadaf,* 29 September 1973; Faruk Qadoumi and Abdul Mohsen Abu Maizar, "The Crux of the Middle East Crisis," *World Marxist Review* 19 (July 1976): 34.
17. "Roundtable: Problems of the National Struggle in the West Bank and the Gaza Strip," *Shu'un Filastiniyya* 118 (September 1981): 48, 49, 53, 58; *Sawt*

Filastin radio (Cairo), 31 May 1974, in which Arafat stressed that the PNF was one among several of the PLO's arms in the territories.

18. *Shu'un Filastiniyya,* 118 (September 1981): 48-49, 61, 67.
19. "Roundtable: West Bank," 50; 'Arabi 'Awwad and Jiryis Kawwas to *al-Nahar,* 30 May 1974; Dakkak, "Back to Square One," 77, 91.
20. "Letter to the Executive Committee of the PLO from the Palestine National Front in the Occupied Territory, 1 December 1973," *Journal of Palestine Studies* 3:3 (spring 1974): 187-91; Dakkak, "Back to Square One," 78, 90. See also Husain 'Awda to *al-Tali'a* (Cairo), March 1974.
21. Dakkak, "Back to Square One," 79, 91.
22. *Al-Nahar,* 30 May 1974; "The Palestine National Front in the Occupied Territories: Its Activities, Goals, and Wave of Arrests against it," *Shu'un Filastiniyya,* 38 (October 1974): 207-11; Sahliyeh, *Leadership,* 61.
23. Frisch, *Institution Building,* 47. For a comprehensive analysis of the elections, see Ma'oz, *Palestinian Leadership,* 135-38; 'Isa al-Shu'aibi, "The Municipal Elections," *Shu'un Filastiniyya,* 57 (May 1976): 166-68; G. KH. "What Position after the Elections?" *Shu'un Filastiniyya,* 57 (May 1976): 168-72.
24. Ma'oz, *Palestinian Leadership,* 141, 145; Halabi, *West Bank Story,* 115.
25. Sahliyeh, *Leadership,* p. 73; Elie Rekhess, "The West Bank and The Gaza Strip," *Middle East Contemporary Survey (MECS), 1979-80* (New York: 1982), 275; Frisch, *Institution Building,* 77.
26. *al-Hurriyya,* 25 June 1979; "Roundtable: National Struggle," 49, 53, 55, 61-62; Dakkak, "Back to Square One," 85; Ma'oz, *Leadership,* 175; Frisch, *Institution Building,* 77; Sahliyeh, *Leadership,* 78.
27. Frisch, *Institution Building,* 70.
28. Elie Rekhess, "The West Bank and the Gaza Strip," *MECS, 1980-81,* 339; Dakkak, "Back to Square One," 86; Ma'oz, *Leadership,* 173-75.
29. Rekhess, *MECS, 1979-80,* 271-72; Dakkak, "Back to Square One," 87.
30. On Sharon's policy, see Elie Rekhess and Meir Litvak, "The West Bank and the Gaza Strip," *MECS, 1981-82,* 363-64, 379. The mayors of Hebron and Halhul had been deported earlier, following a terrorist attack in Hebron in which six Jews were killed.
31. The Palestinian organization within the JCP was allowed to establish a separate party in 1981.
32. On the PLO's efforts to expand its organizational apparatuses in the territories, see Frisch, *Institution Building;* and Joost Hilterman, *Behind the Intifada: Labor and Women's Movements in the Occupied Territories* (Princeton: Princeton University Press, 1992); 'Ali Jarbawi, *al-Intifada wal-Qiyadat al-Siyasiyya fi al-Daffa al-Gharbiyya wa-Qita' Ghaza* (Beirut: Dar al-Tali'a, 1989), 23-24; Sela, "PLO," 75-76.

33. Hillel Frisch, "From Armed Struggle to Political Mobilization: Changes in Fatah's Strategy in the Territories" in Gad Gilbar and Asher Susser, eds., *At the Core of the Conflict: The Intifada* (in Hebrew) (Tel Aviv: Hakibbutz Hameuchad, 1992), 52ff.
34. Ziad Abu-Amr, "Notes on Palestinian Political Leadership: The 'Personalities' of the Occupied Territories," *Middle East Report* 154, (September-October 1988): 23; 'Ali Jarbawi, *al-Intifada wal-Qiyadat al-Siyasiyya fi al-Daffa al-Gharbiyya wa-Qita' Ghaza* (Beirut: Dar al-Tali'a, 1989).
35. Ziad Abu-Amr, *al-Haraka al-Islamiyya fi al-Daffa al-Gharbiyya wa-Qita' Ghaza* (Acre: Dar el-Aswar, 1989), 31-32.
36. 'Ali Jarbawi, "The Geography of the Intifada," *Middle East Report* 20:3-4 (May-June/July-August 1990).
37. Wahid 'Abd al-Majid, "al-Shumuliyya al-Ijtima'iyya lil-Intifada," *Shu'un Filastiniyya,* April 1989; *al-Ittihad* (Abu Dhabi), 9 May; *'Al Hamishmar,* 10 March 1989. For more detailed studies on the composition of this leadership group, see Hillel Frisch, "The Palestinian Movement in the Territories: The Middle Command," *Middle Eastern Studies* 29:2 (April 1993): 257ff., and Meir Litvak, "Palestinian Leadership in the Territories during the Intifada, 1987-1992," *Orient* 34:2 (June 1993): 206-207.
38. See Frisch, "The West Bank and the Gaza Strip," *MECS, 1988* (Boulder, 1990): 278-83; Jarbawi, 74, 78.
39. Meir Litvak, "The West Bank and the Gaza Strip," *MECS, 1989,* 232-35; *MECS 1990,* 246, 249-50.
40. *Al-Hurriyya,* 28 May 1989; *Ha'aretz,* 21 August 1989; *Al-Nashra,* 24 July 1989; Voice of Palestine [VoP] (Baghdad), 17 August; FBIS, *Daily Report*; *al-Ard al-Muhtalla,* 57, September; *al-Hurriyya,* 1 October 1989; *MECS, 1990.*
41. A poll conducted in five refugee camps in the territories was published in *Sawt al-Watan* (January 1991): 12. The great majority, 84 percent, regarded the PLO as the national leadership. However, 14 percent complained of corruption of the leadership, while 64 percent expressed frustration over the Exterior's treatment of the Interior. It is likely that such feelings had existed before, though not necessarily at the same intensity. For an opposing view describing the UNL as merely a "subordinate middle-level command used to obeying orders from the diaspora centers," see Frisch, "Palestinian Movement," 254.
42. "Leaflet No. 2," in Shaul Mishal and Reuven Aharoni, *Speaking Stones: The Words behind the Palestinian Intifada* (in Hebrew) (Tel Aviv: Hakibbutz Hameuchad, 1989), 61-63.
43. The PFLP and DFLP did not practice what they had preached publicly and did not allow their internal wings an equal share in their own decision making, as was shown during the Fifth Congress of the PFLP in March

1993. See Litvak, "The Palestine Liberation Organization," *MECS, 1993* (Boulder, 1995).

44. *Al-Hadaf,* 16 April 1989; *al-Hurriyya,* 5 March and 8 October 1989; *Shu'un Filastiniyya,* October 1989, 105. Whereas the first leaflets were signed by the UNL alone, subsequent leaflets were signed by the UNL and the PLO together, but without a consistent order of precedence.
45. *Filastin al-Thawra,* 23 April 1989; *al-Watan,* 18 February 1989.
46. See UNL activist 'Ata Abu Kirsh in *Shu'un Filastiniyya,* October 1989, 105.
47. *Al-Ittihad* (Abu Dhabi), 21 June 1989.
48. Jarbawi, *al-Itifada,* 81.
49. *Ma'ariv,* 13 January 1989; *al-Watan,* 8 March 1989; *Yediot Aharonot,* 14 May 1989; *al-Hurriyya,* 8 October 1989.
50. *Al-Qabas al-Duwali,* 12 April 1990; *al-Hadaf,* 28 April 1991.
51. Ziad Abu-Amr, *al-Haraka,* 31-32. On the Muslim Brotherhood in the Territories, see also Hala Mustafa, *"al-tayar al-Islami fi al-ard al-muhtalla," al-Mustaqbal al-'Arabi* 13 (July 1988); Mohammad K. Shadid, "The Muslim Brotherhood Movement in the West Bank and Gaza," *Third World Quarterly* 10 (April 1988).
52. See the poll published in *Sawt al-Watan,* January 1991.
53. *The Covenant of the Islamic Resistance Movement* (Beirut, n.d.), clause 2.
54. Muhammad Siyam to *Nida' al-Aqsa,* April 1990; Muhammad Nazzal to *Filastin al-Muslima,* March 1992. See similar arguments among members of the leftist organizations in *Shu'un Filastiniyya,* October 1989, 105.
55. "Whither the Palestinian Political Thought?" *Filastin al-Muslima,* September 1991.
56. "What Is the Alternative?" *Filastin al-Muslima,* February 1992.
57. "Comprehensive Interview with Hamas" *Filastin al-Muslima,* May 1990.
58. *Sawt al-Aqsa,* 13 January 1990; *Filastin al-Muslima,* July 1990.
59. See *Filastin al-Muslima,* May 1990, and *Hamas bayn alam al-waqi'wa-amal al-mustaqbal 7,* a booklet published by Hamas in mid-1990; "An Interview with Four Deportees" *Filastin al-Muslima,* April 1991.
60. *Al-Hadaf,* 19 January 1992.
61. Litvak, "The Palestine Liberation Organization," *MECS 1992";* Litvak, "The Islamic Resistance Movement," *MECS 1993.*
62. *The Islamic Covenant,* clauses 25-27.
63. William B. Quandt, *Revolution and Political Leadership: Algeria, 1954-1968* (Cambridge, Mass.: MIT Press, 1969), 11; Joseph Kostiner, *The Struggle for South Yemen* (London: Croom Helm, 1984), 119ff; William J. Duiker, *The Communist Road to Power in Vietnam* (Boulder: Westview Press, 1981), 214.

64. Quandt, *Revolution*, 96; John Ruedy, *Modern Algeria: The Origins and Development of a Nation* (Bloomington, 1992), 191; Kostiner, *Struggle*, 121-23.
65. Frisch, *Institution Building*, 79, mentions 1,949 activists deported during the years 1967-81. The Jerusalem Center for Human Rights gives a lower number, around 1,600, for the longer period 1967-93. For the Algerian case, see Ruedy, *Modern Algeria*, 169; Quandt, *Revolution*, 115, 127-28.
66. Kostiner, *Struggle*, 71ff.
67. Ruedy, *Modern Algeria*, 176-77.
68. *Al-Fajr* (English edition), 11 and 23 March 1991; *al-Fajr*, 28 March 1991; *al-Hadaf* and *al-Hurriyya*, 28 April 1991; *al-Bayadir al-Siyasi*, 21 September 1991; *Davar*, 17 January 1992; *al-Hurriyya*, 19 April 1992; *Jerusalem Report*, 4 June and 24 September 1992.
69. Meir Litvak, "The Palestine Liberation Organization," *MECS 1993*, 12-13, 15, 19, 27-28.
70. *Jerusalem Report*, 30 December 1993.
71. *The Middle East*, January, July 1992; *Financial Times*, 24 February 1992; *International Herald Tribune*, 6 June 1992; Ahmad Samih al-Khalidi and Husayn Ja'far Agha, *"al-Filastiniyun bayn 'al-dakhil' w'al-kharij"* (The Palestinians between the "Interior" and the "Exterior"), *Majallat al-Dirasat al-Filastiniyya* 12 (winter 1992): 4; 'Ali Jarbawi, *"al-Qiyada al-Filastiniyya wal-tahadiyat al-siyasiyya al-qadima"* (The Palestinian leadership and the coming political challenges," *al-Hayat*, 12 October 1993.

ELEVEN

Intifada Discourse
The Hamas and UNL Leaflets

Shaul Mishal

Social, cultural, or political discourse is composed of thoughts and ideas expressed in speeches, statements, texts, and other forms of communication. A discourse characterizes the social or political world of a certain group or community, its norms and values, its institutions, and the behavior of its members.

Leaflets distributed by Hamas and the United National Leadership (UNL) played a key role in shaping the Palestinian discourse during the Intifada. Their publications dictated a particular way of life and determined the boundaries of permissible action. They brought the people into the streets, instructing them on what to do and when and how to do it. The leaflets were the vital documents of the Palestinians during the Intifada.

In this chapter I will examine the similarities and differences in perceptions of Palestinian national goals as expressed in Hamas and UNL leaflets and consider the leaflets' approach to the day-to-day reality of the Intifada. In so doing I hope to project the possible effects of the Hamas-UNL discourse on the future relationship between the two groups.

UNL and Hamas as Leading Bodies

Four major political organizations prepared leaflets during the Intifada: the United National Leadership *(al-Qiyada al-wataniyya al-Muwahada);*

the Islamic Resistance Movement *(Harakat al-Muqawama al-Islamiyya, or Hamas);* the left-wing Palestinian factions; and Islamic Jihad *(al-Jihad al-Islami).* Each was identified ideologically or linked organizationally with either the national or the religious camp. The two most important groups were the UNL and Hamas.

The UNL was a coalition of supporters of Fatah, the Democratic Front for the Liberation of Palestine (DFLP), the Popular Front for the Liberation of Palestine (PFLP), and the Communist Party. The close relationship between the UNL and the PLO was given explicit expression in UNL leaflets. Beginning with Leaflet No. 3, each communique opened with the same declaration: "No voice can overcome the voice of the uprising, no voice can overcome the voice of the Palestinian people—the people of the PLO." This leaflet and every subsequent one noted that it was issued by the PLO and the UNL, and was undersigned by both bodies.

Hamas became an umbrella organization for activists of the Muslim Brotherhood movement in the Gaza Strip, including the Islamic Community (al-Mujamma' al-Islami) from which Hamas emerged. The Islamic Jihad, whose orientation is also religious, operated separately from Hamas and distributed its own leaflets. The establishment of the Islamic Jihad as an independent organization was originally motivated by a profound disagreement with the Muslim Brothers over how to advance the creation of an Islamic state in Palestine. The Jihad opted for an immediate holy war on Israel whereas the Brothers emphasized the need for social and cultural activities within the community in addition to armed struggle against Israel. The interrelation of the four bodies with either the national camp or the religious camp enabled an intensive level of activity and ensured that a high percentage of the population would perform the directives contained in the leaflets.

Diversity, Frequency, and Effectiveness

The scope of Intifada activities among the groups is reflected in the diversity and frequency of the leaflets, each intended for blanket distribution in the West Bank and the Gaza Strip. In practice, UNL and Hamas leaflets enjoyed the widest circulation. They differed in both style and content. UNL leaflets were longer and more detailed; at the same time, they were phrased more succinctly and their authors endeavored to present political arguments couched in clear language. Hamas leaflets, in contrast, drew heavily on religious images and slogans. With the exception of the UNL, the leaflets of all the groups were homemade; that is, they were drawn up solely by local activists. UNL leaflets were drafted in the territories and then sent to the PLO offices in Tunis for final polish and approval.

Leaflets appeared frequently: In the first year of the Intifada (December 1987-December 1988) the UNL issued 31 leaflets and Hamas 33. (Hamas began numbering its leaflets with No. 21, in May 1988). The average in the first year was therefore two or three leaflets issued by each body per month. During the second year of the Intifada, fewer leaflets were issued: 19 by the UNL and 18 by Hamas. After the third year, the average fell to 12 to 15 leaflets per year. Through May 1994, the UNL had issued 103 leaflets and Hamas 111.

Each group's leaflets set out to dictate the daily routine of the Palestinians. But only UNL and Hamas leaflets proved to have the force of governmental decrees; the response and obedience they elicited were great. Along with offering encouragement and enumerating the Intifada's achievements, the leaflets provided detailed guidelines on what was permitted and what was prohibited. In contrast to the leaflets of the Left and those of the Islamic Jihad, the UNL and Hamas leaflets addressed a broad range of issues: work, health, transportation, education, agriculture, and commerce; whether a strike was to be full or partial; opening hours for shops; how to maintain studies despite the closure of schools; who could travel during a strike; and who could work. The leaflets called for intra-communal help; contributions and donations to the needy and to the families of people killed or imprisoned; a selective boycott of Israeli products; boycotting of work in the Israeli agricultural sector; attacks on Jewish settlers; and the resignation of Palestinians employed by the Israeli Civil Administration, particularly policemen, tax collectors, and members of appointed local councils. Hamas leaflets, which were prepared in the Gaza Strip, also contained religious instructions regarding prayer, charity, penitence, and the need for good behavior (such as obeying traffic rules in the spirit of "Muslim politeness"). The wide range of issues tackled by the UNL and Hamas reflects their respective claims to Palestinian national leadership and their competition for the people's loyalty and obedience.

The UNL and Hamas leaflets influenced the behavior not only of the local population but of the Israeli authorities as well. They became "working papers," guiding the scale and intensity of activity by the army, the Civil Administration and other Israeli security bodies.

In the absence of a formal leadership, the anonymous writers of the leaflets became the "pamphlet leadership" of the Intifada. If effective leadership is defined as the ability to articulate values, define goals, and assure the public's obedience and compliance, the authors of the UNL and Hamas leaflets were exceedingly successful leaders.

THE PALESTINIAN STATE

A content analysis of the leaflets reveals two overriding goals common to the various groups active in the Intifada: undermining the authority of Israeli rule in the occupied territories by means of a civil revolt to force Israel to withdraw from those areas; and preparing the groundwork for the establishment of a Palestinian state.

Hamas and the UNL had divergent visions as to the character of a Palestinian state, and consequently differed in their attitudes toward Israel, the Jewish people, and the peace process. These differences were inherent in each movement's credo. Hamas, with its religious ideology, aspired to establish an Islamic state in all of Palestine. According to the Hamas charter of August 1988, the soil of Palestine is a Muslim endowment *(waqf)* and Hamas is a "distinctive Palestinian movement working to raise the banner of Allah over every grain of soil in Palestine."[1] Hamas saw itself as a link in the chain of jihad against Israel. To forgo parts of Palestine was to forgo part of Islam.[2]

In the eyes of Hamas, the Muslims' right to all of Palestine left no room for dialogue or political settlement with Israel. The following leaflet quotations exemplify this approach:

> Let any hand be cut off that signs [away] a grain of sand in Palestine in favor of the enemies of God . . . who have seized . . . the blessed land (March 13, 1988).

> "Land for peace" and the "umbrella of an international conference" . . . this is no more than a mirage, deceit . . . (March 4, 1988).

> Every negotiation with the enemy is a regression from the [Palestinian] cause, concession of a principle and recognition of the usurping murderers' false claim to a land in which they were not born (August 18, 1988).

> Arab rulers, who invest efforts for the false peace . . . and who entreat Israel to agree to a 'just' peace . . . We hope you will fight at least once

[in order to prove] that you partake of Arab boldness or Muslim strength (January 1988).

And, in a rhetorical appeal to Israel: "Get your hands off our people, our cities, our camps and our villages. Our struggle with you is a contest of faith, existence and life" (undated leaflet).

Hamas also adduced political arguments for rejecting any attempt to achieve a political settlement with Israel. Thus, in Leaflet No. 28: "Israel understands only the language of force and believes neither in negotiations nor in peace. It will persist in its evasiveness and in building a military entity, in exploiting the opportunity for attack, and in breaking the Arabs' nose." And in the same leaflet: "The Arab world is not so weak as to run after peace, and the Jews are not so strong as to be able to impose their will . . . How long can Israel withstand all the forces?"

Furthermore, Hamas ascribed to Israel and the Jews demonic traits that justify a refusal to hold talks: Israel is a "cancer which is spreading . . . and is threatening the entire Islamic world" (May 3, 1988). The Jews, according to another leaflet, are "brothers of the apes, assassins of the prophets, blood-suckers, warmongers . . . Only Islam can break the Jews and destroy their dream" (January 1988).

Hamas often drew on historical personalities and events from Islamic tradition in order to underscore the religious character of the conflict with Israel. Names that frequently cropped up in the leaflets include: Ja'far Ibn Abu-Talib, who fought the Byzantines in the Battle of Mu'tah (629 CE); Khalid Ibn al-Walid, who fought the Battle of the Yarmuk (636 CE) and was called by Muhammad "the sword of God"; Salah al-Din, who vanquished the Crusaders at the Battle of Hittin (1187); and Baybars, the Mameluke sultan of Egypt who fought the Mongols in the Battle of 'Ayn Jalut (1260).

The Khaybar affair has also attracted Hamas's attention. Many Hamas leaflets concluded with the call: *"Allah akbar* [Allah is great]— the hour of Khaybar has arrived—*Allah akbar*—death to the conquerors." Khaybar was a wealthy Jewish colony on the Arabian Peninsula. According to a Muslim tradition, the Jews of Khaybar betrayed Muhammad by serving him poisoned meat that eventually caused his death. The Prophet and his followers had conquered Khaybar in 628 CE, allowing "the Jews their land in return for binding themselves to turn over half their harvests."[3] For Muslims, Khaybar became a symbol of Jewish treachery. Similarly, the Muslims who reside in the territories are looked on as *mujahidun*—the warriors of the holy war—or as *murabitun*—inhabitants of the Ribat, who settled in the countryside during the Muslim conquests to defend the frontier areas and thereby fulfill a religious commandment. Overall, Hamas advocates an exclusively Muslim state throughout Palestine to ameliorate the ills of the Muslim community. The organization thus looks with disfavor on Palestinian Christians and courts the support of Muslims living outside of Palestine.

In sum, Hamas believes that a political solution to the conflict with Israel would violate the religious precept of waging a holy war against the Jewish infidels. Its perception of Israel and the Jews as a religious—not a national—adversary rules out the possibility of a political settlement based on compromise. The alternative to the peace process with Israel, according to Hamas, is "victory or death."

Quite a different picture emerges from the leaflets of the United National Leadership. UNL leaflets, which serve as a mouthpiece for the national camp, have sought to appeal to both Muslims and Christians. "Religion is God's and the homeland is for all" *(al-din li'llah wal-watan li'ljami')*,[4] a UNL slogan, contrasts sharply with Hamas's *'din wadunya'* ("faith is the whole world"). Indeed, UNL leaflets rarely mention heroes or events from ancient Muslim history; their allusions are to modern historical figures who became national heroes. Three names in particular are frequently cited: Shaikh 'Izz al-Din al-Qassam, a pioneer of the armed struggle in Palestine who called for a return to Islamic fundamentalism and was killed by the British in 1935;[5] 'Abd al-Qadir al-Husaini (Husseini), who fell in the battle for the Qastel, outside Jerusalem, in 1948; and the writer and poet Ghassan Kanafani, who was killed in a car explosion in Beirut in 1972.

UNL leaflets stress the ties between Muslims and Christians. Leaflet No. 22 (July 21, 1988), for example, called on the people to "pray for the repose of the martyrs' souls and [to] hold marches and demonstrations in protest at the measures of the occupation authorities against Islamic and Christian holy places." Leaflet No. 30 (December 15, 1988) referred to the forthcoming Christmas celebrations in the following language: "December 24 [is] a day for ringing church bells and calling out *Allah akbar* in the minarets of the mosques, marking the birth of the messenger of peace, the Lord Messiah. We extend felicitations to our Palestinian Christian brothers and urge them to observe the religious rituals."[6]

The UNL perceives the conflict with Israel predominantly in secular-political terms rather than in religious ones. For example, Palestinian society will be healed, Leaflet No. 28 says, through "self-determination and the establishment of an independent state with Arab Jerusalem as its eternal capital," rather than through the imposition of the kingdom of Islam on the Palestinian world.

Like Hamas's leaflets, however, those of the UNL are harsh in their denunciations of Israeli policy and leaders. The detention facilities for Palestinians are "Nazi camps" (Leaflet No. 15); Sharon, Peres, and Rabin are "fascist dwarfs" (No. 16); Rabin is a "shedder of blood" (No. 11); he is a "terrorist" and Shamir is "arrogant" (No. 25); the settlers are "herds" or "rabble" (No. 27); and the Israeli military authorities are a "Zionist machine of oppression and fascist executioners" (No. 28).

Yet the UNL also addresses practical demands to Israel that indicate that it perceives Israel pragmatically, as a political and not demonic adversary. Leaflet No. 26 (September 27, 1988) contained a typical list of such demands: annulment of the 1945 emergency regulations; removal of the army from Palestinian population centers; release of all Intifada detainees and repatriation of the deportees; free elections in all the local governments, urban and rural, under UN supervision; and cessation of punitive measures, such as economic "siege," demolition of houses, torture, deportations, arrest without trial, and building of settlements.

Some leaflets were addressed to the Israeli public in an effort to explain the rationale behind the Intifada and the need for a peaceful settlement. Leaflet No. 28 (October 30, 1988) offers a clear example of this approach:

> UNL stresses to the Israeli street that our blessed uprising . . . did not aspire to shed the blood of Palestinians or Jews, but was a revolution against the dispossession, oppression, and fascism of the occupation, and [a manifestation of] national determination to establish a just peace in our region, [a peace] that will emerge only with the establishment of our Palestinian state on our national soil.

The differences of opinion between Hamas and the UNL regarding a Palestinian state and the role of the political process reflect the ongoing competition between Hamas and the UNL's mother movement, the PLO, over hegemony and national leadership. This has generated continuous friction between the two movements.

Nowhere was the struggle and competition between Hamas and the UNL-PLO more apparent than in the wake of the events at the Palestine National Council meeting held in Algiers in early November of 1988. At this meeting the PNC expressed support for a peaceful solution, declared the establishment of a Palestinian state on the basis of UN General Assembly Resolution 181 of November 1947, and called for the partition of Palestine into two states, one Jewish and one Arab. In response, Hamas issued a Special Leaflet (November 10, 1988) condemning the PLO's decision to accept a peaceful settlement of the Israeli-Palestinian dispute and denying the PLO's right to represent the Palestinian people in the occupied territories:

> Our brothers, members of the Palestinian National Council . . . sons of Qibya and Dir Yasin . . . In this session of your council, there are those who urge agreement on stopping the fighting with the enemy and signing an agreement recognizing him, and an agreement on abandoning the greater part of Palestine . . . Be careful not to be dragged in by the exponents of this inclination, which is dangerous and destructive to our cause . . . And let us say to them . . . In whose name are you condemning to failure the uprising and delivering a death blow to the achievements of the exemplary and *jihadic* achievements?! Which of the martyrs authorized you?! Which of the wounded solicited you?! Which of the widows has approached you in supplication?! Which of the infants has sought your help to conduct negotiations with the Jews, the enemies of peace and of humanity, the murderers of the prophets?! Is it in the name of the suckling babe into whose eye the Jew was quick to fire a bullet while he was in his mother's arms?! Or in the name of the shaikh whom the Jew kicked in the leg and [then] stepped on his forehead, who worships only Allah?! Or in the name of the mother whose son was robbed from her arms and thrown into the black pits of prison?! Or in the name of the youth whose bones Rabin broke?! Or in the name of the youth upon whom they rained blows and electric stingings [beatings] and who are injected with bacteria at the order of Rabin, Shamir, and Peres?! Or in the name of the family whose home the Jews destroyed, leaving [the family] to live under the open skies?! In whose name, O our gentleman, will you conduct negotiations?!

Hamas, according to the leaflet, articulates the true aspirations and needs of the Palestinian people, expressing the real meaning of Palestinian national interests. In appeals to PNC members, Hamas claims that it:

has already made it clear that it posits [as a goal] an all-encompassing jihad until Palestine [is complete], and it decided to launch the uprising, on 8 December 1987, in order to realize this goal. All the members of [the people of] Palestine sided, and continue to side, with it. With the help of Allah, the power latent in our people was able to burst forth, making [the people] the paragons of the century when they confronted the usurping Jewish enemy in daily clashes. We all hope that you will stand behind the aspirations of your people, for the people chose the way . . . the way of jihad, honor, and sacrifice, finding that for the sake of Allah and the liberation of Palestine, whatever is more precious and more valuable than money, than a son and than the soul, is cheap . . . We stress to you that the plan known as a "provisional government," or the "charter of independence," or the "government-in-exile," and whatever includes a plan for a solution, is nothing more than bait with the purpose of sticking a knife in the back of the uprising's achievements; a sword in the back of the children of the stones, and preventing our children from continuing the struggle and [from achieving] martyrdom. Our struggle with the Zionists is not a campaign for a partition of borders and it is not a dispute over the division of land, it is a campaign over entity and destiny. In this stand we see the hope and aspiration of our people everywhere to arouse in you the spirit of the struggle, the spirit of the outbreak of the revolution of 1965.[7] We call on you to take under your wing the spirit of the children of the stones and the continuation of the armed struggle, no matter what the cost. Our people has often confronted plots, and has made many sacrifices to thwart them. Our people is still possessed with the same readiness to make sacrifice after sacrifice, and it expresses this through this blessed uprising which has been recorded as a phenomenon unprecedented in history.

On the local level, the competition between Hamas and the PLO over leadership position and political control exacerbated the power struggle between Hamas and the UNL, increasing the risk of all-out confrontation between the two parties. Yet each side was wary of taking drastic steps that might cause irreparable damage to their relationship. Thus, the UNL and Hamas endeavored to play down the conflicting views and disagreements between them, emphasizing shared values of unity and solidarity. In Leaflet No. 29 (November 20, 1988), entitled "The Joy of the Palestinian State," the UNL appealed to

> a number of fundamentalist elements to prefer the general national interests, our people's national interest, over their basic assumptions and

factional interests . . . and to cease presenting negative stands and manifestations. For they serve the enemy, whether they wish to or not. They must draw the conclusions from the mass celebrations . . . marking the declaration of the [Palestinian] state, reflecting the deep roots of our legitimate leadership and sole representative, the [PLO]. It is still not to late to fuse all the loyal forces in the melting pot of the uprising and its United National Leadership.

In reaction, Hamas declared, in Leaflet No. 31 (November 27, 1988), that it opposed splitting the ranks but that this might result from "leaflets being planted in the name of the Hamas movement which the [Israeli] occupier circulated in order to split the ranks and cast aspersions on the [various] currents." And, above all: "preserve the unity of the people. Pay no heed to the enemy's attempts to cause a rift in families, clans, currents of thought and ideas."

Hamas's response to UNL's charges attest to its complex attitude toward the national camp. On the one hand, Hamas was not eager to aggravate its disagreements with the UNL to the point of a head-on clash. Such a development would have a boomerang effect in the struggle against Israel. On the other hand, Hamas did not undertake to back away from a confrontation in the future, if the UNL, together with the PLO, should assent to a political settlement that jettisoned the principle of liberating the whole of Palestine.

The ideological discord and power struggle between Hamas and the UNL-PLO increased the potential for an irreparable rift between the two camps. Both sides were well aware of the gulf dividing them and the difficulty of reaching an agreement that would enable them to live side by side in political harmony. Still, along with the conflicting interests in the ideological realms, there was an awareness of common interests in the practical domain, namely, in the day-to-day struggle against the Israeli authorities.

The Question of Civil Revolt

A second goal of the Intifada shared by the UNL and Hamas was to undermine Israeli rule in the occupied territories by means of a civil revolt that would force Israel's withdrawal from these areas. On this issue, unlike those noted above, the two groups shared a common approach reflected in their nearly identical directives to the Palestinian public about its role in the uprising.

The population was called on to cooperate in both violent and non-violent actions. The former included throwing stones and firebombs, building barriers, burning tires, wielding knives and axes, clashing with the Israeli forces, and attacking collaborators. In the realm of non-violent activity, the population was called on to take action in three areas: (1) severing economic ties with Israel and building up local institutions to provide alternative public services; (2) engaging in civil disobedience (disobeying laws and regulations); and (3) performing activities that promote solidarity.

The directives on severing ties with Israel called for not working in Israel; not working in Jewish settlements in the occupied territories; boycotting Israeli products; withdrawing deposits from Israeli banks; resigning from the Civil Administration; developing a home-based economy—including growing vegetables and raising domestic animals in one's yard—and for farmers, "to plant cereals and legumes such as lentils, chickpeas, broad beans, garlic, onions, wheat, and so forth, for storage" (UNL Leaflet No. 24, August 22, 1988);[8] expanding local plants and taking on new workers; establishing and expanding popular committees on education, information, guard duty, and agriculture; and setting up and cultivating local bodies for "popular education"—a directive calling on parents, teachers, and students to uphold the routine of studies despite the protracted closure of educational institutions by the Israeli authorities.

Directives regarding civil disobedience called for non-payment of taxes and fines; staging partial commercial strikes; and holding general strikes on specified days. As for activities to enhance solidarity, the population, or at times certain groups, were called on to fulfill the following directives: day-long strikes of solidarity with prisoners; day-long strikes of solidarity with families of victims; memorial days for traumatic events, such as the civil war in Jordan which broke out in September 1970; coordination by lawyers in their dealing with prisoners, and press conferences to expose conditions in the detention camps; sit-down strikes by students, teachers, and parents in front of foreign missions and closed schools; volunteer work to help farmers with the olive harvest; assistance to needy families; refraining from raising rents; reducing medical fees; and writing slogans on walls and raising flags.

An analysis of the first 30 leaflets issued by the UNL and Hamas shows a steady and significant rise, over time, in the number of both violent and non-violent directives issued by both groups. Subsequent leaflets maintained the same high proportion of violent and non-violent directives. Of 315 directives published in the first 30 UNL leaflets, 70 (22.2 percent of the total) were printed in the first ten leaflets, 111 (35.2 percent) in Leaflets 11-20, and 134 (42.6 percent) in Leaflets 21-30.

A similar trend is discernible in the first 30 leaflets put out by Hamas. Of 139 violent and non-violent directives in Hamas leaflets, 36 (about 26 percent of the total) appeared in the first ten leaflets, 40 (29 percent) in Leaflets 11-20, and 63 (more than 45 percent) in Leaflets 21-30.

Statistical analysis indicates a significant rise in the number of directives calling for violent activity in UNL leaflets. In the first ten leaflets, 14.3 percent of the 70 instructions entailed violent action; in Leaflets 11-20, the number had risen to 28 percent; and in Leaflets 21-30, such instructions accounted for a third of the total. Thus, the percentage of violent instructions more than doubled between the first months of the Intifada and the periods to follow.

Concurrently, a dramatic decrease is visible in the number of directives to sever ties with Israel in the realms of the economy and services: from 27 percent in the first ten leaflets, to 11 percent in Leaflets 21-30. The frequency of the two other types of non-violent instructions—civil disobedience and encouragement of acts of solidarity—remained stable.

Where Hamas is concerned, the overall picture regarding violence and the severing of contact with Israel was substantially the same. A comparison of the instructions for violent actions in Hamas and UNL leaflets reveals that the violence level of the former was consistently high from the start of the Intifada. In the UNL the violence level was initially low but gradually crept upward during 1988; after August 1988 it approached that of Hamas. The difference in the amount of violent directives should not cloud the fact that both groups evinced an identical trend: a growing number of violent directives, on the one hand, and a sharp decline in calls to break economic ties with Israel, on the other. In UNL leaflets this trend was discernible as early as the second period, while in Hamas it did not emerge until the third period of 1988.

These trends reflect the contradictory ideologies guiding the groups that were behind the uprising. On the one hand, the Palestinians' growing awareness of the vital role played by violence—in propelling the Intifada and in producing political gains—accounted for the significant increase in the violent directives in UNL leaflets and the consistently high level of violent directives in Hamas leaflets. On the other hand, the

Intifada's real capacity for endurance depended on the Palestinians' economic staying power. In the absence of self-sustaining economic capability, dependence on Israel had become a way of life. Under these circumstances, excessive pressure to sever economic contact with Israel was ineffective. To obey would mean economic hardship for tens of thousands of workers who earned their living in Israel, and a huge loss of revenue for many local merchants and factory owners who maintained commercial ties with Israeli firms. In turn, a severe economic downturn in these sectors could weaken the influence of the UNL and Hamas, stir disobedience, and encourage anarchy. If the Intifada's strength lay in its ability to attract the cooperation of all social strata and age groups, it is easy to see how the ideologically heretical became the economically unavoidable.

The inability or unwillingness of merchants, factory owners, and workers to break off economic relations with Israel forced both the UNL and Hamas to adapt to the circumstances and bow to the economic reality, gradually decreasing in the number of directives urging an economic break with Israel. Instructions in this spirit continued to appear, but more selectively. This was particularly noticeable regarding work in Israel and the boycotting of Israeli products. Later leaflets noted clearly that the prohibition on working in Israel was confined to general strike days or to persons employed in sectors that competed with products of the territories, such as the citrus industry. In the same vein, the leaflets called for a boycott of products for which local substitutes were available, notably milk products, agricultural produce, cigarettes, and soft drinks.

The decline in the number of directives calling for a total economic break with Israel indicates a reassessment by both the UNL and Hamas concerning the limits of strength of the Intifada. This awareness explains why both groups stepped back from declaring a general civil revolt and preferred to hammer home the idea that the uprising was a stage toward a total revolt.

The controlled civil revolt, like the continuous decline in the number of directives calling for the severing of economic ties with Israel, was evidence that the leading bodies of the Intifada had adopted a flexible strategy to further their political goals. The Palestinians were aware of cost-benefit considerations; too many demands would exact too much sacrifice from their constituents. They were avoiding a slide into excess in trying to achieve their political objectives. They recognized the limits of their strength and were careful not to reach a point of no return in the confrontation with Israel. The Intifada had its share of internal contradictions and conflicting interests; nonetheless, it was able to accommodate such contradictions without succumbing to them.

The PLO and Hamas: Toward Relations of Neither Full Acceptance Nor Total Rejection

Hamas's awareness of its inability to achieve the ultimate goal of a Palestinian Muslim state in all of Palestine through all-out struggle with Israel, and the group's social and cultural activities within the Palestinian Muslim community, played a significant role in shaping the relationship with the UNL and with its mother movement, the PLO.

The discrepancy between Hamas's vision and day-to-day reality in the occupied territories led to a crucial dilemma that Hamas could hardly escape. Conformity to its grand design would have demonstrated ideological consistency, thus strengthening Hamas credibility among both its members and its adversaries. At the same time conformity to Hamas's stated doctrine may have weakened its position within broad segments of the Palestinian population who were eager to see an end to their daily agonies and grievances.

Political flexibility and incorporation into the peace process would help Hamas maintain its influence within the Palestinian population for the time being but destroy its uniqueness as the normative opposition to the PLO and increase the risk of friction and disunity within the movement. It is this tension between two competing, sometimes opposing, considerations that led Hamas to shift from its "unrealistic" posture of conflict—that of a total commitment to the vision of a Palestinian Muslim state in all of historical Palestine and a total rejection of any move toward a political settlement—to a more pragmatic posture entailing calculated deviance from its stated doctrine.

Hamas's calculated deviation found its expression in various statements made by its leader, Shaikh Ahmad Yassin, during the Intifada. Following are three examples:

1. Hamas, according to Shaikh Yassin, does not rule out the possibility of a Palestinian state in the West Bank and Gaza Strip as long as it would be considered a first phase on the road to the establishment of a Palestinian state in all of Palestine.[9]

2. Hamas is ready to consider international supervision in the territories after the Israeli withdrawal as long as it would be limited in time and would not require direct and clear-cut concessions to Israel.[10]
3. Hamas will reject any attempt to enter into political negotiations with Israel as long as Israel continues to control the territories. However, Hamas would allow talks after a full lsraeli withdrawal.[11]

Moreover, following the Israeli-PLO agreement of September 1993 to establish a Palestinian interim self-government authority (PISGA) in the West Bank and the Gaza Strip, various Hamas leaders, time and again, stated their willingness to participate in the general elections to be held in the territories, although Hamas continued to criticize the PLO for signing such an agreement.

Hamas's statements reflect a tendency, within the movement, of searching for a conjunction between the poetry of Hamas ideology and the prose of reality. By adopting a strategy of neither full acceptance nor total rejection of the PLO's political perception and policy, Hamas was able to justify its position in normative terms, interpreting such "concessions" as tactical moves.

Hamas's present strategy towards the PLO, and its position toward the political process, will likely continue as long as the Palestinian Authority shows gradual achievements in gaining the support of the Palestinian public. Either a serious stagnation and setback, or rapid progress with clear-cut economic and institutional achievement—both of which may lead to the foundation of a Palestinian state in only the West Bank and Gaza—would increase the dissonance within Hamas.

Under these circumstances, completion of a permanent solution calling for the establishment of an independent Palestinian state in the West Bank and Gaza may carry great risks for the fragile coexistence between Hamas and the PLO. It appears that some sort of political cooperation with Amman, based on a confederation among the parties, may provide a better option to cope with Hamas's political dissonance and its ideological discrepancies.

NOTES

1. Reuven Paz, *"Ha-Amanah ha-Islamit ve-mashm'autah: 'iyun rishoni ve-targum"* (Tel Aviv: The Moshe Dayan Center for Middle Eastern and African Studies, Tel Aviv University, September 1988), 30 (mimeographed).
2. *Jihad,* literally an effort, is a continuous state of holy war against the nonbelievers and is a commandment of Islam. Jihad must end when the nonbelievers (Jews and Christians) have either accepted Islam or agreed to a protected status within an Islamic state.
3. Carl Brockelmann, *History of the Islamic People* (New York: Capricorn, 1960), 28.
4. *Al-Hadaf* (Beirut); PFLP organ, 12 October 1987. Cf. Psalms 115:16, "Heaven is the Lord's, and the earth He gave to man."
5. Fatah views Shaikh 'Izz al-Din al-Qassam as a national hero and not a religious figure. In his memory Fatah issued a special publication, *Thawrat al-Shaykh 'Izz al-Din al-Qassam* (The revolution of Shaikh 'Izz al-Din al-Qassam) (Beirut: June 1977). The Palestinian Left regards Shaikh al-Qassam as a social rebel. Hamas perceives him as a pioneer of the Islamic Jihad according to the fundamentalist interpretation, namely, that the holy war is a duty of the individual, not of the state.
6. The idea was to play down the Christmas festivities and not decorate the streets as in previous years. A similar call to refrain from holding festivities went out to Muslims on the Feast of the Sacrifice *('Id al-Adha).*
7. 1965 marked the beginning of Fatah's guerrilla warfare against Israel. The mention of this date would seem to indicate the national-Palestinian face of Hamas.
8. The subject of a home-based economy rarely appears in Hamas leaflets. The reason is that the population density in the Gaza Strip, which is Hamas's power base, precludes the use of yards for agriculture.
9. *Yediot Aharonot* (daily; Tel Aviv), 16 September 1988.
10. Shaikh Ahmad Yasin to *Al-Sarat* (publication of the Islamic movement in Israel), 10 April 1989.
11. *Yediot Aharonot,* 16 September 1988.

TWELVE

THE ROLE OF WOMEN AND FEMALE LEADERSHIP IN THE INTIFADA AND THE PEACE PROCESS

Naomi Chazan

POLITICAL ACTION BY ISRAELI AND PALESTINIAN WOMEN over the past eight years has proven not only to be a reflection of certain major political processes, such as the Intifada and the peace negotiations; it has served as an actual precursor of these processes. Since the beginning of the Intifada women have systematically been one step ahead of political events on the regional stage. Thus, by looking at what women are doing today, it is possible to get a very good idea of where political processes will be tomorrow.

A number of factors can be offered as a preliminary explanation as to why women have been in the vanguard. First, women's peace actions are characterized by a persistence that is not typical of general peace movements in the region. If we trace the activities of peace movements over a period of ten years, an up-and-down pattern emerges, with peaks and valleys. Women's peace action, on the other hand, has shown a consistent, incremental rate of increase over time.

Secondly, because Palestinian and Israeli women are somewhat outside the dominant political discourse in their societies, they have much greater flexibility in terms of the kinds of activities that they can contemplate and carry out. A third element is women's construction of institutions and structures that enable peace activity to be carried out on an ongoing basis. These structures also attest to a certain pragmatism and the apparent need on the part of women to bring about concrete results stemming from their activity.

The last factor, and a very important element of women's peace and political action on the Palestinian and Israeli front, is the mixture of identities present: feminist identities, political identities, national identities, and geographic identities. Throughout the history of Israeli and Palestinian women's contacts, it has proven possible to find points of communication even when there are direct clashes between elements of women's identities. Overlapping identities offer more possibilities in terms of interaction and connection. Personal ties and large doses of humor have proven successful as mechanisms for overcoming differences at women's conferences, and especially those between Israeli and Palestinian women.

In each of three phases of political action outlined below, there are three critical factors that come into play and, apparently, account for the specific characteristics of the phase. First is the extent to which nationalism motivates each of the partners, second, the extent to which feminism is involved in women's political action; and third, the specific, particular contribution to peace involve in that phase.

THE FIRST PHASE

During the first phase, beginning at the start of the Intifada in December 1987 and continuing until 1992, Palestinian women emerged at the forefront of the Intifada in several respects: in the struggle on the street; in communal organization and grassroots recruitment; and in the formulation of political positions. The involvement of women on the street may be the most obvious—women were visibly at the forefront of demonstrations, sometimes protecting the children, the stone-throwers, from the soldiers; sometimes engaging in their own political actions. But even beyond these overt actions, the galvanization of Palestinian women was absolutely consistent, persisting throughout this period of the uprising.

On the Israeli side, the beginning of the Intifada marked the first time that Israeli women established a sizable number of their own peace movements. Within two or three months after the uprising began, no fewer than six women's peace movements emerged on the

Israeli scene. Women in Black was the best known, but there was also Shani (Israeli Women Against Occupation), the Peace Quilt, and Women for Women Political Prisoners, among others. In fact, there were two movements of women advocating for Palestinian women political prisoners. Within a year of the beginning of the Intifada, the Israel Women's Peace Net (the *Reshet*) was established, and other groups joined in coalitions of women and peace. All of these Israeli women's peace movements were distinct from the general peace movements.

One critical point of convergence between the Israeli and Palestinian developments was that in both camps the barrier between radical women and mainstream women broke down. In other words, the politically oriented women's movements took on a nationalist component. There is considerable evidence that this was as true of the Israeli side as the Palestinian side.

A second commonality was that both Palestinian and Israeli women found it useful, effective, and pragmatic to work in contexts that merged political action and women's action. Some of this action was overtly feminist and some was not. In either case, the convergence of political action and all-women structures came together during this first phase.

A third marker of this first phase is dialogue between Palestinian and Israeli women, exemplified by the Palestinian-Israeli women's meetings that took place in Brussels in May 1989. The Brussels meeting was significant because it established a framework for joint Palestinian and Israeli women's action during much of the course of the Intifada. It was at the end of the Brussels meeting that the Israel Women's Peace Net was established and, more significantly, a Palestinian and Israeli women's coordinating committee was set up. That committee operated throughout the following six years, meeting regularly two or three times a month. Even during difficult periods, such as the time of the Gulf War, when tensions between the two peoples were equally high, it met every two weeks. This could not have happened had a common political platform not been created in Brussels.

At the Brussels meeting Palestinian and Israeli women agreed that (a) Israel should speak directly to "the legitimate representatives of the Palestinian people"; (b) any resolution to the conflict should be based on negotiation; and (c) such a solution could not take place without respect for the mutual political rights to self-determination of both peoples. The participants were relatively mainstream Israeli women and the emerging Palestinian female leadership.

This political platform enabled the continuation of contacts throughout the first phase, which was a very difficult period. For despite the convergences described above, there was an amazing asymmetry between Palestinian women's action and Israeli women's action at the time. The Palestinian women were at the forefront of the Palestinian struggle. Israeli women were active, but they were in opposition to their government, not part of the mainstream. Secondly, the Palestinian women tended to be much younger. Politically, they were in the mainstream of the PLO, but not necessarily socially. Many were single women committed to the struggle and not representative of the mainstream of social norms. Israeli women, from that point of view, are by and large conformist. More important, however, than the political and social asymmetry between Palestinian and Israeli women at the time was (and is) the power asymmetry.

The Second Phase

In the summer of 1992 a second phase began, as a direct outcome of the Israeli elections, that resulted in a power shift, primarily on the Israeli side. A major asymmetry dividing Israeli and Palestinian women was somewhat rectified politically, with Israeli women who were active in the peace movements now no longer in opposition but part of the elected majority. Such women were not only elected to office but also became part of the ruling coalition.

The crucial marker of this phase, which lasted until May 1994, was a second Brussels conference in September 1992. For the most part, the same women who had been at the first Brussels conference were in attendance at the second. The participants decided to move a step forward, from the political pact of 1989 to a social pact in 1992. They were looking one step ahead and saying, at a time when there had not yet been genuine progress in the peace talks, that the next issue on the agenda would be to mold the nature of the peace between the two peoples. They attempted to concretize what was taking place to see if they could not create a paradigm of the kind of relationship that should exist. In doing so they chose to deal with an issue that was not only a political issue but a social issue as well. Thus was created the initiative now known as the Jerusalem Link: two women's peace centers, one Palestinian and one Israeli, each entirely independent, but with a written legal contract between them stipulating cooperation on certain matters.

The Jerusalem Link, which is heavily funded by the European Commission, is precisely such a paradigm of a relationship: equal independent structures, cooperation when necessary, continuation of political work, but at the same time much independent activity by each of the centers around issues that are of concern to women, but do not necessarily have a direct political impact.

Because political developments have been so rapid, the second phase was relatively short. And many of the women involved, on both sides, have monitored the Oslo agreement, and then Gaza-Jericho and the Taba accords. They have begun very seriously to put in place the mechanism of molding and shaping the future peace through the Jerusalem Link.

It was possible to move to the second phase not only because of a power shift, but also because in both communities the Palestinian and Israeli women who were involved in peace activities and national activities were key actors in the first Brussels conference. A number of today's female members of Knesset were key players in the first Brussels conference, though none were in political positions at the time. By 1992 they had achieved leadership positions in their own society. The same holds true for Palestinian women activists, who were involved in the Madrid conference and subsequent negotiations.

Nonetheless, both groups had experienced a process of marginalization as well. Thus, the movement from Brussels I to Brussels II, which came about as a result of the elections and the Madrid process, put women in a very paradoxical situation of being leaders and being marginalized simultaneously. The clear decision by the women was to continue to act, but with a feeling that many of the processes were getting beyond their control. In addition, for the first time there was a feeling of discouragement among the leaders involved—again, on both the Palestinian and Israeli sides: because success had led them to become, or be viewed, as somewhat elitist, they were having a problem with the grassroots women.

The Third Phase

Phase three opens with a conference that took place in May 1994 in Marakesh, the first conference of women from the entire Mediterranean region. It was, to my knowledge, the first conference of any kind that included participants from the Mashreq and the Maghreb as well as participants from Southern Europe. There, once again, the women proved to be one step ahead of other groups.

The purpose of the Marakesh meeting was to create a series of networks between women in the Mediterranean area. For the first time an Israeli delegation was an integral part of this kind of meeting. Four networks were established: an inter-parliamentary group; a group of businesswomen and economists; a media network; and a network of nongovernmental organizations to meet in Tunisia. In each of these networks, an Israeli woman and a Palestinian woman was on the steering committee.

This third phase appears to have two major characteristics, though they are somewhat contradictory. The first is the expansion of relations between Palestinian and Israeli women beyond the specificity of the Palestinian-Israeli conflict to much broader areas. Not only has the scope of interaction expanded for each of the groups; most remarkable is that the expansion is also for both groups together. For example, the stickiest problem at the Marakesh conference was the Greek-Turkish dispute over Cyprus. The Greeks and the Turks agreed to accept the Palestinians and the Israelis together as mediators. Tunisian and Algerian women were totally befuddled by the fact that the Palestinians and Israelis knew each other so well. One characteristic, then, of this emerging new phase is threefold: the expansion of ties for Israelis separately, for Palestinians separately, and for Israelis and Palestinians together.

The second characteristic is very different, one that, for lack of a better term, I call "specificity." It seems that together with the expansion signaled by the Marakesh meeting, there was also a particularism that emanated from the fact that the needs of Israeli and Palestinian women are very different. It is beginning to emerge how different is the mix of nationalism and feminism referred to at the start of this chapter. As cooperation becomes more generally accepted, the differences are becoming more apparent.

In the coming stage it will be important to recognize that the two trends—that of interaction and specificity—are manifesting themselves in tandem. Acceptance of the Israeli-Palestinian relationship is becoming much broader, but at the same time particular needs are becoming more apparent.

To address current needs in the region, the Marakesh meeting led to a new framework that was dubbed WAM: Women's Action for the Mediterranean. The acronym is emblematic of the excitement that this period is generating. Subsequent meetings in Tunisia and Barcelona in 1995 intensified the trend toward regional interaction.

The creation of a regional framework bears out the trends seen since the beginning of the Intifada. First, Palestinian and Israeli women took a pathbreaking role—to the extent that examining what women are doing now is a way of foreseeing what will happen in the future in each of the societies. Second, women have consistently been able to continue their activities separately and together because at each critical point they have institutionalized the relationship: after Brussels I in the coordinating committee, after Brussels II in the form of the Jerusalem Link, and after Marakesh in the form of WAM.

Most recently, in June 1997, the two sides joined together in a local framework, under the banner "Sharing Jerusalem: Two Capitals for Two States," which led to a series of joint activities and plans to work together on permanent settlement issues.

PART IV

Israeli and Palestinian Relations—Between Past and Future

THIRTEEN

THE POWER-ORIENTED SETTLEMENT

PLO-ISRAEL—THE ROAD TO THE OSLO AGREEMENT AND BACK?

BARUCH KIMMERLING

DE-PALESTINIZATION OF PALESTINIANS

SINCE THE FIRST ATTEMPTS by the Zionist movement to settle the territory known by the Jews as "Eretz Israel,"[1] Zionists and the pan-Arab (and before that pan-Syrian) movement have shared a common interest: preventing the rise of a distinct Arab people or entity in Palestine. Both nationalistic movements have stressed that the Arabs of Palestine are an indivisible part of the great Arab nation and their "problem" (no matter how it is defined) must be solved in a framework of Arab nationalism and "Arab-space."[2]

Palestinian identity began in the form of a gradual awareness among parts of the local Arab population who began to consider themselves a distinct society and polity *(wataniyya)*—even as a part of the Arab nation *(al-umma al-'arabiyya)*—like the Arabs of Syria, Iraq, or Transjordan. This dual sense of belonging has made the Palestinian collective identity problematic since it began to form.[3]

The geopolitical situation created by the colonial powers after the first world war meant that the options for joining the pan-Arab movement or achieving a separate polity could not be immediately realized by the Arabs of Palestine, but the problem of dual identity still existed. As the British colonial state was consolidated, the sense of political and even cultural distinctiveness among the Arab population grew, and the colonial state provided them with the final sociopolitical boundaries and identity. The difficulties the local population had in meeting the challenge posed by the growing Zionist settlement contributed to the local Arab population's feeling that theirs was a "unique fate."[4]

Yet after the Jewish-Palestinian civil war and the 1948 war, sociopolitical conditions led to an almost complete disappearance of the Palestinians and of a separate "Palestinian" identity. Several factors contributed to the process of "de-Palestinization" of the Palestinians. Transjordan became the "Hashemite Kingdom of Jordan," annexing the lands that remained from the eastern hilly parts of colonial Palestine, now known as the "West Bank." Granting Jordanian citizenship to the population, which included the original inhabitants and a considerable proportion of the refugees, it claimed to be the only successor of the would-be Palestinian state. The Hashemites used the educational system and techniques of coercive control and surveillance to impose a Jordanian identity. The Israelis treated the Palestinians who remained within the post-1948 boundaries in a similar manner. They granted the Palestinians formal citizenship and equal rights, redefining them as "Israeli Arabs," as Sammy Smooha says, and making a considerable effort at "Israelification."[5]

The Jordanians and Israelis, who controlled most of British colonial Palestine, had a common vested interest: to create and maintain a Palestinian-less sociopolitical reality in the Middle East. The world order generally supported this approach, defining the problem of the Palestinians not as a national problem, but as a "refugee problem." Within the refugee camps under Egyptian control (in the Gaza Strip), in Syria and to a lesser degree in Lebanon, the "Palestinian identity" was preserved and nurtured, but even in the camps of the late 1950s priority was given to pan-Arabism. The precondition for solving the Palestinian problem was seen as "Arab unity," to be followed by the "liberation" of all Arab lands, including Palestine, from colonialism and imperialism. In Gaza the short-lived "All-Palestine Government" was dissolved in 1949, with responsibility for the Palestinian population transferred to the League of Arab States. Under such circumstances the Israeli claim that "there are no Palestinians" came very close to realization. By 1964 the Arab-Israeli conflict was in a great measure de-Palestinized, a conflict between states.

THE MAKING OF A DEMONIC IMAGE

Small Palestinian groups, consisting mostly of young intellectuals, tried to disassociate themselves from the pan-Arab doctrine. One such group was the Fatah,[6] formed in Kuwait in 1958 by a group of former Palestinian students of the University of Cairo. They tried to reverse the conventional pan-Arab rhetoric and wisdom about the need for the liberation of Palestine to be preceeded by Arab unity, maintaining rather that the liberation would come as result of "armed struggle," with the Palestinians themselves as a vanguard, regaining responsibility for their own fate. Such ideas were spread by their periodical "Our Palestine" *(Filastinuna)*, which has been published since October 1959. They represented a revival of an authentic Palestinian voice, but the ideas nevertheless remained a marginal force in Arab politics, pejoratively perceived as "separatist." When the first Palestinian National Council (PNC) was convened in May 1964 and the Palestine Liberation Organization was established, with the veteran Palestinian diplomat Ahmad al-Shuqairi at its head, the yet unrecognized Fatah group comprised about ten of the 422 delegates assembled at the Intercontinental Hotel in East Jerusalem.[7] The newly created PLO drew some attention, but did not manage to achieve an independent status beyond the traditional patronage of the Arab states, and traditional Arab rivalries were reflected in its internal divisions.

However, the existence of the PLO provided the impetus for the Fatah leadership to establish its own "military wing," *al-'Asifa* (the Storm), and to declare on 1 January 1965 an "armed struggle" or "revolution." In their "Communique No. 1," they claimed that guerilla action was needed to prove that "the armed revolution is the way to Return and to Liberty . . . and that the Palestinian people remains in the field . . . has not died and will not die."[8] The Fatah gained a degree of publicity among the Palestinians between 1965 and 1967 as a result of the guerrilla war waged against Israel (including several attempts to sabotage Israel's water-carrier project).

Paradoxically, the glory days of Fatah were in the aftermath of the decisive and degrading defeat over the Arab states by the Israelis in the 1967 war. For the first time since 1948 the entire territory of the British colonial state was once again under the auspices of a single ruling power. Thus three substantial parts of the Palestinian people—those living in the West Bank, those in Gaza, and the "1948 Palestinians" (i.e., the "Israeli Arabs")—were reunited. From a certain perspective, the "colonial situation" had been reestablished, this time under Jewish rule.[9] Fatah's prediction, in the early 1960s, of greater Israeli expansion and the defeat of the Arab states, had come true.

A hinterland population was created that, according to the PLO's vision, would support a "popular guerrilla war" inspired by the doctrines of Vietnamese General Vo Nguyen Giap, the Latin American revolutionary Che Guevara, and the FLN leaders and ideologues of Algeria. Arafat arrived almost immediately after the war in the West Bank to establish underground guerrilla cells. The initiative, however, was crushed by the Israeli security and intelligence, and the leader of Fatah was forced to establish his headqurters in Jordan. In spite of this, an armed resistance and guerrilla attacks against Israeli targets, inside and outside the Green Line (the 1949 armistice-agreement border) began almost immediately, partially inspired by Fatah.[10] Between 1967 and 1970, 115 Israeli civilians were killed and some 690 wounded as the direct result of the guerrilla warfare.

However, the most salient success of Fatah, and the event that put it and Arafat at forefront of the liberation struggle in the eyes of Palestinian public opinion, was the battle of Karamah. Karamah was a Palestinian refugee camp in Jordan, and it was Fatah's headquarters. On 21 March 1968 Israeli troops attacked the camp, but were forced by the Fatah guerrillas (supported by Arab Legion artillery) into a day-long battle. The Israeli forces lost some 25 soldiers and were only able to continue the operation with the aid of artillery and armored vehicle and air force reinforcements. If the Palestinians were shamed by the outcome of the 1967 war, they regarded the *Karamah* battle (honor battle) as a victory over the powerful Israeli armed forces that provided them with a source of pride and hope.

A Palestinian hero emerged—the *fida'i* (the warrior ready to sacrifice himself for the cause)—and quickly gained mythic proportions, sending thousands of teenagers to join the *'Asifa* and propelling Arafat to the top of the Palestinian national movement.[11] In July 1968, at the fourth PNC meeting in Cairo, a coalition of the Fatah and other smaller guerrilla groups occupied half the seats and de facto took over control of the organization, reframing the National Charter. In February 1969 Yasir Arafat was elected as the PLO's chairman.

The revised Palestinian National Charter, to a greater extent than its predecessor, adopted the traditional approach toward Jewish political presence in the Middle East and the existence of a Palestinian polity. Framing it as a zero-sum conflict, the Charter stated that "the partition of Palestine in 1947 and the establishment of the state of Israel are entirely illegal, regardless of the passage of time, because they are contrary to the will of the Palestinian people and to their natural rights in their homeland, and inconsistent with the principles embodied in the Charter of the United Nations, particularly the right of self-determination" (article 19). The charter's theological and historiosophic thesis was: "Judaism, being a religion, is not an independent nationality. Nor do Jews constitute a single nation with an identity of its own; they are citizens of the states to which they belong" (article 20).[12]

The PLO essentially became an umbrella organization of diverse Palestinian political and guerrilla organizations, with Fatah as the predominant force. From the Israeli point of view, the PLO represented the reappearance and revival of the Palestinians as virtually independent political actors on the scene of the Arab-Jewish conflict.[13] At the Rabat summit of Arab states in October 1974, the PLO was recognized as the sole legitimate representative of the Palestinian people. Internal power and ideological struggles—within the PLO and its Executive Committee and between the mainstream Fatah and the Marxist Popular Front for the Liberation of Palestine (PFLP), headed by George Habash, and the Democratic Front for the Liberation of Palestine (DFLP) of Na'if Hawatmah and several other groups—fueled the competition over extremist positions and the need for military success.[14]

One of the controversial issues (at least since 1974) within the PLO was the so-called "external operations" that hit at Israeli and non-Israeli civilian targets, outside of Israel and in the occupied territories. Most visible and popular were the airline hijackings. Among the more spectacular operations were the 1972 Munich Olympics, in which most of the Israeli athletic team was taken hostage and later killed, and the May 1972 collaboration between a Japanese Red Army group and the PFLP in mounting an attack on Ben-Gurion airport, murdering 26 civilians. These actions put the Palestinian issue on the top of the world agenda, but, at the same time, they left the Palestinians demonized as cruel terrorists.

The "inside" operations were also intensified, leading to an uneasy coexistence between the conquerers and the conquered. After 1971 most of the attacks came from Jordan and later Southern Lebanon. Fatah and other guerrilla organizations exploited the weakness of the Lebanese state by establishing a state-within-a-state, building complex social, political, and military infrastructures.[15] This occurred after the abortive attempt to overthrow the Jordanian Hashemite regime in September of

1970. By and large, Palestinian guerrilla warfare met with relative success.[16] Between 1971 and 1982 the Palestinian guerrillas killed some 250 Israeli civilians and wounded more than 1,500.

All these traumatic events were absorbed by the Israeli collective memory. As a consequence, the basic sense of internal and individual security among Israelis was heavily damaged, and the distinction between strategic versus individual security was blurred. Israeli Jewish society began to see the Palestinian guerrilla organizations as a ferocious enemy whose goal was to destroy the Jewish state and "throw the Jews into the sea." They sometimes equated them with the Nazis, who "killed Jews simply because they were Jews." Such a construction of the reality was referred to rather elegantly by one Israeli scholar as "politicide."[17] Although overused, the term had some foundation and served primarily to increase collective frustration and a tendency toward power-oriented solutions.

Under such circumstances, the historical context of the Palestinian struggle was completely erased from Israeli collective memory, history, and awareness, to the point of denying the very existence of the Palestinians on the one hand. Paradoxically, the Palestinians were at the same time perceived as the greatest danger to the very existence of the Jewish state. These feelings were also used for internal political gain by right-wing or "hawkish" Israeli politicians. One limited military operation (Operation Litani, 1978) and one full-scale, bloody war in June 1982 were conducted by Israel on Lebanese territory, against the Palestinian military and political infrastructure. The objective of the Litani operation was to halt the guerrilla war and the bombing of northern Israeli settlements by establishing a limited buffer zone. The 1982 war was conducted in the hope of destroying the PLO, not only militarily, but politically.

Israeli Political Culture

Usually, both the media and the intellectual community depict the Jewish-Israeli political scene—in the context of the Israeli-Arab, and Israeli-Palestinian conflict—as divided between "right" and "left," "doves" and "hawks," with the addition of a recent third category of "Jewish religious fundamentalists." The discourse of a more subtle sociological analysis describes "universalistic" versus "primordial" or particularistic orientations.[18] These cleavages certainly exist, but mainly as self-identities in the ongoing domestic kulturkampf. However they are highly simplistic, serving a stereotyped social order and the need to manage a complex situation of quasi external conflict that lacks clearcut and permanent boundaries or easily identifiable rules of the game.

Israeli political culture is characterized by a mixture of a permanent anxiety and a power-oriented culture. On one hand, the Jewish-Israeli polity is driven by a code of self-perceived weakness, permanent wretchedness, and existential threat. A sense of permanent siege and potential annihilation in a hostile Gentile world of antisemites—be they Christians, Muslims, Buddhists, or agnostics—is perceived as the state of nature, or the cosmic order. Two or three thousand years of Jewish persecution, culminating in the Holocaust, are offered as final proof of the eternal relevance of the particularistic interpretation of history and collective memory, and its relevance to the present time.

On the other hand, Jewish Israelis are well aware of their country's status as a regional military power with one of the best-equipped and trained armed forces. Military service is an important component across the entire spectrum of Jewish-Israeli life (as servicemen and women in both regular service and reserve duty, as the parents of soldiers, and so on). The "new Israeli"—in counter-distinction to the "Jew-of-exile," shaped and disdained by Zionist ideology and mythology—is first and foremost a warrior. Jewish-Israelis adore *macht* (action); they are confident that force, now that they have it, will solve most societal and political problems, making the power-orientation the touchstone of their political culture.[19] There is a deep conviction that "Arabs" in general, and Palestinians in particular, "only understand the language of force." Former Prime Minister Levy Eshkol coined the expression the "poor Samson" syndrome to describe this Janus-faced character of the Israeli political culture.[20] The weakness and power-oriented components of this culture complement each other, yet they are also a source of internal strain within the Jewish-Israeli collective identity.

In Jewish-Israeli culture the Jewish Israeli "man"—especially the Askenazi native-born one—is depicted as modern, educated, sophisticated, highly skilled, motivated, and an omnipotent warrior—in opposition to the Arab (in general and the Palestinian in particular), who is seen as primitive and backward, uneducated, unsophisticated, unskilled, unmotivated, disabled, and militarily inferior. Poor work is labeled "Arab work," and the language—especially Hebrew slang—was once filled with degrading and pejorative stereotypes of Arabs.[21] The wars of 1948, 1956, and 1967 strengthened these stereotypes. A slight change occurred following the 1973 and 1982 wars, accelerating after the popular uprising in the occupied territories.

The reappearance, embodied by the PLO, of the Palestinians as independent actors on the stage of the Jewish-Arab conflict was interpreted by Jewish Israelis to fit perfectly with both components of their political culture. Israeli overreaction was one of the factors that helped to both give the Palestinian organizations publicity and to reconstruct Palestinian identity and nationalism. For example, the first guerrilla attack of *al-'Asifa,* an attempt to install a bomb into a reservoir of the Israeli national water carrier, had been preceeded by several abortive attempts to infiltrate into Israel.[22] These were given a great deal of publicity by the Israeli government. On 1 May 1965 Levy Eshkol, the Israeli prime minister and minister of defense, warned the Arab countries not to give shelter to Palestinian guerrillas, and he filed a complaint to the UN Security Council. Fatah then requested that the United Nations consider its captured gunmen prisoners of war, to be treated according to the Geneva Conventions and international law. Fatah not only gained relatively rapid worldwide recognition, but, moreover, this small group was presented and constructed by the Israelis as a major danger for Israel. This alone operated as a kind of self-fulfilling prophecy, and lay the foundations for a new Palestinian pride.

Israeli oversensitivity was not completely baseless. As we have seen, the de-Palestinization of the Palestinians was the common interest of Israel and at least some Arab states.[23] Any deviation from this process was considered by the Israelis as well the Jordanian regime as "dangerous." Any Palestinian claim as such was perceived in terms of a zero-sum game facing the Israeli as well as Jordanian polities. What must be remembered is that the founder and first chairman of the PLO, the infamous Ahmad al-Shuqairi, the man who gave the PLO its initial shape, declared Jordan as a part of Palestine.[24]

From a political and institutional point of view, the Israeli reaction to the reappearance of a partially independent, Palestine-centered, organization and leadership may have been exaggerated, but from a behavioral point of view the reason for anxiety was evident. From the outset, the PLO—constitutionally, at least—has continued the traditional Palestinian denial of any collective-political rights for Jews in Palestine.

The PLO's argument with the central assertions of Zionist doctrine is also understandable, given the history of both collectivities and the catastrophic outcome for the Palestinians of the encounter with the

Jewish national movement. In view of the Israeli public's acquaintance with the PLO Charter, Arafat's 1994 call for a *jihad* (holy war), which he later attempted to explain as "jihad for peace," and his definition of the post-Oslo Israel-PLO agreements in terms of Muhammed's "Treaty of Hudaybiyya," immediately touched the most sensitive Israeli nerves.[25] The real conflict over a piece of land became a cosmic collision between supernatural powers, uncontrolled by human beings. The Palestinian National Charter's direct assault on the very raison d'être and identity of Jewish collectivity, reflected the nature of the communal conflict, based on the mutual "delegitimation game." Later, both the nature of the conflict as well as the mutual delegitimation drove the partners toward some mutual accomodation.

Personification

Both Israeli approaches toward the Arabs, the Palestinians, and the conflict were embodied in the personality and figure of the Fatah's leader, and later the PLO's chairman, Yasir Arafat. Of course this perception was fueled by Arafat's self-presentation as an ascetic "man of the people," completely dedicated to the "revolution." In contrast, he was perceived and presented by most of the Jewish Israeli media in caricature; shaped as an appalling but ridiculous terrorist, a cunning conspirator with a limited performance record, a loser survivalist, a non-trustworthy consistent pragmatist, and, above all, as the personification of ultimate evil. However, just as Arafat preferred, he remained for most Palestinians and Israelis an enigma. Since his installment in Gaza, and the attempt to establish and efficiently manage the Palestinian National Authority and its routinization, Arafat's enigmatic image has to a large measure disappeared, with his limitations overemphasized both by the Palestinians and Israelis.[26]

Israeli Policy and Palestinian Response

Israel, according to its original field policy, formulated immediately after 1967, was to be that contradiction in terms, an "enlightened conqueror." On the West Bank this meant "open bridges" over the Jordan River and what Moshe Dayan called "functional division." Functional division assumed continuous control, surveillance, and cooptation of the Palestinian population by Jordan, with control over land and water usage by the Israelis. Almost from the beginning, the rules of the game were explicit—the Israelis wanted to keep all or most of the territories of the West Bank and Gaza because, as Eshkol, the pragmatist and dovish premier, put it: "the roots of the Israeli people are in this land, as deep as ancient days."[27] However, from the Israeli point of view, formal annexation of the occupied territories was out of the question (with the exception of East Jerusalem, and the Golan Heights, where most of the Syrian population had left or was forced to leave) as it would have changed the entire demographic balance between Jews and Palestinians, transforming Israel into a binational political entity. Even the right-wing regime that came to power in 1977 was not willing to fulfill the expectations of elements of its constituency by formally annexing the occupied territories.

Despite the fact that the territories were not formally annexed, they were opened up as settlement frontiers[28] and were incorporated within a single economy and military control system. In the first period of the Jewish settlement a grassroots movement sprang up, sporadically supported by the government, or better put, no serious efforts were made to halt it. Later, the government openly supported and encouraged the settlements within the framework of the so-called "Allon Plan."[29] From 1977 to 1987 a concentrated effort was made to create an "irreversible" territorial fait accompli,[30] through the creation of Jewish settlements within a densely settled Arab areas.[31] At this point in time, the West Bank had about 120,000 Jewish settlers, spread over 40 major settlements.

One of the Palestinian responses to the invasion of their land reservoir and the attempt to suffocate any possibility of future self-determination, was to attempt a process of rapid internal institutional and local leadership building[32] or what Salim Tamari perceives as the creation of a Palestinian civil society.[33] The new local leadership was also supposed to prevent any possible settlement in the West Bank and Gaza Strip, such as between Israel and Jordan, without PLO involvement. Initially, the process of local leadership formation did not contradict Israeli policy, which tried not to interfere with Palestinian internal affairs, at least on a local or municipal level. The idea of indirect rule was built into the situation from the beginning of the occupation, but the actual nature of its application varied from time to time. Most of the mayors elected in the 1976 municipal elections were "nationalists," supporters of the PLO, replacing the traditionalist pro-Jordanian leadership.[34] Together with other notables, intellectuals, and professionals, the new mayors tried to establish an "inside" leadership (supposedly subordinate to the "outside" leadership), through the formation of the National Guidance Committee (NGC). The NGC was outlawed by Israel in 1982, and most of its principal members were dismissed from their offices or exiled (two others were attacked by a Jewish underground group). In short, the occupiers could not allow the creation of a country-wide independent Palestinian leadership that was perceived as a kernel of state and nation building, and an extension and arm of the PLO.[35]

However, the complete economic dependence on Israel prevented any real development of the economic and social infrastructure of local institutions. Almost no investments were made in economic or social development. In addition, employment in Israel undermined the traditional family structure; youngsters and women were now earning money outside the control of the elder traditional authority. The recent hopes of certain intellectuals of building a genuine "civil society" built on the ruins of traditionalism and fueled by the Intifada—the uprising that demanded a separation from Israel—also evaporated. The social outcome of the uprising was an internally weakened and divided society.

Under Israeli military government, two kinds of Palestinian heros developed in the West Bank and Gaza—the holy warrior or *fida'i*, whom we encountered earlier, ready for self-sacrifice, and the steadfast one *(samid)*, who endured the hardship and humiliations imposed by the conquerer, staying on the land at all costs in order to avoid a repetition of the 1948 *nakba*. The invention of *sumoud* (steadfastness) in the 1970s, as a response to intensive Israeli settlement, created a limited and conditional legitimacy for cooperating with the conqueror and not escalating guerrilla resistance within the territories.[36]

Despite the assymetrical relationship between ruler and ruled, Palestinian society received a high level of exposure to Israeli society. Many learned the Hebrew language, became consumers of Israeli mass-media, were employed by Israelis (in Israel or in the occupied territories themselves), and formed business ties with Israelis. In addition, generations of young Palestinians spent varying periods in Israeli jails and detention camps. Jewish Israelis encountered Palestinians mainly during their army service—policing and "maintaining security" in the Gaza or the West Bank—or as employers. The Palestinians learned the advantages and limitations of the Israeli system, while the Jews strengthened their stereotypes. As the political stalemate continued, the process of Jewish colonization advanced. The standard of living of the Palestinians rose slightly while the traditional family structure was weakened, and the level of education rose dramatically. In addition, the Palestinian resistance to the occupation became more sophisticated. The *sumoud* civil society became more active and viable, reaching the level of a popular uprising and mass resistance by the end of 1987. The images of the *samid* and the *fida'i* merged into the image and social role of *shahid,* the martyr who sacrificed his (and sometimes her) life for the sake of national liberation.[37]

The Uprising

Since the beginning of the occupation, a revolutionary situation has existed in the West Bank and Gaza Strip. The legitimacy of the occupier was never recognized by the local population. This was expressed by sporadic violence and resistance directed against Israel. Israelis conveniently interpreted these events as disturbances of public order and as marginal phenomena. Thus, it took time for the Israelis to understand the nature and scope of the grassroots uprising.[38] The popular uprising, carried out by youth (the "children of the stones") exemplified a "paradox-of-the-power"[39]: A fundamentally weak partner in a conflict can gain an advantage over a much stronger entity that is limited by the political and moral constraints of its own superior position. The territories became ungovernable and, for the first time since 1967, the cost of holding them exceeded the benefits for most individuals in the Israeli collectivity. Creeping penetration of the guerrilla warfare into the "Jewish Israeli territories" created a picture of the relations between the Jewish Israelis and Palestinians of the West Bank similar to that of intercommunal warfare in such places as Northern Ireland or former Yugoslavia. The focus of the armed struggle shifted inward and the salience of "external operations" decreased correspondingly.

In Israel the difference between "front" and "rear" was blurred, with individual members of each collectivity becoming potential "soldiers" and "victims." Israeli men and women on the streets anxiously began to carry weapons as a matter of routine, thus recruiting themselves into the "war" by the expectation of sudden involvement at any point in time. The Israeli Jewish population was thrust onto the same plane of communal warfare that the Palestinians had already experienced since the beginning of the Israeli (and maybe the Jordanian) occupation.

For the first time since 1967 the Green Line boundary reappeared on the cognitive map of the Jewish population as a result of extended closures and curfews. The necessity of separation—without a concrete specification of how, where and when—crept into Jewish Israeli awareness. Separation became a desired political option, yet the first stage was not neccessarily linked in the public mind with the possibility of withdrawal from the territories or the dismantling of the settlements, let alone the establishment of a Palestinian state.

Within the Palestinian population, the scope of recruitment to the uprising expanded tremendously. One of the most fundamental developments resulting from the popular uprising was the amalgamation of the Islamic elements into the violent struggle and the consequent formation of Hamas. Originally the Islamic elements, the most prominent of which was *al-Mujamma' al-Islami* in Gaza, were an offshoot of the Muslim Brotherhood, which had sponsored sporadical social activities in Palestine following its founding in 1945. The *Mujamma'* concentrated efforts on religious and social activities: building mosques, community centers and youth clubs, and fighting against drugs, prostitution, and other social maladies, as it defined them. In 1979 it was officially recognized by the Israeli military government as a religious association, and until 1983 it had tacit support from the Israeli authorities, who first perceived it as a counterbalance against the nationalistic PLO.

Hamas was founded in January 1988 by the charismatic Shaykh Ahmad Yasin as a political movement in Gaza. At the same time its military wing was established, named after the hero of the Palestinian Great Revolt of 1936-39, Shaykh Izz al-Din al-Qassam.[40] Hamas claims about 30 percent support among the Palestinians of Gaza and the West Bank.[41] The Hamas Convenant, published in August 1988, declares that "the liberation of Palestine in its entirety, from the [Mediterranean] Sea to the [Jordan] River, is the most supreme strategic goal." A smaller rival organization, the Islamic Jihad, founded in Gaza in early 1980, is more interested in pan-Islamism and is influenced by Iranian Khomenism and the Algerian Islamic Salvation Front (FIS). The Islamic Jihad is more militant and is, in fact, responsible in considerable measure for encouraging Hamas's founders to endorse violent activity.

THE 1993 OSLO AGREEMENT
AND THE PALESTINIAN NATIONAL AUTHORITY

The ability of Israeli political culture to adopt an accord with the Palestinians, led by the PLO, with relatively little domestic resistance, was surprising, considering that contact with the organization was prohibited by Israeli law just a short time before. This is even more dramatic if we take into consideration that the consequences of this agreement and its implementation meant not only the acceptance of the PLO and some of its demands, but also entailed a far-reaching change in the political status quo in the occupied territories. The change in the first stage of the interim agreement was in accepting Palestinian autonomy in Gaza and Jericho areas and then extension of that autonomy to most areas of the West Bank and Gaza, entailing a major redeployment of Israeli troops, as a kind of "disengagement" between the two collectivities.

Since the first year following Israel's Lebanon war of 1982, a small (approximately 20 percent) but slowly growing minority of Israeli Jews supported the establishment of a Palestinian state, a rate of support that over time saw more than a net 10-percent growth (and in the first euphoric stage of the agreement reached 40 percent). Support has stabilized at around 33 percent.[42] The acceptance of the autonomy plan is, of course, also considered a revolutionary change in Palestinian political thinking.

From the Israeli point of view, the very conception of the Declaration of Principles (DOP) and its de facto implementation was possible because, contrary to prevailing "common sense" opinion, it was well rooted in the Israeli power-oriented culture. From the beginning of the return of the Labor Party to power in 1992, there was a demonstrated stiffening in the policy toward the Palestinians, which included the mass deportation of Islamic activists and extensions of curfews and closures on the Palestinian population. The macho image of the late Israeli premier Yitzhak Rabin was well established before, by his iron-fist policies in the 1980s and his "break their bones" orders as a response to the Intifada, and he was strongly identified with this power culture.[43] Ironically, the previous right-wing, "patriotic" Likud adminstration, despite some of its rhetoric, was more easily identified with the "weakness" components of Israeli-Jewish political culture, as most of its political moves were based on "anxiety-arousing" sentiments, rather than the "activist" and "security" theme in Labor's message. The final status of the Palestinian entity was conveniently left for another stage of negotiations, dependent on the condition that the Palestinian Authority (PA) "prove" itself through its policies and ability to govern. The major indicator of Palestinian "success" was defined by the Israelis in terms of providing "security" for the Israeli-Jewish population. For this reason, most of the Israelis were ready to accept the formation of several militia units and security forces by the PA.

A major concern for the Israeli public and leadership was that, despite Israel's formidable military strength, its power underwent continuous attrition and slow deterioration, resulting from the need to "police" the occupied territories. As the Palestinian popular uprising continued, the price of direct control of the Palestinian population by the Israeli military system grew, while the gains for the Israeli economy were decreasing. Many Israeli military units drastically cut their basic and advanced training, but worse was the changing mentality of the entire military body from an elite corp, able to conduct extensive blitzkrieg-style large-scale wars, into a static, internal security militia. The Israeli military quickly learned the limitations of a military power facing active civilian resistance primarily composed of stone-throwing children and youth.

Another heavy burden on the Israeli military has been protecting the small Jewish settlements dispersed among the densely populated Palestinian population. According to an obsolete security doctrine, any Jewish settlement in this space is a part of a regional defense system in case of war, granting "territorial depth" for defensive forces. Analysis of the present and future battlefields as well as the lessons of the 1973 war in the Syrian (Golan) Heights, proves the contrary. Settlements and settlers were a burden on the military and limited large-scale movements of armored troops on the battlefield. However, it seems that the Israeli government estimates that public opinion is not ready to tolerate the dismantling of settlements, including those that could be used as bargaining cards vis-à-vis the Syrians and the Palestinians. Even the Netzarim settlement, isolated in the Gaza Strip and entailing a high military and political cost to maintain, is perceived in these terms.

Thus, a power-oriented analysis of the situation, leads to the conclusion that indirect control of the Palestinians is a better and cheaper strategy than direct control,[44] especially in a completely ungovernable area such as the Gaza Strip. The transfer of local rule to a Palestinian authority, police, and secret services was one of the logical conclusions derived from the Israeli power-oriented culture. These arrangements will take at least five years. In any case, a Palestinian "autonomous entity"—or in the worst case analysis, from the current Israeli point of view, a sovereign state—divided territorially between the Gaza Strip and the West Bank and compressed between Jordan and Israel—is for Israel a greater strategic asset than threat.

The Oslo Accord itself includes several "bugs" that contradict the view of Palestinian autonomy just described. The PA desperately needed to gain a legitimacy among the Palestinian population that could only be obtained by holding general and more or less free elections. Elections were finally held in January 1996, in accordance with the Oslo 2 Agreement of 28 September 1995, after major redeployments of Israeli troops from populated areas. The withdrawal of troops in areas of mixed population left behind the seeds of future conflict, such as in the case of Hebron; the redeployment there without evacuation of the small, militant Jewish population is a sure formula for confrontation with the Muslim majority. The Israeli government is too weak to wage an open conflict with the settlers, before a comprehensive "peace package deal" is presented to the public, and is unwilling to do so in any case. However, the "catch-22" is that such a "deal" is not achievable without the "empowerment" of the Palestinian Authority. As the implementation of the empowerment process continued, opposition within the Palestinian camp and among its Islamic components increased the "armed struggle" against Israeli targets within Israel, with the expressed aim of destroying the agreement. A softer interpretation perceives these terror attacks as a signal to the PA, controlled by Fatah, to recognize the Islamic opposition's legitimacy and allow it freedom of political as well as freedom to develop its social and educational activities.

When all is said and done, the Palestinian Authority has been unable to deliver the promised internal security "goods" to the Israelis, and it has failed to deliver tangible and immediate results for the Palestinian population in terms of raising the quality of life, creating better economic conditions, and providing greater freedom of expression. The Western states, which promised massive financial aid to the PA, have hesitated to fulfill their commitments in the absence of clear programs for spending the money for its intended purposes.[45] Much of the aid that did arrive was turned over to supporting the various branches of the PA military. The Israeli leadership, too, was unable to supply the much desired and long-promised internal security, a promise that returned the Labor to power following the 1992 elections. Intensification of the Islamic and other guerrilla attacks left the peace process looking like a "fake" in the eyes of Israeli public opinion, which tended to return to its traditional anti-Arab sentiments. The Israeli government's response to attacks—imposing long closures on the occupied territories—only worsened material conditions for the Palestinians, especially the Gazans, as a considerable portion of the population depended upon work inside Israel. However, the PA's relative success in establishing authority and reducing violence by the Islamists for the most part kept the gradual implementation of the agreement on track.

Pragmatization of the Fatah

The PLO, lead by the mainstream Fatah and Arafat, have already made gradual-yet-essential—although sometimes merely implicit—moves toward coexistence and recognition of Israel. The first was the twelfth PNC resolution (July 1974), "establishing a Palestinian national authority in any liberated area [from Israel]"—the so-called "mini-state option." The second move was made in December 1988 when Arafat declared in Geneva that the PLO recognized the rights of all parties concerned in the Middle East conflict, including the State of Palestine, Israel and other neighbors, to exist in peace and security; denounced terrorism; and accepted United Nations Resolution 181. Despite the fact that these were abstract declarations without any concrete policy and institutional application, they managed to arouse a strident antagonism among many Palestinian groups. The entire process of accepting the Israeli offer and its accompanying details was a revolutionary move for the PLO, as represented by the Fatah leadership and encouraged by part of the local leadership in the occupied territories.

None of this means that Arafat and his colleagues were not aware of the Israeli motives and the unfavorable terms from the PLO's point of view, as well as the danger of becoming the Israelis' soldiers of fortune rather than their equal partners. The Palestinian intellectuals in the West, as well as Palestinians who remained outside Palestine, have become the greatest critics of the agreements, continually reminding Arafat and his colleagues of the faults. The irony is that both the late Rabin and Arafat have been labeled by elements of their own constituencies as "traitors." Indeed, only a weakened Fatah leader, after the major political mistake of supporting the Iraqi invasion of Kuwait, without the Soviet superpower's political and military backing, and threatened by a growing "inside" leadership (graduates of the popular uprising and Israeli interrogation methods, jails, and detentions camps), could be coerced into accepting the near-capitulation terms, in order to survive.

Nonetheless, the ambiguous and foggy deal proposed by the Israelis holds within it the potential creation of a small, independent Palestinian state in the future. As a sovereign state, it will have greater possibilities to maneuver and exploit political or military opportunities (facing its two major potential enemies, Jordan and Israel). No doubt its small size, split into two separate territorial units, internal demographic pressures, economic underdevelopment, lack of natural resources, and pressures from a highly mobilized diaspora will lend this state built-in political and social instability.[46]

The PLO-Israel deal included an understanding that the organization would amend the Palestinian National Charter, in that the preamble of the Washington Declaration stated that "it is time [for Israelis and Palestinians] to put an end to decades of confrontation and conflict, recognize their mutual legitimate and political rights, and strive to live in peaceful coexistence, mutual dignity, and security to achieve a just, lasting, and comprehensive settlement and historic reconciliation through the agreed political process." Interestingly enough, the agreement was made between the government of the State of Israel and "the Palestinian team representing the Palestinian people," and not with the PLO, or one of its organs. In an extensive analysis in *al-Sharq al-Aswat* (April 26, 1994), Bilal al-Hasan, a brother of Khalied al-Hasan, one of the original founding fathers of Fatah, challenged the legal relations between the newly founded PA and its council, which was to be elected by the Palestinian population of the authority, and the PLO organs, questioning the subordination of the latter to the council and the PA. In other words, al-Hasan, like a substantial portion of the Palestinian leadership and intellectuals remaining in *ghurba* (exile), questioned the legality of the amendments to the Charter. To make it more complicated, the Israelis conditioned the holding of elections for a new locally elected self-governing Palestinian council, upon amendments to the Charter, placing the PA in a no-win situation.

THE NEW REJECTIONIST FRONT AND THE HOLY LAND

When, in July 1974, the twelfth PNC adopted the idea of the "mini-state option" (which was in fact a late acceptance of the 1948 partition plan), giving up the traditional claim for "Greater Palestine," many Palestinians perceived it as a betrayal of the cause.[47] Important organizations such as George Habash's Popular Front for the Liberation of Palestine (PFLP) resigned from the Executive Committee, and established the "Rejectionist Front," supported mainly by Iraq and Libya. Every deviation from the traditional total Palestinian negation of the legitimacy of a Jewish polity in Palestine sparked harsh disputes and created cleavages and violent conflicts.

Thus, it is no wonder that a good deal of violence and open criticism accompanied the acceptance of the Declaration of Principles and the other agreements (Cairo, Washington, etc.) with Israel by Arafat. Not only by non-Fatah-affiliated organizations, but even members of his immediate entourage (with such central figures as Faruq Qaddumi and Hani al-Hasan) openly criticized the agreement). Other previously strong supporters of Arafat and Fatah, including such intellectuals as Edward Said, Hisham Sharabi and Elia Zureik, publicly or non-publicly attacked the agreement or quietly withdrew from their positions on negotiation teams (established in October 1991 following the Madrid peace talks), arguing that the agreement gave the Israelis too much. Other prominent Palestinians continued to refuse to accept any recognition of the Jewish state within historic Palestine. Most of the Palestinians who remained in *ghurba* would not benefit in the forseeable future from the agreement, and thus would have no interest in accepting it. For those in the would-be Palestinian territories, it seemed minor compensation for all the humiliations and frustrations that accompanied the years of occupation. For the younger generations it has also been hard to adapt to a routinized life, after the "glorious" days of uprising and "permanent revolution."

Under such circumstances Arafat and the other Fatah supporters of the agreement have relied mainly on the support of the West Bank middle class and the personal loyalty of Fatah military units and security forces brought in from the "outside".[48] The most loyal and enthusiastic Arab supporters of the agreements were the vast majority of Israel's Arab citizens, who had long desired a reconciliation between "their people" (the Palestinians) and "their state" (Israel). In fact, for both Palestinians and Israeli Jews, the agreement hurt longstanding cognitive maps—of who the "enemy" is, of the "intentions" of the "other," and of the imperatives of collective memories and amnesia—without any proper preparation. Moreover, for both parties, many vested interests are sunk into the continuation of the conflict, and the mutual concessions that actually or potentially touched upon the interests of diverse social strata.[49] Intentionally or unintentionally, the tactic of both leaderships was to quickly build a new irreversible social and political reality based on their existing political cultures.

The beginning of the resolution of the conflict between the two national movements—Zionism and Palestinism—exposed an additional layer of this confrontation: the primordial and religious dimensions. For both collectivities Palestine/Eretz Israel was not only a father- or motherland, but the Holy Land.[50] As the conflict's national meanings were reduced, its religious and primordial meanings increased. These trends began much earlier on the Jewish side, when, following the 1967 war and the "reunion" with "holiness of the national cradlelands," a semi-millenarian movement arose among the Jewish population, focused in the later creation of Gush Emunim and a grassroots settler movement in the West Bank[51] that reshaped Israeli society's social and political boundaries. It remains unclear if a real political threat to the Jewish settlements in the Holy Land will lead to violent resistance, and whether there is a potential government that will be ready or able to face such a resistance.

From the Palestinian side, the conflict between the rapidly growing, highly politicized, and armed Islamic movements, and Judaism as a religion and culture is even more prominent.[52] The conflict always had religious roots, and from the beginning religious symbols and terms (such as *jihad, shahid* or *fida'i*) were used to mobilize the peripheries for the struggle. However, the Muslim religion was only one component used for conflict management. From the perspective of the Islamic movement, the religious side of the conflict is the dominant consideration. (Theologically, to give up an Islamic land to non-Islamic people is prohibited.) However, it seems that Hamas's hesitation to join the "peace process" was rooted more in the continuation of the initial Palestinian nationalistic approach, together with an internal struggle that left open an option to participate in the new Palestinian polity. The continuation of guerrilla warfare against Israel in order to blow up the PLO-Israel agreement was a fundamental challenge to the Palestinian Authority. At the same time, this challenge can be seen as an invitation by an Islamic leadership requesting recognition as a partner in the "deal," and treatment as a legitimate actor in the establishment of a new polity.

The Palestinian national leadership, in this situation, has a major dilemma: on one hand to prove its credibility through its ability to implement the agreements with Israel in order that the process continue, and to deliver the goods by being the guardian of Israel's security. At the same time it must avoid a major clash—one that could develop into a civil war—with the Islamic movements and the other opposition elements in Palestinian society. Yet, experiencing the terms of the agreements with the Israelis as humiliating, the PA has to continually test the boundaries of Israeli "permissiveness" and public opinion in terms of granting the use of additional state symbols, nationalist activities in East Jerusalem, and power and institutions that point toward the establishment of a future independent state.

Epilogue

The Israel-PLO agreements are simultaneously compatible and contradictory to both sides' collective memories, cultures, and conventional wisdoms, as well as the interests of different strata and interest groups in each society. They are a kind of political experiment in the making. In social science such an experiment is labeled as a "social construction of reality," giving different interpretations to the sociopolitical facts. The move was taken by two leaderships that tried to provide new solutions to old problems and, in large measure, to force on their own constituencies top-down solutions. Both leaderships had enough power to begin the process, but this power eroded as they tried to convert images to institutional arrangements.

During an international conference dedicated to the Arab-Israeli conflict at Tel Aviv University in late 1992, most of the participating experts agreed that the conflict "was ripe for resolution."[53] However, none of these experts could provide any theoretical conceptualization or historical depth, beyond wishful thinking and gut feelings. No doubt that at that time dramatic changes had occurred in the Middle East; beginning with the Camp David Accords and later accelerated by the collapse of the bipolar "world order" and the dismantling of the Eastern bloc, which was considered the military, ideological, and political "patron" of the Arab and Palestinian causes. The hidden agenda behind the "ripeness theory" was at least partially built on the assumption that the Israeli side of the conflict had attained a decisive power position that enabled it to dictate terms to the Arab side, including the recognition of Israel's right to exist in the region. The other component of this theory was the assumption that from such a powerful position, the Israeli side would feel secure enough to give the Arabs such a generous offer that a revolutionary shift would be created in their political and ideological thought, and would lead to their acceptance of the Israeli state and settler-society in the region.

These ingredients of the "ripeness theory" formed the background dimensions of the settlement, as conducted by the Israeli power-oriented culture vis-à-vis the Palestinians. However, power is a very elusive notion, and in some cases has a "consumer effect": the more that one uses a product, the less it is worth. The Palestinian leadership learned a similar lesson. While trying to convert prestige and image into real power, it discovered that power concomitantly deflates. The result is an open question as to the state of ripeness of the Israeli-Palestinian conflict.

The results of the 1996 elections demonstrated that the Jewish population of Israel indeed was not "ripe" for a reasonable settlement.

NOTES

* The author would like to acknowledge Avraham Sela for his extensive comments on a previous draft of this chapter as well as Samuel Shye, Elihu Katz, and Hanna Levinson of the Louis Guttman Israel Institute of Applied Social Research for their cooperation in supplying survey data for this chapter.
1. That is, "the Land of Israel," or, implicitly, "the land belonging to the Jewish people." The precise scope and boundaries of "the land" were never defined precisely, and were subject to internal dispute and political struggle among different streams of the Zionist movement, as well as the consequence of a number of political opportunities. For an analysis of Jewish territorial behavior see Baruch Kimmerling's *Zionism and Territory: The Socioterritorial Dimension of Zionist Politics* (Berkeley: Institute of International Studies, University of California, 1983). Also see Yosef Gorni's description in *Zionism and the Arabs, 1882-1948: A Study of Ideology* (Oxford: Clarendon Press, 1987) of various streams and attitudes in Zionism toward the "Palestinian question."
2. Jews and Arabs drew diametrically opposite political conclusions from this basic approach. The Arabs perceived all the territory of Palestine as Arab land (in its Islamic version, belonging to God, and legally endowed *[waqf]*. On this land Jews have rights as individuals, but have no basis for any collective, political or nationalistic claims. The Zionists argued that there is no legitimate room for Arab claims for their ancient homeland; rather, the Palestinian Arabs, as a part of the Arab nation, should fulfill and exercise their collective political rights in the framework of the Arab nation and other surrounding Arab states. Those that remained under sovereign Jewish control would enjoy human and civic rights as individuals. This is one facet of the so-called Arab-Jewish conflict. For a full analysis see Mark Tessler, *A History of the Israeli-Palestinian Conflict* (Bloomington: Indiana University Press, 1994).

3. For descriptions of the origins of Palestinian nationalism see Muhammad Y. Muslih, *The Origins of Palestinian Nationalism* (New York: Columbia University Press, 1988), for its development during the British colonial period see Yehoshua Porath, *The Emergence of the Palestinian National Movement, 1918-1929* (London: Frank Cass, 1974) and *The Palestinian National Movement, 1929-1939: From Riots to Rebellion,* 1977), and for a full analysis of its development until 1993 see Baruch Kimmerling and Joel S. Migdal, *Palestinians: The Making of a People* (Cambridge, Mass.: Harvard University Press, 1994).
4. Kimmerling and Migdal, *Palestinians.*
5. Smooha, Sammy, *Arabs and Jews in Israel: Conflicting and Shared Values* (Boulder, Colo.: Westview Press, 1989); Lustick, Ian, *Arabs in the Jewish State: Israel's Control Over a National Minority* (Austin: University of Texas Press, 1980).
6. Fatah is the reversed acronym for *Harakat al-Tahrir al-Filastiniyya,* or Palestine Liberation Movement. Among the initial founders were Yasir Arafat (with the nom de guerre, Abu Ammar), Khalil al-Wazir (Abu Jihad), Salah Khalaf (Abu Iyad), Khalid and Hani al-Hasan, Farouq Qaddoumi, Mahmud 'Abbas (Abu Mazin), Yusuf al-Najjar and Kamal Adwan. There are varying versions about the precise origins of Fatah founders. Cobban probably has the most accurate "inside information" on the mainstream group (Helena Cobban, *Middle East Insight,* 6:3 (1988): 21-28).
7. The PLO was established following an inter-Arab rivalry between the Iraqi president Abd al-Karim Qasim and Gamal Abd al-Nasir in the late 1950s and early 1960s when they competed in declaring support for a "Palestinian entity" (not a state). The PLO was established May of 1964, following the first Arab summit in February of the same year. The Arab summit meetings later approved the creation of the Palestine Liberation Army, ostensibly to recover the rest of Palestine (over and above the West Bank and the Gaza Strip) from the Jews.
8. Cobban, Helena, *The Palestinian Liberation Organization: People, Power, and Politics* (Cambridge: Cambridge University Press, 1984), p. 33.
9. Meron Benvenisti (1986) calls this the return of the "communal warfare" situation, in "Israel's Decolonization Crisis," *New Outlook* (December 1989): 16-19; Emanuel Sivan labeled it a "colonial situation."
10. Ya'ari, Ehud, *Strike Terror: The Story of Fatah* (New York: Sabra Books, 1970).
11. Kimmerling and Migdal, *Palestinians,* 222.
12. These passages are taken from Leila S. Kadi's *Political Documents of the Armed Palestinian Resistance Movement* (Beirut: PLO Research Center, 1969).

13. For many years the official Israeli position was unable to accept the revival of an independent and authentic Palestinian political and military entity, to the PLO as another Arab tool to delegitimize Israel, referring to the population of the West Bank as "Jordanians" and to the inhabitants of the Gaza Strip as "refugees." However, it seems, that the Israeli leadership did understand the real meaning of the post-Shuqairi PLO.
14. Gresh, Alain. *The PLO—The Struggle Within,* trans. A. M. Berrett (London: Zed Books, 1983).
15. See Rosemary Sayigh, *Palestinians: From Peasants to Revolutionaries* (London: Zed Press, 1979); and Laurie A. Brand, *Palestinians in the Arab World: Institution Building and the Search for State* (New York: Columbia University Press, 1988).
16. Operations such as the attack on a school in Ma'alot (15 May 1974), Kiryat Shmona (November 1974), attacks on movie theaters, coffee houses, and hotels (the Hotel Savoy in March 1975), in downtown Jerusalem and Tel Aviv, and a bus on the central coastal highway (March 1978) occupy a salient place in Israeli collective memory. The usual Palestinian response to the accusations that their armed struggle was indiscriminate terror mostly aimed against civilian targets, was that the entire Israeli Jewish society participates in the military effort; thus any distinction between "civilian" and "military" targets is not valid. This argument is sometimes expanded to include the diaspora Jewish community, as well as the "capitalist world order," due to its support of Israel, or because Israel is seen as its "agent" in the region. Only since the late 1980s has an effort been made to primarily hit at military targets within Israel, or settler-targets in the occupied territories.
17. Harkabi, Yehoshafat, *Arab Strategies and Israel's Response* (New York: The Free Press, 1977).
18. Kimmerling, Baruch, "Between the Primordial and the Civil Definitions of the Collective Identity," in *Comparative Social Dynamics,* Erik Cohen, Moshe Lissak, and Uri Almagor, eds. (Boulder, Colo.: Westview Press, 1985).
19. Kimmerling, Baruch, "Patterns of Militarism in Israel," *European Journal of Sociology* 2 (1993), 1-28.
20. In Yiddish, *"der nebech'dicker Shimshoyn."*
21. Zemah, Mina, *Attitudes of the Jewish Majority Towards the Arab Minority* (in Hebrew) (Jerusalem: Van Leer Foundation, 1980); and Smooha, *Arabs and Jews in Israel,* 132-33.
22. The first planned guerrilla operation was thwarted by the Egyptians, who arrested the entire fida'i group in Gaza. In the second operation—apparently against the Israeli national water-carrier project—one guerrilla, Ahmad Musa, was killed by Jordanians and another, Mahmoud Hijazi, was captured by the

Israelis. During this period Fatah received some military training and support from Syria. This was probably the reason to attack the water carrier, which was one of the major sources of conflict between Syria and Israel. However, when in 1966 the Syrians intended to replace Arafat with a pro-Syrian officer, jailing Arafat and Abu Iyad, the cooperation temporarily ceased and Fatah learned how to manipulate inter-Arab rivalries in order to keep its relative autonomy. See Barry Rubin, *Revolution Until Victory: The Politics and History of the PLO* (Cambridge, Mass.: Harvard University Press, 1994), 11.

23. Migdal, Joel S., *Palestinian Society and Politics* (Princeton: Princeton: University Press, 1980); and Kimmerling and Migdal, *Palestinians.*
24. Cobban, *Middle East Insight,* 30-31. Claims for Jordan as a part of a Palestinian state were considered shortly afterward by the Palestinians as "bad politics." First, such claims would turn into a premature total war with the Hashemite Kingdom; secondly, the establishment of a Palestinian state in Jordan could be interpreted as giving up the core lands of Western Palestine. Indeed, the ultranationalist Israeli leader, Maj. General Ariel Sharon, has long asserted that "Jordan is Palestine."
25. Israeli experts rushed to explain to the politicians and public opinion the meaning of this "code." Between 624 (the battle of Bader) and 630 a series of raids between the Meccan Quraysh tribe (Muhammad's original tribe) and the army of Medina (or *Madinat al-nabi,* Yathrib, the place where Muhammed received asylum from persecutions, or performed the *hijra,* which included also a Jewish community). In 627 the Qurayshs defeated Muhammad and his followers, but in a counter attack Muhammad assaulted Mecca. The Treaty of Hudaybiyya reached among the Meccans and Medinans was supposed to end the rivalries and allowed the Medinans to freely perform the pilgrimage to Mecca. In 630, after Muhammad accumulated enough power, he attacked and took over Mecca, consolidating his power in Arabia, and imposed on the nomadic Bedouin tribes the new religion. With this his alliance with the Jews of Medina came to an end. Andrew Rippin, *Muslims: Their Religious Beliefs and Practices,* vol. 1: *The Formative Period* (London: Routledge, 1991), 33-4; and Albert Hourani, *A History of the Arab Peoples* (Cambridge, Mass.: Harvard University Press, 1991), 17-19.
26. Ironically some Israelis titled him "the Mayor of Gaza." This poor image was even strengthened by a comparison with the portrait of Husain, the king of Jordan, who was depicted as a smart and strong gentleman, a man of the world, especially after the October 1994 peace accord with Jordan.
27. Yishai, Yael, *Land or Peace: Whither Israel* (Stanford, Calif.: Stanford University, Hoover Institution Press, 1987), 3.
28. Kimmerling, *Zionism and Territory.*

29. The Allon Plan was never adopted officially, but until 1977 it was a basic guide for the Israeli government. Its basic presumtion was that the densely populated territories should be returned to Arab (Jordanian) control, the Jordan River must be regarded as a "security border," the Jordan valley should be settled by Jews, and the "unified Jerusalem" metropolitan area must be considerably enlarged, through the inclusion of the Etzion bloc.
30. Benvenisti, Meron, *Report: Demographic, Economic, Legal, Social and Political Developments in the West Bank* (Jerusalem: West Bank Data Project, 1986).
31. Ian Lustick opposed the approach of Benvenisti, proposing a highly sophisticated model of thresholds, from simple military occupation to hegemonic control. He explored this thesis in a wide comparative perspective. See Ian Lustick, *Unsettled States/Disputed Lands: Britain and Ireland, France in Algeria, Israel and the West Bank-Gaza* (Ithaca: Cornell University Press, 1993).
32. Migdal, *Palestinian Society and Politics;* and Hilterman, Joost, *Behind the Intifadah: Labor and Women's Movements in the Occupied Territories* (Princeton: Princeton University Press, 1991).
33. Tamari, Salim, "The Uprising's Dilemma: Limited Rebellion in Civil Society," *Middle East Report,* (May-June/July-August, 1990): 7-1l.
34. Bassam al-Shak'a was elected in Nablus, Fahd Qwasmi in Hebron, Karim Khalaf in Ramallah, and Ibrahim al-Tawil in al-Bireh.
35. It seems that the "outside" leadership also felt threatened by the new—and in some cases, elected—leadership.
36. Kimmerling and Migdal, *Palestinians,* 211-12.
37. Hunter, Robert F., *The Palestinian Uprising: A War by Other Means* (Berkeley: University of California Press, 1991); and Kimmerling and Migdal, *Palestinians.*
38. Schiff, Ze'ev and Ehud Ya'ari. 1990. *Intifada: The Palestinian Uprising—Israel's Third Front* (New York: Simon and Schuster, 1990); and Shalev, Arieh, *The Intifada: Causes and Effects* (Jerusalem: Jerusalem Post Press, 1991).
39. Kimmerling, Baruch, *State and Society: The Sociology of Politics,* vol. 2 (Tel Aviv: The Open University Press, 1995).
40. Bowden, Tom, "The Politics of Arab Rebellion in Palestine," *Middle Eastern Studies,* 11:2 (1975): 147-174.
41. Abu 'Ammar, Ziad, *Islamic Fundamentalism in the West Bank and Gaza: Muslim Brotherhood and Islamic Jihad* (Bloomington, Indiana: Indiana University Press, 1994); and Anat Kurz and David Tal, "The Hamas: Islamic Zealotry in National Struggle," in *Islamic Terrorism and Israel* (in Hebrew), ed. A. Kurz (Tel Aviv: Papyrus and Tel Aviv University's Jaffee Center of Strategic Studies), 157-203.
42. The data are based on Al-Haj, Katz and Shye (1993) and data provided to the author of this chapter by the Louis Guttman Institute of Applied Social

Research. Questions about supporting the establishment of a Palestinian state were not asked before May 1989. Generally, the outcomes of surveys that were done by other institutes showed the same trends. In May 1989, 20 percent of the Israeli Jewish population favored the establishment of a Palestinian state (beyond the present autonomy); in July 1990, 22 percent; in November 1990 (the period of Gulf crisis), 17 percent; in May 1991, 22 percent. A dramatic change occurred following the agreement: in September 1993, 40 percent favored a state; in October 1993, 33 percent; in July 1994, 33 percent. The Israeli Arab citizens' support remained very stable: approximately 95 percent. At the same time the majority of the Jewish population supported the Oslo agreement, varying between 62 percent and 54 percent (in August 1994, before the major Islamic terrorist activities). Following the agreement, 57 percent of the Jewish population also supported the cessation of the settlement-building process in the occupied territory, but at the same time opposed dismantling already existing settlements (only 35 percent supported evacuation). Twenty-five percent of the Jewish population believe that Arafat really wants peace—a 15 percent increase compared to May 1989. The public's readiness to make further concessions to the Palestinians increased from 54 percent in June 1994 to 60 percent in August, and approval of the government "handling of current affairs" increased sharply, from 38 percent in June 1994 to 54 percent following the accord with Jordan (Elihu Katz and Hanna Levinson of the Guttman Institute of Applied Social Research, Press Releases, 14 June 1994 and 7-8 August 1994.

43. Yitzhak Rabin was the minister of defense in the National Unity government, under the Likud's leadership, when the Palestinian popular uprising erupted in the Gaza Strip and West Bank in December 1987.

44. The first attempt to use this idea was the establishment of the Village Leagues, quasi military armed groups paid by the Israeli occupation authority and its secret branches, and lead by Mustapha Doudin. This was the initiative of Menachem Milson, a professor of Arab literature at the Hebrew University, appointed as civilian administrator of the West Bank in early 1982. Milson, equipped with the knowledge of the traditional cleavages between the *fellahin* and the city dwellers, made an attempt at "applied Orientalism," hoping to coopt a part of the less nationalistic peasantry, and use them to oppress the more "Palestinized" urban middle classes and intellectuals (Tessler 1994, 549-52). A far more successful move was the establishment of the Southern Lebanese Army, which operates as a soldiers-of-fortune army in the Israeli buffer zone in Southern Lebanon.

45. Some argue that the PA leaders did not establish the requested institutions in order to receive financial resources free of the donor's control. According to this

approach, the PA was also playing the chaos and weakness game, in order to be "saved" financially, without having limits or control imposed on them. This was also done to "recruit" Israeli influence and maximize received resources.

46. In fact, Jordan, with its estimated 60-70 percent Palestinian population, is the best-tailored target for expected Palestinian expansionism. This knowledge made the Bedouin dynasty rush toward a peace agreement with Israel in 1994, as a kind of alliance and insurance that will cement the "traditional" tacit agreements among the two. Israel is also too powerful at this stage, and in the forseeable future, to be threated strategically by a Palestinian state. Paradoxically, the existence of Israel should be the best "insurance policy" for the continuous existence and sovereignty of the Palestinian state vis-à-vis the power of its Arab neighbours.

47. The Israeli interpretation of this historical turn of events was to underplay it as a "tactical move," the adoption of a new doctrine with the aim of dismantling Israel in stages; in such a framework the Palestinians would attain the "mini-state" and have a better power position to conquer the whole of Palestine (see, for example, Harkabi, *Arab Strategies and Israel's Response*). David Ben-Gurion, when accepting the partition plan in 1937 used the same reasoning.

48. This is precisely what raised concern among the educated middle class in the West Bank regarding the formation of a totalitarian and police-state entity.

49. It became clear that the major victims of the settlement from the Jewish side were all or most of the settlers in the occupied territories, including their families. On the other side, millions of Palestinians are called on to give up their hope and right to return to their previous properties, lands, homes and localities. Peace is an abstract notion that is very difficult to exchange for tangible assets (Kimmerling, Baruch, "Peace for Territories: A Macro-Sociological Analysis of the Concept of Peace in Zionist Ideology," *Journal of Applied Behavioral Science* 23:3 (1987), 13-34.

50. For the Jewish religious-primordial relation to Israel see Kimmerling, "Between the Primordial and the Civil Definitions of the Collective Identity." No similar professional analysis exists for the Palestinian or Arab partner.

51. Kimmerling, *Zionism and Territories;* and Kimmerling, Baruch, "Religion, Nationalism and Democracy in Israel" (in Hebrew), *Zemanim* 50 (Tel Aviv: School of History, Tel Aviv University, 1994). Settlement of the Gaza Strip, Jordan Valley, the Syrian Heights, and formerly Sinai, was a completely different case. Most of the initial settlements were initiated and subsidized by the government.

52. Prima facie, Hamas and the Islamic Jihad are a part of the new worldwide wave of so-called Islamic fundamentalism, inspired by its Iranian version, or even a part of a new cosmic "clash of civilizations" (see Samuel P. Huntington, "The

Clash of Civilizations?" *Foreign Affairs* 72:3 (summer 1993): 22-49. However, both movements, and particularly Hamas, in fact have a very local character, and, despite connections with global developments, are a "pure Sunni Palestinian" venture.
53. Hermann, Tamar and Robin Twite, eds., *The Arab-Israeli Peace Negotiations: Politics and Concepts* (Tel Aviv: Steinmetz Center for Peace Research, Tel Aviv University, 1993).

OTHER SOURCES

Al-Haj, Majid. "The Day After the Palestinian State: Arab and Jewish Attitudes in Israel," *Middle East Focus* 13:4 (1991): 23-26.

Al-Haj, Majid, Elihu Katz, Samuel Shye. "Arab and Jewish Attitudes Toward a Palestinian State," *Journal of Conflict Resolution* 37:4 (1993): 619-632.

Bar-Tal, Daniel. "Delegitimizing Relations Between Israeli Jews and Palestinians: A Social Psychological Analysis." In *Arab Jewish Relations in Israel,* ed. John E. Hofman (Bristol, Indiana: Wydhman Hall Press, 1988, 217-248.

Frisch, Hillel. "From Armed Struggle over State Borders to Political Mobilization and Intifada Within It: The Transformation of PLO Strategy in the Territories," *Plural Societies,* 19:2-3 (1990): 92-115.

Kimmerling, Baruch. "State Building, State Autonomy, and the Identity of Society: The Case of the Israeli State," *The Journal of Historical Sociology* 6:4 (1993): 397-429.

Morris, Benny. *The Birth of the Palestinian Refugee Problem* (Cambridge: Cambridge University Press, 1987.

Smith, Pamela Ann. "The Palestinian Diaspora, 1948-1985," *Journal of Palestine Studies* 15:3 (1986): 90-108.

Tibawi, A. L. "Visions of Return: The Palestine Arab Refugees in Arabic Poetry and Art," *Middle East Journal* 17:5 (1963): 507-26.

Turki, Fawaz. "To Be A Palestinian," *Journal of Palestinian Studies* 3 (1974): 3-17.

FOURTEEN

Israel's Policy Toward the PLO
From Rejection to Recognition

Susan Hattis Rolef

I should like to dedicate this paper to the memory of my daughter Anath, a student of international relations, who was killed in Chile on March 19, 1995

It took Israel's leaders 29 years—from 1964 to 1993—to change their basic attitude toward the PLO. They moved from viewing it as nothing more than a coalition of terrorist groups bent on the destruction of Israel to accepting it as the representative body of the Palestinian people, with which Israel must reach an agreement if it wishes to resolve the Arab-Israeli conflict once and for all.

Israel fought against PLO terror, and after 1974—when the PLO started gaining international recognition—against its acceptance as a legitimate actor in the international arena. At various times Israel even carried out assassinations of particular PLO leaders and operatives.[1] On all these fronts Israel's success was only partial, though at least formally its leaders were unwilling to concede that it was a war that could not be won.

In the first ten years of the PLO's existence there was no Israeli of any standing who advocated that Israel establish ties with the PLO. This attitude was a natural reaction to the PLO's expressed desire to destroy

Israel and its refusal to engage in any contact with Israelis—including Israeli Arabs. As will be described below, after 1974 a change began to take place in the PLO itself, and individual Israelis from parties to the left of the Labor Party—and even some Laborites—started to take a more positive look at the PLO and opened a dialogue with its representatives. However, none of this had an immediate impact on the official policy of Israel.

It took the Israeli leaders—especially Labor's Yitzhak Rabin and Shimon Peres—nineteen years, from 1974 to 1993, to finally reach the conclusion that there was no alternative to negotiating with the PLO. This evolution would not have been possible without the changes taking place concurrently within the PLO. Moreover, it appears that the Israelis who played an active role in the embryonic dialogue with the Palestinians contributed both to the changes within the PLO and to the development of a more positive attitude toward it in certain sections of Israeli society. However, the change in the attitude of the Israeli leaders was much less affected by the continuous preachings of the advocates of an Israeli-PLO dialogue than by the development of events and their own perceptions of these developments.

Why it should have been Labor's leaders rather than those of the Likud who made the long journey from rejection to recognition is not difficult to understand. Labor's positions were always more pragmatic than dogmatic, and the principle of territorial compromise with regard to the West Bank and Gaza Strip in return for peace was generally accepted since the Six-Day War, even though it was not until the 1970s that the principle made its way into the Party's platform. Thus, despite the fact that the Labor leaders followed a dogmatic and uncompromising anti-PLO policy (which was not difficult to justify in view of the declared goals and terrorist methods used by the Palestinian organization), this dogmatic policy was the function of a pragmatic approach capable of perceiving alternative negotiating partners for resolving the problem of the occupied territories and its inhabitants. From the moment that it was understood that an alternative did not exist, the way was open for a change of policy. It was only at the final stage that the services of two nonofficial advocates of change in Israeli policy—Ron Pundik and Yair Hirschfeld—were used to effect the breakthrough. It is not without significance that neither was associated with the more radical forces in Israel advocating change.

The leaders of the Likud could not possibly travel the same course as did their counterparts in Labor because of their movement's basic approach. In their way of thinking there could be no or very little in the way of territorial compromise west of the Jordan River; for them territorial compromise had already been made east of the river. The major evolution in Likud ideology was its gradual acceptance of King Husain as a legitimate negotiating partner, or alternatively (especially in the case of Ariel Sharon) its willingness to accept the establishment of a PLO-led Palestinian state in Transjordan, in place of the Hashemite Kingdom. Any Likud member who came to any other conclusion could no longer find his place within the Likud. The purpose of this chapter is to offer an outline of the development of Israel's official policy toward the PLO, charting the main turning points along the tortuous road, and briefly touching also on the efforts of individuals to bring about a change in this policy in the mid-1970s. Special emphasis will be placed on the evolving positions of Rabin and Peres, because they led the country in the last Labor government (1974-77) before the Likud ascent to power when the process started, and they were once again the leaders of the Labor government that enabled the breakthrough to take place (1992-1996).[2]

Obstacles to Israeli Recognition of the PLO

The first obstacle on the road toward Israeli recognition of the PLO as the legitimate representative of the Palestinian people was that initially Israel refused to recognize the existence of such a people. The most outspoken advocate of this rejection was Golda Meir, who had served as prime minister in the years 1969-74.[3]

One might say that Israel had in principle recognized the existence of a Palestinian people and its right to self-determination when it accepted the UN partition plan of 29 November 1947—a plan that spoke of the establishment of a Jewish and an Arab state in Mandatory Palestine. But, formally, the recognition came only in the Camp David Accords of 17 September 1978, which spoke of "the legitimate rights of the Palestinian people and their just requirements."[4] True, Prime Minister Menachem Begin insisted that the Hebrew version of the accords use the term *"arviyei Eretz Yisrael"* (the Arabs of the Land of Israel) rather than *"Palestina'im"* (Palestinians),[5] but this did not change the fact that Israel had recognized the legitimate rights and just requirements of this people. When on 9 April 1986, Shimon Peres—at that time Labor Party chairman and prime minister—declared at his party's conference that Israel recognized the rights of the Palestinian people, he cited the text of the Camp David Accords.[6]

However, recognition of the existence of a Palestinian people with legitimate rights did not lead automatically to a willingness to recognize the PLO as the legitimate representative of this people, or to agree that this people's legitimate rights included the right to establish an independent state west of the Jordan River, as the PLO demanded. The formal Israeli policy, until very recently, held that there was no room for such a state west of the Jordan. Labor spokespeople used to add that a Palestinian ministate in the West Bank and Gaza Strip would serve as a destabilizing factor in the region and would fail to resolve the Palestinian problem.

The first time that a mainstream Israeli leader was reported to have spoken positively of the establishment of a Palestinian state was in April 1995, when Arafat stated that Peres had proposed the establishment of such a state in the Gaza Strip. Rabin's response was "If they will want a state in Gaza, we can talk about it, and this in return for a different political model in Judea and Samaria in which there will be a Palestinian entity which is not a state."[7]

With regard to Israeli recognition of the PLO, other elements came into play. For one, especially within certain secular right-wing circles in Israel, the claim had long been made that a Palestinian state did, in fact, already exist—in Jordan, which had constituted part of Mandatory Palestine (1922-48). Likud Member of Knesset (MK) Ariel Sharon became the main proponent of this concept when he argued in an interview in 1974 that Israel ought to help Arafat take over the Hashemite Kingdom of Jordan in which a majority of the population was Palestinian.[8] The idea of "Jordan is Palestine" gained adherents both in Israel and in Jewish circles abroad; in 1983, when Yitzhak Shamir was still minister for foreign affairs, his ministry considered publishing a historical study proving this thesis.[9] Even Benjamin Netanyahu, when he was deputy minister for foreign affairs, went to great lengths to argue that the Jordanians and Palestinians are a single people who should have a single state.[10] Nevertheless, the concept never really took root among either Israeli decision-makers or the Israeli public.

Another obstacle to a change in the Israeli position vis-à-vis the PLO and its recognition as a legitimate representative of the Palestinians and a negotiating partner was its nature as a terrorist organization whose raison d'être was to establish a Palestinian state in the whole of Palestine. For over two decades Israeli propaganda concentrated on the following themes in its attempt to delegitimize the PLO:

- The Palestine National Covenant denied Israel's right to exist and called for its liquidation. The Israeli Ministry for Foreign Affairs distributed this document in many languages as part of Israel's propaganda effort.[11]
- Every moderate Palestinian statement was invariably followed by an extreme one or a retraction.
- The wording of Palestinian statements and declarations was deliberately ambivalent and could be interpreted in more than one way.
- Most of the moderate members of the PLO, who had held meetings with Israelis, were assassinated by Palestinian extremists (see below).
- An unending series of terrorist attacks was carried out by all sections of the PLO as part of the "armed struggle" against Israel.[12] Israeli leaders were frequently confronted with the argument that peace is made with enemies and that, just as Great Britain started talking to the Mau-Mau in Kenya in the late '50s and France to the FLN in Algeria in the early '60s, Israel had to begin talking to the PLO. Their answer was that while the FLN was not bent on France's destruction and the Mau-Mau was not bent on Britain's, the PLO's raison d'être was the destruction of Israel and its replacement by a Palestinian state.

This distinction raised the issue of to what extent the PLO was capable of changing. Whenever Israeli leaders were asked about the possibility of Israel talking to the PLO if the PLO were to change, the answer was almost invariably: "if the PLO changes, it will no longer be the PLO." Nevertheless, professional PLO-watchers in Israel, who analyzed every word uttered and statement made at each meeting of the Palestine National Council (PNC) and other PLO affiliated bodies, did start noticing changes in PLO positions after the meeting of the twelfth PNC in Cairo in June 1974, which issued the phased political program.[13]

At first the analyses of these changes tended to be conservative and skeptical. Only in the 1980s did they become more optimistic.[14] In fact, it was only after the PNC meeting in Algiers in November 1988, at which the Palestinian state was proclaimed and an implied recognition of Israel was issued, that a growing number of academic observers and political figures became convinced that a real change was taking place within the PLO with regard to the organization's willingness to give up its maximalist goals, and accept a compromise implying coexistence with the State of Israel.[15]

The final obstacle to Israel's acceptance of the PLO as a negotiating partner was the illusion that Israel could find an alternative partner with which to negotiate a peaceful settlement to the Palestinian problem. Here there seemed to be several options. The first, which was popular especially in the Israel Labor Party, evolved around the so-called "Jordanian option." Back in the 1948-49 Arab-Israeli war, the Hashemite Kingdom of Jordan took over those sections of what was to have been the Arab state in Palestine, which were contiguous to the Jordan River, and which Israel did not conquer. In the years that followed Jordan was the only Arab state to grant its Palestinian inhabitants citizenship, which created the reality that a majority of Jordan's citizens were Palestinians. In 1967, Israel took over the West Bank from the Jordanians, and in Labor circles it was argued that if Israel was to return the territories to Arab sovereignty, they should be returned to Jordan.

The fact that the Rabat Arab Summit Conference of 31 October 1974 recognized the PLO as the sole body with the right to negotiate the future of the occupied territories[16] should have convinced Israel that the Jordanian option was an illusion. But it did not. In fact, it was not until after the outbreak of the Intifada in December 1987, and King Husain's declaration in July 1988 that he was washing his hands of responsibility for the West Bank, that the Labor Party finally gave up its Jordanian option.

Besides the "pure" Jordanian option, the Labor Party also played around with the "Jordanian-Palestinian" option, which was first mentioned in a resolution adopted by the first Rabin government on 21 July 1974. This resolution spoke of the establishment of "a Jordanian-Palestinian state east of Israel,"[17] and Rabin conceded at the time that moderate Palestinians could participate in the Jordanian delegation to peace talks.[18]

This formula kept coming up again and again in the form of a joint Jordanian-Palestinian delegation to a Middle East peace conference, where it was repeatedly emphasized that the Palestinian participants would be "non-PLO." In October 1991 it was this formula that enabled the convention of the Madrid Conference, after its acceptance by the Likud government. The bilateral talks in Washington were also based on the same condition.

In fact, the illusion that Israel was talking to a joint Jordanian-Palestinian delegation was kept up until Rabin replaced Shamir as prime minister in July 1992. But then a new illusion took its place: that Israel was talking to a Palestinian leadership from the territories that was not PLO. This illusion held until the middle of August 1993, even though official secret talks began with the PLO in Oslo on May 21-22.[19]

At least in the first ten years after the Six-Day War, successive Labor governments nurtured the pro-Jordanian families in the West Bank.[20] After the Likud took over in June 1977, and especially in the course of Begin's second government, an attempt was made to erode the power and centrality of the nationalist Palestinian leadership by creating an alternative local leadership among the rural population. Such a leadership would favor (so it was hoped) a solution based on limited autonomy in full cooperation with Israel, which would remain the sovereign in the West Bank and Gaza Strip. For this purpose the Village Leagues were nurtured. The Israeli whose name was most closely associated with this effort was Menahem Milson of the Hebrew University, who served as head of the Civil Administration in the West Bank in the years 1981-82. Most Israelis and Palestinians viewed the leaders of the Village Leagues as Israeli stooges. Milson himself disagrees and continues to argue that the failure of the plan was not inevitable. The main problem, he says, was that Minister of Defense Ariel Sharon, who initially supported the idea, became involved in "Operation Peace for the Galilee" in 1982 and lost interest in the Leagues. Milson himself resigned his Civil Administration post following the outbreak of the war in Lebanon.[21]

Palestinians in the territories associated with the PLO argued before the outbreak of the Intifada that there was a discernable Israeli policy, especially in the Gaza Strip, to weaken the PLO by encouraging the activities of the Muslim forces in society.[22] There is very little unclassified information on this subject. However, in two interviews with this writer, retired Brigadier General Binyamin Ben-Eliezer, coordinator of operations in the Territories from 1983 to 1984, implied that such a policy had actually existed, and that the hope was that the Muslim forces would draw the local population back into the mosques and away from the nationalists.[23] As it was from these very forces that Hamas was to emerge after the outbreak of the Intifada, if indeed such an Israeli policy ever existed, it was one of Israel's gravest mistakes.

Advocates of a Dialogue with the PLO in the 1970s

Until 1974 there was no one of any political consequence in Israel who argued that Israel should negotiate with the PLO. At this time retired Major General Mattityahu (Matti) Peled, who was later to become one of the main proponents of talks with the PLO, was still arguing that it was little more than a terrorist organization and did not represent the Palestinian people.[24] Nevertheless, Minister of Defense Moshe Dayan, whose natural curiosity led him to meet all sorts of Palestinian personalities in this period, did try on at least two occasions in the late 1960s to arrange meetings with PLO chairman Yasir Arafat.[25] Nothing, however, ever came of these efforts, not least of all because the PLO in this period rejected all contacts with Israelis of any description, including Israeli Arabs.[26]

The end of 1974 was without doubt a watershed. In the next few years a growing number of Israeli individuals—including *Ha'olam Hazeh* editor MK Uri Avnery, former Secretary-General of the Labor Party MK Arie Lova Eliav, Matti Peled, and former Director General of the Ministry of Finance Yaacov Arnon, who in 1976 founded the Israeli Council for Israeli-Palestinian Peace. These people started meeting with senior personalities from the PLO and advocating a drastic change in the official Israeli attitude. These efforts at "private diplomacy," made possible by a change in the PLO position regarding meetings with Israelis and Zionists,[27] have been well documented by Israeli participants.[28]

The main interlocutors on the Palestinian side were first Sa'id Hammami, Fatah member and the PLO representative in London, and later 'Isam Sirtawi, a highly placed member of the Fatah organization. Both were said to have had Arafat's blessing for holding these meetings and reported directly to him. However, within the PLO leadership there were those who strongly objected to these contacts, including Farouq Qaddoumi (who to the present day is consistent in his opposition to the "Israeli option"). Both Hammami and Sirtawi were assassinated by Palestinian extremists—the former on 4 January 1978, in London, and the latter on 10 April 1983, in Lisbon.[29]

Avnery believes to this day that the contacts were of major importance not only in influencing the more pragmatic elements within the PLO, but in very slowly changing public opinion in Israel.[30] Avnery was also the first Zionist Israeli to meet publicly with Yasir Arafat—in Beirut, on 3 July 1982.[31]

Eliav, on the other hand, concluded after several years that though the Israeli position was shortsighted and rigid, the main obstacle to any progress being made in the course of the 1970s was the PLO's ambivalence.[32] Though Eliav continued to participate in meetings with the PLO throughout the 1980s, his main contribution in this sphere was in contacts he held—with the blessing of Prime Minister Menachem Begin (and later that of his successors)—with various PLO-affiliated and non-PLO Palestinian groups, in an effort to gain the release of Israeli soldiers who had fallen prisoner during the war in Lebanon.[33]

Members of the group involved in the contacts during the course of the 1970s made a concerted effort to meet with government ministers and report to them about their meetings. Curiously enough, Rabin, who was prime minister from 1974 to 1977, was willing to listen unofficially,[34] while Peres, as minister of defense, had a negative attitude toward such meetings.[35]

Especially after 1977 (the year of the upheaval in Israel and the breakthrough in the peace process with Egypt), pressure on Israel to change its attitude toward the PLO also started coming from the member states of the European Economic Community —but especially from various European Socialist leaders. Israel was not successful in preventing the European Community from passing its Venice Declaration of 13 June 1980, in which the nine member states called for the association of the PLO in Middle East peace negotiations, and for the recognition of the Palestinian right to self-determination.[36]

Peres, as chairman of the Israel Labor Party and one of the vice-presidents of the Socialist International, was a little more successful in the latter forum, and waged a persistent battle to stop the SI from recognizing the PLO or granting it any sort of formal status within the organization. This involved constant clashes with prominent European Socialist leaders such as prime minister Bruno Kreisky of Austria.[37]

The Evolving Attitudes of Yitzhak Rabin and Shimon Peres

It is very difficult to gauge the effect of these efforts in the 1970s to broaden the international legitimacy of the PLO and bring about a change in the Israeli policy. As mentioned above, until 1977 Rabin—who less than two decades later facilitated the complete *volte face* in Israeli policy—listened very politely to Peled, Eliav, and others and continued to state that Israel would have nothing to do with the PLO. Though Rabin started to speak of the joint Jordanian-Palestinian option before Peres did, his transformation—from an unwavering opponent of talks with the PLO, to a reluctant supporter—was slow.

A series of interviews he held together with Eitan Haber (who was later to become his close aide) for the daily *Yediot Aharonot* with several world leaders in 1980,[38] apparently left a deep impression on him. Ceaucescu and Kreisky said to him that ultimately Israel would have to enter negotiations with the PLO. But the interviewee who left the deepest impression on Rabin was Egyptian President Anwar Sadat, who apparently convinced him that without a resolution of the Palestinian problem there would be no permanent peace settlement in the Middle East.[39]

However, the main discernable change in Rabin's approach came after the outbreak of the Intifada, by which time Rabin was minister of defense in the National Unity government. It was Rabin who first proposed a concrete plan for starting to resolve the Palestinian problem by holding elections in the territories for an administrative body with which Israel could later negotiate a settlement. His plan, first made public in January 1989, was adopted by the government in May. Rabin believed that through elections an alternative leadership to the PLO would emerge, even though he understood that most of the local leaders in the West Bank and Gaza Strip were linked to the PLO.[40] His basic assumption was that an elected leadership, with the prospect of concrete administrative functions in the territories, would start resenting the orders arriving from Tunis.[41]

At the end of March 1993, Rabin (now as prime minister) had agreed to enable Faisal Husseini—one of the most prominent Palestinian leaders in the West Bank and a resident of Jerusalem—to join the Palestinian negotiating team at the Washington talks, with the hope that this would help solve the problem of the team's impotence and total dependence on instructions from Tunis. But it soon became apparent that Husseini's formal presence changed nothing.[42] By this time Rabin had been brought into the picture regarding the Oslo talks by Peres,[43] and though he continued to deny until August 1993 that there was any change in the Israeli policy regarding talks with the PLO (see above), he was slowly coming to accept the inevitable. Peres's transformation took a totally different course. As already mentioned above, until 1977 Peres seemed much less interested in what the individuals who met with personalities from the PLO had to say about their meetings. However, after assuming the leadership of the Labor Party in 1977, his basic approach to the issue started to change.

Outwardly he continued to fight against pressure to embark on formal contacts with the PLO, especially by socialist leaders.[44] However, already in the late '70s contacts were established by the director of the International Department of the Israel Labor Party, Israel Gat, with PLO representatives such as Nabil Sha'ath. This was done with Peres's full knowledge, though not at his initiative.

Unlike the meetings held by the members of the Israeli Council for Israeli-Palestinian Peace, the purpose of these meetings was simply to exchange views, not to try to reach an agreement or draft joint declarations, and Gat kept no written record of them. According to Gat, Yossi Beilin—at the time one of Peres's aides, who was later to play a vital role in the Oslo talks—also held such informal contacts, with Peres's knowledge.[45] According to Beilin, Peres had said to him as early as 1980 that he knew that Israel would eventually have to deal with the PLO, but that Israeli public opinion was not yet ready.[46] None of this prevented Peres from continuing to pursue the Jordanian-Palestinian option mentioned above.[47] However, by the beginning of 1993, when he was informed by Beilin of the Oslo backchannel and gave it his blessing, he had not only accepted the inevitable intellectually, but was actually prepared to become personally involved in the talks, even before it was certain that anything concrete would result from them.[48]

The Likud's Attitude Toward the PLO

The basic difference of approach between the Labor Party and the Likud regarding the Palestinian issue was most clearly displayed when both parties were vehemently opposed to any type of dialogue with the organization. Though in the mid-1970s the Labor leaders were opposed to meetings with the PLO, and were at best ambivalent toward the contacts developed by individuals from outside the Israeli establishment with members of the Palestinian organization (see above), they did not do anything to stop them. Various personalities in Likud, on the other hand, were determined to stop what they regarded as nothing less than treason. The issue was first brought up in the Knesset by the Likud at the end of 1974 in connection with a reported meeting between Israel Shahak—a professor of chemistry from the Hebrew University, known for his anti-Zionist views—with PLO members in the Hague.[49] It was next brought up by MK Amnon Linn (at this time a member of the Likud) in November 1976. Linn called for the members of the Israeli Council for Israeli-Palestinian Peace who had held meetings with representatives of the PLO to be put on trial. Minister of Justice Haim Zadok, who at the time was not yet identified as a dove though he was one of the few Labor ministers willing to listen to reports by Avnery and his colleagues about their meetings, replied that while politically the government disapproved of these meetings, no evidence had been brought to the Attorney General to indicate that the persons involved had broken any law.[50]

It was only in August 1986, at the time of the National Unity government under Peres's premiership, that the Likud finally managed to pass an amendment of the Order for the Prevention of Terror making unauthorized meetings with members of the PLO, in most forms and for most purposes, an offense punishable by up to three years imprisonment.[51] Despite major misgivings among many members of the Labor Party, the party enabled the amendment to get through in return for the Likud's support for an amendment to the penal code that declared the incitement to racism illegal (this amendment was designed to be used against the extreme right-wing Rabbi Meir Kahane, who had managed to get into the Knesset in the 1984 elections). There is no doubt that it was the Labor Party's ambivalence on the issue of the PLO that enabled the passage of the amendment.

The Likud's position regarding the PLO over the years seems consistently negative, and, in September 1993 (with the exception of three Likud MKs who abstained), the Likud Knesset faction voted against approval of the Declaration of Principles (DOP) with the PLO.[52] Despite this, several interesting episodes took place between central members of the Likud and PLO operatives.

The first episode to recall is Sharon's 1974 proposal that Israel hold talks with Arafat regarding his taking over Jordan. The second is Prime Minister Menachem Begin's July 1981 approval of indirect contacts with the PLO with President Reagan's special emissary Philip Habib, to work out a cease-fire along Israel's northern border.[53] The following year Begin approached Eliav with the request that he establish contact with the PLO and other Palestinian organizations, to try to facilitate the release of Israeli soldiers taken prisoner during the Lebanese War. Begin himself was not interested in anything beyond the release of the soldiers, but over the course of his officially approved meetings with members of the PLO and of the organization of Ahmad Jibril, Eliav discussed not only the fate of the soldiers but political issues as well.[54]

A third incident worth noting took place in September 1987 when a member of the Likud Central Committee, Moshe Amirav, established contacts with persons associated with the PLO in the territories. According to reports, he managed to persuade two Likud MKs and future ministers, Ehud Olmert and Dan Meridor, to do likewise. The upshot of these meetings, however, was that Amirav was ousted from the Likud.[55] Nevertheless, according to certain reports, Meridor later met with two PLO representatives in London.[56] Details regarding the background and purpose of these meetings are not yet available.

Developments After the Mid-1980s that Facilitated the Oslo Talks

The Intifada, which broke out on December 9, 1987, was undoubtedly one of the central events that made possible the breakthrough in Oslo six years later. Though the PLO was not directly involved in the outbreak of the Intifada, it was as a consequence that two highly important changes occurred. The first was that many Israeli leaders, including Defense Minister Rabin, finally realized that there could be no military solution to the Palestinian problem, nor any solution that did not involve direct negotiations with the Palestinians themselves. The second was that despite the initial Palestinian enthusiasm, and the success of the Intifada in bringing the acuteness of the Palestinian problem to the forefront of world attention, the Palestinian leadership was unable to translate this into concrete political achievements. Paradoxically, the PLO's support of Iraqi president Saddam Husain in the Gulf crisis of 1990-91 also contributed positively to later developments, insofar as it resulted in the shutting off of the flow of funds from Saudi Arabia and the Gulf states to the PLO, which threatened the PLO with extinction unless it managed to show some concrete results fast.

In Israel the passing of the amendment to the Order for the Prevention of Terror of 1986 had the effect opposite to that expected by those who had initiated it. After it was passed, many individuals and circles who had never previously taken an active interest in contacts with the PLO started challenging the law, and the number of Israelis who now participated in events at which members of the PLO were also present grew continually. Most of those challenging the law tried to check how far they could go without actually breaking the law and sought to express their opposition to it as an antidemocratic edict.[57] Abie Nathan, the indefatigable peace-seeker, was one of the few Israelis who deliberately and openly broke the law and met Arafat publicly. He served two prison sentences for this—the first in 1989, the second in 1991.[58]

What role did this protest play in influencing Israeli policy? Probably very little, though one might argue that it did help prepare the Israeli public for the news about the Oslo talks and the agreement reached with the PLO. The reaction of the public was much milder than might have been expected after almost 30 years of anti-PLO propaganda.

Furthermore, insofar as a growing number of Laborites became involved in the contacts with PLO representatives and in advocating a change in the position of the Labor Party on the issue, they certainly deserve some credit for the change in the way the Labor Party platform dealt with the issue. The 1988 platform still rejected talks with the PLO, stating that "the PLO, which is based on the Palestine Covenant, and every other organization which denies Israel's right to exist and the national existence of the Jewish people, or acts by means of terror, cannot be a partner to negotiations." The 1992 platform made no mention of the PLO in the chapter dealing with the Palestinians, though the chapter dealing with human rights called for the amendment of the law prohibiting meetings with the PLO.[59] The amendment was in fact cancelled on 19 January 1993, thus making the Oslo talks—which at this point had not yet been officially sanctioned by either Peres or Rabin—legal.

THE OSLO BACKCHANNEL

The Oslo talks started as private meetings between two unauthorized Israeli academics—Yair Hirschfeld and Ron Pundik—and PLO representatives. Beilin, a personal friend of Hirschfeld's, was convinced that something of interest was taking place in these talks. Beilin alerted Peres, who in turn informed Rabin of the talks in the beginning of February. Nevertheless, the Oslo process remained for many months little more than an improvisation, and all suggestions that the move was carefully planned are totally unsubstantiated by the available evidence.[60] The contention that the Labor Party started coordinating moves with the PLO even before the 1992 election is also unsubstantiated. True, the number of meetings between senior members of the Labor Party and personalities identified with the PLO grew, but these were all informal meetings, and none was initiated or approved by Rabin. One episode, which according to opposition circles in Israel proved that there was a Labor-PLO conspiracy to bring down the Likud government in 1992, concerned a meeting held between Ephraim Sneh—a retired brigadier general and former head of the Civil Adminisration in the West Bank later to be elected on the Labor list to the 13th Knesset—and Nablus businessman Sa'id Cana'an.[61] The opposition based its case on the memoirs published in September 1994 by Mahmoud 'Abbas (Abu Mazin), one of the Palestinian architects of the Oslo Agreement, which claimed that 20 meetings had taken place between the two personalities in the course of which policies were coordinated.[62] Sneh himself pooh-poohed the story, stating that he had met Cana'an at the latter's request on 3 April 1992, three days after he had been elected in the primaries to the Labor Knesset list.[63] There had been only one meeting, he said, and since the elections were close Labor's prospects were discussed.

Another story that Abu Mazin seemingly blew out of proportion involved several meetings that took place in July 1993 between Arafat's emissary, Israeli doctor Ahmad Tibi, and the then minister of health and one of Rabin's confidants, Haim Ramon. The meetings had been arranged at the initiative of Tibi, whose main purpose was apparently to try and find out whether Rabin would be willing to meet with Arafat.[64] Ramon, it should be noted, was not privy to the details of the Oslo talks, which were approaching a positive conclusion at the time, and viewing his talks with Tibi as an additional backchannel is a gross exaggeration.[65]

Nevertheless, if the Oslo channel had not turned out as it did, it is very possible that some other channel would eventually have brought about the same results. Both the PLO and Rabin needed an agreement—the PLO because it was in grave financial straits as a result of its catastrophic pro-Iraqi policy during the 1990-91 Gulf crisis, and Rabin because he had during the 1992 election campaign promised an autonomy agreement with the Palestinians within six to nine months of a Labor victory—and by the spring of 1993 it was clear that such an agreement was unlikely to be reached in the Washington talks.[66]

THE ROLE OF THE UNITED STATES

One final subject must be touched upon: the role of the United States in the evolution of the Israeli position regarding the PLO. A study of Israel-U.S. relations in the last twenty-five years suggests that while the

United States has played a major role in the peacemaking process between Israel on the one hand and Egypt and Syria on the other, it played a relatively minor role in the process between Israel and Jordan, whose leaders maintained direct contacts most of the time and rarely needed the help of intermediaries,[67] and between Israel and the PLO.

In the case of the Palestinians, it was Israel that more or less dictated the rules to the Americans, and in the 1975 memorandum of understanding between Israel and the United States, Washington undertook not to recognize or negotiate with the PLO before the PLO formally recognized Israel's right to exist and accepted Security Council Resolutions 242 and 338. The United States also promised that it would not open negotiations with the PLO without Israel's consent.[68]

In fact, over the years the United States did maintain contacts at a technical level with the PLO,[69] and, as mentioned above, in 1981 the president's emissary Philip Habib negotiated a cease-fire between Israel and the PLO in Lebanon. However, even when the United States opened its dialogue with the PLO in December 1988 after Arafat satisfied American demands with regard to his acceptance of Security Council Resolution 242, recognition of Israel, and renunciation of PLO involvement in terror,[70] Israel placed more pressure on the United States to break off the dialogue (which it eventually did, on June 20, following an attempted landing by members of a PLO-affiliated organization on Israel's shores to perform a terrorist attack at the end of May 1990),[71] than the United States did on Israel to change its positions.

The role of the United States in the Oslo talks was virtually nil, though the DOP was finally signed on the White House lawn on 13 September 1993. Though the United States was aware of the existence of the Oslo backchannel, Rabin gave the Americans no indication that something serious was going on: first of all because he was not himself convinced until the middle of August that the talks would lead anywhere, and secondly because he apparently feared American pressure on Israel to concede more than he was willing to concede.[72]

Notes

1. After the massacre of the Israeli athletes at the Munich Olympics, Israeli agents liquidated 12 leading members of Black September—the organization which took responsibility for the massacre (televised interview with retired Major General Aharon Yariv broadcast after his death on the first Israeli TV channel

on 23 July 1994). Israel was apparently also responsible for the assassination of Khalil al-Wazir (Abu Jihad) in Tunis in April 1988. A book published by Mustafa Bakri in Cairo in 1989 dealt with alleged Israeli attempts on the life of PLO chairman Yasir Arafat. Retired Major General Yehoshua Sague, who was head of the IDF Intelligence Branch during the war in Lebanon, claims that in 1983, at the time of the PLO evacuation from Lebanon, Israel deliberately refrained from killing Arafat for political reasons (per Smadar Peri in *Yediot Aharonot,* 22 December 1989).

2. The fact that the leaders of Ratz, Mapam and other left-wing parties "saw the light" before Labor did, is largely immaterial. Neither liberal MKs Shulamit Aloni and Yair Tsaban—nor any of their colleagues—ever influenced what Rabin and Peres thought or did.
3. Meron Medzini, *Hayehudiya Hage'ah* (the proud Jewess) (Tel Aviv: Idanim Publishers, 1990), 403-7; and interview of Arie Lova Eliav by the author, on 20 June 1994.
4. Aryeh Y. Yodfat and Yuval Arnon-Ohana, *PLO Strategy and Tactics* (London: Croom Helm, 1981), 201.
5. See Uzi Benziman, *Rosh Memshala Bemazor* (A prime minister under siege) (Jerusalem: Sifrei Adam, 1981), 287.
6. *Ma'ariv,* 10 April 1986.
7. See *Ha'aretz,* 9 April 1995; and article by Onn Levy in *Davar,* 19 April 1995.
8. *Ma'ariv,* 29 November 1974.
9. This writer was asked to write such a paper, but declined.
10. *Divrei Haknesset* (Knesset minutes) 115, 20 November 1989, 466-8. In answer to a motion for the agenda presented by MK Geula Cohen on the issue of "Jordan is Palestine" on 20 November 1989, Netanyahu stated that "had the Emir Abdallah (King Husain's grandfather) rejected the advice of his English advisor Glubb, and had decided to call his state Palestine rather than Jordan—as he had intended to do—the whole debate today on this issue would not have existed."
11. For example, the ministry distributed Yehoshafat Harkabi's book *The Palestinian Covenant and Its Meaning* (London: Vallentine Mitchell, 1979).
12. See, for example, set of 24 anti-PLO posters distributed by the Israel Labor Party abroad in the course of 1979-80, and an audiovisual program prepared by the Ministry of Foreign Affairs in 1980.
13. See Yodfat and Arnon-Ohanna, 173.
14. Among the most highly regarded PLO-watchers were the late Yehoshafat Harkabi and his student Matti Steinberg, both of whom published numerous articles in the daily press in Israel in addition to their academic work on the subject.

15. For example, Deputy Minister of Defense Motta Gur, a former Israel chief of staff, noted in an interview with the writer on 16 January 1991, that November 1988 had been a definite turning point for him, though he had experienced several disappointments after that.
16. Yodfat and Arnon-Ohanna, 180.
17. *Ha'aretz*, 22 July 1974.
18. *Ha'aretz*, 1 July 1974.
19. In August 1993 Rabin still made very carefully worded statements from which one could gather that the Israeli policy had not changed, though some observers started noting a change in the words he used. In fact, it was only in mid-August that Rabin was finally convinced that an agreement would actually be reached with the PLO. David Makovsky, *Making Peace with the PLO: The Rabin Government's Road to the Oslo Accord* (Boulder, Colo.: Westview, 1995).
20. Yossi Beilin, *Yisrael—40 Plus* (Tel Aviv: Yediot Aharonot Books, 1993), vi.
21. Interviews held by the writer with Menahem Milson on 10 and 21 April 1991.
22. This writer heard such allegations from several PLO-associated activists in the territories in the course of the 1980s.
23. Interviews by the writer of Ben-Eliezer on 25 February 1988 and on 26 January 1993.
24. *Ma'ariv*, May 24, 1974.
25. Moshe Dayan, *'Avnei Derech* (Milestones) (Jerusalem: Idanim, 1976), 511.
26. See for example, Guy Bechor, *Lexicon Ashaf* (Dictionary of the PLO) (Tel Aviv: Ministry of Defense Publishing House), under "Israelis, the meetings with," 169-70.
27. See Alain Gresh, *The PLO—The Struggle Within, Towards an Independent Palestinian State* (London: Zed Books, 1985).
28. See, for example, Uri Avnery, *My Friend, the Enemy* (London: Zed Books, 1986), 119-64; Arie Lova Eliav, *Taba'ot 'Edut* (Rings of evidence) (Tel Aviv: Am Oved, 1984), 239-68; and Mattiyahu Peled, "My Meetings with PLO Representatives" (in Hebrew), *Ma'ariv*, 7 and 21 January 1977.
29. Avnery, 115, 294.
30. Interview of Avnery by the writer on 30 August 1994.
31. Avnery, 3-14.
32. Interview with Eliav on 20 June 1994.
33. Between October 1982 and June 1987 Eliav had held close to 40 meetings with representatives of the PLO. *Ha'aretz*, 21 June 1987.
34. Yitzhak Rabin, *Pinkas sherut* (Service file), Tel Aviv, *Sifriyat Ma'ariv*, 1979, pp. 542-3, and interview with Avnery on 30 August 1994.
35. Interview with Peres, *Yediot Aharonot*, 18 February 1977, and writer's interview with Avnery.

36. Keesings Contemporary Archives, 26 December 1980, p. 30635.
37. Reports in the Israeli daily press, and files of the Labor Party International Department for the relevant years at the Labor Party Archives at Beit Berl.
38. The interviews: with Nicolai Ceaucescu appeared on 6 March; with Henry Kissinger on 31 March; with Bruno Kreisky on 27 June; and with Anwar Sadat on 19 September 1980.
39. Interview by the writer of Deputy Minister of Defense Mordechai Gur, 12 July 1994. Inter alia Gur analyzed Rabin's policy.
40. At the end of 1992 Rabin still argued that after elections were held in the territories the PLO in Tunis would have a status no different than that of the Zionist Organization after the establishment of the State of Israel. See *Yediot Aharonot,* 30 November 1992.
41. This observation is based on statements made by Rabin in the relevant period in public appearances, interviews with the media and in meetings with foreign guests attended by the writer. Also Makovsky, *Making Peace with the PLO.*
42. *Ma'ariv,* 9 May 1993.
43. In interviews with David Makosvky both Peres and Rabin stated that Rabin was first informed of the Oslo backchannel at the beginning of February (Makovsky, *Making Peace with the PLO*).
44. In his book *Battling for Peace* (London: Weidenfeld and Nicholson, 1995) Peres mentions some of the socialist leaders who tried to convince him that talks with the PLO were inevitable. There are also press reports from the period to this effect.
45. Interview of Israel Gat by the author on 30 August 1994.
46. Beilin, p. vii, and interview by the author on 7 August 1994.
47. See, for example, the London Agreement of 11 April 1987 reached by Peres with King Husain.
48. Makovsky, *Making Peace with the PLO.*
49. *Divrei Haknesset,* vol. 72, 6 November 1974, pp. 260-4.
50. Ibid., vol. 78, 10 November 1976, pp. 251-67.
51. The debate on the amendment opened in the Knesset on 31 July 1985 (*Divrei Haknesset,* vol. 102) and ended in its adoption on 5 August 1986 (*Divrei Haknesset,* vol. 105).
52. *Divrei Haknesset,* vol. 131, September 23, 1993, p. 7999.
53. Ze'ev Schiff and Ehud Ya'ari, *Milhemet Sholal* (The deceptive war), (Tel Aviv, Schocken Publishing House), 30-31, and speech by Mordechai Gur, *Divrei Haknesset,* vol. 94, 19 May 1982, pp. 2448-9.
54. Interview by the writer of Arie Lova Eliav on 20 June 1994.

55. For details see articles by Shalom Yerushalmi in *Kol Ha'ir*, 18 and 23 September 1987, article by Dan Margalit in *Ha'aretz*, 23 September 1987, and report in *Yediot Aharonot*, 22 September 1987.
56. Abie Nathan claims to have seen a report of this meeting, which was allegedly arranged by the British Foreign Office. See interview in *Al-Hamishmar*, 3 December 1992.
57. See, for example, article by Arie Palgi in *Al Hamishmar*, 22 February 1989 "Sihot Bezel Hok Mitporer" (talks in the shadow of a crumbling law).
58. See interview with Nathan in *Al-Hamishmar*, 3 December 1991.
59. See *Spectrum,* December 1991, p. 11.
60. Discussions held by writer with several of the personalities involved in the process, and Makovsky, *Making Peace with the PLO.*
61. Unedited Knesset minutes of a debate on motions for the agenda brought by the opposition on this issue on 11 January 1995.
62. See *Ha'aretz,* 8 January 1995.
63. *Ma'ariv,* 8 January 1995.
64. *Ha'aretz,* 9 January 1995.
65. A report on these meetings was first published in *Yediot Aharonot,* 1 September 1994.
66. All these points were repeatedly mentioned in the media reports following the Oslo agreement, and were raised in statements made by both Rabin and Peres. It should be noted that already at the beginning of 1990 Rabin stated that peace negotiations with the Arab states would only become possible after Israel started talking to the Palestinians (*Ma'ariv,* 28 February 1990).
67. See, for example, Yossi Melman, *Shutafut 'Oyenet Baksharim Hasodiyim bein Yisrael leYarden* (A hostile partnership in the secret ties between Israel and Jordan) (Tel Aviv: Meitam, *Yediot Aharonot* edition, 1987) and Moshe Zak, "Kach ze Hit'hil" (This is how it began), *Ma'ariv,* 25 July 1994.
68. See George Lenczowski, *American Presidents and the Middle East* (Chapel Hill, N.C.: Duke University Press, 1992), 150.
69. *Newsweek,* 4 April 1988.
70. *Ma'ariv,* 16 December 1988.
71. *Ma'ariv,* 22 June 1990.
72. Makovsky, *Making Peace with the PLO.*

FIFTEEN

STRATEGIC RECIPROCITY
The PLO and Israel

Leonard Binder

In the Wake of the Assassination

The assassination of Prime Minister Yitzhak Rabin by a Jewish extremist cast a pall of doubt over Israel's ability to proceed to the decisive stages of the peace process. In the immediate aftermath of the assassination, the commitment of the mainstream Israeli parties to the peace process was actually reaffirmed, and a symbolic acceleration of the redeployment of Israeli forces from Jenin took place. But despite the remorse and dismay, the rededication of the centrist groups remains to be tested over the long run.

In the meantime, the strategic aspect of the peace process has been obscured by a paroxysm of emotionalism that has all but recast the adamantine Rabin as a bathetic idealist who was sentimentally rather than strategically committed to peace. The other side of Rabin—that is, his deep conviction that no agreement should compromise or even diminish Israel's net security position—has served as a perfunctory explanation of Israel's readiness to engage in the peace process in the first place. Only Arafat's enemies have been vulgar enough to cite Rabin's orders to deal with the Intifada by breaking bones. Hardly a soul has made the connection between Rabin's readiness to use force to control Arab protests and the possible need to use force to implement the transfer of authority on the West Bank. To the very end, however, and in spite of the epithet of "persecutor" hurled at Rabin, the Labor government refused to consider removing even the smallest and most provocative of the settlements. Still, Rabin was thought by many to be up to the task of making peace—a stable and secure peace—regardless of what it would take.

There were and are greater doubts about Arafat. These doubts included, but went beyond, the fear or hope that Arafat might be assassinated by Palestinians or other Arabs. They included doubts about his capacity to govern, his fiscal responsibility, his willingness to use force against his own extremist opposition, his ability to keep the rejectionist Arab governments from suborning his lieutenants, and, of course, his capacity to give priority to strategic rationality over ideology and emotion.

In the short run, Arafat has been nimble enough to adjust to the Israeli displays of anguish and remorse, and to reinforce Israel's need to make symbolic gestures of persistence in the peace process. That persistence was to be dutifully translated into compliance with the interim agreement on the redeployment of Israeli forces from six West Bank cities and the holding of democratic elections throughout the occupied territories (excluding Jerusalem). But the following steps have not yet been worked out, and, contrary to popular perception, the peace process remains indeterminate. As a consequence, commitments to continue the struggle for peace entail much more than resistance to the extremists on both sides. Such commitments require perseverance in a complex strategic process in which cooperation may sometimes require the appearance of noncooperation. Each side must take account of the other's internal opposition and the minimum requirements for maintaining a majority. Both the capacity and the willingness to play the game of apparent intransigence, followed by what appear to be one-sided concessions, was evidenced by both sides, but, by its very nature such a game should appear to be episodic and uncoordinated. This has been the pattern of border closures, repression of Hamas extremists, regulation of the expansion of settlements, and the *reversal* of those and other measures.

Thus, one of the most insightful observations on the impact of the assassination of Rabin was that many PLO leaders were now better able to understand the constraints under which any Israeli government must act. The reverse is probably also true—or ought to be. As such understanding increases, two types of reaction can be expected. The first is an accommodative response, such as backing off with demands that might embarrass the other protagonist. The second is to press forward with embarrassing demands which may increase the domestic pressure on the other side. Both moves are appropriate in an effort to reach agreement without conceding more than is necessary—assuming that the responsibility of the political authorities on both sides is to maximize the utility of their own citizens, and assuming that the mutual goal is to reach a compromise rather than to validate the claims of one side.

Early public reactions and official expressions of remorse after the assassination of Rabin confused and distorted the atmosphere of Israeli politics. Most importantly, it led to the misconstruction of Rabin's strategic approach to the peace process. Both those who condoned his assassination, and those who mourned Rabin as a martyr for peace, including both Peres and King Husain, found it expedient to represent Rabin's commitment to peace as a moral rather than a pragmatic one. The general public read every conciliatory move as a unilateral concession, and every retaliatory move as a reversal of the peace process. Rabin was not committed to any determined outcome of the final status talks, but it is probably true that he was willing to adapt his policy in response to the unfolding of events.

While Peres was able to seize the moral high ground after the assassination, the announcement of early elections put both Israeli and the Palestinian authorities to a severe test. Arafat was evidently ambivalent regarding whether an increase in terrorist incidents would push Israelis toward a peace-at-any-price policy or whether it would drive up the Israeli price for peace. Consequently he approved the election of a surprisingly representative Palestinian Legislative Council which he has kept under wraps—until the arrest of Daoud Kuttab in May 1997 for broadcasting that Council's debates.

When Peres decided to step up hostilities in Lebanon in order to prove that he was as tough as Rabin had been, he played into the hands of his electoral opponent, Netanyahu. First, Peres lost the moral high ground by a Machiavellian use of force to win the election. Second, the situation in Lebanon was not clearly related to Hamas terrorism and the insecurity that Israelis in the center of Israel began to feel. Third, if the peace process requires an interval of violence and deadlock, then surely, Netanyahu is more credible in that role. The result, of course, was a narrow victory for Netanyahu, the Likud and the right wing, and religious parties. But that narrow victory did not result in the adoption of a cautious policy.

Netanyahu immediately adopted the role indicated by both the events leading up to the elections and by his own rhetoric. Characterizing Labor's policy as giving up more than is necessary to obtain peace from a weaker adversary, Netanyahu also changed the atmosphere and style of the process. Yet, up through the agreement to withdraw from most of Hebron, he pursued the same policy of asymmetrical concessions and refusals to cooperate. Hebron, however, was more of a balanced and reciprocal arrangement, and because of that it aroused more powerful protest within the governing coalition.

Netanyahu felt that he had to make a hasty, unilateral riposte, to which Arafat, misjudging his support in world public opinion, in Israel, and in the United States, decided not to concede, nor even to demand a compensating concession, but to escalate demands beyond the Declaration of Principles in a way that might weaken the Israeli position in the final status talks. Arafat demanded that Israel forswear any action that might preempt the outcome of the negotiations, whereas Israeli policy in insisting upon a transition period was based on the idea that the way in which the peace process itself would unfold would determine the way in which Israel would respond to Palestinian demands. This, it seems to me, was Rabin's position, but it may not be Netanyahu's. Arafat is under no obligation to adapt his strategy to that of Israel, but it seems that it would be rational for both sides to adapt their strategies to that of their opponent. At the present time, the leadership of both sides, with the encouragement of the United States, is moving away from an evolving process of zigzagging, asymmetrical coordination to one of negotiating a contract. But if the general configuration of a final status agreement is not already part of an incipient consensus, they will probably have to back down from their absolute demands and return to an evolutionary process.

There is no doubt that Israeli democracy is undergoing a much more severe test than anyone anticipated at the time of the agreement on the Declaration of Principles. After the Palestinian elections, which sent a few warning signals regarding Arafat's commitment to democracy, the Israelis held elections at which every voter had to consider the cost of peace in terms of the price of national unity. The 1996 elections did not reflect a national consensus, so Israel continues to lurch toward the final status negotiations in a virtual state of denial. Netanyahu's proposal that the final status talks begin immediately foreshadows a showdown and a possible breakdown. Shortcircuiting the process reduces the amount of time the Israeli public will have to get used to the idea of a Palestinian state right next door. It will also shorten the time needed for the Palestinians to realize the benefits of self-rule even under somewhat restricted conditions.

AFTER THE PALESTINIAN ELECTIONS

The appointment of the 24-member Executive of the Palestine Authority (PA) was followed by the election of an 88-member Palestinian Legislative Council. Reduced to a virtual debating society and excluded from serious involvement in strategic decision making, that Coucil has become a repository of resentment against Arafat's monopoly of power and control of whatever assets the PA has acquired. As a consequence, in order to apply pressure for greater involvement, the Assembly casts doubt on the effectiveness of Arafat's strategies as well as upon the soundness of his fiscal management. Arafat's critics in and out of the Council recognize that any agreement with the Israelis will consolidate the leader's power. Consequently, they have some incentive to hold out against any agreement before the powers of the Council or any future legislative body are confirmed in practice.

There is little evidence that Israeli policy makers have taken the Palestinian elections seriously, even though they should be thinking about whether they would prefer a more democratic or more authoritarian regime in a future Palestinian state; a more efficient or a less efficient administrative structure; a more open and direct, multi-level political debate between Israeli and Palestinian opinion leaders or a continuation of secret negotiations and clandestine discussions among hand-picked intellectuals and diplomats. Israel will not be able to decide these issues unilaterally, but an evolutionary process provides for the possibility of a good deal of reciprocal influence on the future political structure of both countries.

The debate on the transitional and final agreements will continue to strain Israeli democracy, and when questions come up such as the disposition of the settlements, jurisdictional arrangements in Jerusalem, the political obligation of religious extremists, and the legitimacy of a government supported by Israeli Arabs, the behavior of Palestinians will influence the outcomes. Israelis and Palestinians will pursue these constitutional quests as though they were in wholly separate arenas, but Israelis should be considering not only the shape of the governing authority that they hope to be dealing with after the treaty is signed, but also the impact of their strategic choice of a form of government for their former enemy upon their own political institutions.

There are good reasons that Israel might prefer an authoritarian regime in the autonomous regions during the transition, but a democratic and pluralist regime after Palestine becomes independent.

The authoritarian regime might be better able to control the extremists and complete a treaty that would include some uncomfortable limitations on the sovereignty of the Palestinian state. A democratic government might be less inclined to attack another democratic state, more inclined to seek peaceful change and accommodation, less capable of pursuing secret or misleading strategies, and, generally, less efficient in implementing any policy.[1]

In the interim, however, it appears that the PLO authority will be neither democratic nor efficient. The 24-member Executive has been more responsive to Arafat than to the Palestinian population, and, given Arafat's political style, even the Executive has been rendered confused and disoriented while Arafat works out his own strategy. The administrative infrastructure in the autonomous regions, still lacking resources, trained personnel, equipment, strong leadership, and clear policy direction, will become even more inefficient under an authority that will be politically rather than service oriented. It may also be expected that Israeli monitoring will further diminish the efficiency of the Palestinian administration and may affect its legitimacy among the Palestinians themselves.

Arafat's style has been reasonably successful in preventing the extremists and the rejectionists from taking over the Palestinian movement, even though he seemed at times to be submitting to them. It may well be that, at least in the first phases of the transition, the PLO will need Arafat's skills in co-opting the Hamas movement and preventing it from being taken over by the advocates of a violent and even suicidal *jihad*. Still, there remains the possibility that supporting a transitional authoritarian regime will lead to the establishment of a permanent authoritarian regime, which is likely to be preferred only under one of two conditions: (1) if the final treaty is exceedingly unpopular among the Palestinian people, and then only for as long as that regime could maintain itself against its internal and external foes—with or without foreign, including Israeli, assistance; or (2) if the process of democratization produces even an ephemeral majority for Hamas, as it has produced significant gains for other fundamentalist movements such as the FIS in Algeria, the Muslim Brotherhood in Jordan and Egypt, the Welfare Party in Turkey, and the MTI in Tunisia. In the latter case, Israeli elites will be forced to join Muslim elites and others in facing the dilemma of whether the long-term prospect of democracy is worth the short-term acceptance of an authoritarian Islamic regime that attains power by democratic means. The answer is likely to depend on whether the popular fundamentalist majority would be ephemeral and whether there would be a realistic long-term prospect for democracy—and we really do not know the answers to these questions.

Because of the lack of historical evidence that might help us answer these questions—and the jury is still out on the Iranian revolutionary experiment—it is likely that many liberals will prefer a risk-averse strategy in which nonreciprocated rewards are given in return for all Palestinian moves that consolidate state power, strengthen the influence of moderates, separate the extremists from the masses, encourage pluralism, diffuse bureaucratic authority, strictly regulate extralegal participation, encourage the growth of a civil society, and expand the "public space" in which Israelis and Palestinians can meet, cooperate, and exchange ideas. In addition, during the transitional period, it might be useful to explore the possibility of establishing common interest institutions—like the forerunners of the European Community—that will be extended into the period of independence, when they may form the basis of an expanding set of cooperative institutions, the withdrawal from which would be costly for both sides.

This liberal strategy is a risk-averse strategy only if it is assumed that a Hamas success would be so much worse than a strong PLO state that it is best to support Arafat and the Palestinian secular elites even without getting anything in return. To elaborate further, a Hamas success can be an electoral victory producing a majority or a plurality of seats in the elected Council, a terrorist campaign that causes a majority of Israelis to vote for parties that will repudiate the DOP, or an anti-Arafat Intifada that makes it impossible for Arafat to govern. The sorts of things Israel might wish to have in return for its support of the PLO include trade, transit, and customs agreements, coordination of foreign policies with Jordan and/or Egypt, special status and protection for Jewish settlers that might remain where they are, and agreements on access to and security within Jerusalem.

If, however, Hamas is seen as the slightly lesser of two evils, then it might be more prudent to consider a strategy conducive to conflict between the PLO and Hamas, weakening both and, should Arafat emerge as the victor by a small margin, rendering him more dependent on international support and Israeli approval. Some critics of Rabin believe that his policy of stopping and starting the process of devolving authority with each terrorist act was a deliberate strategy of weakening the Palestinian authority to the point where Israel would be justified in granting autonomy to a few disconnected enclaves; leaving the settlements and their connecting roads intact. The risk associated with such a strategy is that the PLO will lack the legitimacy and the popular support to carry out the civil and security functions that Israel would like to have implemented in an autonomous or independent Palestinian state. Consequently, Israel will not be relieved of the security burdens it now carries.

Common Interests and Strategic Coordination

When one compares the liberal and the hard-line alternatives with the optimistic plan outlined in the Declaration of Principles (DOP), it becomes readily apparent why many observers have declared that Arafat and Rabin had, or the Fatah and the Labor alignment have, a common interest in making the DOP plan work. From the premise of a common interest, the conclusion is drawn that both should simply follow the timetable laid out in the DOP, regardless of the countermoves made by their respective domestic oppositions or by international actors that may have reservations regarding the beneficence of the peace plan or the way it is being implemented. This "full speed ahead" view is compatible with the view that the post-Oslo peace process can best be translated as a game of pure coordination or pure collaboration in which "the players win or lose together, having identical preferences regarding the outcome."[2]

Of course, the logic of the Israel-PLO relationship is not that of a pure coordination game. A pure coordination game, such as a one-shot Assurance game, without the possibility or the need for communication and with the assumption of a "perfectly symmetrical move structure," is an inappropriate model for understanding the current process, and it leads to the adoption of inappropriate strategies for achieving cooperation.[3] First of all, the game is not a one-shot game but an iterative game that permits both tacit and overt communication as well as the possibility of the evolution of complex strategies and even a change in the payoff structure over time.[4] Second, the players do not have symmetrical characteristics. Israel is clearly the dominant power and the PLO the weaker. There is a strategic asymmetry also, in that Israel seeks to minimize losses while the PLO seeks to maximize gains. Third, the two players have competing interests as well as complementary interests in cooperating. And, fourth, because neither are the transitional deadlines fixed nor is the substantive "final" outcome known, the mutual interest in reaching an agreement may be distinguished from short-term competing interests in controlling the negotiating process.

The significant difference between the power and the status of the two players adds complexity or asymmetry to the move structure of the game. In this case, it appears that the Israel-PLO game is less a pure coordination game than one described by Rasmusen as the Boxed Pigs game (see Figure 1).[5]

FIGURE 1. BOXED PIGS

		SMALL PIG	
		Press	Wait
LARGE PIG	Press	5, 1	4, 4
	Wait	9, -1	0, 0

Source: Rasmusen, *Game Theory*, p. 32

The Boxed Pigs game captures some of the qualities of the Israel-PLO game, especially the possibilities of cooperation with asymmetry of moves based on the differences between the players. It also demonstrates how waiting or inaction can be a cooperative move in a coordination game and the rationality of the stronger yielding to the weaker under certain circumstances.[6] Of course, if both players choose Wait, they will both starve. The importance of coordinated asymmetry becomes clearer still in the games that Schelling describes as bargaining games or games of mixed motives, where both sides will benefit if an agreement is reached, but where each side prefers to maximize its own utility by moving the point of agreement closest to its own ideal.

The Assurance game and the Stag Hunt are examples of mixed-motive games with multiple equilibria, and Rasmusen presents an example, which he calls the Battle of the Sexes: "a conflict between a man who wants to go to a prize fight and a woman who wants to go to a ballet."[7] The two prefer to spend their time together whether at the fight or the ballet or their equivalents, each time they date. The problem is, how do they decide who shall concede? Rasmusen presents the game in normal form as in Figure 2.

FIGURE 2. BATTLE OF THE SEXES

		WOMAN	
		Fight	Ballet
MAN	Fight	2, 1	-1, -1
	Ballet	-5, -5	1, 2

Source: Rasmusen, *Game Theory*, p. 34

In a one-shot game, the one who moves first ("Precedes") is likely to force the other into a concession ("Concedes") for the sake of cooperation; but in an iterative game with possibilities of communication, some explicit coordination of strategies can be achieved.[8] It is neither likely nor necessary that the coordinated strategies will result in a strict alternation between the two equilibria, especially when the players may be playing several coordination games simultaneously. It is to be expected that cooperation between the players will be increased across a range of issues the more they succeed in coordinating strategies. At the same time, a secondary outcome of the game turns on the question of which of the players succeeds in maximizing his or her own utility more of the time.

Certainly, when we consider the problem of the coordination of strategies between Israel and the PLO, given that every communication is either secret or a communication to one's own extremist opposition, it is obvious that tacit communication of threats, promises, and especially of readiness to Concede must be characteristic of the process. Schelling is of the opinion that tacit bargaining is often as important as, and sometimes more important than, overt bargaining. Indeed, he argues that in some situations the outcome in the last moment before a deadline is likely to be the same as in a case with no overt bargaining. It follows that both sides will make many mistakes because they misread signals. Consequently, despite the rationality of cooperation, the correlation of mixed strategies will often fail and the probability of agreement on the selection of one of the two equilibria will be lower than that theoretically attainable.

Because of the widespread belief that the logic of the Israel-PLO game is that of a pure collaboration game and that the preferred strategy requires consistent mutual cooperation, full disclosure of intentions, and equal payoffs to both sides, tacit bargaining and signaling for the purpose of correlating asymmetrical moves and payoffs are generally misunderstood as indications of bad faith or irrational acts of defection. Alternating moves leading to apparently unrequited concessions followed by the assertive pursuit of unbalanced advantage arouse public criticism and suspicion. At the same time, secret communications for the purpose of coordinating alternating mixed strategies deepen anxieties. As a consequence, each side is induced to guess more frequently whether the other intends to defer or take the initiative, and they will seek to minimize their incorrect guesses. The more mistakes that are made on both sides, the more likely the players are to conclude that the structure of the game itself is changing and that mutual cooperation is no longer a joint purpose.[9]

The fact that neither the transitional timetable nor the eventual outcome of the process has been determined also affects the probability of cooperation. Much of the present maneuvering has to do with controlling the transitional process. Presumably, the transition will lead to a stage at which the substantive peace agreement will be negotiated; but, as we have seen, many believe that the transitional process is a slippery slope. This belief is sustained by the arguments of Schelling, who discusses two evolutionary aspects of bargaining games.

The first of these is the evolution of tacit agreements or understandings regarding when to opt for CD and when for DC; in other words, when to Concede and when to Precede. If he is correct, we should see some improvement in this regard on the part of both the Peres government and the leadership of the PLO as they get used to each another. The second evolutionary pattern is more significant because it determines the "focal points" at which eventual agreements to compromise are most likely to be made.[10]

The process by which such focal points emerge as logical or plausible points of agreement or compromise is likely to be the bargaining process itself, whether the focal point is a river or a mountain, a prominent religious site, or a round number of persons, square miles, cubic meters of water, or transitional years. In other words, the indeterminacy of the eventual outcome and the absence of agreed focal points, places a great burden on the bargaining over transitional arrangements; because once people have become used to the transitional arrangements, those very arrangements are likely to establish plausible focal points for the permanent settlement. Issues such as the phasing of elections, the licensing of parties, the size of the autonomous council, the political status of Jerusalem Arabs, control of water resources, the determination of land ownership and use, access from Gaza to the West Bank, the redeployment and re-redeployment of Israeli forces, the rate of release of Arab prisoners, the construction of bypass roads, the admission of Palestinians to employment in Israel are transitional issues, the resolution of which may determine the focal points for later permanent agreement.

The permanent agreement will be devoted to two primary issues, Palestinian independence and Israeli security. Independence will be defined and delimited by Israeli security requirements, and those security requirements will be conditioned by the minimal requirements of Palestinian independence. International agreements will replace the transitional arrangements. For each of these issues there may be objective requirements that each side will consider vital and even non-negotiable, but the transitional experience will establish the heterogeneity of the players' goals and the difficulty of determining whether trade-offs or concessions have really been balanced or fair. The transitional process should also establish the principle that agreement is more important to both sides than insisting on unilateral advantage, except in the most vital questions.

Let us take the Jerusalem question as an example. This issue has been formally deferred to the endgame phase of negotiations, but considerable bargaining already occurs regarding the right of Jerusalem Arabs to participate in West Bank elections as voters and candidates. Additional maneuvering has taken place regarding the status of Orient House as the seat of Palestinian political authority even though it is located in East Jerusalem. There is little doubt that both sides believe that the transitional solution to these issues will contribute to the determination of focal points for the solution of the Jerusalem question.

The most likely alternatives for a permanent resolution of the Jerusalem issue are (a) an independent Palestinian state with part of a divided Jerusalem, (b) an independent Palestinian state without control of any part of Jerusalem, (c) an autonomous Palestinian entity with local administrative control over part of a divided Jerusalem or (d) an autonomous Palestinian entity with all of Jerusalem remaining under Israeli control.

If an independent Palestinian state is a prerequisite for a peaceful solution coordination and the game between Peres and Arafat is a coordination game, it follows that the payoffs for either of the two alternatives (a) or (d) are the most discordant and the least likely to be chosen by agreement. The payoffs for (b) and (c) represent the second-best choices for one or the other and are more likely to be chosen by agreement. (See Figure 3.)

FIGURE 3. FINAL STATUS TRADE-OFFS

PALESTINE

	State	Autonomy
JERUSALEM — Divided	a PLO's best Israel's worst	c Israel's 2nd best PLO's 3rd best
Israeli	PLO's 2nd best Israel's 3rd best b	PLO's worst Israel's best d

Because the PLO is likely to prefer independence to control of part of Jerusalem, (b) is the most likely solution. If Israel grants significant concessions by way of recognizing Palestinian political rights in Jerusalem during the continuation of the process of strategic bargaining, it is more likely that some combination of (a) and (b) will emerge as a focal point for a compromise solution. The formal Israeli position is that Jerusalem must remain united, as it has been since the Six-Day War of 1967, and that Jerusalem must remain the capital of Israel. At least some of the Jerusalem/Ramallah intellectuals have Conceded that Jerusalem can and should remain united, but have insisted that East Jerusalem must be the capital of Palestine.[11] A simple combination of the two positions would place the two capitals in a kind of binationalized, open city. This compromise appears utopian to many observers and is therefore adjudged a maneuver intended to reposition the focal point. The emergent focal point may include a Palestinian enclave in East Jerusalem, joint Israeli-Palestinian security in the Old City, and provision for ease of movement, but not ease of residence, throughout the city. The price for this compromise will probably include the legitimation of the expansion of the Israeli-controlled Jerusalem district.

Of course, there are Israelis and Palestinians who would not be willing to give up their desire for sovereign control over all or part of Jerusalem, just as there are those on both sides who insist on complete sovereignty over all of the land between the Mediterranean and the Jordan River. And if either Peres or Arafat were determined to realize their most preferred outcome, each would be tempted to work with their own domestic opposition groups. Both the threat of their respective extremist oppositions and the temptation to appease opposition groups increase the probability of failure to reach agreement. As a consequence, both sides agreed to postpone the specification of the final agreement. Instead they agreed to agree at some point in the future. Only the stages of the process were specified, and coordination in the participation in the process was required rather than commitment to a substantive outcome. This agreement on a Declaration of Principles transformed the coordination game from a one-shot exchange into an iterative game that might permit deviations and reversals along the way without necessarily leading to an immediate breakdown or cessation of the game. In order to maintain the process, both sides must avoid a simple tit-for-tat strategy, which would permit their respective extremist oppositions to gain control of the outcome of the process.

Since neither side has been able or willing simply to proceed with the process as outlined in the DOP, the coordinating process has become more complicated and even tenuous at times, involving patterns of asymmetrical coordination as well as provocative acts and stonewalling. Because the two parties have agreed to agree in stages that have disputed timetables, they may make both substantive and procedural agreements, or not. They may stonewall or delay, refusing to agree or even refusing to meet. They may also encourage or condone terrorist acts, which threaten the peace process. At any given moment, an act of asymmetrical coordination can appear like an act of self-abnegation or a concession to the other side. Only when the whole game tree can be examined can the pattern of coordination be discerned. But while the process continues, each of the coordinating players must be able to signal the other that they intend to remain steadfast in their agreement to agree. The difficulty in sending convincing signals at the same time that one is mollifying the opposition, has defined and enhanced the role of third parties such as the United States, Egypt, and others.

In sum, we have an overt process that frequently appears to be on the brink of collapse, masking a tacit, covert, but rational process of the correlation of mixed strategies. Often enough, the tacit coordination of concessions necessary for an agreement appear to be no more than a random assortment of last- minute compromises, abetted by third-party incentives and threats.[12]

But the underlying question is, to what extent can Israel and the PLO efficiently coordinate their mixed strategies in order to maximize the benefits to be divided between them? The answer depends, principally, on three further questions:

1. How each deals with their extremist oppositions;
2. The availability of side payments or negative sanctions from third parties; and, most important for our present purposes;
3. How Israel and the PLO actually divide the available benefits.

The issue is clearly stated by Schelling:

Offhand it may seem hard for [the players] to concert on a non-symmetrical pair of strategies. But much the hardest part is just recognizing that they have to; the question of how to do it then becomes a practical matter. They must jointly and tacitly find a clue to the concerting of their choice. Of course, a non-symmetrical solution . . . [may be] a discriminatory one; it quite arbitrarily condemns one of the players to a smaller gain than the other for reasons which may seem purely arbitrary or incidental. But we have to suppose that a rational player can discipline himself to accept the lesser share if the clue points that way. Only a discriminatory clue can point to a concerted choice . . . [which is] far superior to any symmetrical outcome.[13]

The degree to which our two parties are capable of disciplining themselves depends, in part, on how the opposition and international subgames are resolved. But it also depends on whether both players are as rational and imaginative as Schelling requires. Assuming, despite widespread contrary opinions, that our players have these qualities, how should we expect the division of benefits between them to be determined? What is (are) the discriminatory clue(s)?

Schelling discusses the "Nash Point" as a solution to bargaining games—not as theoretically proven, but as a clue that provides for a kind of symmetry that is appealing because it seems fair. He defines the Nash Point as "the outcome that maximizes the *product* of the two players' utilities."[14] The fairness of the Nash Point is derived from the notion that it maximizes the utility of each player within the framework of the rules of the game while diminishing the significance of invidious comparisons of the respective rewards gained by each player. But Schelling concludes that the appeal of the Nash Point ultimately depends on its mathematical aesthetic rather than its practical applicability.

One may, nevertheless, argue that some similarly transcultural concept of fairness and symmetry of payoffs in the face of bargaining asymmetry tends to take the pressure off transitionally determined focal points and turns attention to the aggregate or sum of the solutions to each of the bargained issues. In the Israel-PLO case, the clue seems to derive from the notion of *half a loaf*, that is, each party is to receive half of what they want, even if the payoffs are not 50-50.[15] In accordance with the spirit of Schelling's argument, it might be contended that this solution concept is more important than its practical specification insofar as it can provide plausible justifications for compromise solutions.

This midpoint or half-a-loaf solution concept can be illustrated by means of the following simplification of the Israel-PLO game:

We stipulate that there are three possible moves for each player:

1. P = Precede, in the sense of choosing the most favorable of the two possible equilibrium strategies and thus forcing the other player to choose his or her less favorable alternative.
2. W = Wait, or hold out, threatening to break off the process or to diminish the value of all payoffs, mollifying the domestic opposition.
3. C = Concede, or accept the bargaining demand of the other and with it the less favorable payoff to cooperation.

The resultant coordination game might be represented as in Figure 4.

The payoff structure in this game of correlated mixed strategies adds the complication of "Waiting" to the standard Battle of the Sexes game. Following that pattern of mixed-motive games, the dual equilibria, or preferred solutions, are the cooperative but asymmetrical PC and CP. By contrast, PP and CC are symmetrically detrimental to the interests of both parties. The numbers used, of course, represent ordinal prefer-

FIGURE 4. CORRELATED MIXED STRATEGY GAME

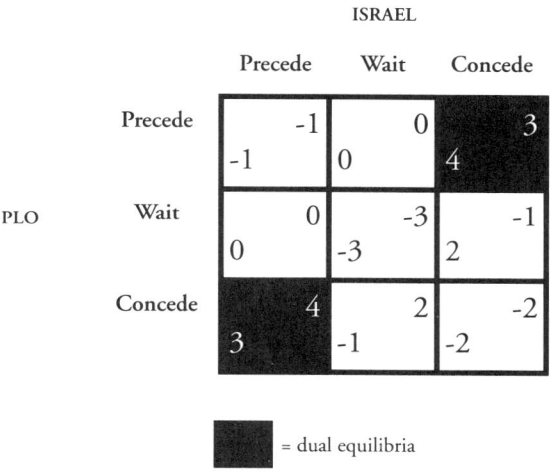

ences and not absolute differences. Hence both players have the incentive to Precede rather than Concede, so they may consider Waiting rather than conceding under a variety of circumstances already discussed.[16] Waiting may be an empty or a real threat. As a response to the opponent's P, W freezes the process and permits additional signals to be sent, provides time for third-party intervention, or allows extremist hotheads to calm down.[17] But W entails certain risks also, in that a reciprocal response of W leads to a possible breakdown of the process, discourages supportive third parties, and encourages extremists and hostile third parties. Waiting can also be a profitable strategy if it leads the opponent to offer a concession, whether procedural or substantive. It would probably be more realistic to suggest that Israel gains more in the short run from Waiting than does the PLO, if only because of the economic conditions prevailing in the occupied territories. Moreover, the real payoff for Waiting might be best measured in terms of the increased frequency with which the Waiting player is then able to Precede successfully. In any case, the more risk-averse player will avoid W if possible. And finally, Concede is a rational strategy if one is relatively certain that one's opponent cannot be deterred from moving

P on this round. The penalty for conceding at the wrong time is very substantial because it suggests that further concessions may be elicited in the next round and weakens the legitimacy of the political leadership. Should both sides Concede, though no agreement ensues, they will both pay a heavy penalty because, in addition to slowing the process considerably, they will affirm the arguments of those who claim that cooperation will in fact be more detrimental to the interests of both sides than was originally claimed by the political leaders of both sides.

We can now return briefly to the matter of the aggregate solution concept, which both sides might use as a rule of thumb in determining when and how often to choose C rather than P and, of course, how to signal the other of their probable choice. Following the standard of mixed-motive games of coordination, PC and CP offer the highest positive payoffs to both players. Using the hypothetical ordinals we have proposed, it is easy enough to calculate, say, over ten rounds, what the payoff to each will be if they always choose C or always choose P. The difference between the two choices will be ten units. If each is acknowledged by the other to "deserve" at least five units, bearing in mind that these payoffs are not interchangeable, then it is considerably more likely that the right signals will be sent at the right time and that direct communication will be fruitful. The correlation of mixed strategies will become even more likely if Israel, for example, is more willing to Concede on questions of Palestinian independence while the PLO is more willing to Concede on questions of Israeli security. Both sides will have to agree on some way of defining these two desiderata, to the extent possible, in mutually exclusive ways.

The model presented has been complicated by the addition of the Waiting move in order to achieve greater relevance to the actual Israel-PLO game. But it is still very simplified because it does not include the opposition subgame nor the international subgame. The model used also ignores orders of magnitude of payoffs and so does not enable us to confront problems of relative versus absolute gains. Israel, for example, probably prefers relative gains, in the sense that it does not wish to have an independent Palestine diminish its relative power vis-à-vis any plausible Arab coalition. The PLO prefers absolute gains because it is starting with almost no resources and will improve its relative and absolute position with every Israeli offer it accepts. While the game model does not lend itself to the analysis of this question, one expects that Israel will be more willing to risk delays, while the PLO will more urgently press for agreements in each round.

As a matter of fact, after the first euphoric ceremonial gestures, both sides have been induced to subordinating the DOP blueprint to tactics of asymmetrical reciprocation, both positive and negative. For the most part, Israel and the PLO have reciprocated in Waiting, but Israel has also closed the border to Palestinians normally employed in Israel while the PLO has only recently attempted to apprehend Hamas terrorist perpetrators.

On the plus side, Israel and the PLO have now agreed to hold elections sequentially in various Palestinian districts while redeploying Israeli forces only partially or temporarily. The PLO is attempting to prevent terror against Israelis even if it does not try to punish terrorists after the fact. Israel and the PLO are trying to come to an agreement on the electoral laws that will be applied and on the question of the exclusion of parties opposed to the DOP. After closing the border to Palestinian workers, Rabin typically reopened the borders after a time, but usually to fewer Palestinian guest workers while seeking to import guest workers from non-Middle Eastern countries. Israel has gone further than might have been expected in allowing Arafat and the Palestinian authority to wield the symbols of sovereignty, but it is also considering sealing the border between Israel and Palestinian territory. These confusing developments suggest that both sides are working out strategies of asymmetrical concession intended to keep the process going and to retain international support while mollifying hostile and skeptical public opinion at home.

Reciprocal Self-Transformation

There is, however, another aspect of the peace process that helps to explain the stalemate and confusion that prevailed before the assassination and will, no doubt, recur as we move from remorse to recrimination. The fact is that cooperation would be much easier to attain if all that was required was that each should deliver goods and services to the other in accordance with a signed agreement. Instead, the DOP envisions each side carrying out functions within its own territory—controlling its own extremists, adapting its own laws, and managing its own economic and fiscal policies—in ways that will benefit the other. Both sides are supposed to change their own societies, laws, and institutions in order to serve the other. Eventually, Israel and Palestine may be able to back away from the currently high degree of involvement in the domestic affairs of one another, but for now, the DOP places them in a position of reciprocally monitoring the other party's domestic policies.

The agreement between Israel and the PLO is like a pair of principal-agent agreements that are primarily concerned with matters of security, economy, public utilities, and communications. Each side acts as agent for the other in protecting the citizens of the other from acts of violence and terror. Each side, as agent, is considered to have more information about the situation prevailing in its own territory, and is therefore more capable of maintaining security in a more efficient way within its own jurisdiction. Both sides will benefit from the transactions cost saving realized because there will be no need to investigate each case and pursue each perpetrator nor interfere with the daily lives of persons under the alternative jurisdiction. Each side will rely primarily on the overall performance of the other in determining whether and how much to reward the other.

The arrangement is asymmetrical, however, because Israel has also imposed an elaborate system of civilian and military monitoring of the performance of the PLO, because Israel's agency contract with the PLO is far more detailed and specific, and because Israel maintains armed forces in PLO territory and has the right to employ those forces under specified circumstances. On the other side, Israel is under an obligation to provide rewards for good performance from time to time over the next few years, culminating in a replacement of the performance-based contract by a treaty. The near-term payoff to Israel by the PLO will be the political assistance provided to Israel as it tries to dispose of the settlements question. Israel probably expects more than the protection of the settlers from harm. It is likely to demand concessions on the distribution of water, guarantees of property rights, the construction of bypass roads, access to sacred sites, and other matters vital to the settlers. The PLO will expect that Israel will at least thin out the settler population, if not agree to the gradual dismantling of the settlements.

But Israel also expects some significant side payments during the transitional period. Chief among those side payments will be improved relations with several Arab countries. The autonomy agreement has already put some pressure on Syria to work out an agreement with Israel. In addition, Israel has already seen the framework for peace with Jordan developed into a full- fledged peace treaty. Israel expected that the PLO (and Egypt) would use their influence to end the Arab boycott or at least mitigate it, and some progress has been made. But the ending of the boycott is likely to occur gradually via a number of steps, and the first steps might involve agreements on specific forms of economic cooperation between Israel and the Palestinian entity, permitting individual firms to make deals that facilitate general Israel-Arab trade. In return, it may be expected that new arrangements will be made regarding the regulation and control of Palestinian labor in Israel. Although the opening of the Israeli labor market to Palestinians is likely to be of mutual benefit, the PLO authority will be expected to screen and license workers who will cross the line on a daily basis.

There are two important strategic consequences of this structure of reciprocal agency. The first is that neither side has the option of simply standing pat (i.e., preferring Wait to either Precede or Concede). The status quo ante, was a kind of state of war, but more like a civil war than a conventional war. If it were possible to freeze all terrorist acts during the standoff period, Wait/Wait might provide interim stability; but freezing extremist acts requires internally directed or reflexive acts of coercive control by both sides and not merely the maintenance of a vigorous external defense. Slowing down the process may please domestic opposition groups, but it will also lead to the demand that sanctions be imposed on the adversary. The demand for sanctions will be increased if the number or intensity of terrorist acts by extremists on both sides surpasses some limit of tolerance. The reciprocation of sanctions is likely to escalate into a complete breakdown of the process, unless the cycle can be broken by the sort of good faith signals that accompany apparently gratuitous concessions (Concede/Concede). Under such conditions, it is unlikely that the game could go many rounds with moves of Wait/Wait not to speak of Concede/Concede.

The second consequence is that the confidence requirements of agency arrangements are much higher than in other forms of transaction. Since mutual trust is not very high, there will be an additional inclination to follow a tit-for-tat strategy, leading to a Wait/Wait outcome. In addition, Israel is unlikely to decrease its capacity for closely monitoring political and administrative activity in the Palestinian territories, while the PLO will increasingly insist on discussing the final rather than the interim arrangements such as the redeployment of Israeli forces.

The logical consequence of the decline in the level of benefits expected from bilateral cooperation is that both sides will turn increasingly to nonregional third parties, urging them to offer side payments to, or impose sanctions on, their adversary. Alternatively, both sides may also explore the possibility of gains that may be realized within the region as a consequence of the realignment of international forces that may result from a broader peace agreement in the spirit of the Madrid process. Presumably, if the benefits that can be realized at the regional level are sufficiently attractive, then at least one side should be willing to play Concede or Precede enough of the time to start a pattern of coordinated asymmetrical cooperation.

The New Regional Balance and Regional Collective Security

In considering the question of the treaty that will end the transitional period and produce a new arrangement, a few preliminary considerations are virtually axiomatic. First, the changed logic of the situation all but determines that the influence of confidence-building concessions under the DOP will wane in the period of independence. Even with the imposition of military limitations on Palestinian sovereignty, the logic of the new situation will derive more from the regional balance of power than from past coordination. Second, the stability of the new arrangement will depend upon a combination of guarantees from third parties—national and multinational, regional and global—and mutual interests in cooperation that are endogenous to the regime constituted by the bilateral treaty. Third, the emergence of a Palestinian state will, by definition, change the balance of power in the region, and it will cause all affected states to make greater or lesser adjustments in their foreign policy strategies. Fourth, to achieve the greatest degree of stability in Palestinian-Israeli relations, the bilateral treaty should be adapted to the postulated prerequisites for the creation of a regional security system. Fifth, a regional security system cannot be based on an externally imposed arms control regime alone but must also take into account the emergent structure of regional relations.

The most important issue to be decided will be the question of the future relationship between an independent Palestine and the Kingdom of Jordan. Presumably, this is a question to be settled by Jordan and Palestine, but given the critical role played by Jordan as a multifunctional buffer state, Israel, Syria, Iraq, and Saudi Arabia have all to be greatly concerned about the consequences of the possible elimination of Jordan from the map. It is, of course, highly likely that the logic of the regional game would induce a unified Palestinian-Jordanian state to continue to play the same role in the future.

But let us suppose that Palestine remains a separate political entity. In that case, the buffering function performed by Jordan will be diminished in its regional importance. The experience of Lebanon demonstrates that Middle East states are quite capable of treating buffers in a disrespectful manner so long as there remains even a sliver of neutral territory or no-man's-land between hostile powers. It might not be as easy to slice up Jordan, but any threat to the integrity of Jordanian territory would pose a serious challenge to Palestine.

The Israeli-Palestinian treaty ending the transitional autonomy arrangement must consider the three-sided relations among Israel, Palestine, and Jordan. Since there is already an Israel-Jordan peace treaty in place, it will be easier to achieve a trilateral agreement. Indeed, it might be prudent to plan to establish a number of trilateral institutions, which would bind the fate of all three to their willingness to resist regional aggression. The pressure on these three small states will be greatly relieved, and the challenge of the integrative force of both Islam and Arab nationalism be avoided, if the removal of international sanctions on Iraq and the Israel-Syrian peace treaty can be conditioned by the need to construct a wider, regional security system in which arms limitations and guaranteed external intervention have a prominent but not exclusive place.

The urgency of adopting a regional rather than a bilateral or a trilateral perspective is already apparent in the way in which Egypt, Syria, Jordan, and Saudi Arabia have attempted to exploit the difficulties that face both Israel and the Palestinian Authority. As the game unfolded originally, Egypt and Syria expected that the weakness of the PLO would guarantee their ability to shape the Palestinian state and use it to bolster their influence with both Israel and Jordan. To the surprise of many, Jordan turned out to be the wild card in this game, fearing more the assertion of PLO influence in Jordanian affairs than the potential costs of an overt alliance with Israel. Jordan hastily entered into peace talks with Israel and concluded an agreement that is likely to reinforce Jordan's status as a neutral buffer and prevent its incorporation into any other Arab state.

Israel had hoped that an agreement with the PLO would open the door to a panoply of relationships with Arab and Muslim states in the Middle East and throughout the world. The invigoration of the multilateral aspect of the Madrid Conference, the November 1994 World Trade conference in Morocco, the mitigation of the Arab boycott, and the peace treaty with Jordan were all part of the expected payoff. Israeli policymakers could begin to contemplate the development of a much more complex regional policy based on the new reality of a multiplicity of diplomatic partners and a profusion of new options. Israel could also entertain thoughts of proceeding to normalize relations with a number of other Arab states without consulting Egypt and without coming to any agreement with Syria.[18]

Although a number of Israeli officials and scholars have expressed their exasperation with Syrian noncooperation, their complaints and those of the United States are often based on the narrow assumption that Syria is seeking an unfair edge in a bilateral negotiation with Israel. If the proposed land (Golan) for peace deal is taken out of the regional context, Syrian hesitation seems irrational; but, in context, Syrian aspirations extend to Lebanon, Jordan, and Palestine, while its security concerns extend beyond Israel to Iraq and Turkey.

A narrowly defined agreement with Israel, limited to the Golan Heights, would leave Israel in a position to thwart Syrian efforts to dominate the "Greater Syria" arena. Moreover, if that treaty included provisions requiring the "shrinking" of the Syrian army in order to allay Israel's security concerns, it might render Syria even more vulnerable to a future Iraqi attack.[19] I think that serious attention ought to be paid to Syrian statements that the return of the Golan is but a precondition of achieving a comprehensive peace based on regional cooperation. I would assume that Syria would like such an arrangement to provide for cooperation against an Iraqi attack and an alternative to Syria's alliance with Iran.

If Jordan surprised us by playing the wild card, Iraq can be predicted to play a similar role in the future, in accordance with the degree of autonomy it is permitted to attain. Despite the continuing efforts of the United States to prolong the neutralization and fragmentation of Iraq, it will return to the regional arena in a more active role in some form. The regime or its leaders may change, and the borders may be altered, but it seems certain that Iraq will be back. Iraq will be able to reestablish working relationships with France, Russia, and other nonregional powers. Within the region, Iraq will be able to forge cooperative arrangements with Turkey and Yemen. Without Saddam, all options are open, including cooperation with Syria, Iran, Saudi Arabia, and Egypt—though probably not all at once. Assuming that Iraq remains intact territorially, and that a Ba'thi successor to Saddam is in power, it is still likely that Syria, Iran, and Saudi Arabia will all view Iraq with suspicion. It is likely that Jordan will remain at arm's length but that Turkey will embrace the opportunity to cooperate against both Syria and the Kurdish challenge.

Israel and Syria are competing for influence in Jordan, Palestine, and Lebanon; but will competition be transformed into cooperation by the reemergence of an Iraqi threat? Does Israel's deterrent strategy and its treaty with Jordan counterbalance the Iraqi threat to Syria, if not to Kuwait and Saudi Arabia? It appears that the Egyptian-Syrian effort to regulate the Israel-Palestine-Jordan (and Lebanon?) realignment is based on short-term assumptions that Iraq will remain in its present state of suspended political animation and that Iranian initiatives in the region will remain limited to arm's-length support of Shi'ite and radical fundamentalist movements. If these assumptions are mistaken, then Egyptian and Syrian policies make little sense except as a throwback to the ideological construction of the Middle East, as though Israel did not exist as a component in the regional balance of power. Such a triumph of ideology over reality actually prevailed during Desert Storm, but is that where the peace process is supposed to take us?

Perhaps that was what was anticipated and even preferred by the Bush administration, when it was postulated that the United States would assume a global hegemonic role. But with the growing belief that the United States and Europe will be more reluctant to intervene in Middle East conflicts in the future, the region will have to rely on its own resources to a greater extent than anticipated. Both Iran and Iraq can be expected to assert their regional aspirations when given an opportunity, and it is difficult to predict which way Syria will jump unless it is bound by security arrangements that will protect it from both temptation and intimidation. The assumption that an Israel at peace with its Palestinian neighbors can be reduced to a subordinate regional role, tacitly supporting an Egyptian-Syrian alliance, is probably a misjudgment of both the intensity and the geographical scope of Israeli security concerns for the long term. It is also a misjudgment of the tacit contribution that Israel makes to the regional balance of power.

Notes

1. For a Palestinian discussion of the virtues of postponing democratic reforms, see Emaddedin Fraitekh, "Democracy First, Elections Later," *Los Angeles Times,* 27 December 1994, B5.
2. See T. Schelling, *The Strategy of Conflict* (Cambridge, Mass.: Harvard University Press, 1960), 84, 86, 89; Eric Rasmusen, *Games and Information: An Introduction to Game Theory* (Oxford: Blackwell, 1990), 35.
3. For a brief characterization of the no-frills Assurance game, see George Tsebelis, *Nested Games: Rational Choice in Comparative Politics* (Berkeley: University of California Press, 1990), 61f. On move symmetry, see Schelling, *Strategy,* 270f.
4. As Tsebelis points out, the simple Assurance game has no dominant strategy. The game has two equilibria: "If one player chooses to cooperate, the other is better off cooperating, but if one player chooses to defect, the other is better off defecting as well." Mutual cooperation is clearly the preferred outcome, so it is highly probable that both players will choose to cooperate. Though both players will benefit most if they coordinate their strategies, consistently preferring to cooperate (C), rather than defect (D), if they both move simultaneously and without communication, they must guess whether the other will choose C or D. In an iterative game with communication, however, coordination of strategies becomes possible and, other things being equal, mutual cooperation should result much or most of the time (Tsebelis, *Nested Games,* 64).
5. Rasmusen, *Game Theory,* 32. Rasmusen describes the game as follows: "Two pigs are put in a Skinner box with a special panel at one end and a food dispenser at the other. When the panel is pressed, at a utility cost of 2 units, 10 units of food are dispensed. One pig is 'dominant' (let us assume he is larger), and if he gets to the dispenser first, the other pig will get only his leavings, worth 1 unit. The small pig does somewhat better if he gets there first, eating 4 units of food, and even if they arrive at the same time, he can eat 3 units. . . . If the large pig picks *Press,* the small pig, who faces a choice between a payoff of 1 from pressing and 4 from Waiting, is willing to Wait. If the small pig picks *Wait,* the large pig, who has a choice between a payoff of 4 from pressing and 0 from Waiting, is willing to press. This confirms that *(Press, Wait)* is a Nash equilibrium."
6. This is a favorite theme of Schelling, who frequently points out that weakness can be strength in a coordination game (Schelling, *Strategy,* 22).
7. Rasmusen, *Game Theory,* 34.

8. Game theorists argue that once a pattern has been established, there is no incentive to change it because there is no alternative equilibrium that is Pareto superior to the one chosen. One can, however, imagine that the quality of the relationship is bound to deteriorate if the couple always goes to the ballet or always goes to the fights. It is more likely that the players will alternate with some frequency between the two equilibria to diminish the probability that one will go off alone at times as a kind of threat. This solution is described as "correlated mixed strategies" (P. C. Ordeshook, *Game Theory and Political Theory* [Cambridge: Cambridge University Press, 1986], 302). Tsebelis defines Pareto optimality as an outcome in which "it is impossible to improve one player's payoff without reducing another's" in any further moves (*Nested Games,* p. 65). Others describe an outcome as Pareto optimal when any further moves will diminish the payoff of at least one player. An outcome is Pareto superior to another outcome when no player is worse off and one or more players are better off with the first outcome. Vilfredo Pareto was, of course, an eminent Italian sociologist.
9. But the obstacles to cooperation should not lead to the conclusion that the Israel-PLO game is best seen as a PD game. The game can evolve, and it can revert back to a zero-sum game. Anything can happen. But the outstanding character of the game is its mixture of conflict and cooperation. If it breaks down, it is far more likely to become transformed into a game of Chicken than a PD game. Consequently, we should not look for or hope for an evolution of strategies (e.g., TFT) toward mutual cooperation as a Pareto optimal outcome. The central distinction to be kept in mind is between a game with a single dominant strategy and a game with multiple equilibria.
10. Schelling, *Strategy,* 70. "Most bargaining situations ultimately involve some range of possible outcomes within which each party would rather make a concession than fail to reach agreement at all. In such a situation any potential outcome is one from which at least one of the parties, and probably both, would have been willing to retreat for the sake of agreement, and very often the other party knows it. Any potential outcome is therefore one that either party could have improved by insisting; yet he may have no basis for insisting, since the other knows or suspects that he would rather concede than do without the agreement. . . . Somehow, out of this fluid and indeterminate situation that seemingly provides no logical reason for anybody to expect anything except what he expects to be expected to expect, a decision is reached. . . . If we then ask what it is that brings their expectations into convergence and brings negotiations to a close, we might propose that it is the intrinsic magnetism of particular outcomes, especially those that enjoy prominence, uniqueness, simplicity, precedent, or some rationale that makes them qualitatively differentiable from the continuum of alternatives."

11. See Edward W. Said, "Projecting Jerusalem," *Journal of Palestine Studies* 25:1 (autumn 1995): 5f.
12. Schelling, *Strategy*, 20-1, 34.
13. Ibid., 286n.
14. Ibid., 287. Schelling goes on to point out: "A distinguishing feature of this particular 'solution' is that it is independent of the exchange rate between the two players' utility scales . . . the Nash theory is not just one that does not need a means for comparing two players' utility scales. . . . Rather, since it uses the arbitrariness of the utility exchange rate as a fundamental principle, the theory must be taken to *depend* on the inherent incommensurability of utilities." Nevertheless, Nash assumes that "both players have perfect knowledge of their own and each other's utility systems (subjective valuations)."
15. As an alternative to the Nash Point, though not much more practical, one might calculate the aggregate payoffs to each party assuming, first, that they each Conceded all the time and, second, that they each "Preceded" or never Conceded. The focal point for an aggregate solution might then fall at the midpoint between the maximum and minimum expected utilities of each as determined by the structure of the mixed-motive coordination game and in accordance with the subjective utility function of each party.
16. See Boxed Pigs game discussed above.
17. The 0,0 payoff prediction for WP/PW indicates that any short-term benefit Israel may gain as the stronger power will probably be overshadowed by gains or losses on the next move.
18. Thomas L. Friedman, "Exodus Part II," *New York Times*, 15 February 1995, A15.
19. See *Los Angeles Times*, 7 November 1994, A6.

Index

1936-39 Revolt, 98, 224, 235
1956 war, 25, 153, 229
1967 war, 14-16, 19, 27, 28, 35, 73, 75, 76, 100, 101, 104, 108, 166, 171, 173, 225, 226, 229, 242, 254, 285
1973 war, xii, 9, 30, 38, 81, 121, 174, 230, 237
1982 war, 228, 230, 236, 259, 261, 264
'Abd al-Rahim, al-Tayyib, 61
Abu al-Abbas, 128, 138n.14
Abu al-'Ala (Ahmad Quray'), 61
Abu Iyad (Salah Khalaf), 148, 149, 154, 245n.6, 247n.22
Abu Jihad (Khalil al-Wazir), 25, 26, 149, 157n.16, 245n.6, 269n.1
Abu Marzuq, Musa, 185
Abu Mazin (Mahmoud Abbas), 245n.6, 267
Abu Musa, Abu Musa faction, 44, 81-82
Abu Nidal group, 116, 127
Abu Salih (Nimr Salih), 44
Algeria, 11, 12, 26, 185-188, 218, 257; FIS, 235, 278; FLN, 186, 187, 257
All-Palestine Government, 25, 28, 224
Amirav, Moshe, 265
'Amr, Nabil, 62, 131, 138n.15, 139n.28
al-Ansar, *see under* communists
Arab Boycott, 292-293, 297
"Arab Cold War," 104, 145
Arab Higher Committee, 11, 25
Arab League, 11, 75, 100, 102, 104, 106, 107
Arab Legion, 226
Arab nationalism, 9, 11, 98, 223
Arab Nationalist Movement, 24, 25, 99
Arab regimes, *see* Arab states
Arab Revolt of 1936-39, 98, 224, 235
Arab states, 39, 41, 47, 77, 78, 86, 88, 100, 103, 104, 131, 144, 145, 183, 230; in Gulf War, 105, 106, 145; funding/support by, 12, 13, 18, 33, 77, 103, 106, 109, 142, 145, 146, 148, 265; and Israel, 100, 115; opposition groups in, 12, 99; and Palestinian cause, 12, 24, 99, 100, 106, 108, 109; and PLO, 99, 102-104, 108, 109, 146, 172, 181, 187, 265; PLO in, 29-30, 179 *(see also* countries by name); and refugees, xi, 24; rivalries among, 28, 31, 75, 97, 145, 247n.22; and superpowers, 144-146. *See also* Arab summit conferences *and* countries by name.
Arab summit conferences, 100, 104, 245n.7; Algiers (1973), 174; Algiers (1988), 158n.32; Amman (1987), 47, 112, 145, 179; Baghdad (1978), 18, 111, 177; Cairo (1976), 41; Fez (1981), 82, 115; Fez (1982), 158n.32; Rabat (1974), 42, 109, 174, 176, 227, 258; Riyadh minisummit (1976), 41, 114
Arab unity, 11, 75, 100, 224, 225
Arafat, Yasir, 14, 15, 16, 29, 30, 39, 41, 44, 50, 84, 239, 256, 269n.1, 274, 277, 279, 291; in Cairo (1983), 79, 82; Cairo Declaration, 49, 149; consolidation of power, 50, 78, 85; and Fatah, 68n.4, 78-79, 111, 113, 241, 245n.6; as guerrilla leader, 16, 226; and Hebron agreement, 276; Israeli perceptions of, 231, 249n.42; and Jordan/King Husain, 82, 109, 111, 112-113, 115, 124-125, 179, 264; meetings with Israelis, 260, 266-267 *(see also* PLO, contacts with Israelis); as PA leader, 55-57, 59-63, 67, 68, 84, 85, 92, 231, 247n.26; and peace process, 166, 189, 280; as PLO leader, 13, 39, 62, 124, 129, 166, 190; strategies of, 276-278; support for Saddam Husain, 188 *(see also* Gulf War); as symbol, 165, 231; and Syria, 44, 116, 247n.22; UN speech (Geneva, 1988) 42-49, 152-153, 155, 239; and U.S., 142, 146-153, 155, 158n.17 *(see also* PLO *and* United States). *See also* Inside-Outside tensions
'Ariqat, Sa'ib, 61
armed struggle, xii, 13, 23-34 passim, 76, 80, 82, 85, 101, 110, 148, 151, 172, 175, 179, 198, 205, 227, 228, 234, 257; as ethos, 179, 202; as means to Arab unity, 100, 225; and nation building, 25, 26-28, 33, 110; shift away from, 39, 40, 42, 46, 49, 50, 82, 127, 173, 179. *See also* Fatah; Hamas; Intifada; *and* terrorism.
al-Asad, Hafiz, 44, 114, 126
Ashrawi, Hanan, 67
al-'Asifa, 225, 226, 230
assassinations, by Israel, 149, 253, 269n.1. *See also* Rabin.
assassinations, by Palestinians, 172, 177, 257, 260
autonomy, 43, 151, 190, 236, 237, 238, 267, 276, 279
Avnery, Uri, 260, 264

Baker, James, 107, 128, 154
balance of interests, 126, 128, 273-297
bargaining games, *see* game theory.
al-Barghuthi, Marwan, 61, 62, 63
Begin, Menachem, 261, 264
Beilin, Yossi, 263, 266
bilateral talks, *see* Washington talks
boundaries, 86, 101, 107, 112, 205, 224, 226, 234, 244n.1, 255; attacks across, 101, 154, 226. *See also* infiltration; of Israel, 46, 73, 109, 122, 234; of Palestinian state, 42, 48, 100, 256
boycotts, 199, 207, 209. *See also* Arab Boycott.
Brezinski, Zbigniew, 41, 143
Brezhnev, Leonid, 43, 45, 53n.14
British Mandate, 9, 28, 97, 98, 165, 224, 256

Brussels, women's joint meetings, 215, 216, 217, 219

Cairo agreement (1969), 114
Cairo agreement (post-Oslo), 57, 241
Cairo Declaration (1985), 49, 149
Cairo summit, *see* Arab summit conferences
Camp David Agreement, 43, 81, 148, 166, 177, 243, 256
Cana'an, Sa'id, 267
Christians, 81, 202, 212n.2. *See also* leaflets.
Civil Administration, Israeli, 199, 207, 259, 267. *See also* occupation.
civil society, Palestinian, 63, 64, 67, 74, 84, 85, 87, 92, 232, 233, 234, 279
clans, *see under* family
collaborator killings, 70n.20, 181
commandos, *see* guerrillas
communists; al-Ansar, 123; Arab parties, 123; Jordanian, 24, 123, 192n.31; Outside Palestinian, loyalty to USSR, 175; PLO faction, 16; UNL, 198; West Bank, 123, 192n.31
cooperation, Palestinian-Israeli, 279, 283, 291-294, 298n.4. *See also* game theory.
corruption, 149, 165, 188; Israeli, 165
Crown Prince Fahd, 44, 119n.35
customary law, 56, 58, 60

Dayan, Moshe, 166, 231, 260
Declaration of Independence, Palestinian, 47, 48, 49, 83, 89-90. *See also* Palestinian state, declaration of.
Declaration of Principles (DOP), 23, 38, 50, 64, 141, 190, 236, 241, 264, 268, 276, 279, 280, 286, 291-292, 294
Democratic Front for the Liberation of Palestine (DFLP), 38, 44, 70n.34, 79, 83, 84, 111, 148, 186, 193n.43, 198, 227; in territories, 177, 178, 180; and USSR, 123, 124, 127, 137n.3
democracy, democratization, 58, 62, 63, 74-92 passim, 166, 168, 193n.43, 278; in Israel, 188, 276, 277
deportations/deportees, 172, 173, 176, 178, 179, 186, 187, 186, 203, 212n.30, 233, 236
dialogue/talks; Palestinians/PLO and Israel, 128, 155, 166-167, 200, 253-254, 260, 263-265, 266; PLO-Jordan, 111, 116; PLO-U.S., 31, 48, 150, 153, 154, 155; women's, 215-219. *See also* Cairo; negotiations; Oslo, backchannel; PLO, contacts with Israelis; *and* Washington talks.
diaspora, Palestinian, xi, xiii, 3, 77, 171, 183, 241. *See also* Outside Palestinians *and* refugees.
Dir Yasin, 9, 204
DOP, *see* Declaration of Principles

early empowerment, *see* interim phase
Eastern Europe, 12, 127, 130, 134, 243
economy, Palestinian, 10, 11, 12, 19, 24-25, 57, 84, 91, 92, 105, 110, 168, 174, 199, 209, 233-234, 238, 240, 293; dependence on Israel, 172, 233; and Intifada, 10, 106, 164, 180, 182, 199, 203, 207-209; PA, 57, 63, 211, 238; PLO as conduit, 18, 172, 178, 179, 182, 185. *See also* Arab states, economies of *and* PLO, finances of; funding of; *and* taxation by.
education, ix, 14, 19, 77, 86, 87, 88, 168, 199, 207, 234
Egypt, 24, 38, 39, 47, 64, 82, 98, 100, 111, 114, 146, 268, 278, 286, 292, 297; control of Gaza, 165; and Gulf War, 47, 106; and Jordan, 11, 108; military aid to Palestinians, 25, 108; and PLO, 41, 44, 100, 102, 108, 111; and Israel, 41, 81, 105, 111, 146, 153, 261, 295, 297; and PA, 295; and Syria, 11, 297. *See also* Cairo agreement.
elections, 61, 85, 88, 89, 181, 203, 262; 1972 municipal, 174; 1976 municipal, 17, 176, 232-233, 192n.23; 1992 Israeli, 216, 266, 267; 1996 Israeli, 244, 275, 276; in East Jerusalem/East Jerusalemites and, 66, 85, 128, 133, 284; Fatah, 61, 68n.4, 190; Hamas support of, 184, 211; Independent Palestinian Group for Elections, 66-67; Jordanian, 113; Palestinian organizations, 61, 88, 89; PA, 56, 63, 65-67, 84, 89, 190, 217, 238, 240, 274, 275, 276, 277, 283
Eliav, Arie Lova, 260, 261, 264
Eshkol, Levy, 229, 230, 232
ethnonationalism, 4-10, 19. *See also* identity.
Europe, 42, 91, 115, 143, 218, 219, 261, 297. *See also* Eastern Europe.
European Community, 63, 261, 279
Executive Committee (EC) of PLO, 16, 29, 42, 77, 81, 123, 125, 150, 175, 186, 227, 240
Exterior, *see* Outside Palestinians

family structures, 55, 58-60, 63, 66, 69-70n.20, 164, 166, 233, 234
Fatah, xiii, 16, 38, 62, 84, 106, 113, 124, 157n.12, 172, 225-226, 239-240, 247n.22, 280; 1983 rebellion, 44, 79, 116; and armed struggle, 12, 15, 23-30, 75, 101, 154, 172, 212nn.5,7, 225-227, 230, 241, 247n.22; and democratization, 62, 188, 190; depoliticization under PA, 60-63, 239-240; elections, 61, 68n.4, 190; factionalism in, 63, 179; Inside-Outside dynamics, 39, 60-63, 178, 179, 180-182, 185; and Intifada, 180-182, 198; leadership, xiii, 44, 79, 172, 225, 239; and PNF, 175, 176; and opposition groups, 30, 79, 83, 84, 111, 177 *(see also by name)*; and PA, 60-63, 85, 238; role in PLO, 75-78, 84, 124, 182, 185, 227; trade union, 178. *See also* al-'Asifa.
Fatah Hawks, 164
Feda, 84
Fez Plan, 44, 45, 82, 115
fida'i, fida'iyyoun (self-sacrificers), 23, 25, 27, 233, 234; myth of, 226
Filastinuna, 25, 26, 225
final status arrangements/negotiations, 236, 276, 277, 280, 283, 284, 295. *See also* permanent phase *and* Jerusalem.

Index

fundamentalism, Islamic, 98, 143, 145, 202

game theory, 279-291 passim, 298nn.3,4,5,6, 299n.8, 300n.14
Gaza, 55-68 passim, 163-168 passim, 238; access from West Bank, 284; Egyptian control of, 107, 165; during Intifada, 163-168 passim; and Jericho First, 67, 217, 236; Palestinian celebration of Israeli withdrawal, 163-164. See also All-Palestine Government and Hamas.
Golan Heights, 232, 237, 296, 297
government-in-exile, Palestinian, 133, 205
Great Revolt, see Arab Revolt of 1936-39
guerrillas, 12, 13, 15, 27, 28, 29, 33, 76, 78, 80, 86, 108, 122, 172, 225-226, 227, 228, 230, 234; operations, 101, 233, 247n.22. See also armed struggle and terrorism.
Gulf states, 10, 12, 47, 105, 106, 114, 144, 177, 103, 265. See also by country names.
Gulf War, 9, 37, 105, 128, 129, 133, 185, 189, 215, 265, 267, 297; impact on Palestinians, 106, 118n.21

Habash, George, 14, 44, 122, 126, 148, 227, 240
Habib, Philip, 264, 268
Hamas, xiii, 66, 70n.20, 84, 85, 89, 106, 183, 185, 189, 198, 201, 202, 204-205, 211, 212n.5, 235, 242, 251n.52, 259, 274, 275, 278, 279, 291; 204-205; challenge to PLO, 112, 183-184, 203-204, 242, 278; dilemmas of, 206, 210, 211; and elections, 184, 211; and Intifada; leaflets, 197-209; objectives of, 185, 200, 206, 210, 211, 235; and PLO, 204, 210-211; social and cultural activities, 185, 210; and UNL, 184, 199, 203-210
Hammami, Sa'id, 41, 260
handbills, see leaflets
Harkabi, Yehoshafat, ix, 269nn.11, 14
al-Hasan, Hani, 149, 241, 245n.6
al-Hasan, Khalid, 41, 150, 151, 152, 240, 245n.6
Hawatmah, Na'if, 14, 44, 123, 126, 137n.3, 148, 227
health services, 9, 15, 16-17, 18, 62, 63-64, 167, 168, 199
Hebron, 135, 140n.37, 212n.30, 238, 276
Hirschfeld, Yair, 254, 266
Hizbal-Sha'b (People's Party), 84
Holst, Johann Jorgen/Holst Fund, 58
Hourani, 'Abdallah, 130, 150
human rights, 85, 87
Husain, Ibn Talal, King, 45, 46, 47, 60, 108-110, 112, 115, 124, 125, 179, 248n.26, 255, 258, 275. See also Jordan.
Husain, Saddam, 129, 155, 188, 297
al-Husaini, Haj Amin, 25, 98
Hussein, Saddam, see Husain, Saddam
Husseini, al-Husaini, Faisal, 61, 262

identity, 4-10; Arab search for, 145, 223-224; feminist, 214; Israeli/Jewish, 227, 229, 231; Jordanian, 224; Palestinian, see under Palestinian identity

Independent Palestinian Group for Elections, 66-67
independents (PLO faction), 16, 84
infiltration, 24, 25, 27, 127, 230; effect on Israeli politics, 188
Inside (West Bank and Gaza) Palestinians, 31, 39, 63, 78, 151, 171-190 (see also Intifada; PNC; and *sumoud*); delegation to peace talks, 83, 107, 189, 258, 259, 262; leadership, see under Inside leadership; PLO and, 33, 34, 142, 171, 174-179, 180-182, 188-190, 239 (see also PLO, shift to Inside)
Inside leadership, xiii, 17, 33, 62, 171-190, 197-211, 232-233, 239, 259, 262; Hamas, see under leadership, Islamic; national elite, 174-178; "organizational," 178-179, 190; traditional elite, 173-174
Inside-Outside equation, Algeria, South Yemen, Vietnam comparison, 185-188
Inside-Outside relations, xiii, 32, 33, 56, 61, 78, 171-190. See also PA.
institution building, 15, 18, 76, 79, 80, 85, 87, 185, 232
institutions; cooperative, 279; Palestinian, 16, 25, 29, 74, 76, 86, 92, 178, 179, 186, 214, 243
intelligentsia, Palestinian, 14, 15, 74, 86-88, 225, 233, 239-241, 250nn.44,48, 285
interim phase, 65, 83, 84, 107, 151, 211, 236, 238, 274, 277, 283, 284, 293
Interior, see Inside Palestinians
international aid, 63, 64, 91, 92, 238
international peace conference, 82, 112, 258
Intifada (uprising), xi, xiii, 18, 67, 81, 106, 166, 168, 197-210, 233-235, 241, 273; background to, 10, 99, 179, 213; decline of, 167, 182, 233; economic hardships, 182, 233; education during, 168, 207; in Gaza, 163-168 passim; and Hamas, 112, 185, 197-210 passim, 235, 259; impact on Israel, 213-216, 219, 234, 237, 262, 265; impact on U.S. policy, 107, 150, 153, 154; imprisonment during, 168, 199, 204, 206, 207, 215; and institution building, 18, 87; and Jordan, 110, 112, 258; and local organizing, 18, 33, 78, 180-182, 197-210, 214-216, 234-235 (see also leaflets); nonviolence and, 207, 208; objectives of, 200, 206; outbreak of, 10, 30, 46, 173, 180, 265; and PLO, xii, 46, 74, 78, 86, 106, 126, 171, 180-182, 265; psycho-political legacy of, 163-168, 233, 241; repression of, 214, 236, 237; Soviet view of, 126-127; violence and, 32-33, 127, 167, 207, 208, 235; women's organizing, 87, 213-216, 219
Iran, 47, 105, 145, 156n.9, 297
Iran-Iraq war, 47, 105, 106, 146, 151, 153, 179
Iraq, 12, 15, 28, 39, 47, 56, 98, 108, 134, 145, 156n.10, 223, 240, 279, 294, 295, 296-297; invasion of Kuwait, 105, 113, 145, 155, 239
Islamic communal activities, 185, 198, 210, 235, 238.
Islamic Community, 185, 198, 235
Islamic Council (IC), 173
Islamic fundamentalism, 143, 145, 202, 251n.52

Islamic Jihad, 66, 84, 198, 199, 235, 251n.52
Islamic movements, 166, 179, 184, 185, 242. *See also by name.*
Islamic opposition groups, Palestinian, 84, 85. *See also by name.*
Islamic Resistance Movement, *see* Hamas
Islamic Salvation Front (FIS) (Algeria), 235
Islamic state, 198, 202, 210
Israel, 25; and 1976 mayors, 176-177, 178, 212n.30; and Arafat, 85, 249n.42; army of, *see* Israel Defense Forces; attacks against, 12, 13, 25, 27, 75, 76, 101, 108, 154-155, 225, 226, 227, 228 (*see also* armed struggle); Civil Administration, *see under* Civil; and Egypt, 41, 81, 105, 111, 146, 153, 261, 297; establishment of, 9, 23, 24, 97, 227; and Hamas, 185, 274; international pressure on, 261; Intifada dilemmas, 237 (*see also* Intifada); Intifada measures, *see under* Intifada *and* occupation; and Iran, 297; and Jordan, 146, 292, 294; Jordanian option, 112; Labor government, *see* Rabin government; Labor party, *see under* Labor; in Lebanon, 31, 41, 43, 45, 78, 81, 106, 114, 115, 116, 124, 148, 179, 268 (*see also* 1982 war); as occupier, *see under* occupation; and PA, 57, 274-297 passim; and Palestinians, 37-51 passim, 68, 228, 234, 257; peace with Jordan, 249n.42, 250n.46, 295, 297; PLO and, 27-41, 43-51, 68, 74-92 passim, 103, 109, 166, 184, 187, 189, 223-244 passim, 253-268 passim, 273-297; and PLO-U.S. relationship, 141-156 passim; Rabin government, 107, 116, 255, 274, 280; recognition of Palestinians, xiii, 240, 256; in region, 99-116 passim, 125, 292, 294-297 (*see also* Arab states); relationship to territory, *see under* land; religious parties, 275; right to exist, 122, 123, 127, 128; search for alternative leadership, 258, 259, 262; security concerns, 228, 230, 237, 238, 280, 284, 297; strategies, 282, 287 (*see also* game theory); support for Palestinian state, 236; and Syria, 99, 146, 292, 295, 297; and U.S. 38, 149, 154, 268; withdrawal from Gaza, 163-164. *See also* boundaries *and* wars by year.
Israel Defense Forces (IDF), 56, 57, 59, 179, 182, 199, 203, 214, 226, 233, 236, 238, 273, 274, 284, 293
Israeli Arabs, 13, 18-19, 224, 225, 241, 254, 277
Israeli collective memory, 228, 230, 241, 246n.16
Israeli Council for Israeli-Palestinian Peace, 260, 263, 264
Israeli Palestinians, *see under* Israeli Arabs
Israeli peace groups, 79, 215. *See also* PLO, contacts with Israelis *and under* women
Israeli policy, 187, 189, 236, 253, 255, 256, 259, 261, 266, 270n.19; Allon Plan, 232, 248n.29; economy, 10; encouraging Islamicism, 259; functional division, 231; indirect rule, 232, 237; open bridges policy, 231; and Palestinian response, 231-234; and PLO, 253-268, 297; security doctrine, 237; separation, 235, 291; territorial compromise, 254

Israeli political culture, 235, 241; and religion, 242; anxiety orientation, 230, 231, 236; divisions, 228-229, 276; power orientation, 228-229, 236, 243-244; role of army, 229
Israeli-Palestinian conflict, 73, 74, 244, 279, 280; Arab perceptions of, 144; religious roots of, 242
Israeli-Palestinian dialogue, *see under* dialogue
Israeli perceptions, xiii, 167, 229-230, 233, 236, 241, 246n.13, 256, 257, 249n.42
Israeli recognition of PLO and obstacles, xiii, 236, 255-259
Israeli right-wing, xiii, 228, 232, 236, 256, 275

al-Ja'bari, Shaykh Muhammad 'Ali, 173-174
Jerusalem, 28, 59, 81, 188, 243, 248n.29, 262, 277, 279, 284-286; East, annexation by Israel, 232, 284; and Palestinian elections, 66, 85, 128, 133, 274; as capital of Palestinian state, 48, 51, 203, 285; in peace talks, 189, 285; sharing, 219
Jewish underground, attacks on mayors, 233. *See also* mayors, 1976.
Jibril, Ahmad, 130, 265
jihad, 198, 199-200, 202, 204, 205, 212nn.2,5, 231, 242, 278
joint negotiating team, *see under* Jordanian-Palestinian delegation
Jordan, 9, 24, 47, 64, 98, 103, 108-110, 111, 114, 145, 172, 173, 227-228, 240, 295, 297; annexation of West Bank, 224, 258; citizenship to Palestinians 13, 112, 224, 258; civil war, 9, 30, 207; communist party (JCP), 123, 175, 192n.31; disengagement from West Bank, 47, 110, 112; and funds for Palestinians, 18, 110; and Israel, 38, 146, 224, 250n.46, 292, 295; Jordanian-Palestinian confederation plan, 45, 82, 109, 151, 211, 258; as Palestine, 230, 247n.22, 256; and Palestinians, 12, 17, 146, 174, 232, 294, 295; Palestinians in, 13, 46, 108, 110; PLO and, 43, 44, 45-47, 82, 79, 102, 107-113, 116, 124, 174, 176, 177, 178 (*see also* Karamah); refugees in, 3, 13, 75, 106, 113; stability after 1971, and Syria, 78-79, 297; and U.S., 46, 111, 268
Jordanian option, 256, 258, 263
Jordanian-Palestinian delegation to peace talks, 107, 258, 259, 262. *See also* Washington talks.

Karamah, battle of, 226
Khalaf, Salah (Abu Iyad), 148, 149, 154, 245n.6, 247n.22
Khalidi, Walid, 41
Kissinger, Henry, 38, 143, 148
Kuwait, 12, 105, 106, 145, 225, 297; Iraqi invasion, 105, 113, 145, 155, 239; Palestinian exodus from, 9, 105; Palestinians in, 13, 105

labor unions, *see* trade unions
Labor party, Israel, 51, 151, 254, 236, 238, 258, 261, 263, 264, 266, 276; dialogue with PLO, 266-267

al-Lahham, Abu Khalid, 59
land, 73-74, 166, 174, 205, 231-233, 254-255, 284; Arab attitudes toward, 200, 242, 244n.1,2; confiscation/loss, 9, 10, 19, 24, 74, 75, 98, 101, 131, 132, 224, 232, 258, 250n.49; Israeli attitudes toward, 232, 242, 244n.1,2. *See also* settlement.
leadership, 7, 8, 185-188, 290; Arab, 101, 102, 155 (*see also* Arab states); diaspora, *see under* "Outside"; Fatah, xiii, 44, 79, 172, 225, 239; Intifada, 180-182, 197-211; Islamic, 173, 174, 183-185, 199, 242; Israeli, 46, 150, 237, 238, 241, 243, 244; local, *see under* Inside leadership; Palestinian, xiii, 13, 14, 15, 19, 24, 28, 29, 40, 47, 50, 75, 98, 168, 244; PA, 165, 166, 242, 243; PLO, 13, 14, 23, 30, 31, 33, 37, 41, 44, 47, 50, 76, 79, 82, 83, 102, 104, 115, 116, 132, 173, 185-188, 206, 241, 260, 265 (*see also* Arafat); women's, 213-219
leaflets (Intifada), 180, 181, 194n.44, 197-209
League of Arab States, 28, 29, 224
Lebanon, 12, 41, 98, 107, 114, 115, 116, 137n.5, 144, 145, 227, 275, 295, 297; 1982 war, 31, 43, 45, 78, 81, 99, 106, 116, 124, 148, 179, 259, 268; civil war, 41, 53n.12, 81, 111, 145, 137n.5; Palestinians in, 13, 31, 127, 148; PLO in, 12, 31, 77, 78, 102, 109, 143, 179, 227; PLO expulsion from, 79, 82, 111, 115, 116, 148, 269n.1; refugees in, 3, 13, 75, 77
Lebanon war, *see* 1982 war
Legislative Council, *see under* PA
liberation models, international, 26, 122, 171, 185-188, 226
Libya, 12, 44, 89, 108, 134, 145, 240
Likud party, 236, 254, 255, 258, 259, 267, 275; ideology, 255, 263-265
local (West Bank and Gaza) Palestinians, *see* Inside Palestinians
local elites, 185-187, 250n.44
local leadership, *see* Inside Palestinians and Inside leadership
London agreement, 112

Madrid Peace Conference and talks, xiii, 12, 74, 84, 107, 135, 139n.30, 187, 217, 241, 258, 294, 295-296, 297
mayors, 1976, 176-177, 178, 212n.30, 232-233, 248n.34. *See also* elections, municipal.
Middle East, 97-116, 134, 143, 297; balance of power, 294, 297; economic dependence of region, 172 ; radicalism in, 56, 100, 102, 115, 143, 144, 145, 146, 148, 173, 177, 297. *See also* Arab states.
Milhem, Muhammad, 150
Milson, Menahem, 249n.44, 259
mobilization, 3-19 passim; armed struggle and, 27, 33; of Israeli Arabs, 18-19; of Palestinians, 9-10, 13-19, 27, 70n.23, 88, 104, 175, 177, 179, 214, 235; of women, 214
mujahidoun, 25, 27, 202
al-Mujamma' al-Islami, *see* Islamic Community
multilateral talks, 38, 107, 133, 142

Muslim Brotherhood Society, 24, 99, 113, 183, 198, 235, 278

al-nakba (catastrophe), 25, 26, 98, 233. *See also* 1948 war and refugees, 1948.
al-Nasir (Nasser), Gamal 'Abd, 11, 28, 29, 75, 100-101, 104, 108, 113, 156n.10, 245n.7
nation building 13, 25-28, 33, 76, 84, 110, 164, 233; and armed struggle, 26-28, 33, 110
National Charter/Covenant, *see* Palestinian National Charter
National Guidance Committee (NGC), 17, 123, 177-178, 180, 233
nationalism, 295; ethnic, *see* ethnonationalism; and feminism, 214, 218; Jewish, 150, 227, 231; Palestinian, *see* Palestinian nationalism
nationalist elites, 174-178. *See also* mayors.
negotiations, 82, 83, 86, 128, 142, 151, 189, 204, 241, 243, 265; final status, 236, 279
neopatriarchy, 55, 56, 58, 60, 65, 67
Netanyahu, Benjamin, 256, 269n.10, 275, 276
NGOs (nongovernmental organizations), 63-65

occupation, 9, 19, 46, 48, 67, 75, 84, 87, 88, 91, 101, 110, 131, 151, 164, 167, 172, 179, 182, 187-188, 200, 203, 206, 231-232, 234, 237, 274; effects on Palestinians, 164, 168, 174, 234. *See also* Civil Administration; Intifada; *and* occupation measures.
occupation measures; bypass roads, 284, 292; closures, 85, 87, 235, 236, 238, 274, 291; curfews, 235, 236; house demolitions, 203, 204; torture, 168, 203
October War, *see* 1973 war
oil, 143, 145, 155
Operation Peace for the Galilee, *see under* Lebanon *and* 1982 war
opposition groups; Israeli, 286; PA, 65, 84, 239; PLO, 13, 15, 16, 30, 42, 50, 51, 79, 82-83, 84, 85, 113, 124, 286 (*see also* PLO, and Islamic opposition)
Organizational Leadership, 178-179
Oslo 2, 37, 50, 57, 59, 62, 66, 103, 107, 238
Oslo Accord, ix, xii, 57, 60, 83, 87, 133, 134, 156, 189-190, 211, 217, 231, 235, 238, 240. 241, 249n.42, 292; backchannel, 84, 259, 262, 263, 265-267, 268, 271n.43; Palestinian opinion, 85, 239, 241, 242
Outside (Exterior, or diaspora) Palestinians, 3, 61-63, 171-190 passim, 241. *See also* diaspora *and* Inside-Outside relations; intellectuals, 239, 240, 241; leadership, xiii, 32, 62, 123, 172, 190, 240

Palestine, 98, 297; and Israel, common interests, 280-291 passim; liberation of as ethos, 98; relations with Jordan, 294 (*see also* Jordanian-Palestinian confederation); as Southern Syria, 146, 297. *See also* Palestinian state.
Palestine Communist Organization, 123, 175, 192n.31
Palestine Communist Party (PCP), 123, 178-180, 192n.31

Palestine Liberation Army (PLA), 29, 56, 59, 75, 245n.7
Palestine Liberation Organization, *see under* PLO
Palestine National Covenant, *see* Palestinian National Charter
Palestine National Council (PNC), 16, 37-51, 74, 77, 80-83, 126-127, 204, 225, 257; 2nd (1965), 80; 3rd (1966), 80; 4th (1968), 80, 226; 5th (1969), 81; 6th (1969), 81; 10th (1972), 175; 11th (1973), 81, 175; 12th (1974), 38, 39, 41, 42, 48, 50, 80, 81, 82, 239, 240, 257; 13th (1977), 41, 42, 43, 82; 14th (1979), 41, 42, 43, 82; 15th (1981), 41, 42, 43, 45, 82; 16th (1983), 41, 45, 82, 148; 17th (1984), 41, 45, 82; 18th (1987), 41, 45, 46, 79, 80, 82; 19th (1988), 40, 41, 47, 49, 79, 81, 83, 152, 182, 257
Palestine National Front (PNF), 16, 39, 123, 175-177, 180
Palestine National Fund, 16, 113
Palestine National Salvation Front, 79
Palestine Red Crescent Society, 15, 16-17
Palestinian Authority (PA), xiii, 55-68, 91, 92, 211, 231, 235, 236, 238-240, 277, 278, 284, 292, 293; attempts to ensure Outside dominance, 61-63; establishment of, 84; Executive, 56, 277, 278; and Fatah, 60-63; finances of, 57-58, 63, 91, 92, 238, 250n.45, 293; Legislative Council, 66, 84, 240, 275, 277, 284; opposition groups, 65, 84, 239, 274 (*see also by name*); security forces, 56, 57, 59, 165, 237, 238, 241. *See also* elections.
Palestinian identity, xi, 3, 4, 9-10, 14, 15, 16, 18-20, 24-33 passim, 74, 77, 80, 90, 92, 98, 100, 101, 103, 164-165, 174, 223-224, 228, 230
Palestinian institutions, *see under* institutions
Palestinian Interim Self-Government Authority (PISGA), *see under* interim phase
Palestinian leadership, *see under* leadership
Palestinian National Authority, *see* Palestinian Authority
Palestinian National Charter/Covenant, 80, 150, 226-227, 231, 240, 257, 266
Palestinian nationalism, xi-xii, 3-5, 8-10, 23-34, 230, 241; and armed struggle, 23-34 passim; Israeli reaction to, xiii, 230; and pan-Arabism, 11, 20, 75, 101; as source of legitimacy for Arab states, 103; rise of, 4, 8-13, 100, 103. *See also* ethnonationalism *and groups by name.*
Palestinian police force, 165. *See also* PA, security forces.
Palestinian Resistance (PR), 100, 102, 103, 108, 109, 113-114, 115
Palestinian society, 9, 19, 24, 25, 32, 55-68, 76, 77, 86, 98, 100, 105-106, 163-168, 216, 225, 233
Palestinian state, 20, 41, 89, 90, 100, 173, 178, 200, 210, 235, 236, 243, 256, 257; boundaries of, 48, 50, 74; confederation with Jordan, 45, 211, 294-295; declaration of, xii, 47, 81, 99, 112, 116, 204, 206, 257 (*see also* Declaration of Independence); as Islamic state, 198, 202, 210; and Israel, 250n.46, 277;

Israeli views of, 236, 237, 249n.42, 276; Jordan as, 65, 247n.22, 255, 256; limitations on sovereignty, 278, 294; obstacles facing, 239-240; U.S. rejection of, 44, 151; UNL and, 200, 203; in West Bank and Gaza, 17-18, 30, 39, 40, 42, 50, 74, 82, 83, 99, 102, 121, 147, 152, 155, 211, 239, 240, 256; in West Bank and Gaza, as phase, 137n.3, 210. *See also* secular democratic state.
Palestinian-Israeli talks, *see under* dialogue,
Palestinians; characteristics of, 5, 19-20, 168, 171; collective memory, 228, 230, 241, 243; "de-Palestinization" of, 223-224, 230; dispersion of, 13 (*see also* diaspora *and by country);* divisions among, xi, 172, 249n.44; economic conditions among, *see under* economy, Palestinian; goals of, 197; grievances of, 5, 10, 19, 77, 210; Israeli, *see under* Israeli Arabs; Israeli perceptions/recognition of, 231, 253; and Jordan, 224, 232; leadership structure, *see under* leadership; links with Arab societies, 24; middle class, xi, 250nn.44,48 (*see also* intelligentsia); perceptions/recognition of Israel/Zionism, 51, 230-231, 241, 243, 257; pro-Jordanian, 259 (*see also* Palestinians, traditional elite); secular elites, 279; sense of victimization, 166, 167; traditional elite, 10, 14, 16; trauma among, 164, 165, 168; West Bank and Gaza, *see* Inside Palestinians. *See also* education, elections, *and* women.
pan-Arabism, xii, 11, 15, 27, 97, 98, 100, 105, 145, 173, 223, 224
peace accords, *see under* name of accord. *See also* dialogue *and* peace process
peace movements, 213; Israeli women's, 214-215
peace process, 65, 67, 92, 109, 133, 136, 151, 238, 243, 268, 273, 280, 291; and Hamas, 242; Israel-Egypt, *see under* Egypt; role of women in, 213-219; strategies, 274, 275
Peres, Shimon, 112, 203, 204, 254, 255, 256, 261, 262-263, 266, 269n.2, 271nn.43, 44, 272n.66, 275, 283
permanent status phase, 83, 219, 236
PFLP/PFLP-GC, *see under* Popular Front
phased political program, 40, 137n.3, 176, 209, 210, 250n.47, 257
PISGA, *see* interim phase
PLO; allocation of funds, 18, 172, 178, 179, 182, 185; and/in Arab states, *see under* Arab states *and countries by name;* assassinations by, 172, 177; Central Council, 77; Charter, *see* Palestinian National Charter; contacts with Israelis, 46, 49, 115, 253-254, 260, 261, 268; decision making, xiii, 44-45, 75, 77, 79, 82, 83, 99, 103, 109, 127, 128, 172, 175; democracy in, *see under* democracy; diplomatic advances, 42, 47, 79, 82, 102, 104, 111, 116, 142, 143, 147, 152; Executive Committee, *see under* Executive; factionalism in, 17, 31, 33, 78, 123, 175-176 (*see also by faction name);* finances of, 11-12, 16, 103, 105, 184, 185, 189, 265, 267; founding of, ix, xi, 16, 75-77, 92, 98, 100, 225, 245n.7; (*see also* Arab

League *and* Nasir); funding of, 11, 12, 13, 57, 103, 105, 109, 265; and Islamic opposition, 183, 238, 242 *(see also factions by name)*; institutions, *see under* institutions *and by institution name;* international status of, 187, 261; and Israel, xii, 37, 109, 280, 291, 292 *(see also under* Israel); Israeli policy toward, 253-268; military factions, *see under* armed struggle *and factions by name;* objectives, 31, 37-51 passim, 81, 83, 99, 147, 190, 254, 257; opposition factions, *see under* opposition *(see also* DFLP *and* PFLP); and other liberation movements, 12, 16, 226 *(see also* liberation models, international); peace initiatives, 37-51, 73-92 passim; perceptions of Israel, 142, 154; perceptions of U.S., 141, 142, 148-152; policies of, 37, 38, 39, 74-92 passim, 147, 150; pragmatism, 38, 72, 74, 78, 81, 83, 86, 102, 149, 176; recognition of Israel, 47, 50, 142, 143, 147, 149, 152, 154, 166, 239-240, 260, 268; in regional Arab politics, 97-116; and Saddam Husain, 105, 155, 265; shift to Inside, 78-79, 99, 175, 180, 182, 185; social services and activities, 11-12, 15, 16-17, 18, 77; as sole legitimate representative, 42, 103, 109, 112, 153, 172, 174, 184, 206, 215, 256, 258; strategies of, 37-38, 42, 43, 46-47, 49, 50, 51, 82, 83, 91-92, 99, 102, 147, 150, 151, 152, 155, 282 *(see also* game theory *and* phased political program); structure of, 16, 17, 29, 76, 77-78, 190 *(see also* institutions); support for, 12, 13, 57, 105, 106, 109, 130; taxation by, 12, 29; and traditional leadership, 173-174 *(see also* Inside Palestinians); in Tunis, 32, 33, 135, 189; and UNL, *see under* Inside *and* UNL; and UN resolutions, *see under* United Nations. *See also* armed struggle; democracy; dialogue; expulsion from Lebanon; Hamas; Inside; Inside-Outside relations; Intifada; Jordan; leadership; mobilization; *and* terrorism.
PLO-Israel accords, 1993, *see* Oslo *and* peace process
PLO-Israel dialogue, *see* PLO, contacts with Israelis *and* negotiations *and see under* Israel
PLO-U.S. dialogue, 31, 48, 150, 153, 154, 155; Soviet response to, 128
pluralism, 74, 76, 85, 86, 88, 89, 279
PNC, *see under* Palestine National Council
PNF, *see under* Palestine National Front
Popular Front for the Liberation of Palestine (PFLP), 15, 16, 27, 29, 39, 42, 70n.34, 79, 81, 83, 84, 85, 111, 122, 123, 177, 178, 180, 193n.43, 198, 227, 240, 157n.16
Popular Front for the Liberation of Palestine-General Command (PFLP-GC), 44, 79
Popular Struggle Front (PPSF), 44
prisoners, 168, 180, 203, 204, 206, 207, 215, 233, 284; Israeli, 233, 261, 264, 266
Pundik, Ron, 254, 266

Qaddoumi, Farouq, 132, 151, 241, 245n.6, 260
Qasim, 'Abd al-Karim, 28, 245n.7
al-Qassam, Shaykh Izz al-Din, 202, 212n.5, 235

Quray', Ahmad (Abu al-'Ala), 61

Rabin, Yitzhak, 51, 116, 135, 136, 203, 204, 236, 239, 254-268 passim, 269n.2, 270n.19, 271n.39, 273-276, 279; assassination of, 273, 274, 275, 291; and Oslo, 271n.43, 272n.66, 280
radicalism, *see under* Middle East
Reagan peace plan, 43-44, 79, 107, 111, 115, 148
reciprocity, 291-294
redeployments, 57, 163-164, 203, 206, 211, 235, 236, 238, 273, 274, 284, 293
refugees/refugee camps, xi, 3, 9, 13, 14, 16, 17, 23, 25, 32, 59, 77, 81, 86, 98, 106, 113, 116, 180, 183, 224, 226; 1948, 13, 24, 98, 106; 1967, xi, 75, 106
regional cooperation, 92, 294-297
Rejectionist Front, 42, 240-241
rejectionists, 42, 50, 51, 79, 133, 240-241, 274. *See also* opposition groups.
resistance fighters, *see* guerrillas
right of return, 81, 250n.49
Riyadh (1976) minisummit, 41, 114
Russia, 91, 121, 132, 133, 134, 136, 297. *See also* Soviet Union

Sadat, Anwar, 81, 102, 114, 115, 153, 262
Saddam Husain/Hussein, *see* Husain, Saddam
Said, Edward, 144, 146-147, 241
al-Sa'ih, Shaykh 'Abd al-Hamid, 186, 187
al-Sa'iqa, 15, 16, 38, 44
Salih, 'Abd al-Jawad , 186
Saudi Arabia, 38, 105, 106, 115, 144, 145-146, 297; and Gulf War, 106, 265; and Israel, 295, 297; Palestinians in, 12, 105; and PA, 294, 295; and PLO, 12, 41, 105
secular democratic state, 42, 80-81, 121, 137n.3
self-determination, 122, 147, 149, 155, 215, 227, 261
self-rule, *see under* autonomy
settlers, settlements; West Bank and Gaza, 199, 203, 207, 232, 235, 237, 242, 243, 246n.16, 249n.42, 250, 251n.51, 274, 277, 292
Sha'ath, Nabil, 61, 70n.20, 150, 153, 263
al-Shabiba (youth movement), 61, 62, 70n.23, 178
Shak'a, Bassam, 178, 248n.34
Shamir, Yitzhak, 128, 129, 131, 204, 256, 259
Sharabi, Hisham, 55, 67, 90, 241
Sharon, Ariel, 178, 203, 212n.30, 247n.22, 255, 256, 259, 264
Shultz, George, 107, 149, 152-153, 157n.11
al-Shuqairi, Ahmad, 28, 75, 225, 230
Sirtawi, 'Isam, 41, 260
Six-Day War, *see* 1967 war
social services and activities, Palestinian, 15, 16, 29, 76, 77; Islamic, 185, 198, 235, 238; PLO-sponsored, 11-12, 15, 16-17, 18, 77; in territories, 18, 65, 89, 178, 207, 214
Soviet Union (USSR), 121-132, 133-136, 144, 145, 146-147, 175; attempt to replace Arafat, 124, 129; breakup of, xiii, 132, 142; Brezhnev plan, 45, 53n.14; competition with U.S., 121,

124, 126, 144; encouragement of moderation, 38, 45, 122, 126; Jewish emigration, 106, 131, 137n.5, 139n.25; media, 127, 128, 129, 130, 131, 139n.32, 140n.37; and PLO, 12, 121-126, 131, 137nn.5,9, 138nn.11,14,15,17, 141, 146, 151, 156n.10. *See also* Russia.
stages, *see* phased plan
state building 28, 32, 33, 60, 68, 166, 190, 233; in East Bank, 112
state formation theory, 58, 67, 100
strategic reciprocity, 273-297. *See also* game theory *and under countries and organizations by name.*
strikes, 199, 207, 209
students, 15, 87, 88-89, 178, 207. *See also* youth.
Sudan, 108, 145, 146
sumoud (steadfastness), 32, 33, 88, 110, 150, 178, 233, 234
Syria, 13, 24, 38, 39, 44, 56, 78, 98, 101, 103, 106, 107, 223, 268, 295, 297; alliance with Iran, 105, 297; attempt to replace Arafat, 116; and Egypt, 11, 115, 297; and Iraq, 106, 297; in Lebanon, 111, 114, 116; and Israel, 99, 114, 146, 292, 297; and Jordan, 12, 108, 294; and Palestinian groups, 9, 13, 25, 113-114, 247n.22; and Palestinian state, 28, 116, 294; and PLO, 12, 41, 102, 108, 111, 114-116, 124, 137n.5; refugees in, 3, 13, 75; territorial aspirations, 114, 146, 297; and USSR, 106, 156n.10; waning influence of, 113-116. *See also* Golan Heights *and* Lebanon.

Tel al-Za'tar, 9
terrorism, 127, 143, 212n.30, 246n.16, 268, 279; Abu al-Abbas attempt, 128, 138n.14; Achille Lauro affair, 149; airline hijackings, 227; Israeli water carrier sabotage, 225, 230, 247n.22; Munich Olympics, 227, 268n.1; Order for the Prevention of Terror, 264-266; by PLO, 127, 143, 148, 149, 154-155, 158n.17, 238, 246n.16, 247n.22, 253, 254, 257; PLO renunciation of, 49, 128, 143, 147, 149, 152, 155, 166, 239, 268, 291
Tibi, Ahmad, 267
trade unions, 87, 88, 178
traditional elites, 173, 174, 184, 232-233
Transjordan, 223, 224, 255
trilateral agreement, 295. *See also* Israel; Jordan; Palestine; *and* Palestinian state.
Tunis, 32, 115, 116, 126, 218, 219, 262, 269n.1, 278
two-state solution, 41, 74, 80, 81, 82, 83, 123, 124, 128; advocacy by DFLP, 137n.3

United National Command (UNC), *see under* United National Leadership
Unified National Front (UNF), 173

United National Leadership of the Intifada (UNL), 180-184, 197-210; competition with Hamas, 199, 205, 206; leaflets, 182, 197-208 passim; and PLO, 181, 198
United Nations, 16, 42, 63, 80, 127, 152, 227; General Assembly Article 194, 81; General Assembly Resolution 181 (partition plan), xii, 28, 48, 49, 128, 204, 239; Security Council, 135, 230; Security Council Resolution 242, xii, 38, 39, 40, 41, 48, 49, 83, 122, 126, 127, 128, 143, 147, 152, 268; Security Council Resolution 338, 48, 49, 83, 147, 268. *See also* Arafat, 1988 address.
United States, 31, 37, 38, 43, 45, 91, 107, 115, 116, 128, 131, 134, 136, 146, 149, 286, 297; anti-Americanism, 143, 145, 147, 152; dialogue with PLO, 31, 48, 79-80, 128, 150, 153, 154, 155; Gulf War, 145; interests, 141, 143, 144, 146, 147, 149, 151; and Israel, 79, 115, 132, 149, 267-268; Jewish community, 149; and Oslo, 268; and PLO, xiii, 41-42, 68, 109, 111, 141-157, 189, 267-268; Palestinian dependency on, 68; perceptions of PLO, 141, 142, 149, 152, 154; policies of, 143, 145, 147, 150, 153, 155, 189; Reagan administration, 144; State Department, 152-153, 154, 155
UNL, *see under* United National Leadership
uprising, *see* Intifada

Village Leagues, 178, 187, 249n.44, 259

War of Independence, *see* 1948 war
Washington Declaration and talks, 135, 240, 241, 258, 262, 267, 294
water resources, 131, 232, 284s
al-Wazir, Khalil (Abu Jihad), 25, 26, 149, 245n.6, 269n.1
withdrawal, *see under* redeployment
women; Palestinian, 87, 89, 168, 178, 213-219, 233; Israeli, 213-219; overlapping identities, 214
World Health Organization, 127
World War I, 8, 9, 97, 223

Yasin, Shaykh Ahmad, 210, 212n.10, 235
Yeltsin, Boris, 132, 133, 135, 136
Yom Kippur War, *see* 1973 war
youth 214, 229, 233, 234, 241; in Intifada, 180, 205, 234, 237; organizations, 15, 87, 178. *See also* al-Shabiba *and* students.

zero-sum equation, ix, 125, 226, 230, 299n.9
Zionism, 18, 43, 229, 230, 231, 241, 244nn.1, 2; perceptions of Palestinians, 223. *See also* nationalism, Jewish.
Zionist movement, 98, 130, 223

Biographies

LEONARD BINDER is the International Studies and Overseas Programs (ISOP) Professor of Middle East Studies in the Department of Political Science at UCLA. A former president of the Middle East Studies Association of North America, he was a Fellow at the Center for Advanced study in the Behavioral sciences and at the Institute for Advanced Study at the Hebrew University. Professor Binder has written extensively on Middle East Politics and on Islamic political thought.

NAOMI CHAZAN is a professor in the departments of Political Science and African Studies at the Hebrew University of Jerusalem. She is also a member of the Knesset (Israeli parliament and serves as a deputy speaker.

EYAD EL SARRAJ, a psychiatrist and director of the Gaza Community Mental Health Program, is an authority on trauma and violence among the Palestinian population. He was a member of the Palestinian delegation to peace talks in Washington.

HILLEL FRISCH, a lecturer in the Department of Political Science at the Hebrew University of Jerusalem, is the author of numerous articles and a book on Palestinian and Arab politics. His book on Palestinian state formation in the West Bank and Gaza is to be published by SUNY Press.

GALIA GOLAN is Darwin Professor of Russian and East European Studies in the Department of Political Science at the Hebrew University of Jerusalem. Academic Director of the Mayrock Center for Eurasian and East European Studies at the Hebrew University, she has written several books on the Soviet Union and Czechoslovakia. Her most recent work is Russia and Iran: A Strategic Partnership or Tactical Alliance?

MANUEL HASSASSIAN is an associate professor of International Politics and Relations at Bethlehem University, where he currently serves as Executive Vice President. He has published extensively on comparative politics, with an emphasis on Middle Eat politics, and on the Armenian national movement and political theory.

DR. SUSAN HATTIS ROLEF is a commentator on Israeli politics who taught International Relations at the Hebrew University. Among her more recent publications are *Israel's Anti-Boycott Policy* and the *Political Dictionary of the State of Israel.* She currently works for the Knesset library information service and a Tel Aviv-based company dealing with Middle Eastern market research. She is an advisor to Israel Television in English on a program for Israel's fiftieth anniversary.

BARUCH KIMMERLING is a professor of Sociology of Politics at the Hebrew University of Jerusalem. Among his books is *Palestinians: The Making of a People* (with Joel S. Migdal; 1994).

MEIR LITVAK is a lecturer in the Department of Middle Eastern and African Studies at Tel Aviv University and a researcher at the university's Dayan Center, specializing in modern Shi'i history and Palestinian politics.

MOSHE MA'OZ, Director of the Truman Institute and professor of Middle Eastern and Islamic Studies at the Hebrew University, has served as an adviser to government officials. A biographer of Syria's President Asad, his publications on Syrian and Palestinian history and politics include *Syria and Israel: From War to Peacemaking* (1995).

SHAUL MISHAL is an associate professor in the Department of Political Science, Tel Aviv University, head of the Institute for Israeli-Arab Studies at Beit Berl, and author of books on the Palestinians in Jordan, the PLO Under Arafat, and the Intifada underground.

MUHAMMAD MUSLIH is an associate professor in the departments of Political Science and Middle Eastern Studies at C.W. Post College, Long Island University, and Sultan Quboos scholar-in-residence at the Middle East Institute, Washington, D.C. He collaborates with A.R. Norton on the Civil Society in the Middle East project, serves on the advisory committee for the Initiative for Peace and Cooperation in the Middle East, a project of Search for Common Ground, and has published widely on the Arab-Israeli conflict and Arab politics.

BARRY RUBIN is a senior resident scholar at the BESA Center for Strategic Studies, Bar-Ilan University, a professor at the university, and editor of the Middle East Review of International Affairs. He is also a fellow at the Hebrew University's Truman Institute and at the University of Haifa's Jewish-Arab Center. His books include: *Revolution Until Victory?: The Politics and History of the PLO* (1994) and a new edition of *The Israel-Arab Reader* (1995).

EMILE SAHLIYEH is an associate professor in the Political Science Department at the University of Texas, Denton. He has published on the Palestinian leadership in the West Bank as well as on Jordan.

DR. YEZID SAYIGH is Assistant Director of Studies at the Centre of International Studies, University of Cambridge. He was an adviser and then negotiator in Middle East peace talks, heading the Palestinian delegation to the Multilateral Working Group for Arms Control and Regional Security (1992-94). His latest publications are *Armed Struggle and the Search for State: The Palestinian National Movement, 1949-1993* (1997) and *The Cold War and the Middle East* (edited with Avi Shlaim, 1997).

DR. AVRAHAM SELA is a senior lecturer in the Department of International Relations at the Hebrew University of Jerusalem. He has published widely on inter-Arab relations, the Palestinian question, Jordan, and other subjects.

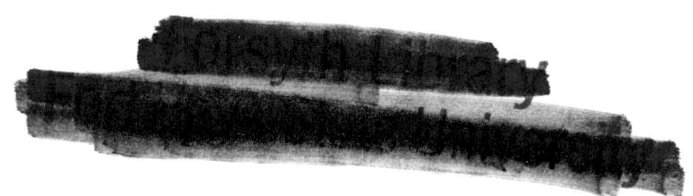